The Industrial Revolution and British society is a wideranging survey of the principal economic and social aspects of the Industrial Revolution in Britain in the eighteenth and early nineteenth centuries. The distinguished international contributors focus on topics currently at the centre of scholarly interest, and draw together the latest research in an accessible and stimulating manner. The intention throughout is to introduce a broad student readership to important aspects and consequences of the first Industrial Revolution. The contributors are acknowledged specialists in their respective fields of economic, social and political history, and employ a variety of different disciplinary skills. Particular attention is paid to the concept and historiography of the Industrial Revolution. Each chapter draws attention to the other literature on the subject, pointing the way to further reading. *The Industrial Revolution and British society* offers the most up-to-date overview of recent scholarship on this subject. It will be widely used as a textbook on advanced courses on British economic and social history.

The Industrial Revolution and British society

The Industrial Revolution and British society

Edited by

Patrick K. O'Brien

Professor of Economic History and Director of the Institute of Historical Research in the University of London

and

Roland Quinault

Senior Lecturer in History, University of North London

CAMBRIDGE UNIVERSITY PRESS

Published by the Press Syndicate of the University of Cambridge
The Pitt Building, Trumpington Street, Cambridge CB2 1RP
40 West 20th Street, New York, NY 10011–4211, USA
10 Stamford Road, Oakleigh, Victoria 3166, Australia

First published 1993

Printed in Great Britain by Bell and Bain Ltd., Glasgow

A catalogue record for this book is available from the British Library

Library of Congress cataloguing in publication data

The Industrial Revolution and British society / edited by Patrick K. O'Brien
and Roland Quinault.
    p. cm.
    Includes bibliographical references.
    ISBN 0 521 43154 9 – ISBN 0 521 43744 X (pbk.)
    1. Great Britain – Industries – History – 18th century. 2. Great Britain –
Industries – History – 19th century. 3. Great Britain – Economic conditions –
18th century. 4. Great Britain – Economic conditions – 19th century. 5. Great
Britain – Social conditions – 18th century. 6. Great Britain – Social conditions
– 19th century. I. O'Brien, Patrick Karl. II. Quinault, Roland
HC254.5.I383 1992
306'.0941 – dc20   92–9649 CIP

ISBN 0 521 43154 9 hardback
ISBN 0 521 43744 X paperback

CE

Contents

Contributors

DUNCAN BYTHELL is a Senior Lecturer in History at the University of Durham, where he teaches both British and Australian history. His publications include *The Handloom Weavers* (1969) and *The Sweated Trades: Outwork in Nineteenth Century Britain* (1978).

ALAN D. GILBERT is Vice-Chancellor of the University of Tasmania. He is the author of *Religion and Society in Industrial England* (1980), joint author of *Churches and Churchgoers* (1977), and a General Editor of *Australians: A Historical Library* (1986–8), an 11-volume history of Australia.

GARY HAWKE is Professor of Economic History and Director of the Institute of Policy Studies at Victoria University of Wellington, New Zealand. He is the author of *Railways and Economic Growth in England and Wales 1840–70* (1970), *Between Governments and Banks: A History of the Reserve Bank of New Zealand* (1973), *Economics for Historians* (1980), and *The Making of New Zealand: An Economic History* (1985).

ERIC JONES is Professor of Economics (Economic History), La Trobe University; Professorial Associate, Graduate School of Management, University of Melbourne; and Visiting Fellow, Center for Comparative Research, University of California, Davis. His work includes *The European Miracle* (1981, 1987) and *Growth Recurring* (1988).

THOMAS LAQUEUR is Professor of History in the University of California, Berkeley. He is the author of *Religion and Respectability: Sunday Schools and the Working Class Culture, 1780–1850* (1976) and *Making of Sex: Body and Gender from the Greeks to Freud* (1990), as well as an editor with Catherine Gallagher and contributor to *The Making of the Modern Body* (1987).

PATRICK K. O'BRIEN is the Director of the Institute of Historical Research and Professor of Economic History in the University of London. He is the author of *Two Paths to the Twentieth Century: Economic Growth in Britain and France 1780–1914* (with C. Keyder) (1978), *The Economic History of Railways* (1977), *The Revolution in Egypt's Economic System* (1966) and *The Economic Effects of the Civil War* (1988).

DAVID PHILIPS is Senior Lecturer in History at the University of Melbourne. His major publications are *Crime and Authority in Victorian England: The Black Country 1835–1860* (1977), 'Good Men to Associate and Bad Men in Conspire: Associations for the Prosecution of Felons in England 1760–1860', in D. Hay and F. Synder (eds.), *Policing and Prosecution in Britain 1780–1850* (1989), and '"A New Engine of Power and Authority": The Institutionalisation of Law-enforcement in England 1780–1830', in V. A. C. Gatrell, G. Parker and B. Lenman (eds.), *Crime and the Law: The Social History of Crime in Western Europe since 1500* (1980).

ROLAND QUINAULT is Senior Lecturer in History at the University of North London and Honorary Secretary of the Royal Historical Society. He co-edited *Popular Protest and Public Order* with John Stevenson (1976), and has also published numerous studies on British politics and society in the nineteenth century.

ERIC RICHARDS is Professor of History at Flinders University, Adelaide. His publications include *Leviathan of Wealth: The Sutherland Fortune in the Industrial Revolution* (1973), *History of Highland Clearances* (2 vols., 1982, 1985), *Cromartie: Highland Life 1650–1914* (with Monica Clough) (1989), ed. *Poor Australian Immigrants in the Nineteenth Century* (1991).

JOHN STEVENSON is Fellow and Tutor in History at Worcester College, Oxford. His publications include *Popular Disturbances in England, 1700–1870* (1979), *British Society, 1914–1945* (1984), and *The Working Class and Politics in Europe and North America, 1929–1945* (with Dr S. Sater). He is currently working on a study of the life and times of William Cobbett and a new social history of Britain.

G. N. VON TUNZELMANN is a Reader in the Economics of Science and Technology at the Science Policy Research Unit, University of Sussex. His publications include *Steam Power and British Industrialisation to 1860* (1978).

Preface

Thirty years ago, Max Hartwell gave new life to the historical study of the Industrial Revolution in Britain. This was rather surprising, because he had grown up a world away from industrial Britain. However his homeland, the New South Wales tableland, had been opened up, a century earlier, in order to supply wool, food and minerals to industrializing Britain. Max Hartwell's interest in the Industrial Revolution stemmed from his initial research on the early economic development of Australia. This led him to study the woollen industry in the West Riding of Yorkshire when he was a graduate student at Oxford. Since then, he has concentrated his historical attention on the Industrial Revolution in Britain, although he has recently published a biographical study of Australian businessmen.

Max Hartwell studied economics in his youth and has a greater understanding of economic theory than most historians. His knowledge of economics stood him in good stead in the 1960s, when he wrote his seminal studies of the Industrial Revolution and was engaged in the Standard of Living debate with Eric Hobsbawm. His command of economics also facilitated his editorship of the *Economic History Review* and his subsequent teaching at the Universities of Virginia and Chicago. But Max Hartwell is not 'a new economic historian' who believes that statistics and cliometrics are a substitute for more traditional historical skills.

Max Hartwell is a social, as well as an economic, historian. As Reader in Recent Economic and Social History at Oxford University, from 1955 to 1974, he gave strong support to the emerging discipline of social history. He has always tried to integrate social, as well as economic, analysis in his study of the Industrial Revolution. He criticised economists for failing to incorporate social forces in their theories of development and stressed the importance of changing social values in promoting economic growth and entrepreneurship. He also explored the legal foundations of Britain's developing market economy.

Max Hartwell is not just a lucid writer and a perceptive scholar, but also a great teacher. He has stimulated and scared, complimented and criticized innumerable students in both hemispheres and in the New and the Old Worlds. Thus it is fitting that ten of Max's former students – from Britain, America and the Antipodes – have collaborated in writing a book which mirrors his multifaceted interest in the Industrial Revolution. They share his belief that a proper assessment of the Industrial Revolution must encompass its diverse economic, social and political aspects. They have sometimes come to conclusions which may not find favour with their mentor, but he is unlikely to be offended; for Max Hartwell passionately believes that argument and debate are essential attributes of a free, vital and plural society.

The year 1992 is an appropriate one in which to publish a tribute to a scholar who strongly believes in free trade and the market economy. It is also over a decade since most of the modern textbooks on the Industrial Revolution were published. In that time, many monographs and articles have appeared with new ideas and information about Britain's economic and social development in the eighteenth and nineteenth centuries. The contributors to this book have tried to link their specialist knowledge with the recent findings of other scholars. They have produced, not a traditional Festschrift, but a 'Textschrift': wideranging surveys which are primarily intended for a student readership. This is an appropriate way of honouring a man who, by both the force of his personality and intellectual conviction, has always been a popularizer – in the best sense of the term.

The speed, scope and even the concept of the Industrial Revolution have recently been questioned by historians. But the editors of this volume make no apology for retaining a term which is still widely used by both academics and the general public. 'The Industrial Revolution' will certainly remain a term in current usage if Max Hartwell has any say in the matter. We dedicate this volume to him in recognition of how much he has done to stimulate interest in and knowledge of the Industrial Revolution.

1   Introduction: Modern conceptions of the Industrial Revolution

Patrick K. O'Brien

A first and very British Industrial Revolution

At a time when the concept of a First and British Industrial Revolution is once again under attack as a 'misnomer', a 'myth' (in both the vulgar and cultural senses of that term) and dismissed as one among a 'spurious list of revolutions', it might seem misleading, certainly provocative, to continue to use the term as the title for a book of essays designed for undergraduates (Cameron 1981; Fores, 1981; Coleman 1989; Clarke 1986, 37–9). Historians certainly need to defend the themes and periods they recommend for study. That task may be straightforward for clearly significant and relatively discrete events such as the defeat of the Armada. But the economic and social changes which have traditionally been encapsulated by historians under the label of Industrial Revolution are so complex that problems of dating, origins, scale, depiction and significance loom as large as they do in those never-ending discussions about the Renaissance and Reformation. Although contemporaries seldom used the term Industrial Revolution before it was made popular by Arnold Toynbee in the 1880s, the generations alive from say 1815 to 1851 were uneasily aware that their economy and society had undergone a profound transformation within living memory (Thomis 1976; Bowditch and Ramsland 1968). After all as Max Hartwell's most famous essay reminds us they began lamenting or defending its consequences almost as soon as the long wars with Revolutionary and Napoleonic France came to an end in 1815 (Hartwell 1959, 1971). Yet many historians, from the vantage point of the late twentieth century and with overwhelming amounts of evidence now before them, question the significance that should be accorded to any one stage in the long-term evolution of a particular national economy. Some are certainly prone to react against several metaphors used to depict and reify the pace and pattern of British economic change as it occurred over several decades after 1750. Their antipathy to describing that period, however dated, as a breakthrough, deep divide, turning point, watershed, take off or even as a great discontinuity is understandable but the label

1

Industrial Revolution is venerable and remains so apposite that recent attempts to write it out of history seem perverse or merely polemical.

By training historians are inclined and indeed are properly concerned to emphasise continuity, to regress backwards in time in search of foundations and to stress the stable nature of economic change. In terms of the years taken for national outputs, capital stocks and the structure of employment to be transformed from an agrarian to an industrial base, the British transition would be ranked well down the lower half of that particular league table. In the context of later and shorter transitions the First Industrial Revolution emerges as rather slow (Maddison 1982; Crafts 1984). Furthermore, and in the long stream of history the first great economic revolution which produced settled agriculture and domesticated farm animals in the river valleys of the Near East might well be regarded as more important than anything that happened in Britain nearly 10,000 years later (Cipolla 1962). Obviously the British Industrial Revolution rested upon the prior accumulation of capital and useful knowledge beyond as well as within the borders of one small European kingdom. It is indeed an example of precocious structural change, in the sense that the release of capital and labour from agriculture (for all kinds of fortuitous geographical as well as institutional reasons) proceeded further and faster in Britain than in other parts of Europe for at least two centuries before 1750. This means that the industrialization of Britain's workforce and the relatively high productivity of its agriculture created conditions for the sustainable, and impressively rapid rates of population growth, urbanization and industrialization that occurred some time after the middle of the eighteenth century and which became obvious when attention turned inwards again when the long wars with France came to an end in 1815.

Although no historian ever claimed that the Industrial Revolution came without antecedents and preparation, at the time the pace of change was not perceived as anything but rapid and astonishing particularly to observers from the mainland of Europe. Furthermore, on all the indicators that have since been constructed and reconstructed for the measurement of rates of economic change, when we compare the first half of the nineteenth with the first half of the eighteenth century, the evidence for an intervening period of pronounced discontinuity still seems unmistakeable. Nothing like that sustained degree of acceleration had ever occurred either in Britain (or elsewhere in Europe and America). In short, between 1750 and 1850 the long-term rate of growth of the British economy became historically unique and internationally remarkable. In recommending this century (or even sub-periods within it) for intensive study economic historians expect to expose most of the forces at work which made the Victorian economy a very different entity from what it had been a century earlier. Naturally, numerous elements of what became outstanding features of that economy had been anticipated, sometimes centuries before. For example, fulling represents a famous example of the mechanization of one process of textile production as early as the thirteenth century. Fossil fuels had been used to generate the energy required by several industries in the sixteenth century (Coleman 1956). Skills, and know-how, and machines imported from beyond the borders of the kingdom had carried the economy forward long before Britain became a major exporter of advanced technology in the later eighteenth century. Antecedents are, however, some distance from quantitatively significant outcomes in the form of high per capita growth rates for industrial and agricultural production and for national income as a whole. That growth took place after 1750 when technical progress, the integration of regional and national markets, foreign trade linked to government policies and further support from agriculture came together to sustain an unprecedented rate of industrialization that still warrants the label of an industrial revolution. Growth on the scale experienced from 1750 to 1850 could not moreover be anticipated but its pace and pattern thereafter became predictable, which exemplifies why the Industrial Revolution marks a decisive 'stage' in the long-run development of the British economy that repays intensive study.

Although the success of the Victorian economy represented a potent 'example' for Western Europe and the United States of what could be achieved, the First Industrial Revolution should not be reified into a 'paradigm' which rival economies emulated. Except in terms of the high level and now commonplace generalizations associated with taxonomies of economic growth constructed by Kuznets, Rostow and Maddison, the ways in which follower countries industrialized and caught up with Britain are now perceived to be more interesting for their contrasts than for their similarities with the experience of the First Industrial Revolution (Kuznets 1966; Rostow 1960; O'Brien and Keyder 1978, ch. 1). Comparative history has revealed numerous 'paths' to the twentieth century that serve to highlight several salient but peculiar features of the British case (Crafts 1989; Sylla and Toniolo 1992). These features include: excellent resource endowments (especially abundant supplies of coal), an exceptionally productive agriculture, a secure system of private property rights and an effective state (Wrigley 1988). These advantages could not be replicated easily or quickly by follower countries on the mainland which disables the idea of a British style Industrial Revolution as an emulatable strategy for those who wished to catch up (Landes 1969; Pollard 1981). Britain certainly prompted other states to support industrialization by its conspicuous and politically challenging economic success. Britain's contribution to their economic growth resided in the export of new technology and skilled labour and in maintaining a liberal international economic order. But as a 'do it yourself' package the First Industrial Revolution seems too British to be of widespread and profound transnational significance. In any case, much of its technical, scientific and organizational elements were international property before 1750 and while the kingdom's early lead was not random or accidental there seems no reason to argue that the industrialization of other European economies would have been long delayed without an earlier British example of success before them. Meanwhile Britain moved ahead by building up and exploiting its comparative advantages (including naval power) and experienced a pattern of long-run development based upon balanced productivity growth between industry, agriculture and transportation and rapid, if confined, advance in a few staple manufactures, sold to foreigners.

Recent debates

Attempts to expunge the term Industrial Revolution from academic discourse also have a history that goes back well before the Second World War, but the recent resurgence of interest is less involved with the semantics that surround the label and more clearly concerned to capture its nature and significance. That interest finds expression in the writings of both historians and economists. As quantifiers the latter have continued to deconstruct and to reconstruct the statistical base for their applications of macro-economic theory to history (Harley 1982, 267–90; Crafts 1985; Hawke, ch. 3 below). By juxtaposing the facts and explanations now available for other European examples of industrialization before 1914, economists have also been concerned to expose what may have been general or particular about the very 'First Industrial Revolution'. Was that transition (as so many British, Continental and American scholars used to claim) a paradigm case? Was it really a pattern for development emulated by 'follower economies' from the mainland of Europe – until alas they eventually caught up and surpassed these off-shore islands? (Senghaas 1982)

As one might expect, historians have been engaged in the exploration of political and legal 'preconditions' which facilitated the establishment of institutions, property rights, good order and political security conducive to the effective operation of commodity and factor markets both inside the kingdom and also within its Atlantic and Indian Empires (Stevenson, ch. 10 below; Philips, ch. 7 below; Sugarman and Rubin 1984). Others have redrawn attention to the rise of an 'aggressive' Hanoverian state, which deployed military power to promote imperial expansion at the expense of European rivals: first Portugal and Spain, then the Dutch; and, from the reign of Louis XIV to the defeat of Napoleon, out competed Britain's 'natural and necessary enemy' – France (O'Brien, ch. 6 below; Black 1986). Historians have long preferred to present British industrialization in 'evolutionary' rather than 'revolutionary' terms. They are predisposed to replace aeronautical metaphors ('take offs') with words drawn from a Darwinian vocabulary. They are inclined to emphasize the agrarian and proto foundations of mechanized factories and corporately organized forms of production, which became such symbolic but untypical manifestations of the mid-Victorian economy (Kriedt et al. 1981; Berg 1984). In brief, current emphasis from both economists and historians is 'back to continuity'. Metaphors such as revolution, great divide, turning point, modern and premodern, advanced and backward should it seems be banished from historical discourse on changes in British economy and society from 1750 to 1850. This fashionable historical 'pointillism' (which blurs all distinctions between old and new, continuity and discontinuity) has been powerfully enforced by monographs on localities and regions conducted in the style of Sir John Clapham (Clapham I, 1930). Such research brings into perspective features of the mid-Victorian economy which had not changed for hundreds of years (Hudson 1990). For example, at mid-century agriculture survived as the dominant component of commodity production and as the major employer of labour. Vast areas of the countryside (including the Highlands of Scotland, mid Wales, Dorset, Suffolk, Westmorland, many other counties and almost the whole of Ireland remained scenically (and mercifully) untouched by the 'vulgarity' of industrial and urban civilization (see Richards, ch. 9 below; Pollard 1981).

At work a majority of men, women and children pursued their jobs in age old ways, without direct help from steam power and unassisted by machinery (von Tunzelmann, ch. 11 below; Samuel 1977, 6–72). Technical progress had neither superseded their skills, alleviated their toil, nor reduced their subordination to the patriarchal authority of 'masters'. Factories and/or large-scale and corporately organized forms of organization employed mere fractions of the nation's workforce and its capital stock. Entire industries and an even greater range of manufacturing techniques remained substantially as they had been when Charles I went to the scaffold.

Considered in international context the 'First Industrial Revolution' is now presented less nationalistically as part of a longer term more pervasively European transformation (Crafts 1989, 415–28). Within that wider perspective the origins of industrial changes in Britain in the eighteenth century are found in a precocious and more complete transition from feudalism to capitalism: that is, as an early and more widespread permeation of social relations by commodity and factor markets (Aston and Philpin 1985; MacFarlane 1978). Furthermore the technology used in Victorian England is seen as the product of a scientific movement which flowered during the Renaissance, and to which minds from most Western European cultures contributed. Furthermore, and as 'les Anglo-Saxons' (particularly our American cousins) learn more about the gamut of European experiences with industrialization, they become less impressed with their mother country as a paradigm case and more aware of several fortuitous and extra economic components of Britain's transition to an industrial economy which could not be replicated by follower countries on the mainland however hard they tried to catch up (Sylla and Toniolo 1992). For example, Britain was well endowed with supplies of cheap coal, fresh water and mineral ores, excellent coastal and internal waterways and a good site at the hub of an expanding Atlantic economy (Guha 1981). The island's soil and climate allowed farmers to take full advantage of a rather limited range of techniques available for raising yields per acre before chemicals, machines and electricity transformed agriculture in the late nineteenth century. Britain's Protestant polity remained a favoured destination for skilled artisans fleeing from religious and political persecution on the mainland. After the Glorious Revolution of 1688 an increasingly powerful state defended the stability and integrity of the kingdom by raising and 'investing' extraordinary amounts of taxes in both sea and land power in order to acquire and hold on to the largest occidental empire since Rome (O'Brien 1988). Nothing is quite so effective as comparative history in making scholars aware of what is geographical, contingent or merely military about a nation's economic achievements.

Reinterpretations of the Industrial Revolution now in vogue reflect contemporary perceptions of Britain at the end of the twentieth century (Cannadine 1984, 149–58; Raven 1989, 178–204). As citizens of a great power in decline British historians are questioning the extent of their country's earlier greatness. Today it is hardly surprising to find liberal intellectuals highlighting the European and international dimensions of their nation's past (Crafts 1989, 415–28). Finally, the transmutation of the Industrial Revolution into a process of slow, stable and beneficial progress is entirely congruent with an anti-Whig and currently prominent school of historians who represent Britain's constitutional and social development (from Charles I right down to 1914) as a process of stable but civilized change (Clark 1985; Beckett 1986). In their view the revolution of the 1640s is seen as an accidental event with insignificant longer term consequences. What survived was an *ancien régime*: an aristocratic oligarchy based on deference, religious precept and mutual respect across and within the estates of an outstandingly cohesive society (O'Gorman 1986). Super and sub-structures are brought felicitously and logically together under labels such as 'gentlemanly capitalism' which seek to project British industrialization as a gradual, civilized and alas ultimately anti-competitive process (Cain and Hopkins 1986 and 1987). To write social, political and economic history in this framework leads to perceptions of British industrialization as a stable process of social change – presided over by a benign aristocratic regime and managed by gentlemen or at least by provincial businessmen who soon matured into paternal Victorians and Christian gentry (Howe 1984; Crouzet 1985).

As usual, critical interpretations of important episodes in national history flow from the pens of younger scholars, attacking the traditions of their elders, many of whom (like Max Hartwell) did indeed represent the Industrial Revolution as a dramatic economic event with widespread ramifications for British society and politics and for the world economy at large (Hartwell 1971). That orthodoxy ('old hat economic history') is still being read and continues to be written by an unrepentant but elderly generation of Anglo-American economic historians (Pollard 1981; Rostow 1975). Thus perhaps it is time to bring old hats and new fashions together and to ask: how far was British industrialization revolutionary, and of transnational significance? Or was it really a protracted process, European in origin but also in important respects peculiarly British and thus of limited significance for other paths and patterns of industrial development pursued beyond Albion's shores?

Rates of economic growth and discontinuities

Behind modern and gradualist perceptions of British economic growth during the period 1700 to 1850 are new population and workforce estimates from Cambridge, revised indices of agricultural and industrial prices and for industrial and agricultural outputs made in Oxford, and reconstituted money wage and cost of living indices from Harvard (Wrigley and Schofield 1989; O'Brien 1985; Crafts 1987, 245–68; Lindert and Williamson 1983, 1–23; Harley 1982, 267–89). It is, however, important to realize that the statistics which appeared in the eighties did not add substantive information to the stock of data available for macroeconomic analysis. They represent reconstructions of rather well-known price, wage, production and population evidence. For example, Harley and Crafts reweighted the limited range of physical output indicators used to measure the growth of particular industries and then rebuilt a macro index for industry as a whole in its three standard forms: Laspayres, Paasche and Fisher Ideal. Their revisions demonstrate just how sensitive the suggested rates of growth are to the unavoidably problematic procedures used for weighting and to the debateable assumptions adopted to deal with the large share of industrial output for which they had no data at all (Mokyr 1987, 293–319). Crafts went on to 'deduce' an estimate for long run changes in agricultural output as a residual in a growth model, in which he deployed data for national and per capita income and estimates for income and price elasticities of demand for agricultural produce (Jackson 1985, 333–51). His interesting results remain subject to the accuracy of the original estimates for national income and to 'best guesses' about price and income elasticities of demand and the latter are 'extrapolations' from modern evidence (Hoppit 1990, 173–93). Crafts's entirely clear methods (used to 'periodize' and 'smooth' revised figures for national output) are particularly sensitive to the treatment of government expenditure, and Jackson's latest 'reworking' of the same data seems preferable (Jackson 1990, 217–34). Crafts's figures and the revisionist tone of his book have, however, been used to underpin the notion of continuity and by more than one historian to deny validity to the very idea of an Industrial Revolution altogether (Clark 1987, 64–75; Cameron 1990).

It is the case that the reworking of Deane and Cole's estimates for the growth of national income over the long span of history from 1700 to 1860 leads to serious downward revisions to their growth rates for the century after 1760. Furthermore, economic historians have been aware of the fragility of the data base at their disposal for exercises in macro-social accounting ever since the publication of Deane and Cole's path-breaking book in 1959. National income figures rest upon contemporary estimates built up mainly from the income side. Apart from industry (which is anyway far from comprehensively covered) there are no independent estimates of production for service outputs and no reliable figures for agricultural production. Meanwhile, economists continue to be ambivalent about the meaning that can be attached to estimates for national product in wartime, which is really a serious problem for centuries punctuated by wars (Higgs 1990). Recent debates among cliometricians have really underlined in red ink Deane and Cole's own original admission that their 'results have turned out to be tentative and questionable' (Deane and Coles 1962, xiii). Anyone using these numbers should at least conduct sensitivity tests. It may well be time to return to the archives and to make one more or less reliable estimate for GNP for, say, 1851 when sufficient data is available.

Meanwhile it is important to emphasize that revisionists (who have indeed 'slowed up' rates of growth) have definitely not undermined extant quantitative evidence for pronounced discontinuities. For example (and even on the most recently revised estimates), between 1831 and 1861 national income was apparently growing 4.3 times and per capita income 5.5 times faster than the rates posited by Jackson for the first six decades of the eighteenth century. Extrapolating forward at the rates of growth experienced immediately before the Industrial Revolution implies that it would have taken national income 120 years and per capita income as long as 346 years to double in size. By the second quarter of the nineteenth century national income could be predicted to double every 28 years and per capita income every 63 years.

On any conceivable revisions to the numbers it will remain clear that something fundamental had happened between the first half of the eighteenth century and 1831–61 to *the rate of change*. Given the quality of the national accounts data at our disposal, it would be unwise (perhaps unreal) to pinpoint or locate a discontinuity within these two periods. Is it not preferable and certainly more historical simply to suggest that between 1750 and say 1825 the growth of the economy visibly accelerated. The ramifications of that 'graphic acceleration' can moreover be easily exposed by constructing a counterfactual statistical portrait of the British economy in 1851 – based on an assumption that national income, population growth and structural change had continued to increase at the rates experienced from 1701 to 1761. Of course the size and structure of that counterfactual economy would have been very different. Britain's economic lead could hardly have astonished visitors to the Great Exhibition if rates of growth had not changed radically over the period. Europeans had become aware that something astonishing was happening for at least two to three decades before the outbreak of the French Revolution. After the long war with France finally ended in 1815 they at least were clear about the political, economic and social implications of British industrialization: the rest of the Continent had either to catch up or avoid the British path altogether in the interest of social and political stability (O'Brien and Keyder 1978). Furthermore, and by 1851, the pace and pattern of economic development for the rest of the century seemed predictable. A similar pattern and equally (if not more) rapid economic change would almost surely continue. Such a prediction could not have been made with any confidence on the eve of the Seven Years War, and was not made after the American War of Independence. Victorians perceived that their economy and society had passed through a revolution and that the experience of their forebears with economic and social change had been qualitatively different from their own (Thomis 1976).

Only those engaged in discourses of their own would wish to reserve the term Industrial Revolution for even more rapid rates of change, for shorter and sharper discontinuities, and will continue to deny the appositeness of that label for the *unprecedented* rates of economic growth experienced by the British economy after 1760.

Yet the label does not denigrate the illumination that may certainly be derived from placing the Industrial Revolution in a global context largely of the Malthusian or geopolitical kind favoured by Braudel, Jones, Komlos and others – who prefer to take a very long run view of economic development (Braudel 1984; Jones 1981). Over spans of economic history going back to Rome or Neolithic times long cycles of expansion in population growth and living standards are sometimes visible in the fragile demographic and real wage data at our disposal (Komlos 1989). Indeed one cycle covering the century or so which succeeded the Black Death carried real wages (and presumably average standards of living) in Western Europe to a level that may not have been surpassed before the mid-nineteenth century (Abel 1980; Campbell and Overton 1991). Over time slow growth occurred and recurred unless checked by political constraints, warfare and natural disasters (Jones 1988). Throughout long spans of history population growth together with urbanization and the contingent economies of scale and lower costs of transacting exchanges across space and time that accompanied more dense patterns of settlement had been restrained and from time to time reversed by periodic subsistence crises. Nevertheless, over the centuries a stock of durable productive assets was formed. Utilitarian forms of knowledge about production and how to cope with difficult natural environments increased slowly and was transmitted from generation to generation. This process of accumulating capital, information and institutions conducive to the spread of markets occurred more rapidly and steadily in Western Europe than elsewhere in the world economy. By the early modern period that geographically favoured continent stood poised to produce (and to procure) sufficient quantities of food and raw materials to support historically unprecedented rates of population growth, urbanization and expansion in industrial production without running into Malthusian checks (Fogel 1990).

Among the politically defined units of Western Europe the British economy probably arrived at a plateau of agrarian capacity to support a rapid ascent to industrial society before most other parts of the Continent (Wrigley 1987 and 1988). Global and meta-historical perspectives do not vitiate but rather highlight the fact that a discontinuity occurred within well defined national (or regional) boundaries and that the productivity of the British workforce producing manufactures and urban services had to advance rapidly enough to procure the food and raw materials required to support themselves and their dependants. Thus while industrialization is a dramatic manifestation of a European escape from Malthusian constraints on population growth and urbanization, that potential for 'escape' probably remained dormant until the productivity of industry increased rapidly enough to support the terms and levels of trade between industry and agriculture required for sustained structural transformation. As the label vividly suggests, when the First Industrial Revolution eventually came it occurred at a rapid pace, was led by industry and took place in Britain.

Capital formation and warfare

Revisionists will stand their ground and point to the unusually long time taken by the British economy to jack up the productivity of its non-agricultural workforce and to raise investment rates in the urban sector. Their comparisons are sometimes with Japan (an economy which experienced spectacular improvements in labour productivity and rates of investment over much shorter spans of time). But comparisons are more often with Britain's industrial rivals of the later nineteenth century – Germany, the United States and Sweden. Compared to France, Holland, Belgium, Switzerland, Italy and Denmark the British 'pace' of productivity change over comparable stages of development does not seem slow. But it must be conceded that it took more than a century after 1760 to double the average level of output per worker employed in the British economy. Between 1761 and 1861 the amount of capital available to each employed worker rose by only a third. Investment ratios (gross domestic capital formation over gross domestic product) took more than a century to double. None of the short, sharp discontinuities suggested by Rostovian terms like 'take off' show up in the revised data. Progression towards a doubling in the share of domestic expenditure devoted to maintaining and supplementing the economy's stock of capital was both slow and steady. Now these 'idealized' facts are reasonably clear they do indeed raise the pertinent question of why it took so long for British capitalists (with all the manifold natural and institutional advantages at their disposal) to raise expenditures on domestic capital formation to a relatively modest proportion of 12 per cent as late as 1851. One traditional hypothesis, once again under active debate, is that potential investments in productive assets were 'crowded out' by wars (Williamson 1984, 687–712). There is something to this recurrent argument because for nearly half the years (from 1688 to 1815) that it took for Britain to achieve the security and status of a hegemonic power, British forces were engaged in armed struggle with the soldiers and sailors of other powers. These conflicts were more or less expensive and led to an ever increasing and (by European standards) an extraordinary appropriation of resources by the kingdom's central government (O'Brien 1988, 1–32). Indeed and for most of this long period the proportion of national expenditure allocated for military purposes exceeded the share allocated for gross investment by multipliers of two to three in wartime and until after mid-century the shares were not far apart even in peacetime (O'Brien, ch. 6 below).

As 'stochastic perturbations' economists find military conflicts difficult to deal with and their attempts to 'factor out' wars from the Industrial Revolution are not convincing (Williamson 1985, chs. 11–12; Mokyr 1987; Crafts 1987). To focus attention exclusively upon the deleterious effects that government borrowing, taxation and more direct manifestations of mobilizing resources for war had upon economic growth is to deal only with the real costs of military expenditures and to ignore their positive connexions with capital formation.

During the second hundred years war with France, 1690–1815, and before Britain's final victories at Trafalgar and Waterloo, free trade within a liberal international order seems as unthinkable as rapid industrialization based upon the kingdom's home market. Britain's navy and its army made both the international and the domestic market safer for British trade. British industries (particularly cotton, metals, engineering and shipbuilding) and British commerce (banking, shipping and insurance) *captured* what we now recognize as 'inordinate' shares of world markets in these commodities and services. Such tangible gains from mercantilism and the spin-offs they engendered for the economy at large represent manifestations of the gains from high rates of public investment in naval and land power from 1688 to 1815 (O'Brien and Engerman 1991). If this perception is granted military expenditures should be aggregated with gross national civilian expenditures on capital formation to obtain a more illuminating assessment of the rise in the overall rate of national investment during the Industrial Revolution? (O'Brien, ch. 6 below).

Productivity changes

Modern interpretations of the Industrial Revolution tend to be presented in the form of growth accountancy stories. Economic historians now find macro-production functions a seductively useful device for ordering their thoughts and for summarizing and aggregating the ever accumulating body of micro-evidence and case studies of economic change. Nevertheless the formidable conceptual, let alone statistical, problems involved in 'decomposing' the growth of Britain's national output during the Industrial Revolution into shares 'imputable' to changes in the quantities of inputs (land, labour and capital) on the one hand, and the share imputable to a residual or changes in the qualities of those inputs on the other, have not been solved (Lave 1966). Theoretical and empirical objections to the method are well rehearsed in the literature and for present purposes I propose simply to review what these exercises purport to say about the nature of the First Industrial Revolution (Nicholas 1982; Geary 1990; Crafts and Harley 1992).

Briefly, the numbers suggest: that accelerated productivity change came some time after the end of the eighteenth century; that the rate of productivity growth between 1800 and 1860 was nevertheless running at about three times the rate for 1700 to 1760; finally, the numbers tell us that although the share of the increment to national output assignable to productivity change varied through time and across sectors of the economy in aggregate terms it remained at or around the 40 per cent mark for more than a century and a half down to 1851.

Such perceptions (derived from this growth accountancy framework) imply that the 'British' economy experienced growth during the Industrial Revolution that can be best depicted as 'extensive' or 'traditional' in the sense that it emanated for the most part (60 per cent on average) from additions to the inputs of land, labour and capital employed in producing national output between 1700 and 1851. Conversely, new technology, ingenuity, improved organization, reductions in market imperfections and other 'residual' elements, which continue to receive much greater emphasis in more historical accounts of the Industrial Revolution, can be relegated to a secondary role in explanations for the long-term growth of the national economy (Berg 1984; Crafts 1985).

It is, however, industry, not the national economy as a whole, that remains as the focus of attention for historians of the Industrial Revolution. Thus I now turn to consider the pace and pattern of growth and productivity changes within the economy's leading sector. Although the new indices to measure the growth of industrial output constructed by Harley and Crafts are the best that could be made, they are not (to repeat a point) comprehensive in coverage. Major industries (shipbuilding, chemicals, pottery, glass, furniture, most preserved foods, finished metallurgy and clothing) cannot be included because we lack data, while numerous sub-sectors of included industries are presumed to grow at the same rate as a single 'representative indicator' for an entire industry. 'Coverage', as revealed by the weights used to construct the overall index, may encompass not more than 57 per cent of total industrial output (Crafts 1985, 22; Deane and Cole 1962, 166). Although recent revisions are clearly important for the analysis of cycles in industrial production and also for the location of turning points in the pace of advance, old and revised indices support impressions of long-term changes that are broadly similar. Both indices suggest industrial growth for 1760 to 1801 proceeded at approximately double the rates for 1700 to 1760. Over the next six decades, 1801–61, industrial output multiplied 6.04 on the original Deane and Cole index and 6.62 on Crafts's preferred index. Differences between older and recent estimates seem to be about timing and the location of discontinuities. The end result for 1861 comes out roughly the same (Crafts 1984, 1987).

Meanwhile the separation of trends from cycles in order to estimate a 'non-stochastic' trend representing the enduring impact of innovations on the future time path of industrial output poses formidable conceptual and statistical problems. Crafts's recent paper applied sophisticated econometric techniques to the data on industrial output which leads to suggestions of trend rates of growth accelerating from around 1 per cent for the years 1700–60, to 1.5 per cent in the 1780s, 1.7 per cent in the 1790s, just under 2 per cent in the early 1800s, 2.5 per cent in 1810, 2.8 per cent for 1820. This new index peaks at around 3 per cent in the mid-1820s, but there is an unmistakeable discontinuity around 1760! (Crafts et al. 1991, 43–60.) No statistical technique, however sophisticated, will persuade sceptics that 'objective historical trends' reside anywhere other than in the eyes of their compilers. Moreover there is still the unresolved issue of 'misplaced aggregation'. When we plot the growth of all the individual industries for which data is available, marked deviations around the average rate of growth for industry as a whole appear on the graph. That variance may well be sufficient to persuade some historians to reject the whole notion of an industrial sector with components growing at comparable rates and along a similar cyclical path. Cotton clearly represents a prominent 'outlier' and during the Industrial Revolution its weight in total industrial output went up from under 3 per cent in 1770 to 22 per cent by 1831. Predictably metal production also stands out, but not to the same degree (Harley 1982; Hoppit 1990). Furthermore, the contribution made by improvements in productivity to the promotion of long-term expansion displayed considerable variance industry by industry and cannot be correlated in any clear way with observed rates of growth of final outputs. For example, the building industry, which increased its weight in aggregated industrial production from 11 per cent in 1770 to 24 per cent in 1841, presumably responded to population growth, family formation, urbanization and rising incomes at constant or even rising costs per unit of output (Williamson, 1990).

For industry as a whole Crafts's estimates suggest an entirely limited acceleration in the rate of productivity change before 1831. But over the next three decades productivity growth advanced at four times the rate experienced over the second half of the eighteenth century which indicates that the famous technological and organizational innovations of that earlier period either diffused slowly across the entire industrial sector or (as Clapham suggested long ago) were confined and industry specific (Clapham 1930).

Unfortunately productivity growth can only be estimated within uncomfortably wide margins of error and for but a tiny number of industries (cotton, woollens, worsted and iron) (McCloskey 1985, 53–74). On the numbers now available these four industries seem to account for most of the productivity gains achieved by manufacturing industry before the mid-nineteenth century. Thus when we focus on industry as a whole, recent reconstructions of indices of industrial production and exercises in growth accountancy have: (a) smoothed the previously 'abrupt' transition between eighteenth and nineteenth-century industrial growth tracked by earlier indices, and (b) suggested that productivity improvements came on stream later than historians had hitherto supposed and were confined to just a handful of industries. Again these revisions represent little more than a qualification to the notion of the Industrial Revolution as a discontinuity. Rates of industrial advance and productivity growth for 1801 to 1861 still proceed on these numbers at four and three times the rates observed a century earlier. Yet industries producing for the home market did not apparently experience conspicuous changes in technology, scale and organization. Thus within an expanding and diversifying industrial sector productivity advance seems to have been 'unbalanced' and concentrated upon 'modern' industries selling relatively large shares of output on foreign markets (Crafts 1985 and 1987; Mokyr 1987).

Indeed it is precisely this 'revived conception' of the 'British' Industrial Revolution as an example of slower, unbalanced and confined improvement in industrial productivity that has generated a counterattack from economic historians, whose detailed research on the development of particular regions, industries and crafts, has led them almost to the point of rejecting the growth accountancy framework as an illuminating way of depicting and understanding industrialization (Berg and Hudson 1990; Berg 1991; Hudson 1990).

At the base of this rejection is the depressingly wide gap that has now opened up between perceptions based upon macro-accounts purporting to measure rates of change in national and sectoral outputs and productivity on the one hand and an impressive body of more traditional historical scholarship on the other. Naturally historians ('on the defensive') have cogently exposed the all too fragile and incomplete statistical evidence to which cliometric analysis is more or less committed (Hoppit 1990, 173–93). Cliometricians have, however, always been entirely clear about the deficiencies of data at their disposal and are much better informed than their opponents about the ambiguities and theoretical difficulties built into macro-modelling and production function analysis (Crafts 1987; Mokyr 1985, 1987). Their enduring contribution resides in attempting to construct a national framework within which the now massive accumulation of research at the local or industry wide level can be generalized and interpreted, in terms of memorable and discussable hypotheses. Thus there can be no logical reason why studies that expose the nature and dynamic pace of change in, for example, the woollen industry of the West Riding or the relative economic stagnation of industry in say Wiltshire could not be accommodated within a national accounts framework (Hudson 1986, 1989). These ostensibly antagonistic perceptions are not irreconcilable but are concerned with the kinds of illumination that can be derived from macro-economic analysis compared with micro and local case studies. Both perceptions address or construct different realities. It seems as absurd to argue that explanations for the growth of the Yorkshire woollen industry could almost dispense with reference to the national (or indeed the international economy within which that industry was embedded) as it is to pretend that general statements designed to refer to the British industry as a whole 'capture' unique elements in the experience of the Staffordshire iron industry during the Industrial Revolution (see Richards, ch. 9 below).

'Our Island's Story' of economic growth is something more than the sum of equally valid histories written about Blackburn weavers, Birmingham button makers, the economy of Kendal, Lancashire or the Lowlands, etc. etc. The problem with micro-history resides in its specificity, its interest to a limited and largely provincial readership and the tendency for the accumulation of detail to obscure and confuse as well as to exemplify the larger national picture. Historians who favour a regional approach rarely confront the problem of how to fit and connect their excellent research with the wider and larger concerns of explaining national economic growth (Langton 1984). Their not entirely misplaced distrust of aggregation and countrywide averages leads perhaps to a proclivity to pile up case studies that either solidify or confront generalizations, without producing any new empirically based hypotheses about the British Industrial Revolution. Has this approach offered a superior framework to national accounts for purposes of interpretation and debateable generalizations?

Yet the data for this period are simply too frail to support accounts of slower and also unbalanced productivity growth, for manufacturing as a whole. The statistics currently available to estimate production and productivity change industry by industry are both too restricted and too weak to gainsay impressions of more rapid and profound changes; gained from well documented investigations into particular industries, regions and manufactured products as well as studies of the changing character and deployment of the kingdom's industrial workforce. In summary: historians tend implicitly to argue that crude indicators used to measure industrial production are neither comprehensive nor sensitive enough to pick up the impact of rather widespread product innovation and improvements to the quality of final manufactured output (Berg 1991). As they see it nearly all of the available physical output or input data used to quantify the growth of industrial production seems biased in the direction of understatement. But they also observe that the equally crude figures used by cliometricians to estimate labour inputs ignore the increasing proportion of female and child labour employed by industry in conjunction with improved forms of economic organization and new machinery (Berg 1987). If the unadjusted index used by Crafts and others to measure the increase in the labour input leads (as this line of argument suggests) to overstatement then productivity changes (flowing from the substitution of lower wage female and child workers for more expensive male workers with traditional skills) may be seriously understated. Thus the low quality of the statistical data available to measure both outputs and labour inputs required for a secure econometric analysis of industrial development means that narrative accounts of British industrialization which implicitly suggest more rapid rates of growth and more pervasive productivity change cannot be ruled out with a dismissive reference to the numbers.

Furthermore, the critique of 'unbalanced' and confined productivity growth will not be resolved simply by refitting production functions to improved sets of data for a wider selection of industries. Even if more acceptable data becomes available (which is doubtful) the demarcation of industries into 'modern' (experiencing relatively high rates of productivity growth) and 'premodern' (utilizing relatively unchanged techniques, scale and forms of organization) is regarded as problematical for this period of transition – when handicraft and mechanized processes of production coexisted decade after decade within a single industry (Berg 1991). On inspection the innovations of the early Industrial Revolution which lowered costs of production tended to effect inputs rather than final outputs (yarn before cloth and clothing, metals before metallurgical products, wood before furniture, etc.) (Samuel 1977). Thus by 1851 particular processes of production rather than entire industries had been transformed and modern classifications of the manufacturing sector into industries distinguished in terms of supposedly homogeneous final outputs may well obscure a more pervasive and significant procrss of productivity change and adaptation (Sabel and Zeitlin 1985, 133–76). That process, this qualitative evidence suggests, effected most industries; should not be associated with any particular organizational form, scale of production or with dramatic examples of mechanization. Thus, productivity advanced on a wide front: in factories and workshops, in smaller and larger scale enterprises, in dispersed and centralized forms of organization. Productivity also advanced in numerous ways – through the slow diffusion of power driven machinery, improved hand tools, cheaper inputs, better organization, the exploitation of female and child labour and the upgrading in skills embodied in the workforce (von Tunzelmann, ch. 11 below; Bythell, ch. 2 below). Finally the interdependence among the several interconnected processes and forms of production required to transform raw materials into finished manufactured goods across and within industries implies that attempts by economists to separate out leading from lagging industries can only obscure significant connexions within and across industries.

The implicit model which underlies the critique of attempts to understand industrialization in terms of industries demarcated in terms of standard classifications employed to organize a modern census of industrial production lays considerable emphasis upon the inseparable and interconnected nature of all the factors promoting productivity changes. At a descriptive level the argument seems persuasive. For example, the realization of productivity advance in the spinning of textile yarns depended upon the accumulation of skills in engineering and the use of improved iron and steel in the manufacture of machinery as well as an intensification of effort on the part of handicraft weavers (Bythell, ch. 2 below). Nevertheless, real costs of production did not decline at a comparable rate across all processes of production. Productivity advanced in an uneven sequence and it continues to be illuminating to try and explain why some segments of the industrial sector were transformed before others. While certain interconnexions were clearly important, not all were equally significant. Input output relationships across industries are, moreover, in principle measurable. Productivity advance may well have been both interdependent and unbalanced. To distinguish 'leading' from 'lagging' processes of production, regions and firms and, where appropriate, industries is difficult but it remains as a major and useful way to analyse the forces behind the transformation of British industry (see Von Tunzelmann, ch. 11 below).

Agriculture and industry

Not surprisingly the same problem about the timing, location and sources of productivity growth has also emerged in recent debates about the contribution of agriculture to British industrialization. Although agricultural output probably increased by a factor of four between 1700 and 1860 while total industrial production rose twenty times the primary sector's rate of productivity advance was apparently more impressive, especially after the turn of the century. According to Crafts (and his figures are only modified by Jackson) the total productivity of the combined inputs of land, labour and capital used by agriculture just about doubled over the century from 1760 to 1860, while industrial productivity rose by about a half over that rate over the same century. Again the accuracy of these estimates (or conjectural hypotheses as Crafts prefers to call his figures) have come into question. There can be no dispute that agricultural productivity increased over the period, what remains in doubt is the precise magnitude and more particularly the chronology of its rise. Alas the data available to measure total farm output is unlikely to improve but the most recent estimates from Chartres and Holderness are at least based upon production figures for major crops and price quotations gathered for the *Agrarian History of England and Wales* (Chartres 1985; Holderness 1989). Although they represent a welcome departure from reliance on less satisfactory estimates for agricultural output measured within a national income framework, their coverage is not comprehensive and gaps in the series for particular crops have been dealt with by interpolation. Fortunately (or fortuitously?) none of the available output indices differ really significantly over the scale of the increase in agricultural production between 1700 and 1860, but their chronologies certainly vary. For example, a historical account based upon physical output indicators exhibits rather steady growth in output and productivity improvements over time, while a chronology, based upon national accounts suggests an alternative sequence of steady productivity growth down to the 1740s, a far slower pace of improvement through to the end of the century and outstanding productivity growth over the next half century (Jackson 1985, 333–51).

That latter sequence seems more congruent with long-run swings in the prices of agricultural and industrial commodities and may turn out on investigation to fall into line with the timing and pace of improvement documented for particular estates and with contemporary perceptions of agricultural developments at regional and local levels (O'Brien 1985, 773–800). Meanwhile, neither the chronology nor the suggested numbers for productivity changes seem secure, not least because their empirical

B

validity, theoretical plausibility and internal consistency are the subject of an unresolved dispute among cliometricians (Williamson 1987, 272–9). For example, Williamson's estimate for productivity change between 1821 and 1861 comes to less than a third of the estimate preferred by Crafts. Furthermore, he finds suggestions of unbalanced productivity growth between British industry and agriculture during a period of rapid structural change to be implausible compared with later case studies of industrialization – which is a *non sequitur* unless economists are prepared to believe in a universal pattern of development. More pertinently, he also enquires why industrialization persisted between 1801 and 1861 if the productivity of inputs of land, labour and capital was growing that much faster in agriculture than industry? Is there a paradox involved in positing relatively fast growth of productivity in agriculture and rapid industrial-ization over the later stage of the First Industrial Revolution? Presumably the question is only relevant for some five or six decades after 1800 when prima facie the data suggest resources might have been flowing into and not away from primary production? (Persson 1991, 91–104). Before that phase there is no evidence that productivity grew significantly more rapidly in agriculture.

If unbalanced productivity growth within industry turns out to be the case, then this paradox arises again in large part from misplaced aggre-gation. The modernizing sectors of industry experienced productivity growth well above the average rate exhibited for the sector as a whole and above the rate estimated for agriculture. Furthermore, rapid productivity growth in agriculture constrained the need to import food and raw materials and thereby reduced downward pressure on the terms of trade between manufactured exports and imports. Thus exporting textiles, iron, ships and commercial services continued to be a profitable strategy for the national economy to pursue despite a rather pronounced decline in Britain's net barter terms of trade (Crafts 1985, ch. 7). Agricultural productivity rose rapidly enough to reinforce conditions for the con-tinued growth of Britain's advanced manufacturing industries, selling high proportions of output on world markets, but not fast enough to shift the country's comparative advantage back towards agriculture.

In any case and for several reasons any shift of that kind seems historically unlikely over the first half of the nineteenth century. First, the Corn Laws of 1815 suggest that the aristocracy, in charge of the tenurial and political framework within which British agriculture developed, had little confidence that their tenants could successfully compete with foreign imports let alone sell much farm produce beyond the frontiers of the kingdom. After agricultural prices had peaked in 1813 their strategy was to stabilize food and raw material prices and (as Ricardo suggested!) to continue to appropriate productivity gains from an inelastic supply of land by raising rents. They had invested heavily in the final wave of enclosures and in fixed agrarian capital during the previous period when the intersectoral terms of trade turned discernibly in favour of agriculture. While they continued to invest in primary production in a period of 'gently' falling prices (referred to at the time as a depression) they were not about to invest massively in order to augment agriculture's already rapid rate of output and productivity growth still further. Between 1815 and 1860 English landowners do not seem to have been under strong pressure to maximize returns. Population growth continued to exert a downward pressure on wage-rates in the rural economy. Enclosure and the consolidation of land into larger farms saved labour per cultivated acre. With the suspension of income tax in 1816 and a harsher regime of poor relief, tax burdens on landed wealth declined. Those responsible for the management of British agriculture could sit back, collect their rents and other positional advantages that accrued from land ownership, while maintaining rather effective barriers to entry from more competitively minded entrants into their gentlemanly sector (O'Brien 1987, 1391–409; Offer 1991, 1–20).

In short, unbalanced productivity growth between agriculture and industry at the kind of differential rates now suggested for the first half of the nineteenth century seems compatible with the *scale* of structural change that occurred over that same period. Presumably these productivity figures imply that although the *gap* in marginal profitability across the two sectors narrowed it was not eroded to a point that seriously constrained the reallocation of labour and capital away from agriculture. Institutional barriers embodied in the English system of land ownership, the Corn Laws, as well as the impressive, if delayed, rise in agrarian productivity growth all operated to contain a potentially more rapid and possibly a politically destabilizing inflow of labour and capital into the urban economy during the later stages of the Industrial Revolution (Williamson 1987, 641–78). At the same time the growth of domestic food and raw material production mitigated potentially unfavourable pressures on food prices, the terms of trade, and upon wage-rates, and thus ultimately upon industrial and commercial profits. Agriculture continued to expand output while reducing its demands on the total supplies of labour and investible resources available to the economy. There seems to be no paradox. Along with expenditures on war, these interconnexions between agriculture and industry help historians explain the particular pace and peculiar pattern of British industrialization as it proceeded between 1700 and 1860. At the same time there should be no derogation of British agriculture's distinguished and highly positive contribution over the long run. Recent research has certainly reinforced perceptions of agriculture as the benign parent of British industry (Beckett 1990). Its role resided in nurturing industry through childhood and adolescence to a stage in the late seventeenth century when about 55 per cent of the nation's workforce producing food and raw materials supported some 45 per cent of the labour force engaged in non-agricultural (but not necessarily urban) occupations. Part of this relatively large share of the population who had already left the farms, serviced agriculture, but the larger part who had severed all *direct* connexions with primary production, resided in towns and produced manufactures for sale on rural, urban and foreign markets. For a national economy to support nearly half of its population outside agriculture as early as 1700 is now recognized as an extraordinary achievement by European standards (Wrigley 1985, 683–728).

Thus a *longue durée* chronology of Britain's conjoined industrial and agrarian development suggests that the nation's agriculture had made a major and enduring contribution to the basis for an industrial revolution long before the growth of manufacturing output, population and towns accelerated in the second half of the eighteenth century. Support from agriculture then weakened for several decades while food and raw material prices went up. But a positive response (based upon a delayed but radical advance in productivity growth) resumed once more during the long wars with France (O'Brien 1985, 773–800). By 1700 the English economy was 'prepared' for an industrial revolution. First and foremost it possessed the agricultural capacity needed to support rapid population growth and accelerated structural change without succumbing to Malthusian crises serious enough to bring development to a halt (Fogel 1990). The economy had also accumulated stocks of skilled and professional labour required to sustain the next phase of constructing an urban industrial society. Institutions and markets needed to cope with the widespread exchange of commodities and with the allocation of labour and capital were already in place and well protected by a strong state from internal subversion and external aggression (O'Brien, ch. 6 below).

If we ignore the special case of the Netherlands, how did England alone in Europe create the agrarian preconditions for structural change by such an early date? The standard explanation stresses institutional changes which altered the organizational framework for the production of food and raw materials in ways that increased crop yields and, more importantly, output per worker and rents per acre to high and distinctively English levels very early on (Campbell and Overton 1991). Institutional reform refers to the familiar history of the long-drawn-out replacement of open field strip farming and communal grazing by enclosed, consolidated, relatively large-scale and individually managed farms (Beckett 1990). England's progressive agriculture was, according to this history, imposed from above by an aristocracy and gentry who retained under their ownership and 'direction' (but not their management) an increasing (again by European standards) quite extraordinary share of the nation's cultivable and most fecund land. Great estates controlled by a commercialized aristocracy who divided their lands into consolidated and large farms, managed by carefully selected tenants who employed hired as well as family labour, are the features still regarded (at least in textbook history) as the key to Britain's precocious agricultural success (O'Brien 1987). Britain's antithesis is France: with its peasantry farming on a sub-optimal scale using backward techniques of cultivation, oppressed and exploited by an urban and courtly aristocracy detached from the land and concerned only to squeeze rents and feudal dues from the system (O'Brien and Keyder 1978, ch. 5; Allen and Ó Grada 1988, 95–116).

Recent research has, however, confronted this traditional history of England's institutional and aristocratic success with several illuminating estimates of how partial productivity indicators pertaining to agriculture changed over the long run. For example, grain yields per acre roughly doubled between the Middle Ages and the beginning of the nineteenth century, but yields rose by approximately the same multiplier on open and enclosed fields alike. Although there is a small differential (of roughly 15 per cent) in favour of enclosed and well drained farms situated on heavy clays, on this particular and important indicator improvements in the physical productivity of arable land cannot be correlated in any direct way with enclosure. After 1800 when grain yields increased at a more rapid rate the apparent advantages of enclosed compared to open fields widen to a differential yield of around 30 per cent to 40 per cent in favour of enclosure (Allen 1982, 937–53).

Before the later stages of the Industrial Revolution the growth of total farm output cannot be explained by enclosure, the consolidation of cultivable land into larger scale farms or by the unusually progressive nature of great estates managed by a commercialized aristocracy. England's peculiar tenurial system can, however, be more readily connected to agriculture's capacity to release labour and capital to the urban sector, while continuing to expand the production of food and raw materials (Crafts 1985, 151–64). This is evident from the trends in the productivity of labour which have now been measured by using demographic arithmetic of the kind propounded by Wrigley (Wrigley 1985). Essentially what his calculation begins from is a series of bench mark estimates for the shares of the English population engaged within and outside agriculture (in industry and services) from 1520 to 1851. From these proportions it is simple to calculate the number of agricultural families required to support one family employed off the land. For example, in a closed economy with 75 per cent of its workforce in agriculture, three units of agricultural labour produce sufficient food for their own families and for one worker and his family outside agriculture. With 50 per cent of the workforce on the land that ratio moves to one to one and productivity per worker in agriculture has risen sharply.

On this arithmetic (which ignores other inputs, prices and differential incomes across the two sectors) the capacity of agriculture to support families engaged in industry and services doubled from 1520 to 1670; doubled again from 1700 to 1800 and doubled again from 1800 to 1851. Thus from the sixteenth to the nineteenth centuries the productivity of labour employed in English agriculture increased at an accelerating and internationally outstanding rate (Campbell and Overton 1991, ch. 1).

Furthermore, labour costs per acre cultivated (i.e. labour inputs weighted by wages) also declined as farms increased in size, up to but not beyond a scale of 300 acres. This arose because larger farms employed more specialized adult males, compared to smaller farms using diversified family workers. Also, and for certain tasks (construction, harvesting and transportation) large farmers employed specialized labour on a sub-contract basis. On such farms, tenant farmers could thus concentrate on managerial tasks and could delegate labour to hired men (Allen 1988). Capital costs per acre cultivated also declined as farms increased in size. Fixed capital (mainly tools, buildings, transport equipment and draft animals) was used more intensively while the amount of circulating capital (i.e. the funds per acre required to pay wages, taxes, seeds and other inputs) declined with increases in the scale of farming (Allen 1989, 69–98; 1991, ch. 9; but see Clark 1991, 248–57).

Although enclosure and the consolidation of the land into larger farms can no longer be represented as institutional preconditions for the observed and rather impressive rise in yields per acre that occurred over the centuries before 1800, thereafter such institutional changes do seem to be more closely related to further advances in the productivity of culti-vated land. Britain's distinctive tenurial system (great estates, enclosed, consolidated and relatively large farms) encouraged agriculture to respond elastically over time to the growing demands of an expanding population and an industrializing economy while releasing capital and labour for investment and employment in the urban sector.

Yet towards the end of the 'classic' industrial revolution, at mid-century, British agriculture still produced 37 per cent of the country's commodity output and continued to employ 26 per cent of its stock of reproducible capital and 22 per cent of the work force. The persistence of a large, traditional (some social historians might say 'feudal') sector in the midst of an urban and rapidly industrializing economy suggests a strong element of continuity in the economic, social and political life of the nation (Quinault, ch. 8 below). Indeed, several historians have argued that the survival of a powerful aristocracy attached to the land did promote a regressive and ultimately inefficient style of 'gentlemanly capitalism' within the most bourgeois society in Europe (Wiener 1981; Beckett 1986; Cannadine 1990). Furthermore, a distinctively aristocratic contribution to the transformation of primary production should not be exaggerated because the role of their agents, tenant farmers and smaller owner occupiers may have been rather more entrepreneurial and inno-vatory (O'Brien 1987).

However important and apposite these perceptions might be for poli-tical and social history, they should not obscure significant connexions between agriculture and the First Industrial Revolution. Agriculture prepared the national economy for that momentous transition decades ahead of other parts of Europe. Except briefly (from 1760 to around 1810) farmers responded flexibly to the demands for food and raw materials emanating from an economy undergoing rapid industrialization, popu-lation growth, urbanization and afflicted by war at approximately the same time. At the beginning of the eighteenth century Britain exported grain. Although the country's small export surplus disappeared and mainland towns relied increasingly upon Ireland, domestic agriculture fed the nation with relatively little recourse to imports down to 1800. There-after foreign supplies rose slowly to account for only 22 per cent of national food consumption as late as the 1850s (Thomas 1985, 137 50).

Agricultural expansion became impressive and between 1801 and 1861 the growth rate ran to two to three times the rate achieved a century earlier and productivity probably grew at least as fast as productivity for the industrial sector as a whole. Agriculture should be ranked among the modernizing and in the long-run perspective as a leading sector for the economy. Productivity growth was accompanied by increases in farm size which allowed agriculture to 'release' factors of production to the rest of the country. Historically the capital and labour saving nature of the expansion in British agricultural output stands out as distinctive; perhaps even as the most significant element for a First Industrial Revolution.

Conclusion

Modern conceptions of the Industrial Revolution continue to develop out of a protracted and illuminating debate that has sensibly moved on from mere semantics and also from an interesting but inconclusive exposé of the contexts in which the term acquired new meanings over time. Historical perceptives are always difficult to delineate but let us stand back and compare the pace and pattern of economic change over half centuries before 1750 with comparable periods say after 1825. Is it really difficult to substantiate a case for discontinuity or to recognize a transition onto a new and different plateau of possibilities for economic development? Victorians, even those apprehensive about social and political consequences, perceived it that way. Nothing could be lost, obscured or denigrated by continuing to label the complex and imperfectly understood economic changes of that transition as an industrial revolution. In summary, the Revolution was: historically rapid, located in Britain, prepared for and sustained by agriculture, concentrated in just a few leading industries linked to foreign trade and state power, and in most analytically interesting respects peculiarly British.

Like a great and innovatory work of art the First Industrial Revolution will stand the condescension of being located within the history of economic growth spanning millennia as well as the cold light of contrasts with outstanding successors. The evidence we now have that something profound happened in Britain between circa 1750 and circa 1825 surely overwhelms the disparagement that attends attempts to dim its colours and place it in one of history's minor galleries?

REFERENCES

Abel, W. 1980. *Agricultural Fluctuations in Europe from the Thirteenth to the Twentieth Centuries.*

Allen, R. C. 1982. 'The efficiency and distributional consequences of eighteenth century enclosures', *Economic Journal*, 92.

1988. 'The growth of labour productivity in early modern English agriculture', *Explorations in Economic History*, 25.

1989. 'Enclosure, farming methods and the growth of productivity in the South Midlands', in *Research in Economic History*, Supplement 5, ed. G. Grantham and C. Leonard.

1991. 'The two English agricultural revolutions', in *Land, Labour and Livestock. Historical studies in European agricultural productivity*, ed. B. Campbell and M. Overton.

1992. *Enclosure and the Yeoman.*

Allen, R. C. and Ó Grada, C. 1988. 'On the road again with Arthur Young: English, Irish and French agriculture during the Industrial Revolution', *Journal of Economic History*, 48.

Aston, T. and Philpin, C. (eds.) 1985. *The Brenner Debate: agrarian class structure and economic development in pre-industrial Europe.*

Beckett, J. V. 1986. *The Aristocracy in England, 1660–1914.*

1990. *The Agricultural Revolution.*

Berg, M. 1984. *The Age of Manufactures.*

1987. 'Women's work, mechanization and the early phases of industrialization in England', in *The Historical Meanings of Work*, ed. P. Joyce.

1991. 'Technology and productivity change in manufacture in eighteenth century England', in *Technology and Innovation from the Eighteenth Century to the Present*, ed. J. Davis and P. Mathias.

Berg, M. and Hudson, P. 1991. 'Rehabilitating the Industrial Revolution', *Economic History Review*, 45.

Black, J. M. 1986. *Natural and Necessary Enemies: Anglo-French relations in the eighteenth century.*

Bowditch, J. and Ramsland, C. (eds.) 1968. *Voices of the Industrial Revolution.*

Braudel, F. 1984. *Capitalism and Civilization*, III, *The Perspective of the World.*

Cain, P. and Hopkins, A. 1986 and 1987. 'Gentlemanly capitalism and British overseas expansion', *Economic History Review*, 2nd ser., 39 and 40.

Cameron, R. 1981. 'The industrial revolution: a misnomer', *Wirtschaftskrafte und Wirteschaftswege*, ed., J. Schneider.

1990. 'La Révolution industrielle manquée', *Social Science History*, 14.

Campbell, B. and Overton, M. (eds.) 1991. *Land, Labour and Livestock: historical studies in European agricultural productivity.*

Cannadine, D. N. 1984. 'The past and the present in the industrial revolution, 1880–1980', *Past and Present*, 103.

1990. *The Decline and Fall of the British Aristocracy.*

Chartres, J. 1985. 'The marketing of agricultural produce', in *The Agrarian History of England and Wales*, V, ed., J. Thirsk.

Cipolla, C. 1962. *The Economic History of World Population.*

Clapham, J. H. 1930. *An Economic History of Modern Britain*, I, *The Early Railway Age, 1820–50.*

Clark, J. C. D. 1986. *Revolution and Rebellion.*

1987. *English Society, 1788–1832: ideology, social structure and political practice during the ancien régime.*

Clark, G. 1991. 'Labour productivity and farm size in English agriculture before mechanisation: a note', *Explorations in Economic History*, 28.

Coleman, D. C. 1956. 'Industrial growth and industrial revolutions', *Economica*, February.

1989. 'Myth, history and the industrial revolution', *Creighton Trust Lecture.*

Crafts, N. F. R. 1984. 'Patterns of development in nineteenth century Europe', *Oxford Economic Papers*, 36.

1985. *British Economic Growth During the Industrial Revolution.*

1986. 'Income elasticities of demand and the release of labor during the British industrial revolution: a further appraisal', in *The Economics of the Industrial Revolution*, ed., J. Mokyr.

1987. 'British economic growth, 1700–1850: some difficulties of interpretation', *Explorations in Economic History*, 24.

1989. 'British industrialization in an international context', *Journal of Interdisciplinary History*, 19.

Crafts, N. F. R. and Harley, C. K. 1992. 'Output growth and the British Industrial Revolution: a restatement of the Crafts-Harley view', *Economic History Review*, forthcoming.

Crafts, N. F. R., Leybourne, S. G. and Mills, T. C. 1991. 'Trends and cycles in British industrial production, 1700–1913', *Journal of the Royal Statistical Society*, 152.

Crouzet, F. 1985. *The First Industrialists*.

Deane, P. and Cole, W. A. 1962. *British Economic Growth, 1688–1959*.

Fogel, R. W. 1990. 'The conquest of high mortality and hunger in Europe and America: timing and mechanism', *National Bureau of Economic Research Working Paper*, 16.

Fores, M. 1981. 'The myth of the industrial revolution', *History*, 66, and see reply by Musson, A., 1982, *History*, 67.

Geary, F. 1990. 'Accounting for entrepreneurship in late Victorian Britain', *Economic History Review*, 2nd ser., 43.

Guha, A. 1981. *An Evolutionary View of Economic Growth*.

Harley, C. K. 1982. 'British industrialization before 1841: evidence of slower growth during the industrial revolution', *Journal of Economic History*, 42.

Hartwell, R. M. 1959. 'Interpretations of the Industrial Revolution in England', *Journal of Economic History*, 19.

    1971. *The Industrial Revolution and Economic Growth*.

Higgs, R. 1990. 'Wartime prosperity during World War II', Cliometric Session, ASSA Meetings.

Holderness, B. A. 1989. 'Prices, productivity and output', *The Agrarian History of England and Wales, 1750–1850*, ed. G. E. Mingay, VI.

Hoppit, J. 1990. 'Counting the industrial revolution', *Economic History Review*, 2nd ser., 42.

Howe, A. C. 1984. *The Cotton Masters*.

Hudson, P. 1986. *The Genesis of Industrial Capital: a study of the West Riding wool textile industry, 1750–1850*.

    1990. 'The regional perspective', in *Regions and Industries*, ed. P. Hudson.

Hudson, P. (ed.) 1989. *Regions and Industries: a perspective on the Industrial Revolution in Britain*.

Jackson, R. V. 1985. 'Growth and deceleration in English agriculture, 1660–1790', *Economic History Review*, 2nd ser., 38.

    1990. 'Government expenditure and British economic growth in the eighteenth century: some problems of measurement', *Economic History Review*, 2nd ser., 43.

    1992. 'Rates of industrial growth during the industrial revolution', *Economic History Review*, 45.

Jones, E. L. 1981. *The European Miracle*.

    1988. *Growth Recurring*.

Komlos, J. 1989. 'Thinking about the Industrial Revolution', *Journal of European Economic History*, 18.

Kriedle, P., Medick, A. and Schlumbohm, J. 1981. *Industrialization before Industrialization*.

Kuznets, S. 1966. *Modern Economic Growth*.

Landes, D. 1969. *The Unbound Prometheus: technological change and industrial development in Western Europe from 1750 to the present*.

Langton, J. 1984. 'The industrial revolution and the regional geography of England', *Transactions of the Institute of British Geographers*, 9.

Lave, L. B. 1966. *Technological Change: its conception and measurement.*

Lindert, P. and Williamson, J. G. 1983. 'English workers' living standards during the Industrial Revolution: a new look', *Economic History Review*, 2nd ser., 19.

McCloskey, D. N. 1985. 'The industrial revolution, 1760–1860: a survey', in *The economics of the Industrial Revolution*, ed. J. Mokyr.

MacFarlane, A. 1978. *Origins of English Individualism.*

Maddison, A. 1982. *Phases of Capitalist Development.*

Mokyr, J. 1987. 'Has the industrial revolution been crowded out: some reflections on Crafts and Williamson', *Explorations in Economic History*, 24.

Nicholas, S. 1982. 'Total factor productivity growth and the revision of post 1870 British economic history', *Economic History Review*, 2nd ser., 35.

O'Brien, P. K. 1985. 'Agriculture and the home market for English industry, 1660–1820', *English Historical Review*, 100.

1987. 'Quelle a été exactement la contribution de l'aristocratie Britannique au progress de l'agriculture entre 1688 et 1789', *Annales.*

1988. 'The political economy of British taxation, 1688–1815', *Economic History Review*, 2nd ser., 41.

O'Brien, P. K. and Engerman, S. 1991. 'Exports and the growth of the British economy from the Glorious Revolution to the Peace of Amiens', in *Slavery and the Rise of the Atlantic System*, ed. B. Solow.

O'Brien, P. K., Heath, D. and Keyder, C. 1977. 'Agricultural efficiency in Britain and France, 1815–1914', *Journal of European Economic History*, 6.

O'Brien, P. K. and Keyder, C. 1978. *Economic Growth in Britain and France, 1780–1914: two paths to the twentieth century.*

Offer, A. 1991. 'Farm tenure and land values in England, c. 1750–1950', *Economic History Review*, 2nd ser., 64.

O'Gorman, F. 1986. 'The recent historiography of the Hanoverian regime', *Historical Journal*, 29.

Persson, K. G. 1991. 'The never ending controversy: agrarian and industrial productivity growth in Britain, 1750–1860', *Institute of Economics, University of Copenhagen Discussion Paper*, 9104.

Pollard, S. 1981. *Peaceful Conquest: the industrialization of Europe, 1760–1970.*

Raven, J. 1989. 'British history and the enterprise culture', *Past and Present*, 123.

Rostow, W. W. 1960. *The Stages of Economic Growth.*

1975. *How it All Began.*

Sabel, C. and Zeitlin, J. 1985. 'Historical alternatives to mass production', *Past and Present*, 108.

Samuel, R. 1977. 'The workshop of the world: steam power and hand technology in mid-Victorian Britain', *History Workshop*, 3.

Senghaas, D. 1982. *The European Experience: a historical critique of development theory.*

Sugarman, D. and Rubin, G. (eds.) 1984. *Law, Economy and Society.*

Sylla, R. and Toniolo, G. (eds.) 1992. *Patterns of Industrialization in Nineteenth Century Europe.*

Thomas, B. 1985. 'Food supply in the United Kingdom during the Industrial Revolution', in *The Economics of the Industrial Revolution*, ed. J. Mokyr.

Thomis, M. 1976. *Responses to Industrialization, 1780–1950.*

Wiener, M. 1981. *English Culture and the Decline of the Industrial Spirit.*

Williamson, J. G. 1984. 'Why was British growth so slow during the industrial revolution?', *Journal of Economic History*, 44.

    1985. *Did British Capitalism Breed Inequality?*

    1987a. 'Did English factor markets fail during the industrial revolution?', *Oxford Economic Papers*, 39.

    1987b. 'Debating the British Industrial Revolution', *Explorations in Economic History*, 24.

    1990. *Coping with City Growth during the Industrial Revolution.*

Wrigley, E. A. 1985. 'Urban growth and agricultural change: England and the Continent in the early modern period', *Journal of Interdisciplinary History*, 15.

    1987. 'Introduction', *The Works of T. R. Malthus*, ed. E. A. Wrigley and D. Souden.

    1988. *Continuity, Chance and Change: the character of the industrial revolution in England.*

Wrigley, E. A. and Schofield, R. A. 1989. *The Population History of England, 1541–1871.*

2   Women in the work force

Duncan Bythell

Introduction

Max Hartwell once suggested that among the major beneficial long-term consequences of 'the Industrial Revolution' was its positive contribution to 'the emancipation of women' (Hartwell 1961, 416). He has not elaborated on the point, but he would no doubt agree with Ivy Pinchbeck who saw in the mill girls of the mid-nineteenth century a shining pointer to the future. The single young women who now went out from the parental home to earn their living in the textile factories of Lancashire and Yorkshire had, she maintained, made 'a distinct gain in social and economic independence ... working the shortest hours and receiving the same rate of wages as men where they were employed in the same kinds of work'; the example of their 'economic emancipation' was 'at once manifested in its influence on better class [sic] women and their demands for a wider sphere and the right to individual independence' (Pinchbeck 1930, 313–16).

Pinchbeck's optimistic views have not gone unchallenged. Perhaps the clearest statement of the pessimistic case has come from Eric Richards. Arguing that 'before the Industrial Revolution (as conventionally dated) the utilization of women in the economy was close to a notional maximum', he was struck by the way in which women's job opportunities actually contracted, so that 'the female participation rate in the British economy seems to have reached its social [sic] nadir in the third quarter of the nineteenth century'. After expressing surprise 'that the unfettered capitalist economy – in the full flood of industrialism in the mid-nineteenth century – should have used a principal supply of labour in so modest a fashion', Richards went on to assert that 'like many other benefits commonly ascribed to the Industrial Revolution, those for female emancipation did not reach recognizable fruition until the middle of the present century' (Richards 1974, 338, 348).

Acknowledgement. I am grateful to Mark Bailey, Anthony Fletcher, and the editors, for their comments on the early drafts of this chapter.

It would, of course, be easy to reconcile the conflicting conclusions of Pinchbeck and Richards by arguing that they were essentially concerned with different things – that Richards was talking about the *number* of women at work, where Pinchbeck (who in fact recognized that, in many areas, women's chances of finding employment did indeed diminish between 1750 and 1850) was thinking *qualitatively* about the improved status and rewards of one distinct group of women workers. But a number of historians since Richards have concentrated their fire specifically on the 'qualitative' aspects of the optimists' case. Thus Patricia Branca pointed out that 'this new sector of the female population [i.e. the textile factory workers] was minute, never comprising more than ten per cent' in the first half of the nineteenth century. Similarly Tilly and Scott, whilst agreeing that, increasingly, women workers were earning an independent wage instead of merely contributing to the efforts of a family work-team, nevertheless argued that, during early industrialization, 'the majority of working women performed jobs with low levels of skill and low productivity similar to those that had characterized women's work for centuries' (Branca 1978, 10–11; Tilly and Scott 1978, 77). However, the pessimists' attack has latterly centred on the Victorian belief in 'separate spheres' and the institution of 'patriarchy', which together are alleged to have limited the *types* of work women were expected or permitted to perform, to have confined them to a marginal and subordinate role, and to have kept down the level of their wages (Hall 1979; Dex 1988).

The ideology of 'separate spheres', with its contingent ideas – 'the angel in the home', 'the sanctity of the family' and the 'cult of domesticity' – is now commonly regarded as one of the fundamental social values of nineteenth-century Britain. From the belief that every woman's destiny was marriage and motherhood, important consequences followed. A married woman's preoccupation with the domestic comfort of her husband and the rearing of her children prevented her from engaging in paid employment. This in turn implied, first, that only *unmarried* women – chiefly young spinsters (widows raised awkward problems) – should be part of the workforce; and second, that a husband's earnings (properly utilized) ought to be sufficient in themselves to support his wife and children at a 'reasonable' standard of living – 'the male bread-winner wage norm' (Seccombe 1986). If women only worked for wages when they were young and single, they were, by definition, without family responsibilities and therefore 'needed' to earn enough merely to support themselves – an argument widely used to justify huge differentials between men's and women's earnings. Moreover, if a woman's working life was limited to a few years before marriage, it followed that there was no point in her being trained for a lifetime's work, except, of course, in such skills as would later enable her to manage her own household efficiently. When coupled with the belief that women were physically and mentally unfitted for certain kinds of employment, the result was a 'gender division of labour'. This not only distinguished many occupations into 'male-employing' and 'female-employing' categories, but also ensured that, even in activities where men and women actually worked alongside each other – as they did in the new textile factories – certain processes and techniques were reserved for men, whilst others – deemed appropriate to unskilled, temporary workers, of limited competence – were left for the women.

As a result of the gradual acceptance of these interlocking values and beliefs, many historians now argue that the changing nature of work in 'the Industrial Revolution', far from 'emancipating' women, served only to redefine and revitalize *patriarchy*. Thus, attempts by organized male workers in *all* modern capitalist economies during the nineteenth century to establish the 'male bread-winner norm', whilst enabling them to mount a strong moral case for being paid higher wages, implied simply the reassertion of paternal authority and male supremacy, and could only be retrograde in their effects on the continued economic and social subordination of women (Taylor 1983, 206–9; Rose 1988, 208).

This essay is concerned *only* with those women, born and raised in wage-dependent households, who would themselves end up as the wives of wage-earning men. Such households may have made up 80 per cent of the population of early eighteenth-century Britain (R. W. Malcolmson 1981, 19). Within this stratum of society, a family's well-being traditionally depended on all its members contributing to supplement the wages brought in by the head of the household, either by being part of a family work-team, or by earning an independent wage which could be surrendered into the common stock. But not all members of a wage-earning family of working age were in fact free to earn by working, because their roles and responsibilities were largely, and necessarily, internal to the household and did not involve making goods or providing services for sale outside it. Wives and mothers, by definition, spent much of their time and effort bearing and rearing children and doing household chores – tasks laborious in themselves, but unrewarded in cash terms by the market economy.

Census takers normally define the 'workforce' as including only those who engage fully in the 'real' economy, and thereby exclude most of the women predominantly engaged in domestic duties from their calculations. Historians have little option but to follow their lead, but they can at least observe, emphatically, that many housewives *did*, indeed, contribute directly to their families' incomes by working for wages, at least on a part-time, casual, or seasonal basis, as opportunity offered or necessity compelled. The tens of thousands whom the mid-nineteenth-century censuses categorized as 'farmer's wife', 'shoemaker's wife', 'innkeeper's wife' and so on, are a powerful reminder of the important contribution which married women made, especially in traditional activities where the workplace still coincided with the home. In addition, particularly in the larger urban communities with their more complex economies, there were many wives who found occasional employment at work which differed from their husbands (Earle 1989, 338–42). Despite the versatility and adaptability they were expected to show in these respects, women's contributions to the workforce at this level have rarely been systematically recorded or accurately measured (Higgs 1987). All that can be said with reasonable confidence is that, until the last fifty years, the contribution of most *married* women to the 'real' workforce has been of precisely this irregular and inadequately quantified sort.

A further conceptual difficulty arises from the imprecise way some historians use terms like 'industrial revolution' and 'modernization'. It would be quite wrong to make vague comparisons between women's role in the workforce in some generalized 'pre-industrial' age and in 'modern times': rather, it is important to be specific about the exact changes which belong to the period 1750 to 1850. It would be misleading to create some timeless, but largely mythical, 'pre-industrial' pattern of women's work which existed unchanged for centuries until rudely shattered in the late eighteenth and early nineteenth centuries. Fortunately, recent writing on the social and economic position of women in earlier periods has given us, for example, a much clearer picture of women's work – and especially of the role of widows – in urban communities in the medieval period (Hanawalt 1986; Prior 1985). Likewise, in the early modern era we now have a better appreciation of the importance of 'living-in' servants in farmers' and artisans' households, and also of the growing involvement of country women in industrial work through the expansion of the 'putting-out' system, particularly in textiles (Kussmaul 1981, 3–11; Berg 1985, 134–9). At *no* time in the 'pre-industrial' past was there a 'golden age' when women were not confined – either by prevailing notions of 'separate spheres', 'complementarity', or 'partnership', or by the institutional structures and mentalities created by patriarchy – to marginal, unskilled and poorly paid work. At the same time, it is obvious that women's participation in the workforce differed significantly by the late seventeenth century from what it had been in the fourteenth.

Finally, even in the period 1750–1850, we must remember the shortcomings of the surviving evidence about women's work. Most women of the labouring poor left no written record of their existence beyond the brief personal entries in the parish registers of baptisms, marriages and burials and – at the end of our period – in the census returns; and these give only a limited account of their experience as workers and wage-earners. Nor, despite the voluminous inquiries which British governments conducted into the condition of the labouring poor, especially in the 1830s and 1840s, are the voices of individual working women heard expressing their hopes, fears and beliefs as often as those of men. Nevertheless, because the evidence *is* fuller and more varied for the end of our period than for the beginning, it seems sensible to start by establishing the chief characteristics of women's role in the workforce in the mid-nineteenth century, and then to work backwards in order to see what changed.

Women's work in 1851

The 1851 census of Great Britain suggests that just over a quarter of the female population – some 2.8 million out of 10.6 million – were at work, and that women made up about 30 per cent of the country's labour force. However, when these figures are broken down region by region, and occupation by occupation, it is immediately apparent, first, that the proportion of the female population deemed to be working – i.e. the participation rate – could vary considerably over the country, and second, that there were very few activities where women actually made up three out of every ten of the workers involved. To take first the participation rate: against a national average of a quarter of the total female population at work, the proportion rose to over one-third in the counties of Lancashire, Nottingham, Leicester, Bedford and Buckingham, but fell to less than one-fifth in Northumberland, Durham, Lincoln, Huntingdon, Cambridge, Glamorgan, Monmouth and Kent. Such wide regional disparities are not simply reflections of a peculiar age-structure, because women's participation in work varied greatly even for the age-group 15 to 24, whose members were mostly unmarried and therefore notionally available to work for wages. Why was the percentage of teenage girls 'not working' more than twice as high in County Durham and Kent as in Lancashire and Bedfordshire? Were there really areas of the country where substantial, but apparently unrecognized, pockets of female unemployment existed? (Jordan 1988, 175–6). To answer these questions, we need to look in greater detail at the kinds of work women were doing in 1851.

Viewed nationally, the picture seems clear enough. Four activities accounted between them for almost 90 per cent of 'women's work': domestic and allied forms of personal service headed the list, employing about two out of every five working women; the textiles and clothing groups of industries together provided employment for a similar proportion, and – lagging a long way behind – agriculture found work for approximately one working woman out of every twelve. This marked concentration in a few sectors had an obvious corollary: there were *other* important areas of economic activity from which women workers were absent completely, or in which they participated only in negligible numbers. Thus – to take the most striking examples – women were virtually absent from the building trades. Except in a few areas where they did surface work, they were not employed in coal or mineral mines. They did not build or sail boats or ships, operate vehicles on land, or indeed have anything to do with the management of horses (which continued to provide so much of the economy's traction and energy long after 1851). They were not to be seen in the great ironworks or machine-shops of the fast-expanding heavy industrial sector; nor were they to be found in the ranks of such traditional rural craftsmen as blacksmiths, wheelwrights and corn-millers. Neither was their exclusion confined to major parts of the primary and secondary sectors of the economy; after all, they do not appear among the clerks and secretaries in the commercial offices and counting houses of Dickens' London. But if they were either excluded from, or greatly underrepresented in, so many economic activities, women certainly dominated others. In particular, they provided 85 per cent of the workers in the country's second largest employment, domestic and personal service, and about half the labour force in what were still very much the principal manufacturing industries, textiles and clothing. Even within these last broad categories, women's participation varied. For example, whereas cotton, the largest branch of textiles, employed almost equal numbers of men and women, silk had a preponderance of women workers, and the wool-using industries a majority of men. However, women virtually monopolized the various stitching and sewing trades, as seamstresses, milliners and dress-makers; and the clothing group of industries was, in fact, the biggest single employer of female labour after domestic service. Taken all round, women were probably underrepresented in the primary sector and overrepresented in the tertiary sector, compared with men: but the outstanding feature of the national employment pattern in the mid-nineteenth century was the way in which so many activities were clearly distinguished as either men's or women's work (Lee 1979).

Once the peculiarly uneven distribution of women workers between various occupations and industries has been appreciated, the marked regional differences in women's participation in the labour force start to make sense. Whereas some of the activities in which female workers were concentrated – such as domestic service and dress-making – were carried on all over the country, others – including textiles and the lesser clothing trades such as hosiery, lace, and straw – were by now confined to particular specialist localities. Regional specialization created marked local divergences from the national norm, not only in the level, but also in the variety, of women's employment. For example, despite the importance of domestic service overall, there were in fact ten counties in England (and three regions in lowland Scotland) where domestic servants were outnumbered by women working in textiles or clothing. In addition to the obvious cases – Lancashire, Cheshire, the West Riding, Derby, Nottingham and Leicester – the list also included the south midland counties of Northampton, Buckingham, Bedford and Hertford. Similarly, in the remoter rural parts of Wales and Scotland, women were as likely to be working on the farm as in house service. On the other hand, there were many parts of England where opportunities outside domestic service were apparently lacking. More than a half of all working women were classed as domestics, not only in London and the counties to the south of it, but also in some mainly agricultural counties along the border with Wales, in Lincolnshire, and in north and east Yorkshire. More surprisingly, servants appear to have made up virtually half the female workforce in the 'coalfield' counties of Durham and Glamorgan, too.

Other unusual features soon emerge when the census figures are perused on a more local basis. For example, although women constituted only one-tenth of the national labour force in agriculture, they amounted to one-fifth or more of it, not only in distant regions such as north Wales and the Scottish Highlands, but also in some agriculturally 'progressive' districts on both sides of the Anglo-Scottish border and in north-eastern Scotland. In a number of lesser manufacturing industries, too, there were cases where, locally, women workers could provide up to a half of the labour force – paper-making in parts of Kent, pottery in Staffordshire, and nail-making in Worcestershire and Warwickshire being notable examples (Lee 1979). Increasingly over the past thirty years, historians have gone behind the printed volumes to the original census enumerators' manuscript books and schedules, in which the details of each household were recorded individually, in order to unravel the complex occupational patterns of particular communities. Armstrong's pioneering study of York, for example, analysed the characteristics of domestic service – which employed almost 60 per cent of the female labour force in this market town and administrative centre in 1851 – and compared them with some of Yorkshire's industrial towns (Armstrong 1974, 179–80). Similarly, following Anderson's classic study of Preston in 1851, historians have used the unpublished census records to explore the nature and the extent of *married* women's work (Anderson 1971). In Leicester, for example, a third of all married women were at work in 1851, about half of them in the hosiery industry; the majority of these women were able to work at home, because the industry was still largely conducted outside the factory system; and women whose husbands were also employed in hosiery were *twice* as likely to be at work as women whose husbands were artisans or general labourers (Osterud 1986, 58–60).

Obviously, local diversity in women's work patterns can be explained partly by differences between town and country, but the picture here is complex. As the implied contrasts between York and Leicester suggest, urban communities could themselves exhibit very different structures, depending on their economic functions and characteristics. The mere fact of living in a town rather than in a village did not in itself guarantee either a wider variety or a greater number of openings for women. Likewise, it is naive to equate women's work in the countryside simply with farm work and domestic service. In the early nineteenth century, many branches of the predominantly female-employing textile and clothing industries were still conducted on the labour-intensive 'outwork' system rather than in centralized and mechanized factories – which meant that country women could be as readily employed stitching, seaming, sewing and plaiting as their urban sisters (Bythell 1978). In some Buckinghamshire villages, for example, over two-thirds of the working women were employed in straw-plaiting and lace-making in 1851 (Horn 1980, 226–7). In short, none of the simple stereotypes of 'women's work in the Industrial Revolution' – least of all that of the millgirl in a cotton factory in some grimy northern town – can convey the complex situation revealed by the 1851 census. What women did depended largely on the peculiar economic structure of the place where they were born, and generalizations based on crude national totals ignore the essential element of regional variety.

Changes during the century before 1851

Despite many ambiguities, the 1851 census provides a reasonable but broad-brush *quantitative* picture of women as full-time members of the labour force. However, it says nothing about such 'qualitative' issues as the status and rewards of women workers compared with men, and nothing about how the patterns of 1851 compared with those of a hundred years before. The lack of national census data on occupations before 1841 makes precise long-term comparisons impossible. Nevertheless, it is not difficult to identify some major developments during a century of unprecedented economic change. The obvious ones include: the decline of women's work in agriculture; the growth of private domestic service, especially in middle-class urban households; and the devel-

opment of mechanized production in textiles, coupled with the nevertheless remarkable resilience and versatility of the supposedly dying
'outwork' system elsewhere. In addition, a number of smaller, more
localized developments – notably the prohibition by law of women
working underground in coalmines in 1842 – had a significance which
cannot be ignored. These developments will now be considered in turn.

Agriculture

Undoubtedly, the years 1750–1850 saw major changes, both in agriculture's place within the British economy and in its internal organization
and methods: but it was already characterized in the early eighteenth
century by relatively large farms, by a high level of production for the
market rather than for self-sufficiency, and by many farmers' reliance on
the services of hired labourers who had to work for wages because they or
their families had little or no access to land, either as owners, tenants or
possessors of common rights. Between one-third and one-half of this
hired labour consisted of 'servants in husbandry': young, unmarried
people of both sexes engaged on annual contracts to work as resident
servants in farmers' households. Such 'servants' must be distinguished
from the married adult male wage labourers who lived in their own homes
and made up the rest of agriculture's permanent labour force. Local
population censuses of rural communities between the late sixteenth and
the early nineteenth centuries indicate that almost a half of all farmers'
households included at least one 'living-in' servant, although the majority
of such farmers employed no more than two. Servants in husbandry
constituted almost 60 per cent of the entire population aged between 15
and 24 in these communities. Remarkably, the ratio of male to female
servants was 121:100 – in other words, about 45 per cent of farm-servants
were young women. But if girls were almost as numerous as boys, there
was a clear distinction between the work done by the two sexes, with girls
generally confined to work in the dairy and poultry-yard, to weeding in
the fields, and to household tasks such as baking and brewing. Likewise,
girls' annual wages were consistently lower, at between one-half and
two-thirds of those paid to boys (Kussmaul 1981, 4, 34, 37).

Why was farm service and its attendant practices – hiring fairs and a
high level of local migration as young people moved on annually from
farm to farm – so widespread in the early eighteenth century? In the
answer to this question lies the explanation of its subsequent dramatic
decline, for, by 1851, resident farm servants were outnumbered by
outdoor farm labourers in the country as a whole by more than three to
one. The effects on the sexual make-up of the agricultural labour force

were striking: among the now more numerous labourers, men outnumbered women by twenty to one, whereas among the residual farm servants the ratio was more like two to one (Armstrong 1988, 94). Over a hundred years, two processes had been at work which together had greatly reduced the female element in the agricultural workforce: first, a marked shift away from living-in servants to outdoor labourers; and second, a fall in the proportion of women even within the remaining group of indoor servants. Nevertheless, this development had not been uniform over the country. Although there were nine counties in the south-east of England where servants had dwindled to less than one-tenth of the total farm labour force, in the south-west, in the northern counties, and in much of Scotland traditional farm service still survived on something like its old scale. As a result, most of these areas still had a relatively high proportion of women farm workers – indeed, more than a quarter of Scotland's farm employees were still female as late as 1871, compared with under 6 per cent in England (Devine 1984, 98).

Why did farm service, and with it women's role in agricultural work, decline so drastically in the late eighteenth and early nineteenth centuries? The process was reflected in a gradually developing sexual specialization of farm work. According to Snell, women in the largely grain-growing south east came to be employed more and more at spring-time tasks such as sowing, weeding and thinning crops – work which was unskilled, labour-intensive and poorly paid (Snell 1985, 21–2, 52–6). Conversely, men came to dominate harvest work, particularly with the increasing use of such heavier tools as the scythe (Devine 1984, 101, 139). The underlying factor behind all this was demographic. A static rural population, based on a regime of relatively high mortality, late marriage and small families such as existed between 1650 and 1750, had made the supply of farm labour uncertain. This situation was made worse in areas where adults could readily obtain farms, access to commons and wastes, or employment in rural trades and crafts and so reduce their need to work for the farmers for wages. An unreliable supply of adult labour made young, unmarried people the farmers' best bet, and made girls as useful and necessary as boys. Thus it is not surprising that the incidence of farm service reached its historical peak in the first half of the eighteenth century (Kussmaul 1981, 100–4). However, in the very different demographic climate of the early nineteenth century, farmers found it less necessary to keep as many resident servants, because continuous population growth in the countryside (coupled with the side-effects of enclosure) increased the number of poor, landless adult male labourers who had little choice but to take whatever work and wages the farmers offered.

Of course, the economics of hiring outdoor labourers rather than resident servants depended partly on other factors. One was the cost of providing board and lodging. When basic foodstuffs were cheap, as in the second quarter of the eighteenth century, it cost relatively little to feed resident servants; but when prices rose sharply around the turn of the century, it made economic sense to hire outdoor labourers at conventional weekly wages, especially when these could be supplemented under the old Poor Law. Another important consideration was the relative returns to the farmer of arable and livestock farming. Because the latter required a constant labour force and the former a more seasonal one, living-in servants were more necessary when farmers were most interested in expanding their animal husbandry, whereas non-resident labour would be preferred in periods when relative price movements made cereal production more attractive. Finally, it should be noted that changes in the long-term rate of population growth and changes in the incidence of farm service were mutually reinforcing. Just as rapid population increase in the countryside made servants less necessary to farmers, so fewer young people in service meant a greater freedom to marry early and, in turn, a still higher birthrate (Kussmaul 1981, 112).

The various forces making living-in servants less necessary to farmers were gathering strength from 1750 onwards. Labour shortages during the war years after 1793 may have delayed their impact, but postwar demobilization after 1815 was the final blow. The banishment of workers from the farmer's table was much lamented by William Cobbett, and its effects on social relationships in the countryside were widely condemned at the time of the 'Swing' riots in 1830 and in the debates which surrounded the reform of the Poor Law in 1834. Nevertheless, despite spells of low grain prices during the 1820s and 1830s, farmers in the arable south and east did *not* revert to using resident servants because, by contrast with a century earlier, continued population growth meant a plentiful supply of cheap adult male labour with few alternative opportunities. However, in other areas, where livestock farming predominated or where adult men could readily find work in industry or services, farmers went on using long-hired, resident servants, both male and female, until mid-century and beyond. Indeed, in parts of south-east Scotland, even the annual hiring of *married* farm servants, on terms which included tied housing and payment in kind, persisted with remarkable resilience (Devine 1984, 1).

It must be emphasized that the *full-time* employment of young women in agriculture was reduced when living-in farm service disappeared from the south east of England. Women and girls continued to be much in demand for part-time and seasonal work – weeding, thinning, stone-gathering and so on. In some eastern districts this led to the organization of the notorious mobile 'gangs' which so outraged respectable opinion around the middle of the century. But those seeking or needing regular and permanent work over much of southern England increasingly found it, not in the fields and farms of their native countryside, but in the middle-class houses and villas of the towns and their suburbs.

Domestic service

For girls in their late teens and early twenties in much of rural England, domestic service effectively replaced farm service as the most common form of paid employment during the period 1750 to 1850. There were obvious similarities between them. In both cases, relatively poor young people, who could not be supported or employed at home by their own families, were transferred to generally better-off households which needed extra labour. In both cases, the servants were hired on long contracts, paid annually, and received perhaps the greater part of their remuneration in board and lodging. In both cases, there were only one or two servants per household and a rapid turnover of personnel. But there were also important differences. In the first place, whereas farm servants had been productive workers in the agricultural sector, domestic servants, certainly in the wealthiest households, did 'useless' labour which simply freed the wife and daughters of their employer from the need to soil their hands with menial tasks. Secondly, domestic servants were overwhelmingly female, as farm servants had not been. And thirdly, whilst farm servants had, by definition, lived and worked in the country, domestic servants were urbanites and suburbanites: indeed, one of the most striking features of domestic service in the nineteenth century was its role in facilitating the long-drawn-out process of townward migration, by removing country girls to work in the towns.

Domestic service employed almost two out of every five working women – over four times as many as agriculture, and twice as many as textiles – by 1851. Yet the *rise* of urban domestic service has been little studied, in comparison with its late Victorian heyday and its twentieth-century decline (Horn 1975). Undoubtedly, the lack of raw census data before 1841 is responsible for this neglect, because the enumerators' records after that date are the main source of information about this ubiquitous type of women's work. Thanks to detailed local analyses, a good deal is now known about who went into service, who hired servants, and how the level and nature of servant keeping varied locally and over time. Some of the findings are not, perhaps, too surprising. London, for example, was the great centre of servant employment, containing over one-fifth of all the servants in England and Wales in 1851; some 60 per cent of them had been born outside the metropolis (McBride 1976, 35–6).

In provincial towns, the incidence of domestic service varied fairly predictably according to the character of the local economy and to the
availability of other employment. Thus almost 20 per cent of York's
households contained a servant in 1851, whereas the figure for Nottingham was less than 12 per cent (Armstrong 1974, 170). Nevertheless, it is
clear that, although servant keeping was perhaps the most obvious
symbol of middle-class-ness, it was by no means confined to such arche-
typal figures as factory masters, bankers, doctors and lawyers. In mid-
nineteenth-century Rochdale, for example, shopkeepers formed 'the
largest occupational group amongst the heads of servant-employing
households'. Approximately one in six of the families which employed a
servant there was headed by an artisan or a manual worker; three out of
every five servants worked in households where they were the only
resident servant; and servant-keeping depended very much on the life-
cycle of the employing family, being most common when the head of the
household was unmarried or when none of the children of the family was
working (Higgs 1986, 133–7). Although resident servants in middle-class
households were the most obvious element within the broad category of
'domestic service', there were also women who provided personal services
for others in (or from) their *own* homes. The census categories of 'servant',
'housekeeper' and 'nurse' could include close relatives of the household
head, and a proportion of the women so described were simply staying at
home and doing the domestic chores for their own families. In addition,
whilst most resident domestics were young and single, older married and
widowed women predominated in such non-resident occupations as laundresses and washerwomen, who were especially numerous in London, the
large seaports, and the spa, seaside and university towns (P. Malcolmson
1981, 442).

Although detailed census studies have revealed much about the
complex character of domestic service at the end of our period, the rise of
this major new type of female employment still poses difficult problems of
historical interpretation. Was it demand-led, reflecting simply the relative
and absolute increase of the servant-employing classes as towns and cities
grew larger and the industrial, commercial and professional bourgeoisie
expanded? Or is it to be explained from the supply side, the result of the
decline in other kinds of female employment? Those who emphasize the
demand side point to the 'unique economic advantages' of domestic
service, which led to its being 'chosen over factory work' (Branca 1978,
34; McBride 1976, 116). Among its alleged attractions was the level of
servants' real incomes, given the value of their board and lodging and the
possibility of saving the greater part of their annual wage. In Rochdale,
however, where local girls really did have a choice between domestic

service and the factory, they opted overwhelmingly for the latter (Higgs 1986, 139, 144). Finally, there is the difficult issue of whether 'domestic service was the chief means by which large numbers of people effected the transition to modern urban society'. Those who see domestic service as an attractive option stress that, in addition to its 'modernizing' effect on girls who entered it, it also 'initiated middle-class women into the role of employer/manager' (McBride 1976, 17, 117). But sceptics are more inclined to argue that 'domestic service may have served to maintain rural deference in the urban milieu and thus to insulate part of the ex-rural population from the dominant ideology of the urban working class' (Higgs 1986, 143). Unfortunately, domestic servants have proved to be silent and self-effacing in this period – as indeed their employers intended them to be; and it is likely that we will always be left guessing about questions like these.

Of course, women who worked in the service sector were not confined to domestic service, as the occupations of some of the best-known women in early Victorian fiction suggest: presumably, Jane Eyre was one of the 22,000 governesses, and Sarah Gamp one of the 2,800 midwives, recorded in 1851. Inns, beershops and lodging houses were particularly dependent on married women and widows. So too were retail shops: a total of over 40,000 women were returned in the categories 'shopkeepers', 'grocers' and 'hawkers' in 1851, *not* including those described as 'shopkeepers' wives'. Two areas, particularly important later on for career-minded women, were already showing strongly by mid-century, when the census counted 47,000 schoolmistresses and 'general teachers', as well as 25,000 'nurses (not domestic servants)'. By contrast, the public sector employed only a few hundred women, in the post office, as workhouse matrons and as prison wardresses. As for the higher professions, the only significant group of women classed as being 'employed in connexion with the learned professions' in 1851 were 658 pew-openers! Interesting and impressive as some of these statistics are, they must be kept in perspective. Charwomen still outnumbered schoolma'ams in 1851; and the 20,000 lodging-house keepers, scattered over the whole country, must be seen in the context of the 28,000 straw-plaiters recorded in the south midlands and the quarter of a million women in the cotton industry.

Finally, we must not forget prostitution – oldest and lowest of the professions – and also the one which dared not speak its name to census enumerators. That many eminent Victorians regarded prostitution as *the* social problem has long been recognized, and we now know quite a lot about the kinds of women who practised it and the pressures which drove them to it (Finnegan 1979). The very existence of prostitution as a last-resort employment raises many important issues about the female job markct in the nineteenth century. But whereas we have a reasonable idea how many Jane Eyres and Sarah Gamps there were, we can hazard only vague guesses at the number of Marthas and Little Em'lys in this often casual and temporary occupation.

Manufacturing industry

More women worked full-time in agriculture and services combined than in manufacturing, even at the end of our period. But how did developments in manufacturing affect women's role in the labour force? Obviously, there were areas of heavy industry – iron-making, machine-making and shipbuilding, for example – and of general outdoor labouring, whose expansion created few, if any, new opportunities for women workers. Similarly, their place in the old-established urban crafts – building, printing, cabinet-making, coach-building and so on – always marginal – was probably even further eroded after the middle of the eighteenth century (Snell 1985, 278–93). But for the most part women's involvement in industrial work fell outside the traditional system of craft apprenticeship. In some cases, it occurred because the wives and daughters of artisans who operated from their own homes necessarily had to lend a hand in the activities of the family workplace, even though they were never formally trained in all the 'mysteries' of the craft. However, it was in the large-scale, capitalist-controlled outwork industries that girls and young women had already come to make their greatest contribution to the industrial labour force by the mid-eighteenth century. During the past twenty years, the historical debate on 'proto-industrialization' as a distinctive aspect of Western European economic development in the seventeenth and eighteenth centuries has demonstrated that mass-production based on labour-intensive techniques and cheap, unskilled labour was the principal means by which merchant-manufacturers increased output and captured wider markets at home and abroad. By bringing together urban capital and commercial expertise with cheap labour, the outwork system permitted many rural communities to reduce their dependence on purely agricultural work and wages. Because women were crucial in supplying this expanding system with its extra hands for basic processes like spinning and knitting, one historian has described the middle years of the eighteenth century as 'a brief but glorious age ... never before did such a large percentage of women participate in productive labour' (Branca 1978, 23). Yet it would be wrong to enthuse about the 'emancipating' effects of outwork on women. Spinning – much the most common type until the last years of the eighteenth century – was extremely badly paid; and the women who did it not only lacked the organizational structures whereby urban craftsmen sought to improve their position, but also remained subordinate members of male-dominated households and family work-teams (Berg 1985, 140).

Because spinning was the first major manufacturing process to be dramatically transformed by new machinery and by the introduction of the factory system, it was often assumed that the late eighteenth century witnessed the end of outwork and the contraction, and ultimate extinction, of this particular type of women's work. It is now clear, however, that outwork continued to play a dynamic role in a number of industries until at least the third quarter of the nineteenth century, and that it lingered on locally, mainly in branches of the clothing trades, into the twentieth century (Bythell 1978). One reason for its longevity was that, in practice, mechanization of one particular process often simply meant *more* hand-work in either the preceding or later stages of production. Thus the rapid adoption of machine-spinning in cotton in the late eighteenth century initially called forth a vastly increased army of hand-loom weavers, amongst whom women and girls bulked large (Bythell 1969, 60–3).

Undoubtedly, when spinning disappeared into the factory, women in some parts of the south and east of England lost the chance of adding to family income. Where this development coincided with diminishing opportunities for agricultural work, especially after 1815, it left these regions with a surplus of unemployed young women who increasingly turned to domestic service as their only resort. Nevertheless, a number of rural areas remote from the new factory towns still maintained their industrial specialities throughout the first half of the nineteenth century. For example, women continued to plait straw and make lace in Bedford and Buckingham, to sew gloves around Yeovil and Worcester, and to knit stockings in the Yorkshire dales. However, outwork was increasingly centred upon the provincial towns of Lancashire, Yorkshire and the east midlands where textiles, hosiery and shoemaking were located, and also on the clothing and needlework trades of London. It was here that women – especially married women, for whom the opportunity to work and earn at home was particularly important – continued to make their main contribution to that part of the industrial workforce which remained outside the factory system in the mid-nineteenth century.

Yet for the most part outwork provided a poor living, which at best merely supplemented a family's other income. Many outwork trades became increasingly feminised by the mid-nineteenth century, as men avoided them when they could. In other cases, a clear gender-based division of labour came to exist: at Leicester and Nottingham, for example, men generally managed the increasingly complex, workshop-based knitting and lace frames, while women were relegated to doing the stitching, seaming and finishing by hand, often at home. In the 'sweated trades' of late Victorian Britain, outwork survived to remind horrified observers of the irregular employment, bad working conditions and low wages which had once been the common lot of working women in industries not subject to legislative regulation or effective collective bargaining procedures.

Where does this leave the small minority of working women – no more, perhaps, than one out of every six or seven by 1851 – who did indeed find employment in the new textile factories? Undoubtedly they enjoyed a new independence which domestic servants, for example, did not. Their earnings for a full week's work, undertaken at regular and limited hours, compared favourably with other women's, and their real level did not depend on the problematic value of payments in board and lodging. Yet a gender division of labour characterized textile factory work perhaps even more than it did industrial outwork. Only in powerloom weaving was Pinchbeck's ideal – of women earning the same wage-rates as men for doing the same work – actually achieved. But even here, because male weavers usually operated more looms, in practice they earned more. Moreover, men monopolized the more responsible jobs in the preparatory and warehousing departments, as well as the key supervisory position of overlooker in the weaving shed. In extreme cases, as at Courtauld's silk mill at Halstead, Essex, in the 1850s, 90 per cent of the workforce consisted of girls employed as winders (at wages of between 2 and 4 shillings a week) and of young female weavers (at approximately double these wages). Only 10 per cent of this company's employees were men, who held all the better paid jobs as managers, overseers, clerks and mechanics (as well, it should be noted, as the unskilled positions of general labourers). Arguably, this situation simply reinforced patriarchy and perpetuated the dependent status of working women, notwithstanding the fact that they earned their own wages outside the family home (Lown 1983, 36–44).

At first sight, the success of adult men in keeping women in a subordinate position in the early textile factories seems at odds with widespread contemporary fears that new machinery would displace men and allow employers to make use of cheap, unskilled and docile female labour. Yet elaborate machines did *not* replace skilled male workers; they merely required new *kinds* of skill in their operators. At a time of rapid technological change in cotton spinning in the second quarter of the nineteenth century, women were unable, probably because of their relatively rapid turnover, to acquire and transmit the skills needed on the self-acting mule, with the result that, by 1850, spinning – traditionally the woman's preserve – had become an elaborately mechanized process where the work was performed by small teams headed by adult men (Freifeld 1986, 320–2).

One feature of factory work which appalled early Victorian observers was the way in which it was alleged to unfit young women for their prime function as wives and mothers. It was even worse when married women, trained to factory work, insisted on going back to it and neglecting their families. The problem was actually less serious than well-meaning contemporaries feared: at Preston in 1851, for example, something under a quarter of wives with children were at work, and fewer than two-thirds of these worked away from home for most of the day (Anderson 1971, 71–4). Moreover, contrary to the modern pattern, it was the younger wives, with few or no children, who were most likely to be working: they gave up permanently as their families became larger, and in due course it was the older children who became the family's extra earners. Nevertheless, the phenomenon of women working away from home, in circumstances held to be physically and morally harmful to their own, and society's well-being, provoked the state to lay down statutory limits on their working hours in the shape of the Factory Acts. The most far reaching of these in its implications – the Act of 1844 – extended the restrictions already imposed on children and young people to all women in textile factories, regardless of age or marital condition.

However, it is Lord Ashley's Mines Act of 1842, banning women and children from working underground, which has been retrospectively accorded the greatest symbolic significance. Although the number of women affected was minute – between 5,000 and 6,000, or about 4 per cent of the total workforce in coalmines in 1841 – and although they had already ceased to be employed both above and below ground in the majority of coalfields, for the first time an Act of Parliament made it unlawful for women to do a particular kind of work. The timing of the Act was determined by the humanitarian outrage which followed the lurid report of the Royal Commission on Children's Employment. But why had many working miners *already* accepted the exclusion of women from underground working, and why were the coalowners willing to deny themselves the use of cheap female labour? According to one modern interpretation, the ban on women underground was yet another example of the collapse of the traditional family work-team and its replacement by the 'male-breadwinner norm'. Capitalist coalowners wanted to deal with a disciplined, reliable workforce, rather than with a collection of independent sub-contractors who controlled work and output through their leadership of family-based work-teams. The miners themselves feared that, if women became free wage-earners instead of subordinate members of a family team, their competition would force down wages and put men out of work. Once again, partriarchy was recreated, this time with the help of the law, in ways which satisfied both the current needs of the employers and the authoritarian instincts of adult males (Mark-Lawson and Witz 1988, 166–73). It should be added, however, that this particular interpretation of events appears to have gone unnoticed by most contemporaries.

Conclusion

Overall, women became a smaller element in the agricultural workforce as that sector declined in relative importance; they came to dominate private domestic service as it expanded; and they maintained a strong presence in the all-important textile and clothing trades by proving adaptable to the changing needs of both outwork and factory systems. There were, of course, both local divergences from these trends and short-term fluctuations in them, the latter most notably between 1793 and 1815, when the wartime shortage of male labour probably meant an increased participation by women in, for example, harvest work and additional branches of industrial outwork (Armstrong 1988, 51; Horn 1980, 59–60; Bythell 1969, 50–1). By the end of the period, too, it is likely that fewer women worked at home in the context of a family-based team, and it had become normal for a full-time woman worker to be employed outside the family home for a personal wage. In consequence there may have been relatively fewer opportunities for women, and in particular married women, to work in a part-time, casual, or occasional fashion by the mid-nineteenth century; and it is therefore possible that many women increasingly faced the stark alternatives of working full-time, or not working at all. If enough work was simply not available in many rural areas of southern and eastern England by this time, it would follow that there *was* indeed an overall decline in women's participation rate, that there *were* pockets of female unemployment, and that employers *were* backward in exploiting this potential resource.

In an abstract world of perfect labour markets, none of this would matter, because regional imbalances would be ironed out by migration. In practice, however, prevailing attitudes to gender roles and to women's status made the female labour market highly imperfect. Obviously, married women – even when not wholly tied to the house by family duties – were restricted to seeking whatever work was available in the vicinity of their husbands' workplaces. Nor were single young women from the country necessarily as mobile as one might suppose. It was neither financially practicable nor socially acceptable for them to establish independent households, except of course on marriage. Thus working away from home generally meant either living with pseudo-parents (as in service) or lodging with relatives or family friends. Similarly, to obtain a 'suitable' post away from home, most girls would initially depend on the network of contacts provided by kin and neighbours, and would subsequently need to maintain a good reputation, not only for hard work, but also for a blameless personal life. By the beginning of the Victorian era, a girl without 'friends' or 'character' could find herself excluded from major areas of female employment, even assuming that her freedom of action had not already been pre-empted by a parental decision that she was 'needed at home'.

All in all, it is remarkable how little many of the basic characteristics of women's work changed between 1750 and 1850. Most obviously, gender divisions, both between industries and within individual workplaces, may have been redefined and reasserted; but they were emphatically *not* a new phenomenon. Contrary to both contemporary fears and later popular beliefs, women workers rarely displaced men in practice – although they sometimes colonized new types of work which men chose to avoid. Because basic gender divisions persisted, women continued to be poorly paid, and there is little to suggest that conventional differentials between men's and women's earnings narrowed, except where work was paid by the piece and women were not debarred from doing it, as was the case in some branches of handloom weaving, for example. Thus the fact that more women workers earned an 'independent' wage by 1850 probably made little difference to their real ability to 'live their own lives', if only because the level of their earnings generally made it impossible.

On the wider question of working women's personal 'freedom', a number of observations need to be made. In the first place, when a girl reached 'working age', in her early teens, it is extremely doubtful whether she was offered or permitted any effective choice of jobs – indeed, even the option of working or staying at home to help mother was probably denied her. Secondly, it would be hard to imagine a less 'emancipated' life-style than that of the average domestic servant in the mid-nineteenth century. Thirdly, even the typical factory girl almost certainly lodged at home and handed over the whole of her wages to her mother and received pocket money in return, probably until the age of 21. The basic fact is that, at least at the outset of their working lives, girls – and boys, for that matter – generally did what they were *told* to do by their parents, no matter how indulgent and affectionate those parents might be. After a few years at work, however, most working girls probably came to enjoy two more substantial 'freedoms'. The first was the freedom to change employer, always assuming that other employment was available: even so, it would be fascinating to discover how the number of girls who ever 'walked off the job' compared with the number who either got the sack or simply bore it all with silent resignation. Secondly, and perhaps more significantly, they had the freedom to chose a marriage partner, or at least to reject an unacceptable one. No doubt for some it was Hobson's choice, and feminist historians would probably argue that to get married at all was simply to exchange one form of male domination for another. But it seems legitimate to ask whether, with all the recent emphasis on patriarchy, the existence of the working-class *materfamilias* who ruled her domestic domain with a rod of iron, or of marriages based on an affectionate partnership, has not been overlooked. It is surely time some courageous historian – male or female – rescued the working-class matriarch from the enormous condescension of posterity!

As with so much about 'the Industrial Revolution', in discussing women's work we should really be asking, not 'why did so many things change', but rather 'why did so much remain the same'. In this case, much of the answer lies in the basic facts of demography. Most women married, and spent the greater part of their adult lives bearing and rearing children, with the result that their availability for full-time and regular employment was necessarily limited. During the second half of the eighteenth century, the marriage rate actually rose, the age of women at first marriage fell, and the number of children born per couple increased in most parts of the country: in other words, an ever *greater* part of the average woman's existence was committed to the responsibilities of motherhood (Wrigley and Schofield 1981, 421–30).

The onset of a new phase of sustained population growth around the middle of the eighteenth century had inevitable repercussions on women's place in the labour market. During the preceding century of negligible population increase, women's chances of finding work improved precisely because men were in short supply; but now the situation was reversed. Once adult male workers became more numerous then, as in agriculture in southern England, women became marginalized. This may seem curious, given that conventionally women's earnings were so much lower than men's. Why did employers – farmers, in particular – not cut their wages bill by employing women rather than men, given that both were readily available? The answer, in Armstrong's words, was that 'there was a sense that males had a prior claim, and anyway would otherwise have to be sustained from the [poor] rates' (Armstrong 1988, 67). Here we are brought face to face with the mixture of ideology and pragmatic necessity that underlay attitudes to women's work. The Victorians may have pushed the doctrine of 'separate spheres' to its limits, but they did not invent it. And if the concept of patriarchy implied male domination, it also involved male responsibilities, not least to maintain their families. To work was both the 'natural' right and the duty of men, but not of women. More prosaically, adult male workers, fearing overstocked labour markets, protected their position from the added threat of women's competition by excluding them from jobs they wished to monopolize for themselves, and then justified their actions in terms of 'the masculine ideal of family provider' (Rose 1988, 208). Needless to say, this ideal generally fell far short of realization. Few working men outside the artisan trades actually earned enough to support a family comfortably from their own wages, and it was still the extra earnings of sons, daughters and wives which made it possible to avoid hardship. Yet if the contribution of women workers remained essential to the well-being of wage-earners' families, it was still the case that women formed part of the labour force only to the extent that men – husbands, fathers, employers and even parliamentarians – allowed or required them to be. In this respect, the 'Industrial Revolution' between 1750 and 1850 had changed nothing.

REFERENCES

Anderson, M. 1971. *Family Structure in Nineteenth-Century Lancashire.*
Armstrong, A. 1974. *Stability and Change in an English County Town. A social study of York 1801–1851.*
    1988. *Farmworkers in England and Wales. A social and economic history.*
Berg, M. 1985. *The Age of Manufactures. Industry, innovation, and work in Britain 1700–1820.*
Branca, P. 1978. *Women in Europe since 1750.*
Bythell, D. 1969. *The Handloom Weavers. A study in the English cotton industry during the Industrial Revolution.*
    1978. *The Sweated Trades. Outwork in nineteenth-century Britain.*
Devine, T. M. (ed.) 1984. *Farm Servants and Labour in Lowland Scotland 1770–1914.*
Dex, S. 1988. 'Issues in gender and employment', *Social History*, 13.
Earle, P. 1989. 'The female labour market in London in the late seventeenth and early eighteenth centuries', *Economic History Review*, 2nd ser. 42.
Finnegan, F. 1979. *Poverty and Prostitution. A study of Victorian prostitutes in York.*
Freifeld, M. 1986. 'Technological change and the self-acting mule; a study of skill and the sexual division of labour', *Social History*, 11.
Hall, C. 1979. 'The early formation of Victorian domestic ideology', in *Fit Work for Women*, ed. S. Burman, 15–32.
Hanawalt, B. A. (ed.), 1986. *Women and Work in Pre-Industrial Europe.*
Hartwell, R. M. 1961. 'The rising standard of living in England 1800–1850', *Economic History Review*, 2nd ser., 13.
Hewitt, M. 1958. *Wives and Mothers in Victorian Industry.*
Higgs, E. 1986. 'Domestic service and household production', in *Unequal Opportunities. Women's employment in England 1800–1918*, ed. A. V. John, 126–50.

1987. 'Women, occupations, and work in nineteenth-century censuses', *History Workshop*, 23.

Horn, P. 1975. *The Rise and Fall of the Victorian Servant*.

1980. *The Rural World 1780–1850. Social change in the English countryside*.

John, A. V. 1980. *By the Sweat of their Brow. Women workers and Victorian coalmines*.

Jordan, E. 1988. 'Female unemployment in England and Wales 1851–1911: an examination of the census figures for 15–19 year olds', *Social History*, 13.

Kussmaul, A. 1981. *Servants in Husbandry in Early Modern England*.

Lee, C. H. 1979. *British Regional Employment Statistics 1841–1971*.

Lown, J. 1983. 'Not so much a factory, more a form of patriarchy: gender and class during industrialisation', in *Gender, Class and Work*, ed. E. Gamarnikow et al., pp. 28–45.

McBride, T. M. 1976. *The Domestic Revolution. The modernisation of household service in England and France 1820–1920*.

Malcolmson, P. 1981. 'Laundresses and the laundry trade in Victorian England', *Victorian Studies*, 24.

Malcolmson, R. W. 1981. *Life and Labour in England 1700–1780*.

Mark-Lawson, J. and Witz, A. 1988. 'From family labour to family wages. The case of women's labour in nineteenth-century coalmining', *Social History*, 13.

Osterud, N. G. 1986. 'Gender divisions and the organisation of work in the Leicester hosiery industry', in *Unequal Opportunities. Women's Employment in England 1800–1918*, ed. A. V. John, 45–70.

Pinchbeck, I. 1930. *Women Workers and the Industrial Revolution 1750–1850*.

Prior, M. (ed.) 1985. *Women in English Society 1500–1800*.

Richards, E. 1974. 'Women in the British economy since about 1700: an interpretation', *History*, 59.

Rose, S. O. 1988. 'Gender antagonism and class conflict. exclusionary strategies of male trade-unionists in nineteenth-century Britain', *Social History*, 13.

Seccombe, W. 1986. 'Patriarchy stabilised: the construction of the male breadwinner wage norm in nineteenth century Britain', *Social History*, 11.

Snell, K. D. M. 1985. *Annals of the Labouring Poor. Social change and agrarian England 1660–1900*.

Taylor, B. 1983. 'The men are as bad as their masters. Socialism, feminism, and sexual antagonism in the London tailoring trade in the 1830s', in *Sex and Class in Women's History*, ed. J. L. Newton et al., 187–220.

Tilly, L. A. and Scott, J. W. 1978. *Women, Work and Family*.

Wrigley, E. A. and Schofield, R. S. 1981. *The Population History of England 1541–1871. A reconstruction*.

3 Reinterpretations of the Industrial Revolution

Gary Hawke

Industrial Revolution: concept and significance

Britain's Industrial Revolution has an enduring fascination. Successive generations of economic historians have reinterpreted the significance of economic change in Britain between about 1760 and 1860. The term, Industrial Revolution, is loose enough to accommodate changes of interest. It was used by a French economist, Blanqui, in 1837 to draw attention to some parallels and contrasts between developments in Britain and the marked and sudden redistribution of political power at more or less the same time in France, for which the term 'Revolution' was well established. There had been changes in Britain which could be seen as at least equally fundamental. Defining and explaining those changes is a never-ending task.

There were big advances in scholarly study in the later nineteenth century. Modern disciplines gradually emerged as convenient sub-divisions for teaching and advancing knowledge. History was separated from current politics, and economics was established as a distinctive specialization. Economic history developed at the same time, although its literature took longer to be readily identified and it never separated from history and economics to the same extent as some other disciplines separated from their parents. Part of the growth of economic history as an academic discipline was study of the Industrial Revolution.

The lectures of Arnold Toynbee, posthumously published in 1884, were especially significant in giving prominence to the term. But Toynbee's focus did not achieve any immediate following. At the centre of his analysis was the comment, 'The essence of the Industrial Revolution is the substitution of competition for the medieval regulations which had previously controlled the production and distribution of wealth' (Toynbee 1884, 58). This points towards a concern with property rights which did not reemerge into such prominence until the 1970s.

In the early twentieth century, most work was on the industrial changes which led to the 'great staples' of Victorian Britain, coal, cotton, iron and steel, and shipbuilding. These gave Britain preeminence in the international economy in the late nineteenth century – and problems in the inter-war years. The focus of interest in the Industrial Revolution was on tracing and explaining their origins. The classic work of the period was Mantoux (1928) which has the subtitle, *An Outline of the Beginnings of the Modern Factory System in England*. Mantoux wrote 'The object of all industry is the production of goods, or to be more explicit, of articles of consumption which are not directly provided by nature. By "factory system" we therefore primarily mean a particular organization, a particular system of production. But this organization affects the whole economic system and consequently the whole social system, which is controlled by the growth and distribution of wealth.' He therefore ranged widely over Britain's experience, but he started with features of European cities in the first half of the twentieth century: 'The great factories on the outskirts of our cities, the tall chimneys smoking by day and glowing by night, the incessant hum of machinery, the bustle of crowds of workmen . . .' T. S. Ashton prepared the edition of Mantoux's book which was published in 1961. He was himself responsible for extending knowledge of how the coal and iron industries grew, and he took a similar approach in his masterly survey (Ashton 1948). But while Ashton was very sensitive to the continuity inherent in historical experience, he was especially interested in the sources of changes. His book includes the memorable reporting of a schoolboy's summing up: 'About 1760 a wave of gadgets swept over England'. Ashton's study goes much deeper, but he would not have repudiated the implicit emphasis on inventive activity: 'Ideas of innovation and progress undermined traditional sanctions . . .'

After the Second World War, interest turned away from questions of stability and the problems of individual industries, and towards issues of economic growth and development. National income accounting had developed, and 'progress' was no longer assessed by indices of output for particular industries, but by the newly refined concepts of economic aggregates. Industrialized countries were preoccupied with postwar recovery and then with disseminating prosperity both directly and through the mechanisms of the welfare state. Poorer countries wanted to reduce the gap between their standards of living and those of industrialized countries. Industrialization was not forgotten, but the focus was on national income. What was it that caused the national incomes of countries to grow? The Industrial Revolution was then approached as the first example of change resulting in higher economic growth rates, and the emphasis shifted from particular industries to aggregate analysis. The book by P. Deane and W. A. Cole (1959) achieved enduring fame by encapsulating this approach.

Questions about industrial organization, technology and economic growth are all likely to be formulated most sharply by people familiar with economics. But there are other questions which can be asked about British experience in the late eighteenth and early nineteenth centuries. The growth of industry was accompanied by an invasion of smokestacks and urban slums into 'green and pleasant' lands (although agricultural life involved much drudgery). The nature of society was changed. Features of modern communities such as a high level of urbanization, concentration of economic activity in large corporations with most people earning wages rather than sharing directly in a family's production, and regulation of activity by mechanical systems of timekeeping rather than by the course of the sun and the natural cycles of the seasons all seemed to originate or at least change markedly at the time of the Industrial Revolution. Indeed, while Blanqui's term seemed to suggest that Britain's Industrial Revolution was an alternative to political upheavals, the nature of political power changed in Britain in the nineteenth century. The Industrial Revolution did have something to do with the progress of democracy.

All of these concerns are overlapping, notably in the question of how the fruits of the Industrial Revolution were distributed. Porter and Engels debated the question in the 1840s, Clapham and Hammond brought to bear on it all the scholarship of the nineteenth and early twentieth centuries, Hartwell and Hobsbawm in the 1960s added that of succeeding generations, and there have been more recent interventions (Williamson 1985). The debate has been far from sterile, but the questions which can be asked proliferate more quickly than balanced assessments can be made.

Porter was a statistician who was keen to document progress; Engels was more philosophical, anxious to trace changes in the nature of society. From its beginning, the 'standard of living debate' was therefore more than a simple matter of deciphering and describing the distributional consequences of the Industrial Revolution. The title of a later contribution, *Capitalism and the Historians* (Hayek 1954) captures the essentially political nature of successive contributions. This was not always immediately apparent. A great deal of effort had to be directed towards elucidating the course of income for some defined group, and not everybody remained aware of the distinction between the *effects* of the Industrial Revolution (however defined) and the course of standards of living *during* the Industrial Revolution. There are further links to be explored before the effects of the Industrial Revolution are identified with those of capitalism. It is precisely in distinguishing more finely between such questions that recent contributions have been greatest.

The Industrial Revolution of the late eighteenth and early nineteenth centuries in Britain did not long remain unique. Experiences in other countries which had parallels were soon drawn into discussion. Britain did not, after all, remain the only industrialized country – or the only one to experience economic growth, urbanization or modernization. But part of the fascination of Britain was that it remained 'first'. Others were following, and following quickly (O'Brien and Keyder 1978). Between 1820 and 1860, Britain's share of the total of industrial production of France, Germany, Britain and the United States fell from 24 per cent to 21 per cent (Capie 1983). But any production by a competitor will reduce the share of a market held by a monopolist. Britain always retained the distinction of being first.

Earlier experiences of unusually rapid growth of at least some industry, even back to the Late Bronze Age, merely qualifies some of that uniqueness. No such experience was as wide-ranging in its effects. Of more importance was the gradual demonstration that much of what happened in Britain in the period of the Industrial Revolution was dependent on earlier developments. Whatever one thought about the appropriateness of the term Industrial Revolution for experiences such as the growth of industries in Britain between 1540 and 1640 (Nef 1934), it could not be denied that what happened between 1760 and 1830 was greatly influenced by what happened in British agriculture, trade and technology in the seventeenth and eighteenth centuries. Furthermore, the consequences of developments between 1760 and 1830 were worked out over a long subsequent period.

For most people, the word 'revolution' has connotations of sudden sharp change. Something that took a long time to evolve, and affected people only over a very long time, does not look revolutionary. In his three volume *Economic History of Modern Britain* published at the end of the 1920s, Clapham seldom used the term 'Industrial Revolution' (except when quoting other authors). Few have followed Clapham's example, but several authors have suggested that this is only because it would be pedantic to avoid a well-known term.

Yet, not too much should be made of semantics. The same kind of discussion takes place about other terms such as 'capitalism' and 'feudalism', 'Renaissance', 'Reformation', 'socialism' and 'colonialism'. Indeed, when a scholarly term becomes part of public debate, it is likely to lose its precision. The terms cited all denote broad concepts. They are not suited to precise analysis because readers bring with them different preconceptions of their nuances. It is certainly right to be sceptical of statements that purport to attribute causal significance to the Industrial Revolution since in the absence of further elucidation it is unlikely to be clear what aspect of the Industrial Revolution is seen as significant.

Joel Mokyr (1985), one of the foremost current writers about the Industrial Revolution, attempts to establish its uniqueness by observing that its effects 'were so profound that even if we divide it by seventy, the per annum change was far-reaching enough to dwarf any economic change in Britain since the Black Death'. But that is unlikely to be true for several aspects of what is written about as the Industrial Revolution, or at least to imply that there have been many subsequent cases of further Industrial Revolutions. Mokyr goes on to identify the fact that 'growth was sustained and even accelerated' as the characteristic which makes the Industrial Revolution unique, but that is subject to the same objection.

In any case, the most fundamental significance of the Industrial Revolution lies elsewhere. Between 1760 and 1830 there were significant developments which continue to preoccupy students of contemporary society. Manufactured products still have an importance difference from agricultural products; those who have any knowledge of agriculture do not share Mantoux's belief that its products come from nature without human effort, but there is still something different about the ingenuity and craft which shapes manufactured commodities. The relative size of agriculture in satisfying consumption demands underwent significant change in the Industrial Revolution. (Now that services are expanding relative to economic activity as a whole, there will probably be more interest in the late nineteenth century and less in the Industrial Revolution, but there is still a widespread belief, perhaps a lingering relic of snobbery in nineteenth-century southern England about trade, that services are less valuable than manufactured goods.) Economic growth, despite concerns about the environment and about non-material values, remains a prime concern for most societies; the Industrial Revolution marked a change in the extent to which economic growth could be regarded as usual. The distribution of income in the face of economic adjustment remains a matter of intense interest; the Industrial Revolution was a major economic adjustment which affected groups differently. And the same kind of point can be made for both social and political aspects of modern human societies. It is the place of the Industrial Revolution in the dialogue between present concerns and past experience that guarantees that it will remain a prime topic for economic historians and others.

Although this is not an especially novel argument, it may still be puzzling to some students of history. Isn't the task of a historian to understand the past in its own terms? Doesn't one incur the danger of anachronism by importing present concerns into past experience? In trying to understand decisions made by individuals in the past, it is obviously wrong to assume that they had information which did not become available until later time. But even when trying to understand past lives, historians have to select which lives they will study, and their choice is likely to be guided, at least in part, by which lives will interest their readers, and that in turn is influenced by how past issues relate to present ones. Furthermore, individuals and their motivations are not the only topic of history. Economic growth existed before it was conceptualized; it is perfectly sensible to ask how it was achieved even when contemporaries were quite unaware that it was happening. But the main point is that present preoccupations influence the choice of what history will be studied. Industrial Revolution denotes a broad set of changes to which historians return frequently. The broadness of its connotations, its 'slipperiness' as a concept, is not evidence of sloppy thinking, but reflects the breadth of the dialogue between past and present which it induces.

Technology

Popular impressions of the Industrial Revolution are likely to be dominated by school textbook accounts of the great inventors. Specific examples of individual action are most easily comprehended. And the great inventions exemplify the key theme of change. Kay's flying shuttle, Arkwright's water-frame and Cartwright's mule are therefore prominent in many accounts of the rise of the cotton industry. Darby's use of coal for smelting iron, successful implementation by the Cort brothers of puddling as the means of refining iron, and Neilsen's hot blast are often presented as the most significant features of the development of the iron industry. The Newcomen engine and Watt's steam engine are likely to be seen as leading to growth in all aspects of industry, culminating in the introduction of railways in the early nineteenth century.

These important inventions raised the standard of living. Improvements in spinning and weaving techniques such as those associated with Kay, Arkwright and Cartwright meant that people could be provided with cheaper cotton textiles. The invention of the Cort brothers had a similar effect through iron products. Their technique needed less effort than the older process of hammering. Similarly, when a cheaper energy source facilitates the conversion of inputs into desired outputs, a community can become richer and have more control over its destinies; Darby's use of coal was therefore important, and recent work has brought the role of coal supplies into prominence again. It was never unrecognized; the other inventions listed above were associated with coal. The Neilsen hot blast was a means of economizing on coal in the process of smelting iron. The Newcomen engine was essentially a pump which made control of water levels in mines cheaper and thereby increased the availability of coal supplies by making it possible to recover what had formerly been inaccessible. Watt's steam engine not only did this better, but when it was combined with skilled engineering, it made the relatively cheap energy stored in coal available for a wide variety of uses.

There is therefore a sense in which such achievements remain landmarks. But they have come to seem less significant as knowledge has grown. There is very little that is indispensable. Most commodities and processes have substitutes, and the critical question is the gap between the best and the next best substitute rather than the existence of the best. Furthermore, those innovations selected for their engineering novelty or their greater impact on the public imagination were supplemented and sometimes surpassed in significance by changes that were not recorded as individual events. For example, the puddling process and the hot blast both reduced the amount of coal needed to make pig iron and were therefore significant in making iron cheaper. But between those landmark innovations, small and varied changes reduced the average amount of coal required per ton of pig iron, and their cumulative effect was more than equal to those of the landmark changes. Nor did the great innovations suddenly sweep all before them. The Newcomen engine remained essentially an adjunct to coalmining; in the late eighteenth and early nineteenth centuries, the steam engine was substantially confined to the cotton industry (von Tunzelmann 1978). While canals carried a great variety of freight, for most of them a large part of their function was reducing the cost of carrying coal from where it was found to where it was wanted. (This was true of railways too.)

But even if the great heroes of the Industrial Revolution no longer seem so heroic, current assessments of the role of technology are still high. As we shall see in the next section, much of the change in Britain in the Industrial Revolution cannot be explained as the result of capital accumulation or an increased labour supply. Technology, in the economists' sense of a gain in output relative to inputs used, remains important. What modern scholarship has done has been to widen the area over which 'technology' is important, to downgrade the importance of particular engineering achievements and to direct attention to the application of ingenuity over a wide area of economic activity.

Where did this ingenuity come from? Few scholars now believe that science had much to do with it in any direct manner. In Britain during the Industrial Revolution, science was essentially a consumer good, a use of resources possible only in a relatively rich society which was able to provide food and necessities for most of the population, and which could therefore support activities which satisfied human curiosity for more than a very select minority. Science was not unlike other cultural pursuits like music and art, although its feedback on systems of production was eventually greater. Science also provided explanations for what had been found to work by trial and error, and this could pave the way for further improvements. But the period when academic knowledge contributed directly to technology began, for the most part, after the Industrial Revolution. This is not to dismiss science, and it is still possible that Britain gained because its scientists were more practical than those of other countries. Their real interests were often broad frameworks of thought just as were those of scientists and philosophers throughout Europe, but they were also willing to solve problems wherever they arose, and they were in contact with people who had those problems. Even Watt's invention of the steam engine owed far more to practical mechanics than to the behaviour of gasses under pressure.

Trial and error is a far more important source of knowledge than is sometimes realized. Knowing that something works may be all that is required; knowing why it works may be an optional extra. Economic historians who reflect on the depth of their understanding of why a motor vehicle responds to its controls or how a word processor works, may recognize the truth of what looks like an anti-intellectual assertion. Intellectual belief often depends on confidence that somebody else could provide a greater degree of understanding. During the Industrial Revolution operatives in industry as much as farming were likely to find the experience of their neighbours more persuasive than the writing and speaking of people who can be recognized as scientists.

This is related to a somewhat more sophisticated point. In a number of contexts, attempts to pierce the 'black box' of technical change and explore the decisions by which innovations were introduced, have resulted in arguments which rest on 'learning by doing'. At a broad level of generalization, there may be a large array of possible ways by which something may be produced. It might even be appropriate to think in terms of a production isoquant with an infinite number of possible combinations of labour and capital as in an introductory economics textbook (e.g. Hawke 1980, 168–70). But at a more detailed level, the degree of knowledge about what combinations of inputs are really needed depends on experience with particular mixtures of them. Thus, when the shift from hammering to puddling was made, it proved possible to use even less coal than was the case initially. The process of change itself induced further change; what we have is less progress in technology for which we need to seek an explanation outside the economy than a process within the economy which included changes which secured more output for given inputs (including inputs of human effort). Older accounts in terms of the great inventions noted that one success sometimes generated pressures for further change – the usual example was an invention that simplified spinning and so put pressure on weavers to find ways of increasing output; reformulation in terms of 'learning by doing' directs attention to the range of endeavour which was affected.

The importance of coal was prominent in accounts of technical inventions and remains so in recent studies. Indeed, Wrigley (1988; see also the paper by Thomas in Rotberg and Rabb 1986) has recently argued that the best conceptualization of the change that occurred is that there were two economies, one in which energy was mostly human and one where exploitation of coal permitted rapid change and the discovery of ways of achieving greater productivity. His title, *Continuity, Chance and Change: The character of the industrial revolution in England*, captures the core of his thesis: much of the economy showed continuity and was only slowly influenced by what was happening elsewhere; chance determined the availability of coal supplies; change occurred where coal was exploited.

There is no doubt that coal was important, and Wrigley's is a sophisticated analysis starting from the importance of coal and the coexistence of old and new. He is well aware of qualifications. Coal had been used for a long time before the Industrial Revolution, and its use increased as it became cheaper than fuels like charcoal. Not all the technical change that occurred in the Industrial Revolution was directly linked to coal. The use of coal increased in agriculture and parts of the economy not usually regarded as those most affected by change in the Industrial Revolution. Britain was less of a divided economy than many which have existed. The central core of Wrigley's vision survives such qualifications. What remains at issue is how much understanding the vision provides. The temptation to oversimplify and see resource constraints removed by a miraculous discovery of new uses for coal should be resisted, but it may well be fruitful to explore how and why working with coal provided examples of successful learning by doing.

In what is an example of a continuing theme in this essay, technology improved in the Industrial Revolution because there was time and opportunity in a relatively rich society to experiment with new ways of doing things.

Economic growth

Once economic historians turned their attention from the classic Industrial Revolution to Britain's economic growth in the late eighteenth and early nineteenth century, the slowness of change became more deeply understood. Earlier scholars like Clapham had set technological change in a wider setting; Clapham was as interested in persisting handloom weavers as in those using new technology and had used census returns to trace the long time during which traditional crafts continued to compete with new industrial activities. But the result of such studies was mostly to establish a more judicious assessment of the way that the new swept all before it, if indeed, it was not understood as a mere qualification to the established picture. When scholars brought the perspective of modern economic development to the experience of the Industrial Revolution, there was a more fundamental reassessment of the speed of economic adjustment. The result is now so familiar that it can be encapsulated in a numerical example (cf. Mokyr 1985, 5).

Consider an economy that can be divided into two parts. One is modernized and grows at 4 per cent per annum. The other is traditional and grows at 1 per cent per annum. Initially, the former composes only 10 per cent of the total. Because of its faster growth rate, its share of the total increases. But as a matter of arithmetic, after twenty years it constitutes only 17 per cent of the total. (And the growth rate of the economy has increased from 1.3 per cent to 1.5.) After fifty years, the modern sector is 32 per cent of the total and the aggregate growth rate is 2 per cent per annum. After 75 years, the modern and traditional sectors are of equal size and the growth rate is 2.5 per cent. And after a century, the modern sector constitutes two-thirds of the total and the growth rate is 3 per cent per annum.

That is delightfully simple, but the initial figures are not unrealistic and it shows why economic change in Britain remained slow in the face of dramatic technical achievements in particular parts of the economy. (It is, however, an aid to understanding, not a finished explanation. In particular, it does not capture the way in which change was diffused. There was no 'traditional' part of the economy which remained unaffected by improved means of production.)

The figures of 1 and 4 per cent per annum for output growth are low relative to some experiences in more recent years, especially that of Japan. It is important, in looking back to the Industrial Revolution to recognize that expectations were then different from those which have become reasonable in years since the Second World War. This observation goes much wider than direct measurement of economic aggregates; it makes sense of the way that many people got satisfaction from placing their children or grandchildren in a better material situation than they experienced themselves, something which is much less prominent in contemporary societies.

It also presents more prosaic problems to economic historians. Changes may be significant even when they are small, but they are necessarily harder to detect and even more difficult to measure with precision. Nor are we assisted by a profusion of contemporary efforts at such measurement. The Industrial Revolution preceded the 'statistical movement' of the 1830s when measurement of sectoral economic and social aggregates became more frequent, let alone the invention of national income aggregates and the estimates of economic variables which are now the standard vehicles for commentary and analysis.

There were a few precursors of statistical monitoring, and their results have been much worked over by subsequent scholars. Squeezing information out of limited evidence is central to the discipline of historians. Economic historians have worked and reworked the efforts of contemporary 'arithmeticians' like King and Colquhoun, rearranging their data so as to fit as closely as possible to modern concepts and removing obvious errors and inconsistencies. Sometimes it appears that the figures are being asked to bear too much weight, and that the guesses of early writers have too large a range of error to permit us to discriminate between alternative possibilities. The reason for this, however, is not excessive zeal by modern scholars but an implication of the arithmetic example we have just discussed – rates of change which imply quite different courses for the economy are themselves close together – the difference between 1.3 and 1.5 is twenty years of unprecedented industrial growth.

To some extent, the problem lies not with the manipulations of those who are entirely familiar with contemporary estimates and modern concepts but with their readers. Those with an intimate knowledge of their sources and methods are aware of their limitations, and they probably approach all estimates of aggregates in the period of the Industrial Revolution (and later) in a probabilistic frame of mind. That is, they automatically associate a range with any numerical estimate. Furthermore, measurement of economic aggregates is not the same as measurement of something like the length of a piece of string. Economic aggregates have more than one dimension and cannot be reduced unambiguously to a single number. Writers can reasonably be asked to minimize the extent to which a figure is misleading, but demands for simple accuracy are unrealistic. All this is well known, and there is a limit to the extent to which anybody who attaches spurious precision to a number just because it is presented in numerical form can be rescued from erroneous interpretations.

Nor should the achievements of modern scholars be underestimated. While the results of arithmeticians continue to underlie modern estimates of aggregates, they have been very greatly refined by drawing on a much wider range of data. Older scholars like Hoffman brought together statistics compiled for other purposes and explored their implications for

Table 3.1. *Estimates of economic growth rates*

	National product	National product per head
1700–60	0.69	0.31
1760–80	0.70	0.01
1780–1801	1.32	0.35
1801–31	1.97	0.52

the growth of output. The process continues – Harley (1985, see also Jackson 1989) has recently shown that the procedures used by Hoffman have misled many people about the change of growth rates within the period 1760 to 1830. The work of Feinstein (1972, 1981) is especially notable not only for the painstaking care with which he has drawn together available information, but for his assessment of the degree of confidence which should be placed in his results. Currently, the best available summary data is that compiled by Crafts which draws together the work of Feinstein and his own reassessment of other data. They result in the following estimates (see Table 3.1) (Crafts 1985, p. 45).

The first column shows annual average growth rates of total output. It suggests that up to 1780 output increased by somewhat less than three-quarters of 1 per cent per year. In the last twenty years of the eighteenth century, it increased to over 1.25 per cent, and then in the first three decades of the nineteenth century rose to nearly 2 per cent. The second column shows annual average rates of output per person. The difference between the two columns is therefore the rate of growth of population. In the first half of the eighteenth century population growth was about half the rates of growth of output. In the two decades between 1760 and 1780, the growth of population increased and came to be nearly equal that of total output. Population growth continued to accelerate, but not by as much as total output so that growth in output per head returned to the level achieved earlier in the eighteenth century, and then reached a higher level in the early nineteenth century. There are puzzles about the implications of these figures, but, consistent with our earlier discussion, the rates of growth are low, and the degree of acceleration is subdued. This can equally be put another way: relatively small differences have major effects when they persist over long periods.

Furthermore, Britain's level of national income in 1760 was high relative not only to contemporary experience but even to what was found in the poor countries of the 1950s. The idea of successive agricultural, commercial and industrial revolutions as expounded in some older studies is no longer regarded as a useful framework of analysis because change was coincident in a number of sectors over a long period rather than separated into distinct periods. But the element which remains important is that changes before 1760 gave a level of income and an experience of change that facilitated the developments of later years.

Processes and causes

We observed in our discussion of Table 3.1 that population growth accelerated after 1760. In the late eighteenth century, it was possible to wonder whether Britain's population was rising or falling, but the first census which was held in 1801 ended the argument. (There was sufficient 'backcasting', collection of information about earlier years, for the census to provide information on growth as well as on levels of population.)

Population growth was probably related directly to economic growth. A more wealthy community could better resist disease, and better distribution systems reduced the effects of harvest failures on mortality (Fogel 1989). But the more important mechanism linking population and economic growth was probably fertility. Britain shared a 'West European Family Pattern' whereby population was subjected to implicit social control according to the resources available to support family formation. A rise in incomes stimulated earlier marriages, an increase in the proportion of the population which married and an increased illegitimacy rate. In shorter periods, the links between income levels and changes in family formation were complicated, and there is no general agreement on the relative significance of possible connections (or indeed on the variables most involved), but Britain's longer term experience was for the rise in population to be a muted reflection of the rise in income so that per capita incomes rose. While this pattern had evolved in primarily rural communities, it was retained as change proceeded, and incomes earned in industry or commerce became the basis for increased family formation (Wrigley and Schofield 1981; Rotberg and Rabb 1986).

Table 3.2 (calculated from Crafts 1985, p. 81) shows the best available partitioning of Britain's growth among increased supplies of labour, capital and land. The first column shows the growth rate of income (as in Table 3.1). The second, third and fourth columns show the percentages of the income growth that can be attributed to increased supplies of labour, capital and land. The final column shows the percentage of the income growth that cannot be so attributed; it is the residual left after comparing output and inputs, and is the starting point for establishing the importance of productivity change.

Partitioning exercises like this have limitations well known to their

Table 3.2. *Growth of inputs and output*

	Income growth	Contribution of labour	Contribution of capital	Contribution of land	Residual
1700–60	0.69	22	36	1	41
1760–1800	1.01	40	35	3	22
1801–31	1.97	36	25	3	36
1831–60	2.50	28	28	4	40

compilers but sometimes misleading to others. This one rests on a constant relative weighting of labour, land and capital. The choice of weights was guided by an intimate knowledge of the available data and a sensitivity towards historical changes and so is far from arbitrary, but it cannot capture all that was involved in securing increased output. The partitioning cannot capture feedbacks such as that just discussed between income and population change (which, after a delay, provides an increased supply of labour).

The role of capital formation has been the subject of a great deal of discussion and controversy. Early accounts of industrialization emphasized mechanization and that looks like more intensive use of capital. Then in the 1950s, development economists put a great deal of emphasis on higher capital–labour ratios, and on a sharp rise in the ratio of investment to income as a key to beginning the process of economic growth. The idea is intuitively appealing. Investment is essentially reserving resources from current consumption in order to achieve a greater level of consumption in the future. Successful investment therefore results eventually in increased consumption, and increased consumption is likely to be dependent on successful investment. Surely, the Industrial Revolution illustrates the importance of investment?

Indeed, it does, but not in the simplest manner. As in many other respects, the slowness of the Industrial Revolution is apparent. There was some increase in the investment ratio and observers can vary in their assessment of whether it included a short sharp surge, but most do not find the kind of increase postulated in the 1950s.

Nor has recent scholarship strengthened the claim of capital accumulation to be an independent initiating force. On the contrary, more significance has been attached to the observation that richer countries are inclined to save more than poorer ones, and the increase in income in Britain during the Industrial Revolution can itself explain a substantial part of the higher level of capital accumulation. This makes more comprehensible the conclusion of earlier scholarship that self-financing was the largest single source of funds for industrial growth, and the even more obvious conclusion that Britain could fund major capital works such as canals without the use of governmental powers to obtain control of resources (even though defence spending remained about two-thirds as much as gross domestic fixed capital formation).

This reinforces another theoretical observation. Investment does not automatically translate into higher growth rates. If savings become more plentiful, capital intensity is likely to rise, but that may produce no more than a change in technology without an increase in the rate of growth (Hawke 1980, 170–3). It is only when we have grounds for thinking that higher capital intensity itself promotes greater efficiency in the use of resources that we can reasonably expect the growth rate to change.

Yet it is important not to diminish too far our assessment of capital formation. Table 3.2 shows that arithmetically capital formation more or less kept pace with output growth in the period 1760–1800 as it did in the earlier eighteenth century. Thereafter, output grew more rapidly than investment. Notice that labour supplies also grew faster relative to output in the earlier years than in the later. Accumulation and recruitment of more inputs were an important part of output growth, and then more efficient use of inputs became more prominent. (Whether it can really be believed that output grew so much more rapidly than inputs before 1760, or whether this reflects deficiencies in the evidence available for that period remains uncertain.)

Increased labour supplies and accumulation of capital explain much of what happened in the Industrial Revolution – or at least direct our attention to what permitted increased labour supplies and investment. We are therefore reminded of the likely importance of a cumulative process whereby greater output encouraged family formation and permitted or at least facilitated redirection of resources from consumption to investment. Especially important in giving the security for both family formation and investment was the performance of the agricultural sector.

Agriculture is important in another way too. The Industrial Revolution was eventually associated with increased productivity, a growth of output relative to inputs of labour and capital (and land). The industrial sectors led the way in productivity advance. One possibility for overall productivity growth is then that resources were redirected from low productivity uses to higher ones. A shift from agriculture to non-agriculture with a concomitant movement of resources to higher productivity uses is sometimes taken to be the key to economic development, and has been so regarded for the Industrial Revolution (Mathias 1969). That certainly happened, but even in the later nineteenth century, at least equally important was the spread of productivity improvement throughout the economy.

It was productivity advance in agriculture which was principally responsible for carrying Britain to a relatively high level of income per capita at the beginning of the Industrial Revolution. It was aided by the gains from international trade (and by early industrial growth), but agriculture was a large part of the pre-industrial economy and necessarily strongly influenced overall productivity trends. Assessments of the course of agricultural change have paralleled those of industry. At one time, it was common to emphasize particular innovations, especially the introduction of turnips and the process of enclosure by which open fields were transformed into individual farms. Again, learning more about what happened in various regions, and asking questions inspired by economists' ways of thinking have resulted in reinterpretations.

Improvement in agriculture was a long and slow process. The main element in it was not the introduction of any particular crop, but a sequence of innovations, varying by region, which permitted a better mixture of arable and pastoral farming. New crops enabled more animals to be carried through winter, improving supplies of food and raw materials such as wool. At the same time, through improved husbandry methods, the rearing of livestock provided manure which increased the fertility of the soil for arable farming and reduced the need for fallow land. This process was widely spread in time, from 'floating meadows' in the seventeenth century, to turnips and the 'Norfolk rotation' which eliminated fallow and was one among many innovations in the eighteenth century, and on to the nineteenth. England shared these trends to a greater or lesser extent with other parts of Europe. Where it was unusual was less in yields per acre than in the number of people employed per acre. Britain evolved relatively large farms, and used an effective combination of skilled labour of farmers and less skilled input of labourers (Allen 1988). By the time of the Industrial Revolution, the agricultural sector was able to feed Britain with a diminished fraction of the total labour force (albeit with some imports of wheat and of other agricultural supplies from Ireland).

The precise role of the 'release of labour' from agriculture remains contested. What can be said is that agriculture experienced productivity increase and was able to supply the community's demand for food with a smaller share of the total labour force. It therefore fitted into a more diversified economy which was better able to use all its resources to provide higher living standards. (For a simple exposition see Hawke 1980 162–5; Crafts 1980 provides a fuller analysis incorporating income elasticities of demand.) But the very growth of productivity in agriculture means that when we measure the ex-post gains from shifting resources from agriculture to other activities, the result seems small.

Simply because before the Industrial Revolution a large part of the population derived their incomes from agriculture, activities with rapidly increasing output looked to the rural population as a market. The income of the country as a whole was increased when agricultural output grew, whether we think of a trend over several years or the result of harvest fluctuations. But its division between farmers and consumers of agricultural products depended on the elasticity of demand and hence on the relative size of variations in prices and quantities (McCloskey 1987, 20–1). The precise effect of any difference in tastes between rural and urban populations cannot yet be assessed, but it is unlikely to be large – industries which were able to exploit productivity gains probably found that their products were in demand in small towns and villages soon after they were fashionable in large towns.

Indeed, what was more important than any special role for agriculture or rural society as a source of demand was that Britain was relatively strongly integrated. At the time of the Industrial Revolution it was far from being as homogeneous as modern societies, let alone having the degree of integration assumed in elementary economics, but contemporary observers and modern studies leave no doubt that the products of different regions were traded among them. The internal transport system was improved, and the distribution system was deepened as traders and shops displaced fairs. The fraction of the total population which was resident in London increased noticeably, and urban life brought a change in material demands strongly disseminated by imitation, but the process spread beyond the capital (Sharpe 1987; Wrigley in Rotberg and Rabb 1986).

There is something similar about current evaluations of the role of agriculture as a source of management knowledge and initiative. Aristocrats were sometimes the source of leadership in the development of coalmining and the iron industry. Landowners were sometimes instrumental in promoting improved agricultural techniques, through the use of agents and through imposing conditions on the tenancies of their farms. But the Britain aristocracy has always been highly varied, and can be seen as the source of what may be called 'Concorde' management, a preoccupation with the new and grandiose rather than with servicing consumer demands. The net effect of its resource allocation remains uncertain, but the best assessment at present is that it probably did no more than share in the process of making more efficient use of resources (O'Brien 1987).

We have already observed that agriculture constituted the largest part of the home market for the increased output of the Industrial Revolution. What then was the role of foreign trade? Building commercial links in the eighteenth century, especially with the US but also with India and the

East, certainly provided gains from specialization. It probably contributed also by providing a variety of consumption possibilities, thereby increasing interest in real income growth. Sugar and tobacco were far from unimportant, but foreign trade provided novelty and stimulated the integration of regional markets as already discussed.

It is the cotton industry which is usually thought of first in relation to foreign trade. It depended for its raw material on imports, although when attention is turned from 'raw material' to 'intermediate inputs', the importance of coal is recognized and the relative size of imports diminished. Britain's development of the cotton industry soon came to encompass export markets. The relative price of cotton goods declined, but would have had to decline considerably faster if the same output had had to be made attractive to an entirely domestic market. International trade provided some of the inputs of the cotton industry and cushioned the fall in prices by which productivity gains in the manufacture of industry were distributed between the industry and its customers. It was important, but not overwhelmingly so.

More generally, Britain's economic growth in the Industrial Revolution was assisted by international trade. But international trade was a means by which resources were used more effectively to satisfy consumer demand and provide higher living standards. Efficiency in the use of resources was important whether or not it involved exchange with other countries.

Consequences of industrialization

One of the longest-standing debates in economic history concerns the consequences of the Industrial Revolution on the standard of living of substantial sections of the population. In the 1840s, Engels wrote about the miserable conditions of industrial workers while Porter used early products of the statistical movement to draw attention to the increased incomes per capita in which all social groups participated. Later literary figures like Carlyle followed the Engels tradition while statisticians and economists refined Porter's analysis. J. L. and Barbara Hammond kept the 'pessimistic' tradition alive in their studies of social history, but when Clapham focused on real income, they conceded his case and sought a reconciliation in a distinction between real income and standards of living. Hobsbawm revived the pessimistic conclusion while Hartwell argued vigorously for an 'optimistic' conclusion on almost any criterion of 'standard of living'. The debate continues. Williamson recently devised ways of assessing how people who chose between rural life and the environment of the early industrial cities themselves valued the disamenities of the latter. Their valuation of clean air and rural poverty relative to urban employment was not necessarily the same as ours; it is not only those without a training in economics who take seriously the idea of understanding the past in its own terms. The evidence suggests that it took only small increases in income levels to outweigh urban disamenities and induce contemporaries to migrate to industrial towns. (It is easy to think of romantic country cottages and forget about the hardships of people who had to earn a living in agriculture.) G. N. von Tunzelmann has reopened and extended a different line of the debate by arguing that what was important was not comparison of changes over time but the gap between the standards of living which were attained and those which could have been gained from the resources available had different government policies been adopted (von Tunzelmann 1985).

Continuation of the debate does not mean that no progress has been made. The early contributions have been absorbed and overtaken. One can always ask for more data in order to discriminate amongst conjectures, but the progressive process is to distinguish questions rather than simply ask for more confidence in answers to existing questions. Thus there is no doubt, as we saw before, that average incomes grew during the Industrial Revolution. Furthermore, investment demands were not such that there is any doubt that average consumption grew. Even for short periods within 1760–1860, these conclusions generally hold.

The issues now at the frontiers of debate fall into two main categories. One can ask about the experience of various sub-groups within the community, or one can refine the general concept, 'standard of living'.

A large number of sub-groups can be defined. First, one can distinguish by relative incomes. It seems likely that incomes did become more unequal during the Industrial Revolution but not sufficiently so for any substantial part of the population not to have experienced rising income. Categorization can also be made by, for example, either occupations or regions. Because aggregates like income are seldom available in sufficient detail, older forms of evidence like wage rates and levels of consumption of particular commodities have usually to be relied on. It is therefore more difficult to reach conclusions which have a high degree of reliability. Nevertheless, the general result of such studies is that individual experiences during the Industrial Revolution were varied, but it was those who persevered with older productive techniques who were most likely to miss out on the general experience of improved living standards. For example, after an initial effect, handloom weavers were not favoured by change during the Industrial Revolution. In any economic adjustment, there are likely to be winners and losers, and those who can adapt to progress are most likely to be among the former.

A slightly more sophisticated point along the same lines is that individual experiences will depend on the timing of change. If an economic adjustment took the form of diverting resources to investment, even when the investment was successful in that it later provided for increased consumption, it would be possible for one cohort of the population to experience a squeeze on living standards but to be dead when its successors enjoyed the increased consumption. (One would then have to ask whether the unfortunate cohort derived compensatory satisfaction from providing for its successors.) Our earlier discussion of investment trends rules out any such analysis applying to Britain as a whole during the Industrial Revolution, but there were clearly differences in the life-experiences of individuals and social groups.

'Standard of living' is open to a range of interpretations. Claims of declining standards of living can be made tautological simply by attaching a high value to what was lost. The stability of earlier communities with families confined to a small geographical area was certainly disrupted, and for some people that may have outweighed increases in material comfort. Even when it is observed that contemporaries made choices which indicate that they did not share such preferences, it can be argued that they were not well-informed about the alternatives available to them and may not have made the same choices in the face of fuller information. There can be no finality of such questions, but it is stretching credulity to think that misinformation could have been so gross and persisted so long that most people did not experience what they themselves would have regarded as an improvement. Change is seldom entirely comfortable; it is always easy to be nostalgic about some loss which is an inevitable part of an overall gain. In this respect, it is unlikely that the Industrial Revolution was at all unusual.

All of this discussion has been about experience *during* the Industrial Revolution. But that involves a lengthy period during which many things happened. If one narrows down the focus of attention from the general process of economic growth to some particular part of it, then one can ask more precise questions about its effects. One might for example want to distinguish the relatively rapid growth of manufacturing industry and ask about its effects on the standards of living. The answer might be different from the conclusions of the previous discussion. Perhaps some adverse effects were outweighed by something quite different – such as increased productivity in agriculture? That is unlikely, but the point being made is that there is an infinity of possible questions related to the link between the Industrial Revolution and standards of living. They cannot all be pursued here, but it is worth making one observation. Standards of living were more likely to have been improved by the Industrial Revolution than to have risen during the Industrial Revolution when Britain needed extra resources for the contemporaneous Revolutionary and Napoleonic Wars. The net effect of warfare on living standards was probably adverse.

A great discontinuity?

Modern studies of economic growth pay a great deal of attention to government policy. After the 1930s, there was a consensus that the responsibility of government included the achievement of economic goals like income growth and employment. Most relatively rich countries developed some form of 'Welfare State', going beyond the provision of 'safety nets' for minorities unable to look after their own welfare to offering increased security for all at something like the level of income they had earned for themselves. At the same time, economic development for countries other than the relatively rich often focused on government planning. Therefore a natural question to pose about Britain's experience during the Industrial Revolution was how it had been achieved without much government action.

In the 1970s and 1980s, many governments found it less easy to influence economies in the manner they intended. Reactions to policy measures became more sophisticated, and it was more likely that policy intervention would be anticipated or frustrated, not by deliberate obstruction but as a consequence of the actions of individuals and corporations protecting their own interests. Economists' attention turned much more to issues of property rights, how individuals' interests could be aligned to be consistent rather than mutually destructive, and how some individuals as principals could ensure that they were well served by others as agents.

This line of theoretical enquiry makes contact with a longstanding issue in study of the Industrial Revolution. It was once not uncommon to think that the growth of industry had been assisted by the enclosure movement which was thought to have transformed British agriculture, especially in forcing people to move from the countryside to industrial towns. The argument has been undermined in several ways. First, the rural population continued to grow in enclosed villages. Enclosure itself probably increased the demand for agricultural labour as field boundaries were reorganized, and although that makes only a difference of timing, the more intensive agriculture facilitated by enclosure readily accounts for an increase in the absolute number of agricultural labourers employed. As we saw above, there is still a sense in which labour was released from agriculture and so that objection is not as fatal as it was once understood to be.

Secondly, earlier accounts of the timing of enclosure were misleading because they relied too quickly on parliamentary sources. There was a remarkable growth of acts of parliament empowering enclosure at the end of the eighteenth century (codified into a general Enclosure Act in 1801) but these acts often endorsed and finalized enclosures that had been carried out much earlier. Enclosure was a more localized and extended process than was the process of parliamentary confirmation.

There are interesting implications of these conclusions. Rights to land were rearranged as agricultural production was raised. Institutional barriers to taking advantage of new knowledge were not insuperable. Enclosure was by agreement, but in agreements not all parties were necessarily equal. The process was not so much a reallocation of property rights as a defining of property rights, and 'rights' which had been based on customary tolerance were not necessarily recognized (Hay, Linebaugh and Thompson 1975). The eighteenth century was also a period when the Church of England was at a low point of social and political influence (at a local as well as a national level). It is possible that its rights to tithes were not only converted to a commercial basis but diminished in the process of enclosure, although some Church assets were controlled by people who looked after its interests.

There was therefore some conflict of property rights but this was small relative to a mutually beneficial reorganization of agriculture and there was time for conflicts to be worked out. The same conclusion applies elsewhere in the economy and society. A growing economy required more transport services, and use of roads ceased to be overwhelmingly local. It became unreasonable to expect local communities to bear the cost of road maintenance, especially on roads which carried a lot of through traffic, the main beneficiaries of which lived elsewhere. A solution was found in turnpike roads, highways for which tolls were charged. Again, the process was not entirely smooth and there were riots against loss of traditional rights of passage, but economic progress was not frustrated by inability to find a generally acceptable distribution of its costs (Hawke and Higgins 1983).

Other transport developments illustrate the same theme. In the building of canals, landowners shared in the gains from cheaper transport by becoming shareholders in canal companies and through increased land values. Earlier worries about the trustworthiness of company organizations were overcome. The process continued when in later years railways led gradually to adoption of limited liability, a reallocation of rights between trade creditors and shareholders adopted as compatible with the national interest.

The relative slowness of the Industrial Revolution in Britain, so frustrating to economic historians seeking precise measurement of significant changes, gave contemporaries time to construct and implement new compromises so that the essentially coercive power of the state played a small role and social dislocation was constrained.

The internal logic of the discipline of history, exploiting newly explored evidence and reconciling apparently puzzling implications of different bodies of evidence, continues to throw new light on the experience of the Industrial Revolution. So does the formulation of new questions often suggested by thinking which uses terminology and concepts fashioned to address the problems of a much later age. The general thrust of reinterpretations has recently been to emphasize the continuity and slowness of what happened in Britain in the late eighteenth and early nineteenth centuries. There is a lot to be gained by thinking in terms of an inherent tendency towards gaining the control made possible by higher per capita real income, often offset by marauding expropriation of some kind (Jones 1988), with Britain in the period of the Industrial Revolution benefiting from a process of cumulative causation free from such imposed restraints.

Yet, not everything has changed since Toynbee and Mantoux were writing. Many features of the modern world did undergo a significant phase of development during the Industrial Revolution. It was, in Hartwell's phrase, a 'great discontinuity'. The balance between the importance and the speed of the changes depends on the questions being asked, on the perspective of the historian rather than the experience of contemporaries. While we now understand more of the mechanisms involved than was possible before recent studies, it can be predicted with confidence that reinterpretation will continue. Before current debates are played out, new questions will arrive. Environmental issues which have been discussed among academics for some time are now becoming central to policy debates and to everyday discussions; we can expect a new interest in how property rights were defined during the Industrial Revolution so as to get a balance between effective use of resources and recognition of externality effects or implications for the wider society (cf. Humphreys 1990). In many countries, the role of the state is under new scrutiny; we can expect innovative approaches to the extent to which individuals and groups responded autonomously to opportunities during the Industrial Revolution and the extent to which they had to be guided by people with better access to or understanding of centralized information. We can also expect increased knowledge from further exploitation of new and old data about those people who lived during a period of immense change.

REFERENCES

Allen, R. C. 1988. 'The growth of labour productivity in early English agriculture', *Explorations in Economic History*, 25, 117–46.

Ashton, T. S. 1948. *The Industrial Revolution 1760–1830*.

Capie, F. 1983. 'Tariff protection and economic performance in the nineteenth century', in J. Black and L. Winters, *Policy and Performance in International Trade*, cited in Williamson, 1987.

Crafts, N. F. R. 1980. 'Income elasticities of demand and the release of labour by agriculture during the British Industrial Revolution', *Journal of European Economic History*, 9, 153–68.

1985. *British Economic Growth during the Industrial Revolution*.

Deane, P. and Cole, W. A. 1959. *British Economic Growth, 1688–1959*, 2nd edn 1967.

Feinstein, C. H. 1972. *National Income, Expenditure and Output of the United Kingdom 1855–1965*.

1981. 'Capital accumulation and the Industrial Revolution', in *The Economic History of Britain since 1700*, I, ed. R. C. Floud and D. N. McCloskey.

Floud, R. and McCloskey, D. N. (eds.) 1981. *The Economic History of Britain since 1700*.

Fogel, R. W. 1989. 'Second thoughts on the European escape from hunger: famines, price elasticities, entitlements, chronic malnutrition and mortality rates', NBER Working Paper Series on Historical Factors in Long Run Growth, no. 1.

Harley, C. K. 1982. 'British industrialization before 1841: evidence of slower growth during the industrial revolution', *Journal of Economic History*, 42, 267–89.

Hawke, G. R. 1980. *Economics for Historians*.

Hawke, G. R. and Higgins, J. P. P. 1983. 'Britain', in *Railways and the Economic Development of Western Europe 1830–1914*, ed. P. O'Brien.

Hay, D., Linebaugh, P., and Thompson, E. P. 1975. *Albion's Fatal Tree*.

Hayek, F. A. 1954. *Capitalism and the Historians*.

Hoppitt, J. 1990. 'Counting the Industrial Revolution', *Economic History Review*, 2nd ser., 43, 173–93.

Humphries, J. 1990. 'Enclosures, common rights and women: the proletarianization of families in the late eighteenth and early nineteenth centuries', *Journal of Economic History*, 50, 17–42.

Jackson, R. V. 1989. 'Measuring Britain's industrial growth 1700–1841: problems and implications', *ANU Working Papers in Economic History*, no. 128.

1990. 'Government expenditures and British economic growth in the eighteenth century: some problems of measurement', *Economic History Review*, 2nd ser., 43, 217–35.

Jones, E. L. 1988. *Growth recurring: economic change in world history*.

McCloskey, D. N. 1987. *Econometric History*.

Mantoux, P. 1928. *The Industrial Revolution in the Eighteenth Century*, ed. T. S. Ashton, 1961; 1st French edn, 1905.

Mathias, P. 1969. *The First Industrial Nation: an economic history of Britain, 1700–1914*; 2nd edn 1983.

Mokyr, J. 1985. 'The Industrial Revolution and the new economic history', in *The Economics of the Industrial Revolution*, ed. J. Mokyr.

Nef, J. U. 1934. 'The progress of technology and large scale industry in Great Britain, 1540–1640', *Economic History Review*, 5.

O'Brien, P. K. 1987. 'Quelle a été exactement la contribution de l'aristocratie britannique au progrès de l'agriculture entre 1688 et 1789?' *Annales ESC*, 1391–1409.

O'Brien, P. K. and Keyder, C. 1978. *Economic Growth in Britain and France: Two Paths to the Twentieth Century*.

Rotberg, R. I. and Rabb, T. K. (eds.) 1986. (Schofield, R. S. and Wrigley, E. A. guest eds.). *Population and History: from the traditional to the modern world*.

Sharpe, J. A. 1987. *Early Modern England: a social history 1550–1760*.

Stavins, R. 1988. 'A model of English demographic change: 1573–1873', *Explorations in Economic History*, 25, 98–116.

Toynbee, A. 1884. *The Industrial Revolution*, new edn 1956.

von Tunzelmann, G. N. 1978. *Steam Power and British Industrialization to 1860*.
  1985. 'The standard of living debate and optimal economic growth', in J. Mokyr (ed.), *The Economics of the Industrial Revolution*.

Williamson, J. G. 1985. *Did British Capitalism Breed Inequality?*
  1987. 'Debating the British Industrial Revolution', *Explorations in Economic History*, 24, 269–325.

Wrigley, E. A. 1988. *Continuity, Chance and Change: the character of the industrial revolution in England*.

Wrigley, E. A. and Schofield, R. S. 1981. *The Population History of England 1541–1871*.

4 Religion and political stability in early industrial England

Alan D. Gilbert

Historians, like other detectives, deal with facts. But establishing the facts is often a matter of supposition and conjecture, of adducing and testing hypotheses. The relationship between religion and politics in early industrial England is a case in point. The fact is that many informed observers, contemporaries of the early industrial period as well as later historians, have considered the political stability of the society remarkable in an age when scarcely any other society in Europe avoided serious political violence. It is also a fact that England during the late eighteenth and early nineteenth centuries had flourishing and variegated traditions of religious dissent without parallels in contemporary Europe. It has been a matter of frequent supposition – also by contemporaries as well as later historians – that these two things were related. This study revisits the intriguing hypothesis that a unique religious culture somehow meliorated the threat of serious political instability and violence in early industrial England.

That threat exemplified the truth that for every generation the future remains open, inescapably hypothetical in its myriad possibilities and probabilities. It also illustrated the way in which unrealized hopes and fears help shape the course of history. The spectre of an English political revolution, and the possible futures it implied, shaped political agendas, social developments, public policies and private behaviour in numerous ways during the early industrial age. With the luxury of hindsight we may conclude that the threat was in fact minimal, and that political extremism was mere froth on a surface below which deeper socio-economic developments flowed inexorably in a quite different direction. In the contemporary society, however, many did *not* think so, and their conflicting hopes and fears entailed important social and cultural choices.

That 'revolution inevitably must come, and in its most fearful shape', was Robert Southey's melancholy conclusion about the English society which he described anonymously in *Letters from Spain*, published in 1807 (Simmons 1951, 375). Throughout the early industrial period others remained equally fearful. Sydney Smith remembered the agitation surrounding the passage of the Great Reform Bill as a time for 'the old-

fashioned, orthodox, hand-shaking, bowel-disturbing passion of fear'
(Flindall 1972, 76). Julia Peel, the wife of a prime minister facing the
threat of political violence and the reality of widespread unrest across
much of the midlands and the north in August 1841, collected her servants
into Drayton Manor, near Tamworth, and, armed with carbines sent
from the Board of Ordnance in London, spent anxious days preparing to
repulse a 'vile mob' expected to attack in numbers as high as 'three or four
thousand' (Gash 1976, 222). From Pitt in the early 1790s to Sir Robert
Peel during this peak of Chartist agitation, politicians never took political
stability for granted. Aware of the existence of small groups committed to
revolution, they knew that such groups succeeded at various times
between 1789 and 1848 in producing embryonic revolutionary organizations and plotting violent political activities. They knew too that early
industrial England harboured a much larger reservoir of less focused
political frustrations and radical aspirations.

Successive British governments therefore feared revolutionary violence, and as apparent need called, the authorities used military force,
political surveillance and legal repression to contain it. Had circumstances conspired differently during one of the crises of the 1790s, or in
the Luddite years, or during the postwar discontents of 1816–21, or while
the Reform Bill had its tense passage through parliament in 1832 or in
August 1841, or when Chartism wracked the country with large and
hostile demonstrations, then generalized radical inclinations may have
nurtured a serious revolutionary movement. Such crises certainly produced a flood of extremist pamphlets, placards and newspapers advocat-
ing the overthrow of the state. They also produced genuine revolutionary
conspiracies. We can presume that the Cato Street conspirators actually
intended to assassinate the British cabinet in 1820, and that their plot,
however ineffective, was merely one dangerous eddy amid others in the
political turbulence of a volatile society.

Yet that identikit would fit many societies in which revolution never
developed. What remains elusive in the case of early industrial England is
a convincing evaluation of how serious the revolutionary situation actually became at any stage during the half-century after 1789. On certain
obvious criteria England seemed, in the words of the famous French
historian, Elie Halévy, 'above all other countries, destined to revolution'
(Halévy 1961). Pervasive social and economic pressures associated with
industrialization, a prolonged confrontation with revolutionary and
Napoleonic France and mounting pressures at home for constitutional
reform were *prima facie* likely to combine to generate great social stress
and instability. Yet there were in fact remarkably few English manifestations of the disorder and bloodshed marking the volatile, extremist

politics of Continental Europe's 'age of revolution'. Halévy devoted his considerable analytical skills to this paradox, adducing a 'thesis' about English religious culture which has intrigued subsequent historians for more than three-quarters of a century.

In retrospect, Halévy greatly underestimated the meliorating influence of rapid economic growth. Whereas in the France of 1787–9 socio-economic dislocation had been exacerbated by national bankruptcy, urban under-employment and accumulating agrarian crises, in early industrial England there was a long-term buoyancy in key sectors of the economy. Economic opportunities and prospects of social mobility were perceived to be growing significantly. Great dislocation accompanied industrialization, and during cycles of economic depression, great hardship too; but the underlying trend was uniquely buoyant. Rapid, if sectoral, economic growth was an important antidote for political frustration. Nor was war so dislocating an experience for England as it was after 1792 for almost every other country in Europe, for England alone remained uninvaded and unvanquished.

Yet while he underestimated such considerations, Halévy's underlying questions are still worth pursuing. The absence of a major revolutionary crisis and the ineffectiveness of political extremism *may* be wholly explained by the constitutional peculiarities, the rapid economic growth or the military inviolability which set England apart from that of the Continent. But it is unlikely. The stationed troops; the legal system with its quasi-political prosecutions, transportations and executions; the government spy networks and embryonic police forces; the immense authority which the magistracy retained into the early industrial age – these may have been able to cope with almost any form of insurrectionary activity, especially in a society as decentralized and constitutionally 'anarchic' as the English society was at the end of the eighteenth century. What remains puzzling, however, is not so much the maintenance of public order as the ease with which order was maintained. The extrinsic mechanisms of social control were remarkably little tested. Thus Halévy's original question about England's avoidance of revolution leads to a deeper cultural problem: the remarkable tolerance of this early industrial society to social and political stress.

Many historians who have sought this missing piece in the jigsaw of early industrial history have found it in the special character of English religious culture. As early as 1878 William Lecky stressed the role of Methodism in England's relatively peaceful progress in the previous century (Lecky 1878), and before he developed the thesis in *England in 1815*, Halévy had portrayed Methodism as a source of political quietism in two articles on 'La Naissance du Methodisme en Angleterre', published in 1906. Half a century later E. J. Hobsbawm (1964, 23–33) revisited the thesis in a short article on 'Methodism and the threat of revolution in England', and E. P. Thompson (1968) undertook a brilliant and precarious reconstruction in *The Making of the English Working Class*. Thompson's twin conclusions were that Methodism 'may have inhibited revolution', and that 'we can affirm with certainty that its rapid growth during the Wars was a component of the psychic processes of counterrevolution.' (p. 419). The provocative nature of his work, combined with his lack of specialist knowledge of religious history, gave specialists in the field an invitation to enter the mainstream of social and cultural history by reexamining the politics of Methodism. Despite John Kent's exasperated advice to Methodist historians in 1974 that 'references to Halévy should be sternly avoided', the role of religious deviance in the national politics of early industrial society was too intriguing to ignore. A range of analyses followed. David Hempton's *Methodism and Politics in British Society, 1750–1850* (1984), a work of considerable scholarship, produced a political portrait of Methodism which Halévy would have found complex and inconclusive. Hempton stressed the political ambiguity of a movement torn between the conservatism of its founder and his ministerial successors and the radical proclivities of many of its rank-and-file members.

A fascination with links between Methodism and early industrial politics is readily understandable. By the 1790s Methodism was the most conspicuous and successful manifestation of a spectacular social and religious movement that had swept large areas of eighteenth-century England, creating unconventional forms of association, social behaviour and modes of thought among artisans, tradespeople, small freeholders, labourers and a sprinkling of professional people. This new popular evangelicalism, by challenging the spiritual and ecclesiastical authority of the Church of England, had already assumed considerable social and political significance by the end of the eighteenth century. That was inevitable in a society with an Established Church. For a church by law established, as the Church of England had been since the Reformation, is by virtue of its establishment a social and political institution, not just a narrowly religious one. The Church of England had immense social and political authority. It was literally part of the state. Its bishops sat in the House of Lords. By family ties, education and tradition, as landowners and in many cases also as magistrates, its parochial clergy were important authority figures in English local society. 'Very few in the Church of England before the eighteen-thirties', G. F. A. Best has pointed out, 'thought that the church, in its functions as an established church, could have any higher aim than complementing the work of the civil power and

– what it alone could do – toughening the fabric of society' (Best 1964, 153).

Methodism, born in the 1730s under the influence of John Wesley, Charles Wesley, George Whitefield and a growing band of less famous itinerant followers and emulators, was quite different in conception to the older dissenting traditions of the Presbyterians, Congregationalists, Baptists and Quakers. Old Dissent had maintained an ecclesiastical opposition to the Anglican Establishment since the Reformation, but with diminishing fervour and effectiveness under the aegis of the Act of Toleration of 1690 and the political latitudinarianism of the Hanoverians. By the 1730s Old Dissent was stubborn, inward-looking, essentially marginal, nursing old political and ecclesiastical grievances but no longer offering any viable political alternative or serious challenge to the Established Church.

Methodism had little in common with Old Dissent. It began as a conversionist evangelical movement *within* the Church of England, and under John Wesley, a Tory gentleman by inclination and manner, it remained as quiescent politically as a vigilant leadership could make it. In his profound support for the idea of the Established Church, Wesley was as much as any other Anglican clergyman an opponent of organized dissent. He wanted only to revitalize the spirituality and purify the theology of Anglicanism, and was committed to the point of holy obsession with the 'Methodist' mission of 'spreading scriptural holiness throughout the land'. But that obsession made him finally and reluctantly schismatic. For when the institutions, conventions or values of the establishment came into conflict with his evangelical mission they came off second best. Wesley saw the world as his parish, and from the outset Methodism was driven by an itinerant evangelism which undermined the parochial system of the Church. Its prodigious growth rested on the enthusiastic labours of unauthorized preachers who affronted the parochial clergy by ignoring parish boundaries and defying clerical authority whenever it stood in the way of Methodist evangelism.

The result was mounting conflict between the Established Church and the Methodists. Countless Methodists suffered injury, indignity and loss during the eighteenth century at the hands of anti-Methodist mobs whose activities were usually connived at by the local clergy, if not actually instigated by them. At least seven Methodists were killed by such mobs. The vehemence of the anti-Methodist reaction suggests that something more than personal religiosity was at stake. It was evidence of a widespread perception that the new movement was a form of social as well as religious deviance. Whether Wesley liked it or not, once his movement came to be seen as subversive of the religious establishment, being a

D

Methodist took on social and political meaning. This was true not least because social and political persecution is a self-fulfilling prophecy. Social harassment and political opprobrium ensured that increasing numbers of Wesley's followers really did become *de facto* dissenters. Itinerant preachers were prosecuted under legislation requiring anyone wishing to preach outside the confines of the Church of England to seek registration as Dissenting Preachers. Before Wesley himself died in 1791 the movement was also being forced to register its meeting places as 'places of dissenting worship', and Wesley was flouting the traditions and authority of the Church in other ways as well, ordaining deacons and superintendents and taking legal action to ensure that when he died formal authority in Methodism would pass to a Conference of travelling preachers.

There was thus a tendency for Methodism to converge with older traditions of Protestant Dissent, and to be stigmatized as a socially deviant type of behaviour at a time, on the eve of the French Revolution, when extra-establishment religious activities were about to become less and less acceptable politically. Historians still differ about the extent to which this convergence carried Methodism away from the political quietism of its Tory founder, but the tendency was patent. At the same time, another convergence was taking place. Old Dissent was greatly influenced by the theological preoccupations and conversionist zeal which gave Methodism its dynamism. In 1814 an ageing, unreconstructed Dissenter, Walter Wilson remarked ruefully that 'the Independents have gone over to the Methodists. Indifference [towards theological issues once regarded as vital] and enthusiasm have thinned the ranks of the old stock, and those who remain behind are lost in a crowd of modern religionists.' Viewed from a rather wider perspective, Methodism and New Dissent had converged to form a popular extra-establishment evangelicalism which amid the political unrest of the period after 1791 could readily be construed as a threat to the political as well as the religious establishment.

That is why the present study rejects not only the 'Halévy thesis', but also any other interpretation portraying early industrial Methodism as an essentially conservative movement; and why it attempts to go further than Hempton in offering an alternative understanding of the movement. Halévy actually misunderstood the politics of Methodism. Hempton, by leaving certain ambiguities in Methodist culture unresolved, left unresolved also many questions as to how, if at all, Methodism influenced early industrial politics. His caution is understandable. Aware of the complexity and diversity of 'chapel culture', he judiciously avoided too many generalizations about the role of Methodism at a national level. Yet the fact remains that Methodism was a genuinely national movement.

Questions about its role in national politics are valid and important, even if the answers must in places remain speculative.

No one has identified the terms of the argument more clearly than Hempton did in *Methodism and Politics in British Society*. He was aware that there are three fundamental propositions that need somehow to be integrated into a coherent analysis of early industrial religion. The first is that, in a society with an Established Church, there was something inherently radical about religious deviance. 'However conservative they [Wesleyans] claimed to be in social and political terms,' Hempton (1984, 226) explains, 'they were seen by the established order in Church and State as a radical challenge to its authority.' Secondly, at the level of the Wesleyan leadership, Methodist politics were quite as reactionary as Halévy believed. Determined to inculcate and maintain conservative political values within the movement, the Wesleyan Conference and its ruling oligarchy made it 'crystal clear', in Hempton's words (1984, 108), that the working classes in the manufacturing districts 'could be radicals *or* Methodists, but not both'. Yet – and this is the third proposition – connexional discipline broke down on precisely this point. Hempton would not go as far as to see Wesleyanism as a moderately radical movement with an incongruously reactionary leadership, but he does concede that the number and vehemence of efforts by Wesleyan leaders to stultify radical political tendencies among the rank-and-file 'testify to their ineffectiveness' (1984, 104).

Understanding the contribution of Methodism to the political stability of early industrial England is a question of balancing these three propositions. Halévy was satisfied that the conservatism of Wesley and his successors in the leadership ultimately shaped Methodist politics. Hempton tolerates a scholarly ambiguity on this point. The following argument suggests that it was moderate radicalism, not reactionary conservatism, which gave early industrial Methodism its essential political significance. The argument can be elaborated by exploring in turn each of the three fundamental propositions.

The first proposition needs little further elaboration. Because the politics of Methodism evolved in a religious culture dominated by the Established Church, religious deviance seemed politically dangerous because its very existence interfered with the capacity of the Church to function effectively. 'Every kind of separation from the Established Church', Anglican clergy were told in 1800 (Anon. 1800, 21), 'by narrowing the ground on which that Church stands, tends to weaken the foundation on which the government of this country is built.' To defy the Church was therefore an act of social as well as religious deviance. In principle it was a politically radical act. Wesleyan leaders could continue to argue, as

Thomas Allen, a Methodist solicitor, did during an hour-long session with the prime minister, Spencer Perceval, in February 1812, that 'Mr Wesley never intended to form a distinct sect', and that therefore 'members of our Society consider themselves as members of the Establishment and do not choose to rank with Dissenters . . . ' (Hempton 1984, 11). The Establishment disagreed, and the social and political implications of its attitude were realities which the Wesleyan leadership fought in vain to deny.

It is therefore a measure of Halévy's great historiographical importance that the debate about the role of Methodism in early industrial politics has been preoccupied largely with the effectiveness of the movement as a conservative force, and specifically with the extent to which it succeeded in 'holding the lid' on simmering lower and lower-middle-class disorder. Wesleyanism, thought Halévy, was 'conservative on principle' (1961, 11). His 'thesis' was that potentially revolutionary sections of the society were 'imbued' by Methodism 'with a spirit from which the established order had nothing to fear' (1961, 425). Religious deviance – on this view – injected what Hobsbawm (1964, 32) has called an 'anti-radical' element into popular political consciousness. Too little attention, however, was paid by either Halévy or Hobsbawm to the prima-facie implausibility of such a role for a movement at odds with a conservative politico-religious Establishment. Perhaps both were overly impressed by the vehemence with which the Wesleyan leadership sought to impose political quietism on the rank-and-file.

The second proposition, that the Wesleyanism leadership was anti-radical throughout the early industrial period, has thus distracted attention from the political significance of Methodism's extra-establishment status. As a statement about leadership attitudes and values, Halévy's interpretation of Methodism as a conservative political force certainly is valid. John Wesley's own Tory sympathies and autocratic instincts had been strong and genuine, and as far as possible he had instilled into his followers deference towards established social and religious authorities. He emphasized political quietism. His mission he saw as strictly spiritual, and his own inherently conservative political instincts and social values reinforced a pragmatic concern to give as little offence as possible to a suspicious wider society.

These same motives influenced the ministerial oligarchy which, working through the self-perpetuating Conference which Wesley had established, assumed the very considerable vestiges of his personal authority after the founder died in 1791. The new generation also inherited Wesley's politics. 'Methodism', said Jabez Bunting, its most redoubtable figure in the next half-century, 'hates democracy as it hates sin.' Pragmatism conspired with principle to make it so. For in the reactionary political climate of 1791–1821 the very survival of Methodism seemed to its leaders to depend on its being above reproach politically. The Conference adopted a 'no politics' rule, and encouraged the travelling preachers it posted to circuits throughout the country to brook no deviation from it. The leaders themselves meanwhile practised the politics of conservatism and reaction. In 1812, for example, with Lord Sidmouth seeking to check the spread of radical political ideas by outlawing itinerant preaching (a central principle of Methodist polity), Wesleyan leaders lobbied effectively in Whitehall, pressing the point that through their control of a national 'connexion' they were powerful allies of the status quo. Itinerancy survived, although not necessarily because Sidmouth and his colleagues were entirely convinced about the capacity of Methodist leaders to control their followers. The government had also to weigh the possibility that a ban on itinerancy, unless entirely effective, might radicalize religious deviance without sufficiently weakening it.

How effectively could Methodist leaders shape the political values and behaviour of the Methodist laity in manufacturing towns, industrial villages and rural hamlets across England? From its first decade Methodism had faced insinuations of disloyalty to the established order, and however much Wesley denied suggestions that he was creating a haven for Jacobitism, radicalism or lawlessness, hostile parochial clergy and violent anti-Methodist mobs remained unpersuaded. So did ministers of state like Lord Sidmouth. In the connexional polity Wesley had created the leaders wielded considerable authority. Ownership of Wesleyan chapels was vested in the Conference, and ministers carrying out Conference policy had extensive powers of expulsion and discipline over ordinary members and lay preachers. There is no question that throughout the half century after 1791 this Wesleyan 'establishment' was, in Halévy's words, 'conservative on principle', or that to the extent that they had their way, the contribution of Methodism to national politics was 'anti-radical'. The validity of the 'Halévy thesis' thus rests initially on a judgement about the extent to which the politics of the leadership were normative throughout the movement.

That is the crux of the argument. The persistence, despite the 'no politics' edict, of an incorrigible radicalism among the rank-and-file can be interpreted in either of two ways. The common tendency has been to accept the official policy of Wesley and his successors as the norm and to regard grass roots deviations from it as the exception. This has led to some interesting conclusions. As we have seen, in his influential article on 'Methodism and the threat of revolution in England', Hobsbawm (1964) assumed that if Methodism had played any part in helping England avoid revolution it was as an 'anti-radical' force. So he viewed the radicalism that so often went hand-in-hand with Methodist commitment as something that vitiated its essentially anti-radical influence. Radical 'heresy', this argument goes, was too widespread for Methodist conservatism to be of much assistance to the forces of reaction.

But what if radicalism was itself the norm? Turn Hobsbawm's argument on its head, and the facts suddenly fit a quite different interpretation. There are two kinds of counter-revolutionary politics, broadly speaking. One is the politics of reaction; the other involves the existence of moderate radicalism as an alternative to revolutionary extremism. Whereas the first seeks to hold the lid tightly on revolutionary movements, the second offers a safety-valve for the relatively harmless release of pent up social tensions. Paying too little attention to the inherently provocative social meaning of deviation from the Established Church, and too much attention to the strident official conservatism of Wesleyan leaders, many historians from Halévy onwards have misinterpreted the politics of Methodism in the early industrial age. Efforts to gauge the 'anti-radical' influence of the movement amount to testing the wrong hypothesis. The evidence fits better a 'safety-valve' theory in which a rank-and-file proclivity towards moderate radicalism offered an effective alternative for many in the society who may otherwise have gravitated towards extremism. Did the political and social behaviour of ordinary Methodist members reflect the fears of an Establishment which saw them as renegades or the hopes and prescriptions of a conservative connexional leadership? The 'safety-valve' theory requires us to demonstrate the former.

It is a theory which rests on the logistical and cultural limits to ministerial and Conference authority in Methodism. The ruling oligarchy was constitutionally paramount but numerically weak. There were many more chapel communities than there were ministers, and in much of England the possibility of adequate ministerial surveillance and control over the attitudes and activities of the laity simply did not exist. In any case, where their commitment is more than perfunctory the members of any voluntary association inevitably exercise a powerful influence on the character of the associational culture, even if it is not their views which are articulated in official pronouncements. In early Wesleyanism the tensions between ministry and laity, chapel community and Conference, tended to be resolved at the local level with engaging practicality. If sufficiently determined, and willing to face the prospect of schism, a minister generally could impose his will on a local society in a direct confrontation; *in absentia*, however, he could virtually be ignored. The Wesleyan ministers were itinerants: while they came and went the chapel communities persisted.

The social consequence of this polarity had been characteristic of Methodism since its birth. In Wednesbury, Staffordshire, for example, Wesleyanism had been introduced by Charles Wesley's fervent, evangelical, apolitical preaching in the early 1740s. But no sooner had Wesley departed, after assuring the local parson that the new movement was a simple, voluntary effort to strengthen the Church and augment its ministry, than the local converts were listening to a bricklayer, and then a plumber and glaiser, voicing the notion that the clergy were 'dumb dogs', and generally disrupting the social order of the town (Anon. 1744). Social and political reality looked very different to artisan lay preachers in places like Wednesbury than it did to a London-dominated ministerial elite. It is a commonplace of religious sociology and geography that Methodism flourished, not where the Church of England was strong and traditional social values and institutions unquestioned, but in gaps in the parochial system, where clergy were absent, or parishes too large or too populous for effective pastoral care. Typically, these conditions obtained in the new settlements and growing towns of the industrializing society, and among elements of the population least deferential to the traditional hegemony of squire and parson. The labourers, artisans and tradespeople, the school teachers and other minor professionals, and even (albeit to a much lesser extent) the merchant and manufacturing groups who became Methodists in early industrial England (Gilbert 1976, 59–67), were the kinds of people who, in matters of politics, industrial relations or social status, often found themselves at odds, in one way or another, with the norms, values and institutions of the ruling classes.

Consequently, the Methodism which the ruling classes knew, as distinct from that which Wesley or his successors endorsed, often seemed belligerent, intransigent and overly egalitarian. Not only were the social groups from which the movement drew the bulk of its members already predisposed towards radical or independent politics, but the very act of becoming a Methodist was often interpreted by non-Methodist neighbours and local civil authorities as one of social defiance. Characterizing Methodism as politically unreliable and socially unacceptable doubtless dissuaded the least independent, most conformist elements in society from joining; but it also created a natural constituency for the movement among people with a measure of social and political independence, for it made Methodist commitment temperamentally satisfying for those at odds with dominant institutions and values. Conservative leaders seeking to impose a 'no politics' rule on rank-and-file members often found themselves defied by the very independence of mind which had predisposed such people to Methodism in the first place.

According to the Duchess of Buckingham, the movement seemed

'strongly tinctured with impertinence and disrespect ... towards super-iors, in perpetually endeavouring to level all ranks, and do away with all distinctions' (Seymour 1839, 27). In an open letter to his local squire in 1805, an East Anglian clergyman agreed, claiming that after becoming Methodists people were usually less deferential than they had been before. Inviting the squire to remember the pre-Methodist situation in the parish, he wrote:

I would now ask you Sir, whether our servants or labourers were not at that time more content with their wages, less ready to murmur on accidental advances in the price of provisions, and more willing to work extraordinary hours as the exigencies of their masters might require, than they are at present. (Anon. 1805, 41–2)

This kind of testimony about the grass-roots reality of Methodism contradicts official assurances of political quietism. Thomas Allen may not have been being dishonest when he told the prime minister in 1812 that Methodists were 'not a political people' and that they had 'been the steady friends of government ... ', but he was wrong about many Methodist people (Hempton 1984, 102). While it is no easy task to measure the extent to which protest and 'independence' pervaded the movement, examples of social belligerence are numerous. A meeting of Lincolnshire clergy summed up the situation in that county at the end of the 1790s. Some Methodists, they conceded, were unaggressive, and a few even attended Church as well as chapel, but in too many others there was 'a determination to calumniate the clergy, and revile the Establishment' – a quasi-political position which they articulated 'with unrelenting vio-lence and malice, at all times and in all places' (Anon. 1800, 11). Lin-colnshire, moreover, was far less troubled by political unrest than many other counties.

Methodism's unwilling drift into a nonconformist relationship with the Establishment had become irreversible in the 1780s, partly because county magistrates in many parts of England prompted its convergence with traditional religious Dissent through a more or less concerted campaign treating Methodist activities as a form of deviance open to prosecution under the long-standing Uniformity Laws (Gilbert 1976, 78). The polari-zation of popular politics in the 1790s hastened this process. A few years later a Methodist pamphleteer (Nightingale 1807, 471), conceded ruefully that to an outsider at least Methodists and 'evangelical dissenters' belonged 'more or less, to the same body'. They were lumped together in the public mind as 'The combined armies against the Church of England.' Thus in the face of legal harassment and social opprobrium Methodist commitment was forced to become precisely what the authorities feared:

a symbolic act of social deviance, an assertion of socio-political 'independence' and, depending on local circumstances, of protest.

If there is substantial truth in this characterization of the movement, not only Hobsbawm's argument about anti-radicalism, but the 'Halévy thesis' itself, becomes untenable. Methodism may have been fraught with acute tensions and contradictions, and the residual influence of Wesley's Toryism and authoritarianism may have persisted in official policies, but as far as the social and political history of early industrial England is concerned, it was the radical element, the undercurrent of protest, the reformist sympathies and egalitarianism – the attitudes and concerns of the ordinary chapel folk – which determined the primary political significance of the movement.

So it is noteworthy that even Jabez Bunting came close to recognizing the radical incorrigibility of grass-roots Methodism. He served as an itinerant in the Halifax district of the West Riding in 1812–13. Luddism was rife, and instead of political quietism, Bunting found considerable sympathy among local Methodists for the Luddite machine-breakers whose assault on the new industrial processes of framework-knitting represented a major law and order problem for the government. In the Sowerby Bridge circuit the preachers closed Wesleyan chapels to Luddite orators evidently welcomed by the rank-and-file, and in Holmfirth a close associate of Bunting, Robert Newton, had to discipline members apparently willing to permit the local chapel to be used as an arms store (Hempton 1984, 104). In his own circuit, Bunting became so unpopular after refusing to conduct Luddite funerals that he was afraid to go abroad alone at night. At York, in 1813, six men hanged for Luddite crimes turned out to be the sons of Methodist families, a development which left Bunting feeling profound alienation from the chapel culture of the region. The growth of Methodism in the West Riding of Yorkshire had been 'more swift than solid; more extensive than deep', he wrote to George Marsden, a ministerial colleague, on 28 January 1813 (Methodist Archives, Ministerial Correspondence). But the problem was much wider than the West Riding during periods of radical political agitation, and the obverse of ministerial criticism of the rank-and-file radicalism was rank-and-file animosity towards the official position. As a delegation of lay Methodists told a Manchester circuit superintendent during the aftermath of the Peterloo Massacre of 1819, 'Methodist Preachers were as bad as the Church ministers in supporting government' (Ward 1972, 24).

Shortly after Peterloo, in a letter to Bunting, a superintendent of the Wesleyan North Shields district wrote:

On Monday the 11th instant a meeting of reformers was held at Newcastle for the purpose of expressing their opinion on the Manchester Murders as they call them.

50 or 60,000 people attended, amongst whom were a great number of our people, several of our leaders [that is, Class Leaders], and some of our Local Preachers. One of the latter William H. Stephenson, a young man who teaches a school at Burton Colliery in this Circuit went upon the hustings and made a speech, condemning in strong terms the conduct of the Manchester magistrates: this has given very great offence to most of the Travelling Preachers and respectable friends in this neighbourhood ... and I have been advised at all events to put him off the plan [the schedule of local preaching engagements] ... He replied that he would never give up his plan until he was compelled, that he would be tried by his peers and did not fear the result, that if they expel him he will publish the cause to the world, that I had better let it quietly pass as three quarters of our people are radical reformers, that if he be tried so must hundreds more, that he only went to plead the cause of suffering humanity, that he believed it his duty to go, that he never joined himself to the reformers, nor attended any of their private meetings. (Ward 1972, 21)

What was being described was the recurrent ministerial dilemma that had confronted Bunting himself six years earlier in the West Riding. The radical sympathies of men like William Stephenson formed an incorrigible element of Wesleyanism at the level of the chapel community.

One final question remains. To what extent were the politics of early industrial England influenced by the existence of such a religious culture. In the first place, it is important to see Methodist commitment, even in its most overtly radical forms, as an essentially moderating force. The evidence of the Bunting correspondence, for example, clearly indicates that William Stephenson, the recalcitrant local preacher, did feel that his Methodist commitment placed certain restraints upon his political actions and sentiments. On the one hand he felt that it was legitimate for Methodists to join the 'radical reformers' in denouncing the 'Manchester Murders', and indeed he believed that this was a duty which most of the Wesleyan rank-and-file also recognized. On the other hand, however, part of his defence against the threat of connexional discipline was the accompanying guarantee that 'he never joined himself to the reformers, nor attended any of their private meetings' (Ward 1972, 21). The implication was that while the role of a Wesleyan local preacher might be compatible with public protest at a radical meeting, it was incompatible with the conspiratorial and potentially subversive associations of 'private meetings'.

There was, in short, a new kind of 'moral economy' operating upon those sections of the population that had been caught up in the religion of the chapel. Precisely how the constraints worked in any given case is immaterial. What is significant is that religious affiliations did exercise moderating influences over those numerous radical sympathizers who, like Stephenson, became lay preachers or ordinary members in the chapel communities of the early industrial age. Sometimes the protest associated with Methodism was purely symbolic, involving, in Everett Hagen's words, a 'withdrawal of status respect' (Hagen 1962, 185–236). Some converts presumably were forced into this quasi-political position by the reaction of a local squire or parson to what initially had been a purely 'religious' commitment. They abandoned deference as part of the social cost of becoming a Methodist. For other Methodists, the assertion of 'independence' implicit in membership was part of the attraction of the movement. Recognizing this, a contemporary Baptist leader, Robert Hall, called religious dissent generally an 'asylum' for people wishing to affirm their emancipation from the authority of squire and parson (Hall 1791, 29). This fact alone implicated religious deviance deeply in the political evolution of English society, and the availability of a semi-legitimate alternative to the increasingly anachronistic politics of paternalism became an important factor in the peaceful transformation of the political system.

A 'safety valve' theory of religious deviance as a moderate alternative to revolutionary politics would have held no novelty for such people. In 1821, for example, in a strong defence of non-violent opposition to the reactionary Liverpool ministry of the previous decade, a Dissenting journalist writing pseudonymously as 'Christophilus' explained that it was

to prevent revolution, and to avert its attendant horrors, that all religious and enlightened men seek to overturn a party, which for its own sinister ends, monopolizes all the patriotism and religion of the country – but bids fair, nevertheless, to extinguish both; which, by its conduct, has excited a spirit of party violence unknown in any former times, and too likely, if it continues, to prove the prelude of civil contention and bloodshed. ('Christophilus', Anon. 1821, 11)

There was a conscious recognition here that moderate radicalism could contribute to the maintenance of public order in a polarized society. It could preempt radical extremism by expressing more or less legitimate opposition to a reactionary regime; and what is more, it could exercise a form of social control over the political behaviour of those attracted to it. The importance of this relationship remains problematical, however. Was Methodism strong enough in the right places to have made a significant difference to the national political culture of early industrial England?

Writing just of Methodism, Hobsbawm argued in 1957 that it is unlikely 'that a body of, say, 150,000 out of 10 million English and Welsh could have exercised decisive importance' (1964, 29). But this is a question-begging conclusion. For while on the one hand the effective influence of Methodism extended well beyond the limits of full membership (ticket-bearing members probably represented no more than one-third of those caught up in Methodist chapel communities), on the other hand Methodism was merely the largest component of a wider phenomenon of extra-Establishment evangelicalism. Halévy was virtually obliged to concentrate solely on Methodism in developing his thesis, for if the political orientation of Methodism was somewhat problematical, the other dissenting bodies certainly could not be construed as 'anti-radical'. Having adopted a 'safety valve' hypothesis, however, it is appropriate to include the members and adherents of Congregational and Baptist chapels along with Methodists in any quantitative assessment of the capacity of extra-Establishment religion to influence the domestic politics of the early industrial age.

At the middle of the eighteenth century scarcely 2 per cent of the adult population was sufficiently influenced by Methodism or evangelical Dissent to maintain an active association with a chapel community. But between 1750 and 1800, despite rapid population growth, Methodists, Congregationalists and Baptists increased as a sub-group within the adult population from 2 per cent to between 8 and 9 per cent. By the late 1830s this quantum of full members and more loosely associated 'attendants' and 'adherents' was about 20 per cent (Gilbert 1976, 36–41).

Yet even that index of Methodist and Dissenting strength does not measure adequately its quantitative significance as a factor in popular politics. For if Hobsbawm's decision to concentrate solely on Methodism makes his equation misleading, so does his practice of relating the strength of the religious movement to the total population of the wider society. The critical constituency from which threats of revolution or political disorder might have emerged was limited both in socio-economic and geographic terms. The danger may have been exaggerated, but what the Commons Committee of Secrecy reported in February 1817 – that the problem of public order was greatest 'in the great manufacturing districts' and among 'the lower order of Artizans' – was certainly true (*Parliamentary Papers* 1817, IV, 6). Artisan occupational groups constituted less than 25 per cent of the total population of early industrial England, and, equally significantly, they were disproportionately strong within chapel communities. A sample of more than 10,000 occupations of births, deaths and marriages listed in non-parochial registers in the half-century before 1837 has indicated that about 60 per cent of all chapel adherents were artisans or skilled operatives (Gilbert 1976, 67). The implication of these figures is that, instead of a ratio of 150,000 to 10 million in 1811, which was Hobsbawm's quantification of Methodist strength (1964, 29), the historian ought perhaps to think in terms of something approaching 20 per cent of the most politicized section of the adult 'lower orders' being associated with chapel communities.

Hobsbawm, of course, was aware of the correlation between Methodism and Dissent, on the one hand, and on the other the socio-occupational groups most prone to radicalism. In terms of a conservative understanding of the chapel's political function it furthered the view that religious commitment did little to curb radical behaviour. Hobsbawm made this point explicitly about the geography of Methodism. Explaining that Methodism tended to be strongest in parts of the country most agitated by political radicalism, and that the most disturbed populations in places like the West Riding and the north midlands often supported exceptionally large Methodist communities, he conceded that in such areas the movement 'had no more chance of preventing large numbers of them from being rebellious than had the Archbishop of Canterbury'.

But unlike the archbishop of Canterbury or the Anglican religious culture over which he presided, the chapel community did not function, at the grass-roots level, to 'hold the lid' on popular radicalism. And if Hobsbawm had been considering the 'safety valve' hypothesis, the geography and social composition of chapel going would have provided confirmatory evidence of Methodist political influence. Its very existence expressed mildly radical protest, and its rapid growth in radical strong-holds was evidence of a capacity to attract the kinds of people who were inclined also towards radical politics. So the choice is whether religious deviance was an ineffective anti-radical force (Hobsbawm's view), or a potentially effective 'safety valve' for radicalism.

If, as argued here, it was the latter, the question remains whether the 'safety valve' actually succeeded in curbing extremism. In the case of some individuals, such as the North Shields preacher, William Stephenson, we know the answer. Involvement in a chapel community did place con-straints on radical or revolutionary tendencies, but it is possible that the involvement (and hence the constraint) was in many other cases severed or suspended during phases of intense political excitement. E. P. Thomp-son, in one of his most famous arguments, has suggested that this in fact happened, and has stressed what he has called the 'oscillation' of indi-viduals between religion and politics. Oscillators, he has explained, were 'floating voters', people who 'would now flock to the chapel, now would follow the Jacobin or Radical hard-core' (Thompson 1968, 922). In response to fluctuations in the political climate, such people would find associational satisfactions in either religion or radical politics – but not both simultaneously. Instead of inhibiting their political involvements, religious deviance would simply lose relevance for oscillators whenever social conditions appeared to favour direct political or industrial action; and it would revive 'just at the point where "political" or temporal aspirations met with defeat' (Thompson 1968, 919).

To the extent that oscillation of this kind was prevalent in Methodism or evangelical Dissent, grounds for regarding involvement in a chapel community as a moderating influence in domestic politics are eroded. But there are two serious objections to the 'oscillation' theory. In the first place, Thompson failed to support it with adequate evidence. He may be justified in claiming (Thompson 1968, 919) that there are 'scores of life-histories of individual oscillators', but the subjects of biographical evidence are not, in most cases, very representative samples of their contemporary society, and this is especially true when the subjects are artisans, factory operatives, tradesmen or labourers. Indeed, the very fact that their life-histories have been so long preserved suggests that their experiences were atypical in various ways, including, perhaps, their proclivity for oscillating between religious and political associations. Certainly so small and particular a sample cannot substantiate the notion that oscillation was widespread in the chapel communities of the early industrial period.

Oscillation almost certainly would have differed both in frequency and in significance in relation to the level of commitment of the individuals concerned. Important distinctions can be made between the commitment of adherents, full members, lay preachers, elders, deacons, class leaders or other part-time officials, and that demanded of the professional ministry. That large penumbra of adherents whose attachment to their chapel community fell short of full membership – who simply attended chapel services, regularly or irregularly, or who simply enjoyed sharing the excitement of 'special occasions' – these people could have 'oscillated' virtually without restraint, although there is no evidence that many of them actually did. Full membership, however, was less likely to have been associated with oscillation.

To carry a Methodist membership ticket was to have made a commitment not to be lightly relinquished or casually reaffirmed: the discipline and cohesion of the early industrial chapel community guaranteed that. The same was true of evangelical Dissenters. What relevant evidence there is about their commitment – an annual series on 'Lapsed Members Restored' collected after 1834 by churches associated with the Baptist Union (*Baptist Handbook* 1970, 70) – scarcely sustains the idea of widespread oscillation at the level of full membership. The data unfortunately cover only the concluding years of the period under review. But they indicate that for every person reviving a previous commitment to membership, between five and ten people became members for the first time. It is unlikely, moreover, that many 'Lapsed Members Restored' would have been oscillators in Thompson's sense. And if oscillation by rank-and-file members had relatively little quantitative significance, oscillation among lay leadership groups would have been rarer still.

Yet Thompson explicitly linked the concept with this higher ministerial level, concentrating his analysis of oscillation on the behaviour of Methodist lay preachers. The idea of widespread oscillation within this group is simply implausible. Methodism and Dissent were sectarian phenomena in early industrial society. They were totalitarian religious cultures. Defection did occur, but its overall incidence was low; leaders, lay as well as ministerial, occasionally were expelled because of radical political views or associations, but memories were long. Such people seldom could reasonably hope to resume a religious leadership-role abandoned previously in favour of unacceptable political activism. The implication is unavoidable: contrary to Thompson's suggestion, the political significance of leadership in an early industrial chapel community – as indeed of full membership generally – was vitiated little, if at all, by oscillation.

The point has been worth pursuing, however, partly because whatever influence Methodism and Dissent did exert in English domestic politics rested heavily upon the role of lay leadership groups within local chapel communities. It was the activities of potential political leaders among the 'lower orders' which the authorities most feared during the 'age of revolution'. For unless the 'masses' were mobilized by such leaders, the House of Commons was told by its Secrecy Committee in 1817, popular discontent could not actually endanger the constitution. 'The character of the danger', the committee explained, lay in

the indefatigable exertions of persons in the lower ranks of life, or but a little above them, of some popular talents, inflaming and aggravating the actual distress of a numerous manufacturing population, by exciting hopes of an immediate remedy to all their sufferings from a reform in Parliament, and preparing them (in despair of obtaining that object) to attempt by force the total subversion of the established constitution of government. (*Parliamentary Papers* 1817, IV, 12)

But if popular leaders bent on political activism were particularly dangerous, they were also notably thin on the ground; and among the strongest reasons for official confidence in the political order was the belief that, in the words of the same Parliamentary Report, 'The Disaffected appear to want leaders to conduct such enterprises as they have conceived' (p. 13). A 'safety valve' theory of religious deviance as a political force is highly significant in this context. For while an essentially conservative movement would scarcely have attracted many potential radical leaders, a moderately radical movement might very well have done so. Indeed, if in fact a leadership role in a chapel community inhibited or moderated radical political inclinations (and we have established that in certain cases it certainly did so), then the quantitative strength of the popular religious deviance offers a strong prima-facie explanation for the recognized dearth of extremist radical leadership among the 'lower orders'.

For in 1851, at the very end of the period under review, the official Census of Religion enumerated more than 11,000 separate Methodist, Congregational and Baptist chapels in England, each of them a social microcosm offering a plurality of leadership positions for its lay members (*Parliamentary Papers* 1852–3, LXXXIX, clxxviii). The 1840s was the zenith of Methodist and Dissenting strength within the wider society; but it is clear that throughout the 'age of revolution' there had been considerable and expanding opportunities in chapel communities for members of the labouring, artisan and trading classes to exercise that elusive amalgam of ambition, initiative, popularity and egotism which sets apart 'natural leaders' in any social group.

Because the deployment of its resources made religious deviance strong in areas of the country where tendencies towards political disorder actually existed, and granted that it was indeed a politically moderating force, there can be little doubt that the movement had the numbers to make a significant difference in the domestic politics of its contemporary society. To be more precise we need evidence not currently available, particularly about the significance of chapel-going in specific instances and at critical stages of the shaping of popular political opinion and behaviour. But on the reading of existing evidence there would appear to be good grounds for conducting discussions of the religion-politics nexus, not in terms of the traditional conservative characterization of Methodism, but in terms of the alternative possibility that religious deviance was a political 'safety valve' for the pressures of early industrial politics.

REFERENCES

Anon., 1744. Some Papers Giving an Account of the Rise and Progress of Methodism at Wednesbury in Staffordshire, and other Parishes adjacent: as likewise of the late riot in those parts.

Anon., 1800. Report from the Clergy of a District in the diocese of Lincoln. Convened for the Purpose of Considering the State of Religion in the Several Parishes in the said District as well as the best Mode of Promoting the Belief and Practice of it, and of Guarding as much as possible against the Dangers arising to the Church and Government of this Kingdom. From the Alarming Increase of Profaneness and Irreligion on the one hand, and from the False Doctrines and Evil Designs of Fanatic and Seditious Teachers on the Other.

Anon., 1805. A Letter to a Country Gentleman on the Subject of Methodism. Confined Chiefly to its Causes, Progress and Consequences in his own Neighbourhood. From the Clergyman of his Parish.

Anon., 2nd edn 1821. Christianity Interested in the Dismissal of Ministers. A

Vindication of the People from the Charge of Blasphemy, and a Defence of the Freedom of the Press. In Six Letters. Addressed to W. Wilberforce. Esq. M.P. and the Religious Public.

Best, G. F. A. 1964. *Temporal Pillars: Queen Anne's Bounty. The Ecclesiastical Commissioners, and the Church of England.*

Christie, I. R. 1984. 'The churches and good order', in *Stress and Stability in Late Eighteenth Century Britain*, 183–214.

Flindall, R. P. 1972. *The Church of England, 1815–1948: A Documentary History.*

Gash, N. 1976. *Peel.*

Gilbert, A. D. 1976. *Religion and Society in Industrial England, 1740–1914.*

    1979. 'Methodism, Dissent and political stability in early industrial England', *Journal of Religious History*, 10.

Hagen, E. 1962. *On the Theory of Social Change: how economic growth begins.*

Halévy, E. 1906. 'La Naissance du Methodisme en Angleterre', *Révue de Paris*, 1 and 15 August 1906 (trans. B. Semmel in *The Birth of Methodism in England*, 1971).

    1961. 1st French edn 1913. *England in 1815* (trans. E. I. Watkin and D. A. Barker).

Hall, R. 1791. *Christianity Consistent with a Love of Freedom: being an answer to a sermon, lately published by the Rev. John Clayton.*

Hempton, D. 1979. 'Wesleyan Methodism and educational politics in early nineteenth-century England', *History of Education*, 8:1, 207–21.

    1982. 'Thomas Allen and Methodist politics, 1790–1840', *History*, 67:219, 13–31.

    1984. *Methodism and Politics in British Society 1750–1850.*

Hobsbawm, E. J. 1964. *Labouring Men: studies in the history of labour.*

Itzkin, E. S. 1975. 'The Halévy thesis – a working hypothesis?' *Church History*, 44:1, 47–56.

Lecky, W. E. H. 1878. *History of England in the Eighteenth Century*, III.

Moore, R. 1974. *Pit-men, Preachers, and Politics: The effects of Methodism in a Durham mining community.*

Nightingale, J. 1807. *A Portraiture of Methodism: being an impartial view of the rise, progress, doctrines, disciplines, and manners of the Wesleyan Methodists.*

Piggen, S. 1980. 'Halévy revisited: the origins of the Wesleyan Methodist Missionary Society: an examination of Semmel's thesis', *Journal of Imperial and Commonwealth History*, 9:1, 17–37.

Semmel, B. 1974. *The Methodist Revolution.*

Seymour, A. C. H. 1839. *The Life and Times of Selina, Countess of Huntingdon*, I.

Simmons, J. (ed.) 1951. 1st edn 1807. *Letters from England.*

Stigant, P. 1971. 'Wesleyan Methodism and working-class radicalism in the North, 1792–1821', *Northern History*, 6, 98–116.

Thompson, E. P. 2nd edn 1968. *The Making of the English Working Class.*

Ward, W. R. 1972. 'The religion of the people and the problem of control, 1790–1830', *Studies in Church History*, 8, 237–57.

Ward, W. R. (ed.) 1972. *The Early Correspondence of Jabez Bunting, 1820–1829.*

5   Sex and desire in the Industrial Revolution

Thomas Laqueur

Introduction

Neither 'sex' nor 'desire' appear in textbooks of the Industrial Revolution and yet contemporaries, as well as subsequent historians, talk about them endlessly. Thomas Malthus made the seemingly irrepressible power of sexual desire the central axiom of his work on population, one of the foundational texts of nineteenth-century political economy. The classical sources on the social history of the period – Engels, Gaskell, Kay-Shuttleworth, not to speak of parliamentary investigations, medical tracts and novels – revel in observations on the subject: on prostitution (newly christened *the* social evil); on lasciviousness among the young and especially young working-class girls; on scarcely novel domestic practices like the sharing of beds and sleeping rooms by parents, children of both sexes, and lodgers which now deeply shocked middle-class witnesses; on masturbation; and generally on a diffusely but powerfully felt loss of social control over sexuality.

Moreover, as contemporaries well understood and philosophers since Nietzsche have emphasized, sexual desire is not simply a measurable biological property but itself a product of historical forces. It is both generated and deployed by social practices and by the vast array of often contradictory literature of which it is the focus. Factories, cities, shops, markets, novels and medical tracts were all themselves engines of desire and not just sites for indulging or writing about it.

This chapter asks why two seemingly distinct histories – of the Industrial Revolution on the one hand, and of sexuality on the other – should be so thoroughly imbricated. The general answer is that talk about sex in the Western tradition has always been talk about society and so too during the Industrial Revolution. Marriage, sexual intercourse and reproduction form the most basic connections between individuals and generations, the microcosmic arena where the most intimate aspects of human existence intersect with the demands of the culture and society beyond. (Their meaning and consequence, of course, vary significantly over time,

100

between men and women, and amongst different social strata.) Little wonder that one of the great transformations of human history would be refracted in both how humans managed their sexuality and how they understood it.

More specifically, I will offer an answer in two parts: the first in terms of what 'really happened', the second through an examination of the relationship between discourses of the marketplace on the one hand and discourses of sex and desire on the other. There was, in fact, a demonstrable, dramatic lowering of the franchise for access to heterosexual intercourse, a sort of sexual democratization, which made it easier to couple and which constituted for contemporaries a frightening sign that the bonds of the old social order had come asunder.

But there was also a deep and pervasive understanding that economic rationality alone could not motivate capitalism and market behaviour. There was more to industrialism than science in the service of progress. Passion and desire were integral to the new order and there was no clear conceptual boundary between the sexual kind and that which fuelled consumption. There was nothing in principle to distinguish the openness of a marriage regime relatively unfettered by constraints of land or fixed livelihood and the free market in labour; the freedoms of the marketplace in goods and services and the marketplace of sex; the threats posed to the family by an explicitly amoral public economic sphere and the threats posed by prostitution; the loneliness that was built into a model of society that emphasized individual autonomy and the socially corrosive power of autoerotic self-absorption; the rapid circulation of money and commercial paper – so enticing and yet so seemingly ephemeral and ungrounded – and the effervescent qualities of eros.

In an economic and social order where, as Marx noted, 'all that is solid melts into air', where 'man is at last compelled to face with sober senses his real conditions of life and his relations with his kind', the discourses of sexual passion and desire reiterate, reinforce and intertwine the imaginative connexions between the worlds of the body and the worlds of the market (Marx, *Communist Manifesto* 1976, 476). Even in the early eighteenth century, when social theorists looked for metaphors through which to understand the exuberant new marketplace, they turned to the realms of eros: the future is sought passionately and inconstantly in love and speculation; credit is a woman and like Fortuna (Pocock 1985, 99).

What happened to sex and desire?

Some contemporaries certainly thought that the Industrial Revolution brought welcome increases of libidinal repression. Francis Place, for example, one of the leading working-class radicals of the period, wrote his autobiography as an instance of this development, an exemplary story of rising moral standards from his boyhood in the 1770s and 1780s to the post-Napoleonic era. 'Smirched but not deeply stained' he tells how he was saved by his wife from a brutal low life and entered triumphantly into the new world of respectability where the drunkenness, sexual licence and general dissipation of the decadent old world were but quaint bad memories. Numerous working-class autobiographies, not to speak of conversion narratives of the period, tell the same story. In his influential articles on eighteenth-century plebeian life as well as his magisterial account of working-class formation, E. P. Thompson is more sympathetic than was Place to popular culture but he nevertheless traces the same trajectory: from 'picaresque hedonism' to class self-consciousness and political discipline (Thomson, 1965; 1974).

This story, albeit in a new register, gains credibility from social theorists who raise it to a more abstract level and argue that it is precisely what they would have predicted. 'Economic action', of the sort appropriate to a capitalist economy, Max Weber writes, requires 'instrumental rationality', which supersedes both an 'instinctual reactive search' for the immediate gratification of wants and 'inherited techniques and customary social relations'. The new mode of production, in this model, depends on the spread of a new personality type, one able to control animal urges and to delay the satisfaction of present wants for future gains, one governed by internal constraints and the capacity to abandon old practices for new and more rational ones (Weber 1978, I, 63, 70).

Freud translates this moral odyssey into a universal truth: the intensity of the pleasure to be had from psychical or intellectual labour – the sort of labour that makes human progress possible – is 'mild as compared with that derived from the sating of crude and primary instinctual impulses'. It is quite simply part of the order of things that civilization should be antagonistic to sexuality and that progress is bought at the price of 'great sacrifices' of sexual gratification (Freud, 28).

Furthermore, one might adduce a variety of cultural developments that could be interpreted as both causing and reflecting a new era of sexual repression. Censorship played its part. Bowdler's *Family Shakespeare* appeared in 1804 without the intolerably lewd Doll Tearsheet in *Henry IV* or the word 'body' anywhere; Jane Austen was criticized for allowing Lydia in *Pride and Prejudice* to happily survive her elopement. This was also the age of the masturbation phobia with its endless jeremiads on the mortal dangers of solitary pleasure; of the Society for the Suppression of Vice, founded 1802; of woman supposedly unencumbered by lust – a putative angel in the house – and of the companionate marriage; of

Methodism – Wesley himself preached celibacy and regarded marriage as a distinctly second best even if many of his followers did not agree (Abelove 1991); and of Anglican Evangelicalism with its stern moralism – thousands of copies of Hannah More's tracts preached restraint, on all fronts, to the working classes. 'Rational recreation' made headway, at least in the public sphere, against the old blood sports. The body, in short, was at a discount; 'repression' and the new bourgeois world order seemed to fit very comfortably together.

Or did they? Certainly much qualitative evidence could be adduced for quite the opposite case. Parallel to the high and dry tradition of a Francis Place, chronicled most recently by Thompson, there subsisted a lowlife realm of London radicals who lived from pubs, pimping and pornography (McCalman 1988). If certain prescriptive texts suggest that the bourgeois family was at its core desexualized others claim that its men folk at least profligately spent their newly gained money in a hugely increased libidinal economy. When Flora Tristan, the French socialist and feminist, visited England's 'chief city' she reported that 'there are in London from 80,000–100,000 women – the flower of the population – living off prostitution'; on the streets and in 'temples raised by English materialism to their gods ... male guests come to exchange their gold for debauchery'. The number is exaggerated, probably wildly so, but the point is made nevertheless that where some saw repression others saw an intimate link between an expansive sexual and economic life.

The working classes, we are told by other bourgeois observers, were apparently no more chaste than their betters. Frederick Engels in 1844 was repeating a longstanding commonplace when he noted with just a hint of envy that 'next to the enjoyment of intoxicating liquors, one of the principal faults of the English working-men is sexual license'. Just as novels were said by some to have corrupted the morals of impressionable young girls of the middling sort in the late eighteenth century, it was supposed that 'certain books [for example, the radical Richard Carlile's *Everywoman's Book* (1828) a guide to birth control for the working classes] have gone forth to inform depraved persons of a way by which they may indulge their corrupt passions and still avoid having illegitimate children' (SCHC 1831–2, 706 xv, q. 3468). The seemingly rootless denizens of the city suggested nothing so much as illicit, uncontrolled desire to bourgeois commentators of all ideological proclivities.

Statistics showing a remarkable rise in illegitimacy, particularly during the period 1750 to 1850, seem to lend credence to such views. One historian, for example, from a very different moral perspective than nineteenth-century observers, categorically interprets these numbers to mean that the 'liberation of the young' was finally nigh (Shorter 1977). He claims that the freeing of working-class youths from the sexual control of family and community led to a veritable 'unleashing of sexuality' destroying 'all competing passions (such as avarice or familial egoism) in the area of courtship'. (Shorter seems to mean by this that they increasingly had intercourse as part of dating without concern for property or parental approval. It signals, for him, the first phase of the two-part libidinal revolution that would be completed in the 1960s.)

As for masturbation, Shorter argues that far from being suppressed during the Industrial Revolution it was largely unknown before and really only came into its own then as part of the 'premarital sexual revolution' that did so much to 'modernize' affective relations generally. Shorter's evidence, like that of Jean-Louis Flandrin who makes a similar argument, is the silence of the sources. Almost nothing was said in medical literature about masturbation before the eighteenth century and even in prescriptive religious texts it is lumped with other sexual sins: fornication, sodomy, adultery. (Even if we do not accept the assumption that discursive silences entail an absence in life the question remains: why 'self abuse' suddenly became such a pressing, much written about, topic.) In any case, Shorter briefs a case that, far from ushering in a new era of sexual repression, the Industrial Revolution struck a blow for liberation. It first freed, not the middle class but the working class generally and working-class girls in particular who, through work outside the home, were supposedly emancipated from their pre-industrial subjugation.

Moreover, the old stereotype of a sexually repressed and repressive Victorian and even pre-Victorian middle class has recently been shown to be a gross simplification (F. B. Smith 1980) and Peter Gay in particular has accumulated considerable evidence to the contrary. He argues that the anti-bourgeois diatribes of a Marx or a Flaubert, and of subsequent attacks on bourgeois sexuality as well, were either versions of their more general criticism of the bourgeois as hypocritical – fine upstanding men seeing prostitutes and reading pornography in private – or were simply fanciful (the bourgeois wife silently suffering the attention of her husband). Gay paints a more nuanced picture of a generally healthy and varied sexual life in which married couples were likely to enjoy, and be advised to enjoy by their doctors, both foreplay and intercourse. After analysing the extraordinarily explicit diary of a mid-nineteenth-century woman's sexual desires and satisfactions Gay concludes that 'the bourgeois record [diaries, medical accounts, marriage guides, novels] is full of such passions' (Gray, 1984).

Faced with qualitative evidence which seems to both confirm and deny the 'repressive hypothesis', we turn to quantitative, 'hard' data in an effort to resolve the question. This will not be easy. It is even today notoriously difficult to secure reliable statistics about sexual desire or behaviour using current survey techniques and virtually impossible for the nineteenth century. 'Would more time have been spent on collecting the actual experiences of human beings', lamented comparative anatomist and birth control advocate Richard Owen; but, in a field 'so characterized by delicacy and silence' it was not (Laqueur 1990, 190). Modern demographers, moreover, have been relatively uninterested in the proximate cultural determinants of fertility, those which might translate as affect or desire: 'although [they] deal with sex and death', notes one of them, 'they characteristically eliminate the pleasure from the former (hiding it under the category "fecundability") and the terror of the latter (death tables being euphemistically called "life tables")' (Smith 1982). Still, there is important demographic research relevant to our question and we turn now to it.

There is no doubt that the population of England rose rapidly during the 'long eighteenth century': 133 per cent, from 4.9 million in 1680 to 11.5 million in 1820. Between 1791 and 1831 alone, the core years of the Industrial Revolution, it grew 72 per cent from 7.7 million to 13.28 million, the fastest rate of increase anywhere in Western Europe with the possible exception of Ireland (Wrigley 1983). Ever since Thomas Rickman collected vital statistics from a sample of parish registers in the early nineteenth century demographers have been debating whether this unprecedented growth was due primarily to changes in mortality – in which case it would reflect various environmental factors but tell us nothing about sexual behaviour – or fertility, in which case it might. With the publication of Wrigley and Schofield's *Population History of England 1541–1871* – the fruits of over a decade's work by the Cambridge Group – the question seems finally laid to rest: mortality did fall, that is, life expectancy at birth increased by over six years from about 32 in the 1670s and 1680s to almost 39 in the 1810s; but more importantly fertility rose and its contribution to population growth was of the order of two and a half times more important than mortality. Wrigley and Schofield's conclusions on this point have been remarkably robust in the face of over a decade of scrutiny. Debate however continues about final *ad hoc* correction for underregistration of births and deaths in the parish registers which are their primary source. Peter Lindert, for example, troubled by the differences between demographic patterns in Britain during the Industrial Revolution and in the third world today, has argued that they increasingly overestimate crude birth rates for the period 1740–1815, resuming the correct level by 1840. While this leaves their overall population estimates standing – crude death rates for infants were also underestimated – and also leaves intact the overall estimate for the relative importance of mortality and fertility over the whole period 1680–1840 it would affect discussion of the 1740s to 1810s (Lindert 1983). No one, however, has proposed a compelling alternative to the Wrigley/Schofield model and recent work on Germany (Knodel 1988) has tended to support their emphasis on fertility.

Specifically marital fertility, however, did not change much between the seventeenth and the nineteenth century; that is, women were not having more children for any given number of years at risk. But they did marry earlier and fewer of them remained celibate than before, which meant that a larger proportion of women were likely to become pregnant in the first place. Between the middle of the seventeenth and the early eighteenth century the celibacy rate seems to have been a more important variable as the percentage never married declined from about 25 per cent in 1641 to around 10 per cent c. 1690–1710 where it remained, except for a low of around 5 per cent in the cohort of 1741, for most of our period. After 1700 the drop in age of women's first marriage came to have the dominant effect: 26.6 for 1675–99; 25.7 for 1725–49; 25.3, 24.7, 23.7 respectively for the next three quartiles to 1824. But even if the precise contribution of marriage age and percentage never marrying is still being debated and even if manipulation of necessarily incomplete data yields different abso- lute values there is little question that changes in nuptiality were critical to population growth (Wrigley 1982; Weir 1984; Schofield 1985).

But sexual behaviour was changing outside of marriage as well. Despite a higher proportion of women marrying and marrying younger there was also what might seem, at first blush, a surprising increase in illegitimacy and prenuptial pregnancy. The illegitimacy ratio (illegitimate to all births) rose from 1.5 per cent of births in the 1670s and 1680s to 3 per cent by the middle of the eighteenth century to 6 per cent by 1810 and almost 7 per cent by 1850 after which it declined to around 4 per cent by the end of the century. In Western Europe generally during the late nineteenth century both illegitimate and legitimate fertility again moved together, this time both downward (Shorter 1977; van der Walle and Knodel 1980). Mean- while the percentage of first births resulting from prenuptial conception rose from a little over 15 per cent at the beginning of the period to between 30 per cent and 40 per cent by the end of the eighteenth and early nineteenth century (Wrigley 1982).

Wrigley and Schofield estimate that the fall in marriage age and in percentage never married, the rise of the illegitimacy ratio, and the fall in the mean age of maternity contributed 52 per cent, 26 per cent, 15 per cent and 7 per cent respectively to the fertility component of the population growth rate. But, whether these precise percentages are ultimately sustainable or not, the critical and seemingly inevitable conclusion for our purposes is that a complex, interconnected set of social, economic, political and cultural developments between the late seventeenth and early nineteenth century lowered the barriers to reproductive sexual intercourse generally, marital as well as extra-marital.

Thus, for example, the age at first birth for married women was more or less the same as that of women who bore illegitimate children, which does not, however, mean that having children was generally divorced from marriage. The usual practice was for parents of illegitimate children to marry later: 4/5 of illegitimate children were also first children (Wrigley 1982). But it does mean, to put the case conversely, that whatever had limited entry into full reproductive life, across the board, in the seventeenth century had lifted considerably by the early nineteenth. (Poor Law records also suggest that the ability of individual women, communities or parish authorities to enforce marriage after prenuptial pregnancy declined with the increased mobility of commercial and industrial society and this would account for some of the increase in bastardy.)

So much is clear. So too is the fact that population continued to increase without the preventive checks that had sustained a more or less homeostatic system before. But why and how nuptiality functioned, what caused the decline in age of marriage and rates of celibacy, is still very much debated.

Certainly efforts like Shorter's to deduce the libidinal liberation of working-class women from rising rates of illegitimacy are seriously weakened by historical evidence. Tilly and Scott (1976) point out that except in a few sectors, more women did not, in fact, work outside the home than before; and that when they did, it was out of necessity – out of a need to fulfil traditional family obligations in new settings – not the desire to be rid of them. Illegitimacy rates, moreover, were no higher in new industrial than in rural areas. And finally, illegitimacy cannot be considered on its own but is part of a far broader, nuptiality-driven, increase in fertility patterns.

Wrigley and Schofield's explanation is essentially Malthusian: rising wages make it easier for couples to accumulate enough resources to marry: people marry earlier, fewer remain unmarried, they have more children. Consequently, labour supply increases, real wages go down and the opposite happens: later marriage, higher celibacy rates, a lower gross reproduction rate, i.e. fewer children for each couple. There are several serious problems with this view however. In the first place, the empirical connection between wage-rates and population, although plausible, remains weak in part because historical wage series themselves are flawed, in part because economic analysis has suggested that if population affected wages at all it did so indirectly through influencing prices

(Lindert 1985). The Wrigley–Schofield model also demands an unaccountably long and difficult to explain, forty to fifty-year, lag between changes in wage-rates and changes in marriage behaviour. And, the two nuptiality indicators, a lowered age of marriage and a smaller proportion of the population remaining celibate also do not move consistently together as the model would predict (Goldstone 1986). Finally, regional studies show that something else is at work. In the agricultural south, where wage-rates were notoriously depressed, the female age of marriage probably dropped because of the sheer need to survive: there was a sharp decline in the demand for live-in female servants who before had remained single until they had saved a nest egg; a depressed demand for labour due to changes in farm size which lowered wages so far that single people, especially women, could not earn enough to survive alone; and Poor Law policy – subsidizing family but not single people's income in proportion – may well have kept depressed wages from having their 'natural' demographic effect as Malthus had feared. One recent study, for example, of 214 parishes in south-east England found that family allowances positively affected birth rates and accounted (when other variables were controlled) for most of the increased marriage fertility in a period of falling, or at best, stable real incomes (Snell 1985; Boyer 1989).

Proto-industrialization, and the resulting proletarianization of labour, i.e. dependence on wages, has also been adduced as the critical social and economic change effecting nuptiality and hence population growth. The argument has two pillars. First, since marriage age and the celibacy rate were supposedly kept relatively high by the difficulties of accumulating sufficient scarce resources – land or money – to set up an independent household, anything which would make such accumulation easier, i.e. would make people less dependent on, say, land, would make access to marriage easier which would be reflected in lower ages for marriage and for the percentages never married. Second, empirical work shows that in fact the age of marriage did drop precipitously in a community like Shepshed, from a medium for women of 26.8 in 1600–99 to 23.2, 1700–49 and 20.6, 1750–1824 – seemingly in response to dramatic new opportunities in rural industry (Levine 1977). A number of other studies for specific locales, in Britain and on the Continent, present similar evidence (Gutman and Leboutte 1984).

But there are also difficulties with proletarianization as a general explanation. Marriage age dropped in parishes where there was no rural industry; and conversely in certain Belgian parishes, for example, studied by Gutman and Leboutte, marriage age remained high despite new industry. At the national level, proletarianization and proto-industrialization can be associated in England both with declining fertility in the sixteenth and seventeenth century and increasing fertility in the eighteenth. This does not mean that there is no connection between industrial change and family strategies and certainly contemporary observers lamented the ease with which young couples could enter into a sexual relationship under the new economic dispensation. But the mechanisms are far more complex than have been portrayed in any of the available models.

In response to the absence of any clearly validated relationship between wage-rates or other underlying economic changes on the one hand and nuptiality on the other, Henry Abelove has argued recently that the problem has simply been misconceived by demographers. It is not a question of nuptiality but of sexuality; not 'what changed constraints on entry into marriage?' but what made 'sexual intercourse so called more popular in late eighteenth century England?' (Abelove, 1991). The rise in production and the increased popularity of a sexual act 'which uniquely makes for reproduction', he speculates, are part of the same phenomena which could 'be called either capitalism or the discourse of capitalism or modern heterosexuality or the discourse of modern heterosexuality'. The attraction of this reformulation is that it forces us – as I will argue in more detail below – to think about the economic and the sexual sphere as connected.

The problem is that while there is certainly increased open hostility to non-reproductive sexuality – masturbation and homosexuality, if not openly to foreplay – and while the incidence of 'intercourse, so called' per capita is certainly higher than it was before because the barriers to marriage were lowered there is little evidence for the increased 'popularity' of a specific reproductive act among those with rising, falling or stable real incomes.

Within marriage, where the vast proportion of reproductive intercourse took place, the sexual regime was largely unchanged. Based on the timing of first births nine or more months after marriage, demographers can calculate fecundability, i.e. the chance of becoming pregnant in the absence of birth control or post-partum non-susceptibility, during a menstrual cycle or month. Since women are, in fact, fertile only during a finite number of days in the middle of the menstrual cycle the chances of becoming pregnant are greatly increased with frequency of coition. Using a widely accepted range of mathematical models demographers can work outwards from the actual data on fecundability to the coital rate that would be consistent with the data (Potter and Millman 1985). In the case of England, the estimate is disappointing for Abelove's hypotheses: fecundability for every marriage cohort after 1600–49 remains stable at or about 0.23 (23 out of 100) which corresponds to a constant coital rate of about 0.25 or once every four days (Wilson 1986). There are European populations where Abelove's hypothesis *might* prove true. For example, Knodel found a sizeable increase in age standardized fecundability from 0.21 in the cohort 1750–74 to 0.282 in 1875–99 in the fourteen German villages he studied but he attributes the shrinking birth interval not to more frequent intercourse but to changes in breast feeding practices which in turn affect fertility because the hormone that induces milk production reduces the likelihood of ovulation.

Furthermore, not only did age-specific marital fertility not change dramatically during the long eighteenth century but neither did the general pattern of reproductive behaviour. England, and indeed Europe generally, until the late nineteenth century remained a 'natural fertility' regime, one in which there was no discernible effort at family limitation, i.e. stopping childbearing completely after a given number of children had been born; so that women would tend to have their last children near menopause at around 40 no matter how many they had had before. This does not mean that the actual level of fertility did not vary between societies and that individual couples – or women – did not try to space births according to various cultural, economic, or idiosyncratic personal considerations. Indeed the method most within the control of women – the duration of lactation after each birth – seems to have been the most important of the means used. Effective surgical abortion was extremely dangerous and the widely sold abortifacients, when not also poisonous, were of doubtful efficacy; coitus interruptus and abstinence required the problematical cooperation of men and may even have been generally 'unknown'; birth control devices, especially those controllable by women, like the sponge, were next to useless. During the Industrial Revolution, in other words, sexual intercourse was still inextricably bound up in the consciousness of the great majority of men and women with babies. We of course do not know whether a new family limitation regime would have come earlier if the technology had been available. But, demographers tend to see it as a product of new mentalities not technologies because it depends on widespread knowledge of, and also adoption by couples – perhaps men only since women had long been willing to do so – of behaviour or devices to stop reproduction entirely once a certain family size has been reached. This step, in contrast simply to birth spacing, constitutes a radical and irrevocable shift in reproductive behaviour – the so called 'fertility transition' – which falls outside our period (van de Walle and Knodel 1980; Watkins 1980).

We have now advanced somewhat in our pursuit of what happened to sex during the Industrial Revolution. Within marriage, the evidence suggests, there was little change. But, as the barriers to nuptiality eased, access to sexual intercourse did become greater, the franchise, so to speak, for indulging in it was lowered. Beginning in the late seventeenth century and continuing well into the nineteenth – precisely how and why remains unclear – the social and economic constraints on marriage diminished. Sexual intercourse was thus literally 'freer' because there was a freer market in matrimony to which it was still inextricably linked.

But perhaps we should rephrase the question. Instead of asking whether there was more or less sexual intercourse, greater or lesser opportunities for the fulfilment of sexual desire or for its repression, or more or less desire itself, we should ask instead why there was such a vast outpouring of talk on the subject during this period, how it articulated with other discourses, and how the various discourses of sexuality served to constitute, rather than merely reflect, their object.

Discourses of sexuality and desire

'The central issue' the philosopher Michel Foucault argues, 'is not to determine whether one says yes or no to sex ... whether one asserts its importance or denies its effects ... but to account for the fact that it is spoken about, to discover who does the speaking, the positions and viewpoints from which they speak ... ' (Foucault 1978, 11). In this account desire is not a constant biological given that is more or less repressed; talk about sex produces desire and allows for a new sort of political control of the body. Specifically, Foucault argues that there was a vast expansion of the 'discourse of sex': medical texts, tracts about masturbation, the initiation and elaboration of censuses, discussions about vital statistics, marriage manuals, moralistic pamphlets; that this varied and multi-voiced literature – this discourse – imbricated the body in a new 'technology of power'; and, that while the old 'absolutist' state displayed its authority by actually punishing the bodies of offenders, the new bourgeois order produces a vast 'will to knowledge' about sex (among other things) which both incites the body's sexuality and allows it to be controlled by various sorts of experts.

The history of discourses about sex is thus very much part of the history of the Industrial Revolution and of the nineteenth century generally and does not constitute a separate subject from that of this paper. But my concern in what follows will be to show, more specifically, how social, cultural and economic concerns were thought about, imagined through, and given a special emotional urgency by, an erotically charged body.

The Tory poet laureate Robert Southey hated Thomas Malthus' *Essay on the Principle of Population* in part because he detested political economy generally. But, more particularly, Malthus profoundly threatened the traditional Christian view of a well ordered, beneficent universe that reflected God's foresight and judgement. No matter how much the productivity of agriculture might be improved, no matter how much better humanity became, fertility would inevitably outstrip resources. To obey God's command to Noah that man be fruitful and multiply could lead only to disaster. God, as the saying went, appeared to have invited too many mortals to nature's feast.

Of course, theologians and other evangelical thinkers worked to repair some of the damage that Malthus had wrought to their well ordered world. In the first edition he admitted only the positive check of famine and the preventive check of ascetic abstinence as means of keeping the birth rate in check. But if, as he admitted in later editions, moral restraint, i.e. postponing marriage in the face of one's inability to provide adequately for children, could work as well then perhaps there was moral purpose in the universe after all. Either overpopulation was God's incentive to labour more, acquire more, conserve more so as to be able to have children later; or, it transformed the spiritual virtues of prudence and chastity into secular values which would be more easily practised as economic progress brought moral and cultural improvement in its wake (Hilton 1988).

But the worm was in the bud and people like Southey knew it. He is appalled that Malthus would consider lust and hunger as equivalents, both equally independent 'of the reason and the will'. He is outraged that a book in which sexual reproduction looms large and vice figures prominently 'for the preservation of good order', should be written in the vulgar tongue, available to everyone including women: 'These were not subjects to be sent into circulating libraries and book-societies, and to be canvassed at tea-tables.' How could it be 'heard without indignation by one who had a wife, a sister, or a 'daughter' (Southey 1832, 82)?

Perhaps, too, Southey is upset that Malthus is so insistent on the absolute primacy of sex in political economy. Against Godwin, who held that in a perfectly rational society sexual passion would disappear, Malthus argues not only that sex is here to stay, and a good thing besides, but also that there is absolutely no reason whatsoever to believe that matters could be otherwise. The fact that 'the passion between the sexes is necessary and will remain nearly in its present state' is as obvious, and requires as little apology, as that food is necessary for human existence. 'No move towards the extinction of passion has taken place in the five or six thousand years that the world has existed'; why should it take place now? Sexual pleasure indeed is so satisfying that its deferral through late marriage – he thinks of it only in this context – is one of the 'miseries' that might curb population growth: 'Perhaps there is scarcely a man who has once experienced the genuine delight of virtuous love ... that does not look back to the period as the sunny spot in his whole life, where his imagination loves to bask ... and which he would most live over again.' No pleasures, he concludes, are 'more real and essential' than the pleasures of the flesh. And, no-one understood better than Malthus their relation to economy and society (Malthus 1970, 146–7).

The reproductive capacities of the body are, for Malthus, the sign of its individual well-being but also, paradoxically, of society's present or future sickness (Gallagher 1987). Healthy bodies reproduce themselves geometrically; food supplies increase arithmetically and as a result the bodies of future generations are less healthy – since they have less nutriment per capita available to them – than the ones that came before. The old healthy body/healthy society homology has broken down, but the reproducing body has become the lens through which the conditions, and tensions, of political economy could be viewed with great clarity.

And nowhere was Malthus' vision darker than when discussing the Poor Law. People are given money which stands for value – in this case of food – while in fact they contribute no labour to produce it or anything else for that matter. Indeed the poor are encouraged by child allowances, he fears, to reproduce in direct violation of the law of the body, i.e. they are being artificially allowed to escape the misery of sexual abstinence. In a world without effective birth control each act of heterosexual intercourse represents a potential claim on sustenance. More profoundly, however, for Malthus human sexuality is the mark of our essential corporeality of the body, which, mixed through labour with external matter, is after all what produces value in a *labour* theory of value.

Malthus' theoretical commitment to such a corporeal standard is evident too in his critique of Adam Smith's view of money as a way of representing the comparative values of different products for purposes of exchange. According to Smith a shilling's worth of wheat is by definition of the same value, and exchangeable for, a shilling's worth of lace. But not so for Malthus. He argues that Smith is wrong in holding that increases in the productivity of labour are equivalent to increases in the productivity of land. All increases in revenue are not the same and in fact a stock or a revenue will not be 'real and effectual' in terms of maintaining labour, will not be 'convertible into a proportional quantity of provisions' if it has 'arisen merely from the produce of labour, and not from the produce of land'. Buying, selling, trading – the activities of the marketplace – are in short less 'real' in terms of the body than actually growing food. Malthus frames the distortions of the market in an extraordinary image of the beef cow fattened on food that should go to men. The very high price of beef today, he argues, makes it profitable to raise such a beast not only on the best of grazing land but even on land that could, and formerly did, grow corn for human consumption. Fattened beef feeds far fewer labourers and their families than would the grain it consumes, i.e. it is produced with a net caloric loss in the stock of food available for humans, and consequently 'may be considered, in the language of the French economists, as an unproductive labourer' (Malthus 1970, 184, 187–8; Gallagher 1987, 96–7). In other word the chimerical, unreal, incorporeal qualities of circulation and exchange, of money and especially paper money, lead to a distortion of the regime of sex: men and women indulge in the pleasure which – based on tangible nutritional resources – they have no claim to. The changes in nuptiality discussed above, are, therefore, like the fattened cow, evidence for the dangers of unproductive exchange, of bodies tricked into profoundly impermissible intercourse.

Desire, whether for sexual gratification or for consumer goods, lies still more deeply at the heart of theories of capitalism. A market economy and especially an industrial economy is predicated on social openness, on the notion that the satisfaction of desire – for goods, prestige, services – through labour is beneficial to both the individual and society. It stands in stark opposition to a society of ranks and orders in which convention and sumptuary legislation is meant to keep desire in check. But once the genie of desire is let out how is it to be restrained when its attention turns to sex? A free labour and free exchange were to be sought after, one of free love was clearly not.

David Hume, the eighteenth-century Scottish philosopher and historian, lays out the theoretical grounds for the connexion; nineteenth-century observers squirm when confronted with its implications. 'Everything in the world', Hume points out, 'is purchased by labour', the cause of which are 'the passions' – pain and aversion in the old, pre-commercial world; pleasure and desire in the new. In the old world there was little to work for, little to buy, sumptuary restrictions on what one could own even if it were available and within financial reach, and a moral predisposition against the exercise of desire: a low wage economy with a backward sloping supply curve of labour to put it in modern terms. The state or a feudal lord, Hume argues, can always extract a certain amount of labour by taxes or dues and can try to prevent consumption through legislation but theirs is an uphill battle against the resistance of men and women who have no attractive reasons to work. Employers or the state have to contend with the high marginal utility of leisure and use force, of arms or of hunger, to compel effort.

But 'furnish him [the producer] with manufacturers and commodities, and he will do it himself' (Hume 1898, 294). The carrot replaces the stick not only externally but in the realms of the psyche: 'govern men by other passions and animate them with the spirit of avarice'. Both consumption and production thrive – and overall wealth grows – as a result of the unshackling of desire and the breakdown of restrictions on the passions and on social mobility. Desire stimulates supply by making labourers produce for the market rather than only for home consumption or the state and the consequent growth of 'industry, art, and luxury' in turn stimulates further desire by providing it with new objects for purchase: a high wage economy and a wage elastic supply of labour in modern terms. (Hume here is taking the side of 'high wages' in the eighteenth-century debate that raged between those who believed that the poor worked only to avoid starvation and if paid more would work less – the low wage faction – and those who thought that they worked in order to consume and would work more if they had more money to spend – the high wage faction.) (Gilboy 1967 in Hartwell, ed.)

At its most general level, this is a brief for the new social order in which a boundless drive towards self-improvement, imbedded in every breast, was thought a virtue that redounded to the benefit of both the individual and society. It is also an argument about morality. Hume, like other early theorists of capitalism, wants to rescue avarice from its moral dungeon and show it to be a passion fit to govern other less benign ones like aggression. The exercise of economic self-interest becomes a beneficent and peaceful foil against dangerous, anti-social human propensities (Hirschman 1977).

But Hume's new positive valuation of desire does not stop with the less overtly carnal passion for clothes. There is psychologically only one sort of desire. So, for example, he argues that 'the natural appetite betwixt the sexes' is the 'first and original principle of human society' because men in their wild uncultivated state would never be compelled by reason to join together. Love, of the sort that 'arises betwixt the sexes' is more complex. Of all the 'compound passions', none 'better deserves our attention' 'as well on account of its force and violence, as those curious principles of philosophy, for which it affords us an uncontestable argument'. He goes on to propose that it is derived from the conjunction of three different passions: the 'pleasing sensation arising from beauty; the bodily appetite for generation; and a generous kindness or goodwill' (*Treatise*, 394).

The critical point here is not Hume's benign attitudes towards a passion more often condemned than so neatly dissected but the fact that his mode of analysis applies equally well to consumer goods. Thus he explains the relation of the direct to the indirect passions by the case of a 'suit of fine cloths': 'It produces pleasure from their beauty' which in turn produces the direct passions of volition and desire; but since the clothes belong to

E

us they also raise the indirect passion of pride which in turn gives new impetus to the original direct passion of desire and the will to satisfy it (*Treatise*, 438–9).

The connexion between desire for clothes or indeed any other personal adornments on the one hand and sexual desire on the other is not new. It is standard fare among seventeenth-century moralists: outward adorning of the hair leads to 'whoredom' not to speak of 'drinking, stealing, lying, murder, and HELL'; 'vain apparel leads to whoring, drinking, gluttony, and envy'; 'rolling in foreign silks and linens' is likened to 'blind sodomites groping after their filthy pleasures' just as wearing French clothes is tantamount to getting a venereal disease. Ambition itself was regarded as but the vanguard of all other vices, especially those of the flesh: 'wherever you see pride in the front, sure lust marches in the rear'. But by the late eighteenth century moral valences had changed; desire itself was not intrinsically bad; it could not be condemned *tout court* but had to be judged by its objects on a case by case basis.

And, under the guiding moral assumptions of commercial society 'unnecessary expenses' and the desire to live always a little above one's station was far from a vice. It was a virtue. Bernard de Mandeville in the 1720s had already argued that if pride and luxury were banished goodly numbers of artisans would be starved within half a year. But more pointedly when observers in the 1780s and 1790s noted that the rural poor 'pant to imitate' London fashions; that girls in the country had 'the most longing desires' to ape their urban betters; that Wedgwood's customers for pottery or Foster's for carpets had 'caught from example the contagion of desire' they were doing so with approval (McKendrick et al. 1985, 28, 95). The language of the marketplace speaks of a more open libidinal economy generally: 'longing desires', 'panting', the sense of being caught up in a maelstrom of want, bridges the apparent chasm between material objects and the flesh.

But therein lies the mortal danger for many nineteenth-century bourgeois observers. The old elision of the difference between consuming goods on the one hand and consuming sex on the other could not be raised to the level of a general principle. And while these middle-class observers seem to have regarded their own class as sufficiently rooted in home, work and family to resist the slide from one side to the other, the same was not so for the working class. They were perceived generally to be rootless and uncontrolled – a sort of social correlative of unrestrained id – and working-class women in particular were seen as dangerously vulnerable to the freedoms, the allure, of the marketplace. Girls' love of 'dress and finery', the source of the effective demand which kept the cotton and silk mills, the ribbon and lace workshops going, also led them, so it was said, into prostitution, 'adding to their legitimate earnings in the mills, with which alone they could not indulge their passion to show' (Parliamentary Report 1843 [431] xiv, A6 para 42). Prostitutes may be distinguished from factory girls by their clothes 'though the costume and head-dress of the factory girls is not altogether different' (E 38). Hetty Sorel in George Eliot's *Adam Bede*, as she is contemplating illicit sexual intercourse with the wealthy landowner Donnithorne, dreams vacantly about all the wonderful clothes she will have when she becomes lady of the manor. Working-class women specifically were seen to bear the dangers of uncontrolled desire that seemed to flow freely from one domain to another, from legitimate consumption to illegitimate sex.

But, more generally, bourgeois observers of all stripes looked at the working class through the prism of illicit sex. Engels' reproaches on their 'unbridled search for pleasure' – one detects a certain wistfulness here – or indecent sleeping arrangements – couples sharing their beds or their sleeping rooms with lodgers and children of both sexes – find echoes everywhere. Here the offence is not simply wearing jewelry or dresses; nor are comments like Engels' simply a response to measurable increases in vice. By their own admission social commentators found these difficult to come by. James Kay-Shuttleworth, the Manchester physician and reformer, notes that while crime can be 'statistically classed' 'the moral leprosy of vice can not be exhibited with mathematical precision'. 'Sensuality has no record . . .' he concludes (Kay-Shuttleworth 1969, 62). The Manchester surgeon Peter Gaskell provides a long footnote to explain why statistics on illegitimacy are 'worse than useless' – they, in fact, show a higher rate in agricultural than in manufacturing districts – and that one must look beyond them if one is to appreciate 'the general licentiousness and illicit intercourse which prevails' there (Gaskell 1968, 100).

Neither absolute nor relative rates of anything are centrally at issue here. But working-class sexuality, in itself, represents in passages like these the exhilarating yet also terrifying lability, flux and movement of a capitalist economy and rapid industrialization. The social discourses of sex during this period make starkly accessible what is omnipresent and, at the same time, but indistinctly perceived. Examples abound. Navvies, itinerant workers *par excellence* who built the railroads, also had a reputation for exceptional potency, 'a fine muscled animal . . . grasping in one hand a pick by the shaft, and in the other a woman by the waist' (Coleman 1965, 162). Specifically in an industrial context, the moral nightmares of middle-class observers like Peter Gaskell readily translate their fears about mobility, individual and social, into accounts of the 'almost entire extinction of sexual decency' among mill artisans. The problem is not directly the democratization of access to sex; it is the democratization of access to respectable social position and authority. It is as if seemingly unbounded upward mobility pollutes the social and specifically the sexual body.

Parvenu master manufacturers – so Gaskell's analysis goes – 'sprung from the ranks of labourers ... uneducated, of coarse habits, sensual in their enjoyments' are presented with 'the facilities for lascivious indulgence afforded by the number of females brought under their immediate control'. These rootless master manufacturers, desperate for supervisors in their mills, invest their sons – mere children – with authority and money: 'Boys, at an age when they would have been sedulously kept apart from opportunities of indulging their nascent sexual propensities, were thrust into a very hotbed of lust.' Accustomed to 'unbridled indulgence', they do not marry their partners in crime although these females, 'known to have lived in a state of concubinage', have no problem in finding husbands. The licentious new economy has no bounds as it destroys what Gaskell imagines was the old market in marriage.

One could go on and on pointing to the discursive connexions made by nineteenth-century observers between the sexual on the one hand and the social or economic realms on the other: the sexual dangers of unsupervised movement of the young and of adolescents with money of their own, the heated atmosphere of mills (70–5 degrees F!) producing early puberty and desire in girls, the 'bringing together of numbers of the young of both sexes in factories', etc. Probably the most famous and guilt-inducing picture in nineteenth-century social reform literature – from the investigation of women's and children's labour in mines – is of a girl, bare to the waist, pulling a loaded cart. The text emphasizes over and over again the nakedness, the violations of the modesty, of female workers. Everything in the new social order was heated up, changeable, morally shaky and sex was the prism through which its dangers were imagined.

At a more general level too, perverted sex was the sign of perverted social relations; the bodies of the dangerous classes were imagined as preternaturally fecund and productive of monsters. Thus Edwin Chadwick cites with approval the fantasies of a negative utopia voiced by a stipendiary magistrate of the Thames Police Office. From the 'indigent and profligate generally', he moves to the case of a fish hawker – again note that an itinerant occupation is fastened upon – to the image of a race of 'tub men' 'lower than any yet known', who would somehow spawn if 'empty casks were placed along the streets of Whitechapel'. In a few days each tub would have a tenant; they would breed, they would prey upon the community; and in the end 'there is no conceivable degradation to which portions of the species might not be reduced ... savages living in the midst of civilization' (Parliamentary Report, 1842, xxvi, p. 135).

The leading Manchester sanitary reformer, Dr James Kay-Shuttleworth, goes on a similarly Rabelaisian revery about a 'licentiousness
capable of corrupting the whole body of society, like an insidious
disease'. The notion that cities generally, industrial cities in particular,
and perhaps even industrial society as a whole, is somehow dangerous,
dark, and 'unreadable' – so powerful in Engels' encounter with the
walled-off courts of Manchester – is evident here too. Moral contagion is
an evil in its own right but Kay gives it an economic twist. Ultimately
productivity suffers: 'the population becomes physically less efficient ...
politically worthless as having few desires to satisfy, and noxious as dissi-
pators of capital accumulated'. Finally a dissipated race multiplies,
'licentiousness' continues to 'indulge its capricious appetite' and a great,
dense, morally impotent, stagnant blob of flesh is all that remains.
Lesson: 'Morality is worthy of the attention of the economist' (Kay-
Shuttleworth 1969, 81–2).

Masturbation and prostitution are also, as their new names – the *solitary* vice, THE *social* evil – imply primarily social pathologies that are
understood through the perverted sexualized body. The political and
sexual radical Richard Carlile's treatment of the solitary vice makes a
kind of *reductio* argument for how it must be construed as a threat to the
nature of human solidarity, and how little it appears to be a problem of
excess or wicked sexual desire. Sociability and not repression are at stake.
Carlile's *Every Woman's Book* (a reprint of a special issue of the *Red
Republican* which he published with his wife Jane) is a sustained attack on
conventional sexual morality, a plea for freeing the passions, and a practical guide to birth control. Love is natural and only its fruits can and
should be controlled, marriage laws constrain excessively a passion that
should not be forced or shackled and so on. Carlile proposes that
Temples of Venus be established, places where young men and women
could enjoy safe, non-reproductive, health preserving, *extra-marital*
sexual intercourse. (Five-sixths of deaths from consumption among young
girls resulted from want of sexual commerce, he thought, and perhaps as
much as nine-tenths of all other illness as well, he points out as one of the
selling points for this utopian scheme.)

But on the subject of masturbation Carlile the sexual radical is as shrill
as the most evangelically inspired moralist or alarmist physician. Born of
the cloister or its modern equivalents where a diseased religion turns love
into sin, 'the appeasing of lascivious excitement in females by artificial
means' or the 'accomplishment of seminal excretion in the male' is not
only wicked but physically destructive as well. Masturbation leads to
disease of mind and body. Indeed the 'natural and healthy commerce
between the sexes' for which he offers the technology is explicitly linked

to the abolition of prostitution, masturbation, pederasty and other unnatural practices.

The contrast could not be clearer between a fundamentally asocial or socially degenerative practice – the pathogenic, solitary sex of the cloister – and the vital, socially constructive act of heterosexual intercourse. But the supposed physical and even moral evils of masturbation seem almost secondary to its status as a sign of underlying social pathology. The emphasis in 'the *solitary* vice', should perhaps be less on 'vice', understood as the fulfilment of illegitimate desire, as on 'solitary', the channelling of perfectly healthy desire back into itself. The debate over masturbation which raged from the eighteenth century onward might therefore be understood as part of the more general debate about the unleashing of desire upon which a commercial economy depended and about the possibility of human community under these circumstances – a sexual version of the classic 'Adam Smith Problem'.

Prostitution is the other great arena in which the battle against the destructive power of un-socialized sex was fought. 'Whoring', of course, had long been regarded as wicked and detrimental to the commonweal, but so had drunkenness, blasphemy and other disturbances of the peace. Not until the nineteenth century did it rise to being '*the* social evil', a particularly disruptive, singularly threatening, vice. How this happened is a long story of which I tell only a small part here. The critical point is that the social perversity of prostitution was thought to be visited on the individual bodies of prostitutes: they were generally regarded as an un-productive commodity. Because they were *public* women; because so much traffic passed over their reproductive organs; because in them the semen of so many men was mixed, pell-mell, together; because the ovaries of prostitutes, through overstimulation, were seldom without morbid lesions; because their Fallopian tubes were closed by too frequent intercourse; or, most tellingly, because they did not feel affection for the men with whom they had sex, they were thought to be barren, or in any case very unlikely to have children.

Money, or more precisely a somehow illegitimate exchange of money, is the root of their strange biology. Prostitution is sterile because the mode of exchange it represents is sterile. Nothing is produced because, like usury in medieval Christian theology, it is pure exchange. A deep cultural uneasiness about money and the market economy is thus couched in the metaphors of reproductive biology. But, more to the point here, fear of an asocial market takes on a new avatar in the claim that sex for money, coition with prostitutes, bears no fruit. By the nineteenth century the trope of the barren prostitute had a respectable pedigree reaching back to the early commercial cities of Renaissance Italy. But the boundaries which it guarded – between home and economy, between public and private, self and society – were both more sharply drawn and more fraught in the urban class society of the industrial and commercial revolutions than ever before. Or at least so thought contemporary observers. Society seemed to be in unprecedented danger from the marketplace. And the sexual body bore the widespread anxieties about this danger.

While masturbation threatened to take sexual desire and pleasure inward away from family, prostitution took it outward. Perhaps even more than masturbation it broke the barrier between home and market which, in much social thought, was regarded as the safeguard for human solidarities against the disintegrative forces of the market. The sterility of prostitutes – and their other biological defects and dangers (as well as the illnesses resulting from self-abuse) – are in this context not warnings against undue sexual pleasure or inadequate sublimation but rather representations of the dangers of withdrawal from family and other supposed shelters from money (Laqueur 1990).

But all is not discourse. Recently the social history of class formation and especially of middle-class formation has been brought together with the history of gender relations and thus also of sex. Changes in the gendered division of labour in various industrial pursuits, mining and agriculture have long been a staple of economic and social historians although this history has figured relatively little in how labour and cultural historians have understood the making of the working class. Davidoff and Hall's *Family Fortunes* (1987) demonstrates, however, with a massive amount of empirical data, 'how middle class men who sought to be "someone", to count as individuals because of their wealth, their power to command or their capacity to influence people, were in fact, embedded in networks of familial and female support which underpinned their rise to public prominence'. Theirs is a history of the making of new, gendered, public and private spheres in the context of specific middle-class economic and social circumstances. Its major historiographical contribution is to show that a history of class formation must also be a history of gender formation.

But my point here is to link gender, which is the central concern of Davidoff and Hall, back to sex. The middle classes, through the writings of moralists like Sarah Ellis, and of a host of doctors and other professionals, sought to understand new gender relations not as the vagaries of social change, as mere cultural artefacts, but as the consequences of biology. Women were intrinsically suited to their roles in the home, their place as guardians of morality, their intimacy with children. Gender, in short, could be translated – if not always with complete conviction – back into sex.

The easing of access to marriage, the paradoxes of commercial society which had already plagued Adam Smith and his colleagues, the nagging doubts that a free market economy could in fact sustain the social body, haunt the sexual body. Or, the other way around, the sexual body haunts society and reminds it of its fragility. Thus, thinking through what happened to sex and desire is part of a far more general effort to think through the human meanings of the Industrial Revolution.

REFERENCES

Abelove, H. 1989. 'Some speculations on the history of "sexual intercourse"during the "Long Eighteenth Century" in England', *Genders*, 6, November.

1991. *The Evangelist of Desire: John Wesley and the Methodists*.

Boyer, G. 1989. 'Malthus was right afterall: poor relief and birth rates in south east England', *Journal of Political Economy*, February.

Coleman, T. 1965. *The Railway Navvies*.

Davidoff, L. and Hall, C., 1987. *Family Fortunes: men and women of the English middle classes, 1780–1850*.

Engels, F. 1962. 'The condition of the working class in 1844', in *Karl Marx and Frederick Engels on Britain*.

Foucault, M. 1978. *The History of Sexuality*, I, trans. Robert Hurley.

Freud, S. (1962) *Civilization and its Discontents*.

Gallagher, C. 1987. 'The body versus the social body in the works of Thomas Malthus and Henry Mayhew', in *The Making of the Modern Body*, ed. C. Gallagher and T. Laqueur.

Gaskell, P. 1836. 1969. *Artisans and Machinery*.

Gay, Peter. 1984. *The Bourgeois Experience*, I, *Education of the Senses*.

Gilboy, O. 1967. 'Demand in the Industrial Revolution', in *The Causes of the Industrial Revolution*, ed. R. M. Hartwell.

Goldstone, J. A. 1986. 'The memographic revolution in England: a re-examination', *Population Studies*, 40, 5–34.

Gutman, M. P. and Leboutte, R. 1984. 'Rethinking protoindustrialization and the family', *Journal of Interdisciplinary History*, 14, 587–607.

Hilton, B. 1986. *The Age of Atonement: the influence of Evangelicalism on social and economic thought*.

Hirschman, A. 1977. *The Passions and the Interests*.

Hume, D. 1739. 1965. *A Treatise on Human Nature*, ed. L. A. Selby-Bigge.

1898. 'On commerce', in *Essays: Moral, Political, and Literary*, ed. T. H. Green and T. H. Grose, I.

Kay-Shuttleworth, J. P. 1832. 1969. *The Moral and Physical Condition of the Working Classes Employed in the Cotton Manufacture in Manchester*.

Knodel, J. E. 1988. *Demographic Behavior in the Past*.

Laqueur, T. 1990. *Making Sex: Body and Gender from the Greeks to Freud*.

Levine, D. 1977. *Family Formation in an Age of Nascent Capitalism*.

Lindert, P. 1983a. 'English living standards, population growth, and Wrigley-Schofield', *Explorations in Economic History*, 20, 134–49.

1983b. 'English population, wages and prices', *Journal of Interdisciplinary History*, 20: 4, 609–34.

McCalman, I. 1988. *Radical Underworld: prophets, revolutionaries, and pornographers in London, 1795–1840*.

McKendrick, N., Brewer, J. and Plumb, J. H. 1985. *The Birth of Consumer Society*.

Malthus, T. 1798. 1970. *An Essay on the Principle of Population*.

Marx, K. 1976. *The Communist Manifesto*, in *The Marx-Engels Reader*, ed. R. Tucker.

Pocock, J. G. A. 1983. *Virtue, Commerce and History*.

Potter, R. G. and Millman, S. R. 1985. 'Fecundability and the frequency of marital intercourse: a critique of nine models', *Population Studies*, 39: 3, 461–70.

Schofield, R. 1985. 'English marriage patterns revisited', *Journal of Family History*, 10:1, 2–20.

Shorter, E. 1977. *The Making of the Modern Family*.

Smith, D. S. 1982. *William and Mary Quarterly*.

Smith, F. B. 1980. 'Sexuality in Britain, 1800–1900: some suggested revisions' in *A Widening Sphere*, ed. M. Vicinus.

Snell, K. D. M. 1983. *Annals of the Laboring Poor*.

Southey, R. 1832. 'On the state of the poor, the principle of Mr. Malthus's Essay on Population, and the manufacturing system (1812)', in *Essays, Moral and Political*, I.

Tilly, L. A., Scott, J. W. and Cohen, M. 1976. 'Women's work and European fertility patterns', *Journal of Interdisciplinary History*, 6: 3, 447–76.

Thompson, E. P. 1965. *The Making of the English Working Class*
1974. 'Patrician society, plebeian culture', *Journal of Social History*, 7:4, 382–405.

van der Walle, E. and Knodel, J. 1980. 'Europe's fertility transition: new evidence and lessons for today's developing world', *Population Bulletin*, 34: 4.

Watkins, S. C. 1986. 'Conclusion', in *The Decline of Fertility in Europe*, ed. A. Coale and S. Cotts Watkins, 420–49.

Weber, M. 1978. *Economy and Society*, ed. R. Guenther and C. Wittich, I.

Weir, D. 1984. 'Rather late than never: celibacy and age at marriage in English cohort fertility, 1541–1871', *Journal of Family History*, 9, 341–55.

Wilson, C. 1986. 'The proximate determinants of marital fertility in England 1600–1799', in *The World We have Gained*, ed. L. Bonfield, R. M. Smith and K. Wrightson, 203–30.

Wrigley, E. A. 1982. 'Marriage, fertility and population growth in eighteenth century England', in R. B. Outhwaite, *Marriage and Society: studies in the social history of marriage*, 137–85.
1983. 'The growth of population in England: a conundrum resolved', *Past and Present*, 98, 121–50.

Wrigley, E. A. and Schofield, R. 1981. *The Population History of England 1541–1871*.

6   Political preconditions for the Industrial Revolution

Patrick K. O'Brien

State intervention and the national economy, 1688–1815

After the Glorious Revolution of 1688, a stable political order gradually took shape, referred to hereafter as the Hanoverian state. Inside the boundaries of the ancient 'kingdoms' of England, Wales, Scotland and Ireland, as well as within the borders of the Empire, over which that state also exercised jurisdiction, private investors took responsibility for all but a fraction of the nation's capital formation. Private businessmen (not servants of the state) organized the kingdom's production, distribution and exchange. Businessmen and investors looked to central governments primarily for the provision of security. They expected to be protected from risks and losses emanating from warfare on British soil or in home waters around the isles. From the time of the Interregnum onwards, an influential minority of businessmen, including traders, shippers, brokers, bankers, insurers, planters, investors, indeed everyone engaged with the international economy, expected the state to go beyond the mere defence of their ships, merchandise and wealth located beyond the kingdom. After King William took the throne they confidently intensified pressures on their rulers to use diplomacy and armed force, whenever necessary, to extend opportunities for British enterprise overseas.

Somehow a succession of governments (overwhelmingly aristocratic in make up and uninvolved in any very direct way with trade and industry) managed to sustain political and legal conditions, which turned out on balance to be conducive to the rise of the most efficient industrial market economy in Europe. Yet their actions should not be interpreted as a far-sighted 'strategy' for the long-term development of the British economy. Although Hanoverian ministers and parliaments allocated an overwhelming share of the taxes raised from 1688 to 1815 for military purposes, this does not imply that their foreign and imperial policies should be represented as somehow derived from a 'mercantilist vision' for empire and the domination of world commerce.

But this chapter intends to bypass the concerns of political historians with the motivations and perceptions of Britain's political elite, as well as the short-term impact of changes in public policy upon economic growth and stability. Its focus is upon the long run. An attempt will be made to appreciate how the outcome of major initiatives taken and not taken by the state may have affected the management and development of British industry, commerce and agriculture. No doubt Orange and Hanoverian kings, their ministers and parliaments supported the Industrial Revolution. They may even be depicted as the closest approximation to a 'businessman's government' among the *ancien régimes* of Europe. But how exactly did the Hanoverian state assist in carrying the British economy forward to its status as the first industrial nation?

One obvious way to answer that question is to ascertain how much money central governments spent and how they allocated taxes and loans at their disposal. Budgetary data will not encapsulate the economic significance of the state. Some important functions were performed at very little cost but runs of figures for civil and military expenditures do help us to 'quantify' changes in the scale and scope of its 'fiscal impact' on the economy. For example, when deflated by indices of wholesale prices, the statistics 'track' the ever increasing and potentially destabilizing role of the central government. In real terms its 'normal' or peacetime expenditures on goods and services climbed by a multiplier of three from around £2 million in the mid-1680s to just over £6 million a century later. Wartime expenditures jumped even more – from around £4 million per annum in the 1690s to nearly £17 million in the war against Revolutionary France in the 1790s and by a factor of five if we compare average annual expenditures during the war against Louis XIV, 1689–97, with the war against Napoleon, 1803–15. Estimated as a share of gross national income at current prices the activities of the state accounted for a tiny percentage of national expenditure just before 1688 and that proportion rose to reach nearly a fifth in the years immediately before Waterloo.

However defective statistics for national income may be there can be no doubt that for more than a century the government's revenues and expenditures are assuming a place of increasing significance for the growth and fluctuations of the British economy. Thus the period cannot be presented as one of transition to the economic domination of private enterprise. For long-term development the point about significance emerges clearly in Table 6.1 which compares the shares of national income devoted to aggregate private expenditures on capital formation with shares allocated to the purchase of goods and services by the government. Even in peacetime years the proportion of the nation's resources absorbed for military and (to a smaller degree) for civil purposes by the state often exceeded the ratio devoted to gross private investment expenditures on

Table 6.1. *Estimates for total expenditures on goods and services by the central government of Great Britain, 1688–1815*

Peace and war	Year (5-year average centred on)	Military[b] expenditures £m	Civil[b] expenditures £m	Total[b] expenditures £m	Military[c] expenditures deflated £m	Proxies for[d] national income at current prices £m	Private[e] investment expenditures £m	Private investment as a share of national income %	Military expenditures as a share of national income %
P[a]	1685[b]	1.11	0.79	1.90	1.15	50.00	2.00	4.0	2.0
W	1690[b]	3.30	0.73	4.03	3.30	50.21	2.04	4.0	6.4
W	1695	4.78	0.87	5.65	4.23				
P	1700	2.13	1.08	3.21	2.04	56.00	2.24	4.0	3.8
W	1705	4.47	1.22	5.69	4.81				
W	1710	8.77	1.22	9.99	8.05	60.39	2.54	4.2	14.5
P	1715	2.37	1.38	3.75	2.35				
W	1720	3.18	1.48	4.66	3.24	62.38	2.81	4.5	5.1
P	1725	1.84	1.48	3.32	1.79				
P	1730	2.51	1.46	3.97	2.61	63.31	3.10	4.9	4.0
P	1735	2.46	1.40	3.86	2.59				
W	1741	4.31	1.32	5.63	4.27	72.74	3.92	5.4	5.9
W	1745	6.43	1.46	7.89	6.77				
P	1752	2.52	1.57	4.09	2.40	79.26	–	–	–
W	1760	12.88	1.77	14.65	12.63	82.90	4.68	5.6	15.5
P	1766	4.43	1.74	6.17	3.78				
P	1770	3.77	2.15	5.92	3.17	103.78	6.71	6.5	3.6
W	1780	19.79	2.48	22.27	16.49	112.22	8.86	7.9	17.6
P	1786	5.37	2.75	8.12	4.04				
P	1790	5.27	3.12	8.39	3.85	146.06	12.90	8.8	3.6
W	1796	28.22	3.56	31.78	16.70	–	–	–	–
W	1800	30.59	5.30	35.89	15.06	264.74	17.04	6.9	10.4
W	1805	35.96	6.43	42.39	17.63				
W	1810	50.89	7.29	58.18	20.94	358.98	28.50	7.9	14.1
W	1813	64.36	8.07	72.42	29.12	–	–	-	–

Notes and sources: ^a 'P' relates to 5-year periods when the armed forces were not mobilized for war. 'W' is a war period.

^b Annual expenditures figures are from British Parliamentary Papers 1868–9 (XXXV). Appendix 1 contains data for 1685–8 and 1688–91 which were majorated to three complete fiscal years. Expenditures figures refer to GB but the Act of Union with Scotland did not come into effect until July 1706. The separate *revenue* accounts for three years to October 1705 show English revenues amounted to 97 per cent of total revenues for England plus Scotland. Thus the English expenditure figures for 1685–1705 above will serve for Britain. Ireland also complicates the table. The two countries were united in 1801. Their Exchequers remained separated until 1817 but during the war the London Exchequer transferred money to Ireland to fund military expenditures there. I have included these sums as part of Britain's military expenditure.

When necessary the 'Issues from the Exchequer' for military expenditures have been adjusted to include military purchases on credit in the form of Navy bills, Ordnance and Army debentures which were later 'funded' or converted into funded debt. Such purchases effect the timing of military expenditures year by year but do not qualify the long-term trends displayed in this table (Jackson 1990).

Civil expenditures as reported in the Parliamentary Papers for years before 1800 are net and do not include costs of revenue collection and other payments out of revenues before they reached the Exchequer. I have estimated the proportion of taxes disbursed before payments into the Exchequer from the known ratios of around 5 per cent 1800–15, on a straight line interpolation back to an assumed 10 per cent for 1685. My estimates represent *gross* expenditures on civil government.

The figures for expenditures on goods and services military and civil include a small and probably constant proportion of transfer payments (pensions, gratuities, gifts, percolation, etc.) which are impossible to sort out.

^c Deflated by an index of wholesale prices reprinted in O'Brien (1988).

^d From O'Brien (1988) English estimates were majorated to include Scotland on the assumption that the populations of the two countries maintained a consistent proportion to each other and that per capita income in Scotland remained at 60 per cent of British levels throughout the period.

^e Based on estimates in Feinstein and Pollard (1990, T. 17) and the proportions cited in Crafts (1985; 73). The figures before 1700 are interpolated backwards at 4 per cent.

productive assets required for the long-term development of the British economy; while wartime allocations for the army and navy amounted to multiples of private expenditure on domestic capital formation and the acquisition of wealth located beyond the borders of the kingdom.

Fiscal records expose one very large (and by no means unknown) fact about the Hanoverian state: its preoccupation with national security and imperial expansion. Regardless of the rhetoric or pretensions of politicians to intervene in other areas of economic life, that state was in no position to regulate a national economy. This means that ministers and civil servants could spend something (but not much) to make markets operate more efficiently; to further the construction of social overhead capital; to safeguard internal law and order; to raise the quality of the work force; to foster technical progress or to engage just a little more seriously with almost any policy of a developmental nature. Parliament pushed an increasing volume of economic legislation through to the statute book, and repealed several laws perceived to constrict private enterprise (Lieberman 1989, 61; Lambert 1971). From time to time ministers in London despatched orders to justices in the countryside. But the executive machinery and fiscal resources required to actively promote the development of the economy were not available, either in England or for that matter in any other part of Europe. Only an 'integrated package' of strategic, diplomatic, imperial, commercial and fiscal policies could be formulated systematically and implemented more or less effectively from the centre. As far as domestic policies (social as well as economic) were concerned *laissez-faire* proved to be not merely ideologically attractive, but emerged as the only practical strategy for governments to pursue (Taylor 1972; Mathias 1983, 76–84).

Over this long span of time, military imperatives commanded shares of the public revenue that simply 'crowded out' possibilities for the contemplation of a more interventionist, economic stance. Thus, in contrast to other countries that industrialized later, British businessmen and investors shouldered the costs and managed the initiatives required to build up the realm's network of roads, navigable rivers, canals, ports and other forms of social overhead capital. Their governments devoted almost no public money to education and training, to research and development or even to the dissemination of scientific and technical knowledge. Patrick Colquhoun's estimates imply that only 0.5 per cent of total public revenues collected during the long reign of George III was devoted to objectives that might nowadays be defined as developmental (Colquhoun 1814, 205–32). Monarchs, ministers and their parliaments preferred to leave the promotion of science and technology to the patronage of aristocratic, commercial and professional associations with an amateur interest in 'natural philosophy' (Allan 1974, 434–52). They persisted, however, with Tudor and earlier traditions of encouraging foreigners to bring novel products and technologies into the realm while actively prohibiting the emigration of skilled artisans and the export of machinery (Gwyn 1985, 60–76; Jeremy 1977, 1–34). They also continued to rely on that other 'cheap' but rather 'ineffective' method of encouraging technological progress – the Elizabethan patent system – as codified in the Statute of Monopolies of 1624 (Dutton 1984, ch. 9; MacLeod 1988, 10–57).

Integration, good order and authority

On the credit side this inescapable fiscal constraint on potentially more active governmental interference with the economy provided 'space' or freedom for private enterprise. On the debit side it left the framework of law and order within which factor and commodity markets operated within the realm in an unsatisfactory condition. For example, while the new regime which developed after the revolution of 1688 successfully maintained a free trade area within England and Wales it took several decades to integrate Scotland politically into a single market and more than a century to incorporate Ireland into a unified kingdom and economy. Parliament deposed James II peacefully but his departure from London provoked civil war and considerable destruction of life and property in Scotland as well as Ireland. Despite the achievement of political union in 1707 the 'pacification' of Scotland (and thus the stability of the regime itself) was not secured until Cumberland's troops had savagely repressed a second and serious Jacobite rebellion in 1745 (Lenman 1977, 44–99; Levack 1987, 138–68). William of Orange's victories at the Boyne and Limerick created conditions for a sullen acceptance of established property rights and Protestant authority in Ireland. Nevertheless the persistent threat of sedition as well as isolated outbreaks of disorder remained strong enough for governments in London to station a permanent garrison of troops in Ireland. The survival of religious antipathies, problems of internal security as well as the English parliament's failure to liberalize trade between the two nations precluded their full integration into a common market until after the Union of 1801 (Cullen 1987, 35–76, 97–8; Devine and Dickson 1983, chs. by Devine and Smout).

Meanwhile, inside the less than united Kingdom (and if those highly imperfect statistics can be interpreted correctly) the well protected patricians who ruled the realm left businessmen and investors to cope with the conduct of their economic affairs against a discernible rise in the tide of crimes against property (Beattie 1986, 200–32; but see Innes and Styles

1986, 380–435). Furthermore, social and labour historians have now uncovered and explained too many episodes of collective protest, intimidation and violence for historians to assume that the landowners, farmers, millers, bakers, transporters, industrialists, merchants and retailers of Hanoverian Britain used their assets and managed their enterprises in the climate of security, approval and autonomy enjoyed by their counterparts during the heyday of Victorian capitalism. Unfortunately (as with criminal activity) no way exists of measuring the scale or severity of these ostensibly real social constraints on managerial authority and the rights of property owners to allocate their resources to uses that they perceived to be profitable (Rudé 1981; Bohstedt 1983; Charlesworth 1983; and see Stevenson, ch. 10 below).

This should not lead us to underestimate the willingness and capacity of 'paternal' governments of the day to deal viciously with the lower orders. Hanoverian authority came down persistently, and effectively in favour of property and against customary rights; in support of masters and against the traditional expectations of workers and consumers who appealed to an older, more 'moral economy' (Emsley 1983, 10–21, 96–112; Hayter 1978, 9–74). Liberal historiography which portrays the eighteenth-century economy as a 'free' market system, has neglected the experience of large sections of the labour force (young people, women, semi- and unskilled labourers of all kinds) who lived out their working lives within an 'authoritarian' framework of law which severely curtailed their rights to work or not to work, to select occupations, to withdraw their labour to search for alternative employment or to engage with impunity in 'insubordinate' behaviour towards their bosses. Englishmen may have been freeborn but traditional statutes of the realm dealing with masters and their servants, apprenticeship, poor relief for the able bodied, vagrancy and delinquency gave employers political and judicial authority over their workers which left the labour market in a state of suspension between feudal servitude and the free contractual system of nineteenth-century political economy (Innes 1987, 42–111; Haines 1980, 262–97; Kussmaul 1981). Meanwhile parliament did everything required to keep the legal and political framework for labour relations in a condition that preserved hierarchy, authority and the extraction of optimal work loads. For example and to counterbalance the paternalism and flexibility occasionally displayed by justices at local level, from Westminster there came streams of injunctions designed to tighten up on the allocation of poor relief, and the execution of vagrancy laws in order to force 'idle' able-bodied workers, dependent juveniles and women to take up or return to virtuous toil at low wages (Innes 1985). Parliament legislated to transpose traditional perquisites attached to particular jobs into criminal acts of embezzlement (Styles 1983, 173–205). Recognizing that the, already hostile, common law had not proved to be a sufficient deterrent to the formation of combinations of skilled workmen, the House of Commons also enacted no less than forty statutes prohibiting unions in particular crafts and locations before it passed the Combination Act of 1800 which outlawed all forms of collective bargaining (Dobson 1980, 112–50; Rule 1986; Orth 1987, 123–50).

Although the rights of property and the autonomy of masters could not depend on anything that would nowadays be recognized as effective support from local police forces, manifestations of serious challenges that could not be settled by established local authorities were on the whole quickly and effectively put down by the military forces of the Crown. It can no longer be claimed that Britain's constitutional regime lacked the legal authority, the will or the force required to deal with a so-called 'ungovernable people'. Local militias and yeomanry could be embodied fairly quickly at the request of magistrates. The War Office displayed little reluctance to despatch troops to meet demands for armed force from any part of the kingdom, particularly after the rebellion in America, and even more enthusiastically after the outbreak of revolution in France. With British troops mobilized for war for such a large part of the century, parliament's antipathy to a standing army looks increasingly irrelevant – at least when it came to coping with serious economic losses from problems of internal disorder (Palmer 1978, 198–214; Hayter 1978, 57–74).

In general the Hanoverian State presided successfully, and in fiscal terms at minimal cost over a society on its way through an industrial revolution. It dealt with crime on the cheap by enacting a bloody code of punishments for the unfortunate minority who happened to be convicted, it suppressed disorder, and supported authority and hierarchy easily in the countryside and without much difficulty in the growing towns and industries of the realm.

Perhaps its 'success' in maintaining the good order required for the spread of markets rested in large part on the polite and peaceable behaviour of the population at large. Loyal to the Protestant succession, patriots of a nation acquiring an Empire and almost perpetually at or on the edge of war, open to persuasion from the Established Church, deferential towards birth, respectful to wealth and power, those who actively resisted the encroachments of capitalism upon customary rights rarely confronted their superiors with anything more challenging than a dereliction of duty. Even then protestors could often be placated by minor concessions offered to uphold a dying moral economy or the common law.

Such concessions were, moreover, graciously extended by a hereditary ruling class – enforcing traditional and widely accepted codes of conduct. That elite's reward for running the offices of state, church, law and local government had long been secured as a substantial charge (a rent) levied upon agricultural production. Aristocratic authority could be extended at small fiscal cost to include new tasks involved in maintaining law, order and hierarchical systems of command over production and exchange during the long period of transition to an industrial society (Christie 1984; Clark 1985; O'Gorman 1986, 1005–20; Colley 1986, 97–117). As Shelburne so complacently put it 'providence has so arranged the world that very little governance is necessary' (Porter 1982, 131). The compliant behaviour of the majority of the populace coupled with the acceptance of aristocratic government ensured that a potentially unfavourable coincidence of rapid population growth and urbanization, on the one hand, and serious challenges to established authority, on the other, did not occur. Unlike France (or so many developing countries in our own time) political disruption did not frustrate the course of economic change until it became irreversible.

Law and the operation of commodity and factor markets

Nevertheless, the combination of strong authority coupled with the enviable political freedoms and civil rights achieved by Englishmen in 1688 should not be conflated with the legal conditions required for the operation of competitive markets. For example, liberals have long welcomed the stance taken by the Hanoverian state in allowing industries to escape from the fetters of gild controls by relocating beyond the boundaries of corporate towns, but the economic costs of permitting gilds to survive in a very large number of towns right down to 1835 have not been assessed. They have also praised Hanoverian parliaments and ministers for recognizing the futility of attempts to regulate prices and wages and for resisting pressures for the enforcement of rules for apprenticeship embodied in the Elizabethan statue of 1563. In general the commendation is merited but parliament did not repeal the Statute of Apprentices until 1814, and the powers conferred on Justices of the Peace to assess wages and regulate food prices continued to be used from time to time (Kelsall 1938; Lipson 1934, 251–92). Meanwhile parliament's failure to sweep away a penumbra of obsolete statutes and to push the courts towards an assertion of free market principles maintained a climate of uncertainty surrounding businessmen and traders and gave semblance of legality to the actions of disorderly crowds and combinations of workers seeking to use collective forms of organization, intimidation and violence, to change prices and wages in their favour (Rose 1961, 277–92).

Neglect might certainly be preferred to a vigorous implementation of the state's extant powers to interfere with factor and commodity markets but its *laissez-faire* stance was in these and several other respects less than masterly. For example, as markets widened and specialization increased the costs of transacting business across time and space went up. Well defined and enforceable rules were required to make impersonal exchanges work efficiently. In England private property rights to land, minerals, houses, transport facilities, agricultural, industrial and commercial capital and to human skills and labour power had become legally enforceable under common and statute law decades before 1688. Rules governing trade, exchanges and the extension of credit had also evolved over the centuries into modes of conduct widely accepted by businessmen, workers and consumers at large. Thus during the Industrial Revolution the kingdom's factor and commodity markets continued to operate within a long-established framework of law and extra-legal codes of conduct. From 1688 onwards parliaments can be perceived to be engaged in a process of rescinding and amending a traditional body of law and adding new rules for the conduct of economic relations at the margin (Lieberman 1989, 14, 17, 61; Lambert 1971). Throughout the period their intentions continued to be interpreted by the 'King's' less-than-compliant courts and laws were put into effect within wide margins of flexibility by the incompetent administrative machinery available for their execution. Whenever their transactions with each other broke down Hanoverian businessmen could certainly appeal to the common law and turn to the established courts to safeguard and to indemnify them against risks from fraud, bankruptcy and breaches of contract. But on all such matters (of abiding concern for the conduct of a functioning market economy) historians who have recently examined some of the evidence related to the day-to-day work of the courts suggest that the English legal system did not offer speedy, cheap and economically efficient ways: of minimising risk and settling breaches of contract between firms; of dealing with disputes between businessmen and their customers, or in making arrangements for economically efficient settlements between creditors and debtors. Reforms occurred but the jurisdiction on offer in Hanoverian England continued to be unpredictable and expensive to procure and was suffused with considerations of custom, equity and other anachronistic obstacles to the diffusion of competitive markets (Atiyah 1979). Fortunately (and perhaps this occurred for an overwhelming share of their transactions?) businessmen abided by codes of practice, backed by sanctions which rested upon mutual interdependence and upon the preservation of 'reputation'. When necessary, they resorted to their own system of arbitration, conducted by trade associations, gilds, chambers of commerce and other peer groups who applied commercial rules to disputes and breakdowns in normal business relations (Sugarman 1983, 213–66; Baker 1986, 341–68; Arthurs 1984, 380–404).

From time to time parliament stepped in and legislated, for example, to compel the courts to recognize promissory notes as assignable instruments of credit and in 1776 and 1779 passed bills designed to protect small debtors from the risks of imprisonment (Hoppit 1987; Cohen 1982, 153–72; Atiyah 1979, 134–6; Innes 1980, 253–59). Alas such interventions did not always operate to improve efficiency. Parliaments of landowners (antipathetic to forms of ownership that were not proprietorial or family based and hostile to commercial dealings in 'paper' assets) passed the Bubble Act of 1720 and outlawed the 'infamous practice' of jobbing in stocks and shares thirteen years later. With these two acts the Commons placed legal barriers in the way of an ongoing evolution towards corporate forms of business enterprise which operated to depress the rate of investment, and to maintain the capitalization of industrial and commercial firms (particularly banks) at a scale which contributed to cyclical instability. What was ultimately more baneful, this legislation sustained a tradition of family based business organization in Victorian Britain that proved itself to be ill-adapted to meet competitive challenges from American and German corporations during the second Industrial Revolution of the late nineteenth and twentieth centuries (Dubois 1971, 1–25; Dickson 1967, 516–21).

In 1688 parliament took over responsibility for the management of the money supply from the Crown, but it failed to meet demands from the growing economy for increasing supplies of coins or to establish a framework of legislation for the regulation of bank money and paper credit. Parliament's *laissez-faire* stance towards the money supply left the economy exposed (at one and the same time) to unnecessary inconvenience and deflationary pressures from shortages of coin, and to potential instabilities associated with uncontrolled extensions of credit (Ashton 1955, 167–79). Eighteenth-century governments certainly managed the nation's coinage with manifest incompetence. They maintained fixed mint prices and parities which encouraged the export of gold and silver bullion and melted down coins. This left the domestic economy chronically short of small change, especially silver coins of low denomination (Styles 1983, 177–240; Feaveryear 1963, 109–64; Craig 1953, 180). Fortunately a network of financial intermediaries (merchants, bill brokers, London and provincial bankers) developed to fill the gap and to provide convenient and elastic forms of paper substitutes (banknotes, bills of exchange, book credit, cheques) for metallic money. By default virtually unregulated private commercial enterprise assumed responsibility for the expansion required in the nation's money supply and a financial system evolved that carried the British economy through eight wars and an industrial revolution without widespread breakdowns, serious episodes of inflation or loss of confidence in paper credit. Although several short-lived cycles of economic instability which occurred long before the famous financial crises of the years after 1819 can be associated with imprudent extensions of bank credit, the system worked largely because bankers, businessmen and above all politicians exercised a strong degree of caution with respect to the use and extension of paper credit (Pressnell 1956; Ashton 1955, 177–88). Throughout the period (indeed until well into the nineteenth century) neither the central government nor the governors of its chartered Bank of England wished to manage the 'money' supply. Classical economists remained unwilling to hand over such 'awesome' power to the state or the governors of the Bank of England. Although most of them also expressed grave doubts about an unregulated system of free and occasionally 'wildcat' country banking (White 1984; Clapham 1944).

The political economy of foreign and strategic policy

By 'governance' eighteenth-century writers meant governing the internal affairs of the realm but the overwhelming preoccupation of the Hanoverian state was with funding and directing the kingdom's foreign, strategic and commercial policies. Something like 83 per cent of all public money spent on goods and services between 1688 and 1815 can be classified as military in origin and purpose. On a per capita basis (and almost certainly as a share of national income) Britain's military expenditures headed European league tables for the period. They swamped by a large margin the funds allocated by private investors for the formation of capital and the promotion of technical change upon which the progress of the economy so directly depended.

Between 1688 and 1802 Britain declared war against foreign powers no less than eight times and mobilized its troops and sailors for about half of all those years between the Glorious Revolution and Waterloo. Oscillations in the economy connected to these unpredictable political events did not provide anything like an optimal environment for development. But the ups and downs in economic activity can only be analysed cycle by cycle, war by war. In this central section I propose to discuss the 'huge and possibly unmanageable' question of how an 'interconnected sequence' of wars (beginning in 1689 and ending finally in 1815) can be related to the long-term progress of the economy. Such an attempt presupposes that the economists' heuristically powerful tools of cost benefit analysis might be applied to the assessment of decisions made by the state to allocate such a high share of the nation's resources to military objectives. In turn that assumes that national gains from, as well as the costs of, strategic policy might in principle be measured – which is palpably absurd. Even a qualitative historical assessment of the economic benefits imputable to military expenditure is predicated upon an assumption that an alternative set of foreign and strategic policies were actually on offer, and which might also have carried the British economy to the plateau of development it had attained when Viscount Castlereagh signed the Treaty of Vienna in 1815. In retrospect conceivable options seem difficult to discern – even though dissent from the broad aims of foreign policy frequently appeared in the arena of public debate between 1688 and 1815 and conflict with the thirteen colonies came nearer than any other war to dividing the nation.

Whatever else it may have signified, England's Glorious Revolution certainly marked a decisive shift in favour of a more active and fiscally more costly involvement in European power politics. For several decades that quantifiable outcome of the Revolution aroused 'Tory' antipathies and Jacobite hostility (Black 1987, 128–41; Black 1989, 139–58). But diplomatic historians wisely refuse to entertain a 'counter-factual' scenario for the kingdom's foreign policy based upon the survival of the Stuart dynasty. Accepting the Revolution and the consequences of the Protestant succession, their narratives present the foreign policies of Hanoverian monarchs and statesmen as a prolonged response to the realm's 'natural and necessary enemy' – France (Black 1986; Black 1987, 128–41). To check the ambitions of the Bourbons (especially Louis XIV) and of Napoleon to hegemony in Europe – linked to a contingent expansion of the French Empire in the Americas and India – turned out to be *unavoidably* expensive. Over what is now loosely referred to as the 'Second Hundred Years War', intervals of cordiality, even alliance, marked relations between the two states, but while the power of France waxed and waned it never ceased to threaten the interests and security of the British economy until after the defeats of Napoleon, first at Trafalgar and finally at Waterloo (Black 1986).

Over this period the House of Commons voted for the supplies requested by ministers to confront the king's enemies almost without serious demur, because members of parliament appreciated the realities of power politics faced by the Crown and its political advisers. They grudgingly recognized that Britain's monarchs and ministers had to cope with a complex and unstable international environment. They appreciated the problems caused by the ambitions of France, Austria, Prussia and Russia; the slow decline of Spain; the vulnerability of dependencies and allies such as Hanover, Portugal and Holland, as well as the series of succession crises that afflicted most of the royal houses of *ancien régime* Europe (Jones 1980; Langford 1976).

Taking the international order and the enmity of France (and Spain) as the inescapable givens of power politics, economic historians must also contemplate (and not continue to ignore) those vast sums of public money allocated in order: to preserve the security of the realm; to seize and defend Atlantic and Indian empires, to safeguard the kingdom's increasing commitment to foreign trade; and to weaken the competitive power of rival economies. They might at least enquire if the money was well spent? How far did the broad thrust of foreign and strategic policy pursued by successive Hanoverian governments contribute to the industrialization of the economy? Perhaps a great deal of the public revenue they raised was (as radicals so often insisted) wasted in pursuit of dynastic aims with no obvious spin-offs for economic growth and the welfare of the British people? Such questions rejoin serious eighteenth-century discussions concerned with the political economy of diplomacy and military strategy (or what is nowadays analysed as strategic trade policy). This discussion should not only lead to a reengagement with the problem of analysing the potential benefits of state expenditures but to an escape from that entirely unbalanced preoccupation of liberal thought since the time of Adam Smith with the costs of taxes and loans.

Mercantilists certainly looked hard at public expenditure and argued a great deal about 'power and profit' (Gomes 1987; Schaeffer 1981, 81–96). In going over debates of the day, modern military and diplomatic historians have distinguished two persistent and antagonistic refrains among the cacophony of eighteenth-century voices that can be heard discussing the economic implications of Britain's contentious military and diplomatic relations with the rest of Europe. Their heuristic separation between 'blue water' and 'continental commitment' schools of thought represents a viable counterfactual (or at least a relevant argument) to pursue (French 1990).

Adherents of blue water strategy defined their premises fairly clearly during the course of three short and inexpensive conflicts with Holland in the 1650s, 1660s and 1670s. Briefly the 'predatory' proponents of this school of thought pressed Cromwell and then Charles II to use the navy to countervail the competitive edge of Holland in international trade, shipping and finance and if possible to conquer Dutch possessions overseas. Their expectations of real maritime and colonial gains turned out to be overestimated. English admirals (preoccupied with more urgent military problems) did not use their men-of-war to inflict the maximum possible damage on the Dutch mercantile marine. Apparently, on balance, the total losses suffered by England's merchant ships and their cargoes did not fall far enough short of similar losses suffered by Holland. Peace treaties signed twice at Westminster and once at Breda provided disappointing gains; Dutch recognition of the Navigation Act of 1651, a small indemnity, Jamaica (taken from Spain in 1654) and New York – regarded at the time as a rather worthless piece of real estate (Howat 1974; Jones 1980; Padfield 1979).

In its pure form, blue water strategy recommended that British governments should avoid expensive embroilments in continental power politics, advocated the use of force to maximize profits for minimal amounts of military expenditure, expected English diplomats to cash in on the 'spoils of war' and pressed for naval actions which might permanently weaken Britain's economic rivals.

Fortunately, Hanoverian monarchs and their aristocratic advisers proved to be more farsighted. They formulated longer term, more realistic and, as we now see, more profitable strategies for the kingdom to pursue. They accepted a major role for sea power and throughout the period allocated some 60 per cent of revenues available for military purposes to the royal navy. At the same time they realized that seapower alone would not be sufficient to preserve the security of the realm, to safeguard the Empire or even to protect Britain's growing share of world trade (Baugh 1983, 1–46; 1988, 1–58).

Navies operated off-shore and only the commitment or threat of deploying ground forces could prevent the armies of France and her allies from securing Bourbon or Napoleonic supremacy in Europe. Only the need to countervail rival powers and their armies on the mainland limited the aspirations of French ministers to allocate a greater share of their limited fiscal resources to the construction of a fleet and to the training of sailors with the guns and skills necessary to mount a serious challenge to the royal navy and menace the kingdom's trade with Europe, the Americas and India (Meyer 1980, 139–63). Only allied troops (reinforced from time to time by regiments from Britain) could check French forces from occupying strategically placed ports along the opposite side of the North Sea – from which to launch an 'Armada' of soldiers and their equipment capable of establishing a bridgehead along the east coast of England (Duffy 1989, 127–46).

Between 1688 and 1815 the Hanoverian state lacked the authority to conscript manpower on a large scale as well as the fiscal base and political will to maintain ground forces on the Continent for any length of time. Just as British governments carefully nurtured the nation's comparative advantages in seapower, its enemies, France (and Spain) sustained their martial traditions on land. To lend support to the 'foreign' armed force perceived to be necessary to counter the ambitions of these formidable enemies on the mainland turned out to be the most controversial aspect of Hanoverian foreign policy and repeatedly gave rise to pressure for the more 'cost-effective' blue water option. It would be difficult to estimate the share of public revenue that was allocated over time in order to build up and maintain military alliances with European powers – prepared for their own national interests to confront France and her allies in Europe. In fiscal terms that aspect of British 'grand strategy' involved three exposed and politically contentious categories of military expenditure. First and foremost (and this occurred on three occasions 1689–97, 1702–13 and 1808–15) it led to the serious commitment of British infantry and artillery to long campaigns on the Continent. Secondly, it involved the allocation of direct subsidies transferred in the form of bullion into the coffers of so-called friendly emperors, kings and princes. Thirdly, British taxes were spent on hiring less than dedicated regiments of Hessian, Hanoverian, Swiss and other mercenaries. While commitments of manpower in European theatres of war were often requested by Britain's Dutch, Austrian, Russian, Prussian and other allies, that tactic was only rarely agreed to by governments in London, who sensibly sought to keep their options open. Prudently they manoeuvred to retain troops at home in case enemy soldiers managed to land on English beaches. Ministers also sought to retain a position which would allow them to turn off flows of subsidies (or exports of military hardware) as and when it suited their own perceptions of Britain's economic and strategic interests to so do. Finally, they preferred to be able to wind up a war at their discretion by serving short notice on regiments of mercenaries, thereby avoiding the serious problems of crime and disorder associated with demobilization of masses of British troops in home ports. Furthermore, the decisions by William of Orange, Anne and George III to commit ground forces to campaign in Europe are all associated with drastic and sudden rises in the level of military expenditures, balance of payment problems, currency depreciation and an intensification of 'war weariness' among public opinion at home (Cookson 1982).

On the other side of the North Sea, Perfidious Albion's devious diplomacy and the use of its wealth and fiscal advantages to 'buy' foreign armies to do its dangerous and dirty work inspired deep distrust and growing resentment. As Europeans correctly observed, while their own manpower, capital assets, agricultures, towns and trades bore the brunt of armed attacks from France, Spain and their allies, Britain preserved its island security and exploited its naval superiority to expand territorial possessions and commercial opportunities overseas. No wonder all Europe gloated when George III lost his thirteen colonies in 1783 (Mackesy 1989, 147–64; Schmitt 1953).

Thus it is no surprise to find that many Englishmen hankered for a simple and profitable blue water strategy. Did not European allies distrust their intentions, take their money and all too often fail to deliver promised amounts of force to the fields of battle? Yet continental commitments represented an integral component of Britain's grand strategy. Of course from time to time (examples are too numerous to list) British revenues, equipment and lives were wasted in ill-conceived or badly executed amphibian landings or longer term military campaigns on the mainland. But the Hanoverian view that rather high levels of expenditure on the ground forces of Britain and her allies were essential for the protection of the realm, for the support of the navy and the containment of France turned out to be correct in the long run. Along the way and to the predictable chagrin of merchants and mercantilists diplomatic policy involved the acceptance of peace treaties and the granting of economic concessions to European powers that did not appear to 'cash in' on the spoils of victory (Kennedy 1983, chs. 3–5; Horn 1967).

Meanwhile the altogether more massive and consistent investment by the Hanoverian state in naval power paid off. Through eight wars (with three, perhaps four, conspicuous lapses when the incompetence of French and Spanish admirals saved the day) the royal navy remained in command of the Channel and the North Sea. Its blockades and occasional first strike actions prevented the combination of hostile fleets with sufficient fire power to outgun the Admiralty's men-of-war stationed in home waters.

European perceptions that the British economy gained more or perhaps suffered less from warfare are surely correct? Between 1688 and 1815, foreign troops never ravaged the nation's towns, destroyed its capital equipment or ransacked inventories of grain, animals, industrial raw materials and transport equipment. In wartime, the share of the English workforce (particularly artisans) drafted into the army remained at small and manageable proportions because troops were recruited overwhelmingly from among the unskilled, potentially underemployed (often from the colonial and Celtic) fringes of the workforce; because the War Office and Admiralty hired large numbers of foreign mercenaries and seamen; because monarchs and ministers concentrated the bulk of 'military investment' in waging more capital intensive – that is to say naval – campaigns to secure national objectives.

In several significant respects this 'British way of warfare' complemented and sustained the long-term progress of the economy and that makes it sensible to conceive of military expenditures as the Hanoverian state's 'implicit agenda'; or as the bill for an integrated package of strategic, imperial and commercial policies for the long-term development of the kingdom. Even its most famous critic Adam Smith argued for 'defence before opulence', which is not perceptive enough. Within that international order defence formed an integral part of opulence. As mercantilists recognized military expenditures in general (and the strategic concentration of the navy in particular) can be seen to have provided 'preconditions' for an unquantifiable but possibly significant part of the economic growth achieved between 1688 and 1815 (Anderson 1787; Knorr 1944).

Obviously the tangible links between 'power and profit' connect the navy through the defence of the realm and foreign trade to the ongoing industrialization of the economy. Naval power forestalled, repelled and protected the British Isles from invasion and provided its capitalists with the security required to invest in the long-term future of their economy and Empire. True a larger, more professional army stationed in barracks within the kingdom might have provided a cheaper and comparable measure of security but that unpopular option could never allay the anxieties of businessmen and investors about the potential stability and predatory intentions of the Crown, acting as the commander-in-chief of a larger standing army. After all, at the end of those wars demobilized merchant seamen went back to sea (Blackburn 1984, 167–72).

Furthermore, several well documented overlaps between public investment for the construction of warships, royal dockyards and naval organization on the one hand and the mercantile marine, shipbuilding and foreign trade on the other suggest that the 'unavoidable' commitment of merchant seamen and other scarce resources to the royal navy carried in its train some long-term benefits for the civilian economy. Several examples of such 'externalities', including improvements to the design of ships and their sails, to nautical instruments, maps, metallurgy, food preservation, to training in seamanship, even to medical care, have been listed by historians as byproducts of naval expenditures. Such expenditures almost certainly generated more spin-offs than can be found to have accrued from public money allocated to feed, clothe and arm soldiers (John 1955, 329–44; Trebilcock 1969, 474–90; Saville 1984, 2–12).

Finally, well-known connexions between expenditures on the navy and the growth of the nation's commerce with foreign and above all with imperial markets should not continue to be derogated. Exports, imports, capital flows, shipping, services, marine insurance, international banking and commodity exchanges, the growth of London, Liverpool, Glasgow, Bristol and other ports are all related in so many ways to the Hanoverian navy. In that age of mercantilist warfare and piracy, economic development that can be linked directly and indirectly to an ever widening and deepening commitment to foreign trade and to the servicing of the international economy is almost inconceivable without persistent and increasingly effective support from British seapower. As Pitt's secretary for war, Henry Dundas, observed in 1801 'It is obvious that the present strength and pre-eminence of this country is owing to the extent of its resources arising from its commerce and its naval power which are inseparable' (Dundas 1801).

Only the preoccupation of nineteenth-century liberals and modern economists with the 'costs' of taxes and loans required to pay for it all makes it necessary to remember that ships-of-the-line and frigates kept open trade with Europe, even in those difficult years of Napoleonic blockade (Crouzet 1988). The navy contained enemy attacks on British ships in the Channel and North Sea. The navy captured and recaptured and maintained a fortified network of bases in the Mediterranean and along the perimeters of the Atlantic, Pacific and Indian Oceans to protect British ships and their cargoes sailing in blue waters far from home (MacKay and Scott 1983). Naval organization (convoys) eventually defeated the long running *guerre de course* waged with great skill by French (but also from time to time by Spanish, Dutch and American) privateers against British trade. In most wars and thanks to naval superiority, the balance sheet of prizes (ships and their cargoes taken) probably exceeded domestic losses to enemy privateers by a considerable margin (Mackesy 1989; Crowhurst 1977). That represents a victory for British public enterprise over the daring individualism of French privateers. Despite all the obstacles, interruptions and risks associated with the conduct of international trade in that dangerous international economic order, British exports continued to expand. Thanks to the royal navy, the nation's commerce was never crippled or even for long arrested. The outward orientation of a relatively small economy on the edge of Europe persisted as an endurable and effective strategy for its long-term transition to the status of a hegemonic power and workshop of the world

There are well rehearsed objections to presenting foreign trade conjoined with the royal navy as the engine of Britain's economic growth from 1688 to 1815. Trade, goes the opposite argument, was but 'the handmaiden of growth'. Did not the increased volume of sales overseas flow from the growing efficiency of the economy rooted in technical progress and entrepreneurial vigour? Furthermore, and in theory, there are always other growth paths to follow. In a fully employed economy, close to equilibrium the gains from trade (exporting in order to consume imports at lower cost) are likely to be 'small'.

Monocausal explanations of the kind implied by such ill-defined terms as engines or handmaidens of growth have fortunately all but disappeared from academic discourse. The substantive issues behind these two metaphors which involve attempts to specify and estimate the gains from trade are dealt with at length elsewhere (O'Brien and Engerman 1991, ch. 8). Our exposition estimates the rather large share (roughly 40 per cent) of the increment to industrial output that was sold outside the kingdom over the eighteenth century and rejects Ricardian models of the connexions between trade and growth based upon untested theoretical assumptions that the Hanoverian economy was fully employed and close to a state of competitive equilibrium. Furthermore, the counterfactual scenario for the long-term growth of the economy implicit in Ricardian theory diminishes the role of trade in the Industrial Revolution to little more than a marginally preferable option that the country could have been abandoned without serious economic cost in favour of a hypothetical strategy of selling a far higher proportion of industrial output on the home market (Thomas and McCloskey 1981, 88–102). Alternative (let us label them as Stuart) notions for the long-term development of the British economy are certainly interesting to reflect upon. But contemporaries would have found it difficult to envisage how industrialization and urbanization as well as the penumbras of favourable spin-offs that flowed from closer involvement with the world economy might have emerged if the state had radically constrained that involvement from the reign of William III onwards. Between 1688 and 1815 as the economy became more committed to international commerce (and increasingly vulnerable to hostile forces outside the kingdom) the taxpaying public became more compliant towards the expenditure of ever-increasing amounts of revenue in order to expand and defend Britain's interests in the Atlantic economy, the Mediterranean and the Indian Ocean. Only Jacobites fumed in the wilderness against the ever-increasing burden of taxation. Aristocratic politicians (who disdained 'trade') entertained few doubts about promoting and protecting the nation's commerce. Merchants and industrialists lobbied for the use of force and diplomacy to open markets, to acquire territory overseas and to compel their colonial cousins to buy British. Mercantilists wrote pamphlet after pamphlet to extol the pursuit of power and profit (Brewer 1989; Coleman 1969). Was all this expenditure of political effort, bourgeois money and intellectual propaganda unnecessary and possibly an economically flawed way to defend the realm and develop the economy? Or can strategies actually pursued by the Hanoverian regime for protection of the home market and for safeguarding and expanding the nation's commerce with the rest of the world be more realistically represented as the creation of political conditions for the industrialization of a relatively small market economy, trading at the core of the largest occidental Empire since Rome?

Along the way 'some' misallocation of resources certainly occurred.

Historians have exposed numerous examples of: inept diplomacy, military disasters, the loss of thirteen colonies, profligate expenditure, and, by Gladstonian standards, the corrupt misappropriation of taxpayers' money raised in theory to fund the army and navy. Spending by military departments of state, commanders of ships and gentrified but greedy colonels of regiments proved to be extremely difficult to control everywhere in Europe in the eighteenth century (Ekelund and Tollison 1981; Binney 1958). Historians of public finance will wish to follow up radical critiques of Britain's aristocratic governments and guess (or rather guestimate) at the proportion of public money that they 'wasted' and percolated from all those millions of pounds raised and spent to carry the state and the economy through to that more peaceable international order which succeeded the decline of French power after 1815. Meanwhile economic historians can only presume that expenditures on military force by the Hanoverian state were basically unavoidable; and for the most part a profitable investment for the economic development of the kingdom.

Taxation

Nevertheless, the liberal preoccupation with the economic costs of the taxes and loans raised to pay for it all must also be discussed simply because Hanoverian governments raised taxes and borrowed sums of money way beyond the administrative capacity or the political comprehension of Tudor and Stuart regimes. Taxes rose in real terms by a factor of sixteen between the reign of James II and George IV. Stable inflows of revenue into the Exchequer formed the indispensable basis for the accumulation of the perpetual national debt, which proved to be such a potent weapon for the rapid and sustained mobilization of financial resources in wartime. To some extent the fiscal prowess displayed by Orange and Hanoverian regimes can be regarded as fortuitous. A Dutch king took over an 'undertaxed' economy from an unpopular Stuart monarch, secured a political settlement with parliament and embarked upon war to defend the Protestant succession. This enabled his ministers to 'jack up' revenues to previously unthinkable levels. Taxes never again fell back to anywhere near the modest exactions 'extorted' (at least in the eyes of their opponents) by Charles and his brother James (O'Brien 1988, 1–33). Fortunately, the economy and its tax base continued to grow. Did that occur despite or because of the 'depredations' of the state? Industrial development, the spread of internal markets and growth of foreign trade certainly assisted eighteenth-century governments to innovate taxes and levy ever higher rates of duty. But estimates for the shares of national income appropriated as taxation (even in peacetime) went up by multipliers that confirms a discontinuity in politics and fiscal administration. That unmistakable outcome of the Glorious Revolution also points to the 'compliance' of England's taxpaying public with the aims of the new regime, as well as a shrewd recognition by those who managed its fiscal policy that indirect taxes levied on imported (and, in growing proportion, upon domestically produced goods and services) would provoke less resistance than attempts to assess potentially more progressive, but ultimately unacceptable, direct taxes on income and wealth. Until Pitt the Younger introduced the first income tax in 1799 the fiscal system shifted steadily in favour of taxes on commodities and services. Furthermore, all but the most flexible of chancellors recognized it would be expedient to tolerate rather high levels of fraud and evasion, particularly in Scotland and other potentially seditious and virtually untaxable provinces of the realm. Perhaps that is why (apart from the costly exception of the American rebellion) no tax revolts marked the upward rise in military expenditure.

Meanwhile industrialization progressed in an economy 'afflicted' by ever-increasing 'burdens' of taxation. For the times the British enjoyed the distinction of being the most highly taxed nation in Europe, even if their government's military-fiscal matrix was transparent and widely admired (Mathias and O'Brien 1976, 601–50; Fritschy 1990, 58–79). Taxes went up in wartime to fund interest bills on loans floated to cover suddenly enhanced levels of military spending. Taxes remained at higher levels over subsequent interludes of peace in order to service an irredeemable public debt accumulating over time as a direct consequence of successful (and with the thirteen colonies unsuccessful) engagements in warfare. What can we conclude about the economic effects of rising taxation? Not much! There were literally hundreds of taxes of every kind and their incidence is extremely difficult to determine empirically. To say anything at all, tax burdens must be related to social groups, sectors, economic activities and to types of expenditure liable for taxation.

For example, the land and other directly assessed taxes, levied upon the wealthy, were increased radically and collected far more effectively during the wars against Louis XIV from 1689 to 1713. Thereafter, and especially when land values began their long upward climb from mid-century onwards, the nation's propertied elite transferred a diminishing share of their incomes to the state in the form of direct taxation. For political reasons such taxes levied directly on the rich could not be imposed at anything like progressive rates. All in all Hanoverian politicians did not use the fiscal system to check growing inequality in the distribution of wealth and income. Apart from the very poor, all groups in British society found themselves paying ever increasing absolute amounts in direct taxes but the non-progressive nature of this form of taxation miti-gated potentially deleterious effects upon incentives to save and invest.

To make even tentative statements about the social and economic incidence of that more important and extraordinary range of customs, excise and stamp duties, imposed by successive chancellors over this period is extremely difficult. In their thrust in favour of indirect taxes, and their attempts to spread the burden across all ranks of society, Hanover-ian governments maintained a fiscal strategy that became more and more regressive. But we must be clear what we mean by that loaded epithet. Necessities of the poor (their basic foodstuffs, clothing and shelter) remained exempt. Chancellors and their advisers selected commodities and calibrated rates of taxation in order to take more money away from those with higher incomes. (Thus brandy and silk carried higher rates of duty than beer and linens.)

Assuming, along with politicians of the period, that indirect taxes were in general passed on in the form of higher prices, enables us to estimate that between 1755 and 1815 the share of consumers' expenditure, appro-priated as customs, excise and stamp duties, may have risen three to four times. An earlier jump from 1670 to 1720 could have been even more pronounced.

Most of the revenues passing through the hands of tax collectors circulated back into the domestic economy as military expenditures for the food, clothing, equipment, ships and weapons supplied by British firms to keep navies at sea and armies in the field. Unfortunately, a not insignificant proportion 'leaked out' of the realm into expenditures on imports and to fund mercenaries and British forces serving overseas. It is this 'share' that represents the macro squeeze on consumption and which operated, particularly in wartime, to depress the home market for British industry and agriculture.

Furthermore, the entire budgetary process of taxing and spending by the state altered patterns of demand and supply for goods and services. Indirect taxes did not fall with equal weight upon value added so demands for more 'heavily' taxed commodities (such as beer, spirits, tobacco, salt and tropical groceries) were restrained while other goods and services (textiles, processed foodstuffs, paper, metallurgical and engineering goods, household utensils and furniture and internal transportation) escaped with lighter taxation (Beckett and Turner 1990, 377–403). Rapidly growing and innovative industries were not seriously burdened by taxes on their final outputs or raw materials. From the 1690s onwards nearly all sectors of industry also enjoyed higher levels of protection in home and imperial markets. Despite a never ending search for new taxes chancellors avoided whole areas of manufacturing activity. Their 'depredations' and 'distortions' tended to fall on well-established and eminently taxable agro-industries – beer and its ingredients, spirits, vinegar, cider, salt, refined sugar, tobacco, soap, starch and candles. They also hit rapaciously at bourgeois families with aspirations to reside in more comfortable, spacious and civilized homes, to dress with style and to emulate the consumption patterns of those above them in the social scale. England's so-called consumer revolution occurred in the teeth of taxmen.

Yet British businessmen could avoid taxes entirely by exporting their wares to foreign and imperial markets. Export duties almost disappeared in the late seventeenth century. If the mounting burden of indirect taxes narrowed the home market, drawbacks, bounties, imperial preference and attacks on enemy (and even on neutral) commerce secured and safeguarded markets overseas. Britain's fiscal policy (which complimented strategic, commercial and imperial policies) seemed designed to promote exports and to encourage the development of the mercantile, shipping and financial services required to integrate the populations of the kingdoms, the Empire and (after 1846) peoples everywhere into a common and effectively policed international market (Williams 1972; O'Brien and Pigman 1992).

Borrowing and the national debt

Many an eighteenth-century commentator can be cited to support recent exercises in cliometric history which purport to show how the massive rise in borrowing by the state (in order to provide immediately for cash required to wage war) 'crowded out' the formation and maintenance of the stock of capital upon which the progress of the economy depended. Crowding out almost certainly accompanied all Hanoverian wars, which were waged largely on borrowed money. Dampening effects on private investment usually appeared in construction or similar lines of capital formation connected to urbanization that were particularly responsive to variations in interest rates, and where investors competed directly with the state for loanable funds on the London capital market (Williamson 1984, 687–712; Ashton 1959).

The Treasury experienced no difficulty in that competition because if necessary it could offer rates of interest above the legally allowable maximum of 5 per cent and because investors in the national debt could reasonably anticipate capital gains at the end of hostilities. Securities or bonds sold by the state developed into relatively risk-less and highly attractive assets for nationals and foreigners alike, not simply because the Hanoverian regime (unlike its Stuart predecessor) repaid debts and met its interest bills but also because English statesmen devoted borrowed money to winning wars and strengthening the economic and fiscal base upon which the servicing of government loans depended. Despite the accumulation of a national debt which rose from a nominal capital of less than £2 million in 1688 to £834 million in 1816 (from less than 5 per cent of GNP to over twice its level) the cost of borrowing (on comparable public securities) declined from around 8 per cent to 9 per cent in the wars against Louis XIV from 1698 to 1713 to below 5 per cent in the war against the French Emperor, Napoleon, from 1802 to 1815. Corrected for movements in prices, interest rates decreased even more sharply particularly in those welcome interludes of peace when the consol rate hovered at or around the 3 per cent mark (Ashton 1955, T. 13).

Thus between the Glorious Revolution and Waterloo competition for loanable funds between the government and the civilian economy diminished as savings rates rose to accommodate voracious demands from the military forces of the Crown to fund their activities in wartime. In the short run (and again in a counterfactual sense) some potential capital formation failed to occur particularly during the wars against France from 1793 to 1815 when inflows of foreign capital may possibly have met a smaller proportion of the government's demand for loans than had been the case in previous conflicts? Modern economic theory suggests that military expenditures tend over the long term (but particularly in wartime) to depress consumption rather more than investment expenditures. That almost certainly occurred during most of the wars engaged in by Britain from 1689 to 1815 (Neal 1990; Barro 1987, 227–48).

Trends in the cost of borrowing certainly indicate that the British economy (perhaps with hitherto underestimated assistance from inflows of foreign and refugee capital from Europe) found it progressively less difficult to fund the military investment upon which its development depended. Furthermore, the accumulation and careful management of the national debt crowded 'in' as well as 'out'. It is not difficult to mention some positive as well as the familiar short-term and negative economic consequences that flowed from public borrowing. For example, the debt diffused a habit of impersonal investment, and encouraged saving, particularly in wartime when appeals to the propertied elite by buy bonds could elicit 'patriotic and prudential' as well as economically rational responses to help their armed forces defeat foreign enemies who threatened their own wealth and status. Sales of bonds, of Exchequer and military bills provided British capitalists with portfolios of low risk and liquid paper assets – on the base of which they could afford to venture more of their savings into commerce, industry and agriculture. Dealings in 'sound' governmental paper also helped to integrate segmented capital markets within the kingdom. While metropolitan financial intermediaries developed the expertise required to attract Dutch, French, Swiss, German and even American capital into that reliable and militarily safe haven for money – the City of London. Is it not plausible to regard the national debt as the motor of an eighteenth-century revolution in public and private finance? Could the rise of the City, first to become the hub of national capital market, and in short compass to surpass Amsterdam and all other European cities as the centre of the international monetary system – could that development be envisaged without a century or more of profitable and educational interactions between the Bank of England, London banks, and the Stock Exchange on the one hand and Hanoverian public finances on the other? Spin-offs for industry, agriculture and trade from the steady growth in London of institutions that matured into the most efficient capital market in Europe in some degree compensated for crowding out effects in wartime (O'Brien 1989, 335–83).

Furthermore (as radicals noticed) the burden of debt servicing charges went up and up and laid prior claim to an ever-increasing proportion of taxes collected in peacetime. That significant fiscal constraint on central government's room for manoeuvre rose from something negligible in the reign of James II, to around a quarter of tax receipts at the turn of the eighteenth century and up to reach 55 per cent of total receipts in the aftermath of the Revolutionary and Napoleonic Wars. As everyone remarked at the time, the social effects of transferring income through a budgetary process, which collected revenue from taxpayers distributed across income bands in general, and transferring it to holders of the national debt (concentrated in higher income brackets) could only be 'regressive' – and that effect would be intensified whenever price levels declined at the end of hostilities. Politically the regime survived persistent attacks made on its debt by radicals, Tories and other believers in 'real' as distinct from 'fictitious property'. Economically that regressive fiscal process associated with the rise of the national debt operated to raise rates of saving, investment and economic growth over the longer run (Crouzet 1989, 189–210).

Conclusions: Industrialization and the state

A liberal world economy of the kind that prevailed from 1846 to 1914 formed a superior environment for Victorian economic development than the mercantilist order within which British governments, merchants, industrialists and farmers operated from 1688 to 1815. Yet on balance (and not by any grand design) the outward orientation of the Hanoverian regime's foreign policies promoted structural change and the long-term growth of per capita incomes.

That orientation almost precluded domestic expenditures on social overhead capital, research and development, education and training and probably crowded out any serious contemplation of reforms to the legal system within which markets for commodities, factors of production and for money and credit evolved over this period. By default successive Hanoverian governments tolerated: anachronistic common and statute laws, an expensive and unpredictable judicial system, inadequate policing against crime, incompetent local authorities and other traditional institutions that were in many respects inimical to effective operation of a market economy. On the credit side the state slowly became immune to Jacobite sedition and other threats to good order. Gradually, first Scotland and then Ireland were incorporated into a single market. Throughout the period the regime sustained hierarchy and authoritarian (and perhaps, alas, economically efficient?) codes of control over a potentially unruly workforce at minimal fiscal cost. Acting as a hereditary ruling elite, Hanoverian monarchs, ministers, members of parliament and Justices of the Peace successfully exploited feudal powers, status, deference and Anglican religion to maintain political and managerial power over a population growing rapidly in size, younger in age and more urban by the year. They secured order at home while spending ever increasing amounts of public money on strategic and imperial objectives overseas. But if, as most mercantilists, as well as Malthus, believed the economy operated for long stretches of this period below full employment levels, then enhanced levels of military expenditure pushed the economy closer to full capacity utilization and thus in some degree the wars of the age not only helped to maintain security and expand the Empire but paid for themselves (Anderson 1972, 1–18). Even so, by any standards the expenditures on the armed forces required to underpin the kingdom's foreign, strategic and commercial policies look massive, and possibly profligate. I have argued that on balance the money seems to have been well spent because between 1688 and 1815 no invasions of the homeland wasted the domestic economy. Before 1805 no great power emerged on the mainland of Europe capable of obstructing the kingdom's trade with the continent. Foreign aggression against British commerce and territories overseas declined in significance. After the recognition of its independence in 1783 the United States was gradually 'reincorporated' into the Atlantic economy with Britain at its hub. Meanwhile diplomacy backed by military force had compelled the rival Empires of Portugal, Spain and Holland in the South Americas and Asia and the Mughals in India to concede entrée to British trade and ships. British privateering, together with blockades and assaults upon the mercantile marines of Holland, France and Spain by the royal navy (coupled with the vulnerability of

Amsterdam and Frankfurt to invading armies on the continent) formed 'military preconditions' for the City of London's domination of international services by the late eighteenth century.

Apart from the unmeasured windfall associated with the loot from India (which flooded in after Plassey) gains for the national economy took eight wars and decades of diplomatic activity to achieve; even longer to mature into secure markets for exports and imports and into flows of private profits, rents, wages and jobs for the surplus population from the Celtic and other underemployed regions of the economy. During the eighteenth century mercantilist intellectuals and aristocratic politicians claimed that the security of the realm and the expansion of its Empire and markets overseas represented real and sustainable returns for the ever-increasing burdens of funding defensive and offensive expenditures borne by British taxpayers. Their arguments have been ignored for too long by the proclivity of liberal political economists to concentrate only on the costs rather than the benefits of military force.

During that long (but still by historical standards rapid) transition Hanoverian statesmen entertained no illusions about the international order their businessmen had to operate within. For more than a century, when the British economy was on its way to maturity as the workshop of the world, its governments were not particularly liberal nor wedded ideologically to *laissez-faire*. Like the proverbial hedgehog of Aeschylus the Hanoverian governments knew some big things, namely that security, trade, empire and military power really mattered. In fruitful (if uneasy) partnership with bourgeois merchants and industrialists they poured millions into strategic objectives which we can see (with hindsight) formed preconditions for the market economy and night-watchman state of Victorian England, as well as the liberal world order which flourished under British hegemony from 1846 to 1914. By that time men of the pen, especially the pens of the political economy, had forgotten, and did not wish to be reminded, what the first industrial nation owed to men of the sword (Silbener 1972).

REFERENCES

Allan, D. D. G. 1974. 'The Society of Arts and government', *Eighteenth Century Studies*, 8.

Anderson, A. 1787. *An Historical and Chronological Deduction of the Origins of Commerce* (4 vols.).

Anderson, J. 1972. 'Aspects of the effect on the British economy of the war against France, 1790–1815', *Australian Economic History Review*, 28.

Arthurs, H. W. 1984. 'Special courts, special law: legal pluralism in 19th century England', in *Law, Economy and Society*, ed. G. Rubin, and D. Sugarman.

Ashton, T. S. 1955. *An Economic History of England: the 18th century*.

1959. *Economic Fluctuations in England, 1700–1800.*

Atiyah, P. S. 1979. *The Rise and Fall of Freedom of Contract.*

Baker, J. H. 1986. 'The law merchant and the common law before 1700', in *The Legal Profession and the Common Law*, ed. J. H. Baker.

Barro, R. J. 1987. 'Government spending, interest rates, prices and budget deficits in the United Kingdom', *Journal of Monetary Economics*, 20.

Baugh, D. 1983. 'Towards a blue water defence policy in seventeenth-century England: its political and social significance', Princeton Davis Center, unpublished paper.

1988. 'Great Britain's blue water policy, 1689–1815', *International History Review*, 10.

Beattie, J. M. 1986. *Crime and the Courts in England.*

Beckett, J. and Turner, M. 1990. 'Taxation and economic growth in eighteenth century England', *Economic History Review*, 43.

Binney, J. E. D. 1958. *British Public Finance and Administration, 1774–92.*

Black, J. 1986. *Natural and Necessary Enemies.*

1987. 'The British state and foreign policy in the eighteenth century: a survey', *Journal of British Studies*, 26.

1989. 'The revolution and the development of English foreign policy', in *By Force or by Default? The revolution of 1688*, ed. E. Cruickshanks.

Blackburn, R. 1984. 'The armed forces in legal history', *Journal of Legal History*, 5.

Bohstedt, J. 1983. *Riots and Community Politics in England and Wales, 1790–1810.*

Brewer, J. 1989. *The Sinews of Power: war, money and the English State, 1688–1783.*

Charlesworth, A. (ed.). 1983. *An Atlas of Rural Protest, 1549–1900.*

Christie, I. R. *Stress and Stability in Late Eighteenth Century Britain: reflections on the British avoidance of revolution.*

Clapham, J. H. 1944. *The Bank of England. A history* (2 vols.).

Clark, J. C. D. 1985. *English Society 1688–1832.*

Cohen, J. 1982. 'The history of imprisonment for debt and its relation to the development of discharge in bankruptcy', *Journal of Legal History*, 3.

Coleman, D. C. (ed.) 1969. *Revisions in Mercantilism.*

Colley, L. 1986. 'Whose nation? Class and national consciousness in Britain, 1750–1830', *Past and Present*, 113.

Colquhoun, P. 1814. *Treatise on the Wealth, Power and Resources of the British Empire.*

Cookson, J. E. 1982. *Anti-war Liberalism in England, 1793–1815.*

Crafts, N. F. R. 1985. *British Economic Growth during the Industrial Revolution.*

Craig, J. 1953. *The Mint. A history of the London Mint from A.D. 286 to 1948.*

Crouzet, F. 1988. *L'Économie britannique et le blocus continental.*

1989. 'The impact of the French wars on the British economy', in *Britain and the French Revolution, 1789–1815*, ed. H. T. Dickinson.

Crowhurst, P. 1977. *The Defence of British Trade, 1689–1815.*

Cullen, L. M. 1987. *An Economic History of Ireland since 1660.*

Devine, T. M. and Dickson, D. (eds.). 1983. *Ireland and Scotland, 1600–1850: parallels and contrasts in economic and social development.*

Dickson, P. G. M. 1967. *The Financial Revolution in England.*

Dobson, C. R. 1980. *Masters and Journeymen. A prehistory of industrial relations.*

Dubois, A. B. 1971. *The English Business Company after the Bubble Act.*

Duffy, M. 1989. 'British diplomacy in the French wars', in *Britain and the French Revolution, 1789–1815*, ed. H. T. Dickinson.

Dundas, A. 1801. 'Memorandum for consideration of His Majesty's Ministers', 31 March 1801, Duke University Library.

Dutton, A. 1984. *The Patent System and Inventive Activity during the Industrial Revolution.*

Ekelund, R. B. and Tollison, R. D. 1981. *Mercantilism as a Rent Seeking Society.*

Emsley, C. 1983. 'The military and popular disorder in England, 1790–1801', *Journal of the Society for Army Historical Research*, 51.

Feavearyear, A. 1963. *The Pound Sterling. A history of English money.*

Feinstein, C. H. and Pollard, S. 1988. *Studies in Capital Formation in the United Kingdom.*

French, D. 1990. *The British Way of Warfare.*

Fritschy, W. 1990. 'Taxation in Britain, France and the Netherlands in the eighteenth century', *Economic and Social History in the Netherlands*, 2.

Gomes, L. 1987. *Foreign Trade and the National Economy.*

Gwyn, R. D. 1985. *Huguenot Heritage: the history and contribution of Huguenots in Britain.*

Haines, B. W. 1980. 'English labour laws and the separation from contract', *Journal of Legal History*, 1.

Hayter, T. 1978. *The Army and the Crowd in Mid-Georgian England.*

Hoppit, J. 1987. *Risk and Failure in English Business, 1700–1800.*

Horn, D. B. 1967. *Great Britain and Europe in the Eighteenth Century.*

Houlding, J. A. 1981. *Fit for Service. The training of the British army, 1715–1795.*

Howat, G. M. D. 1974. *Stuart and Cromwellian Foreign Policy.*

Innes, J. M. 1980. 'Debtors and the law', in *An Ungovernable People: the English and their law in the seventeenth and eighteenth centuries*, ed. J. Brewer and J. Styles.

    1985. 'Social problems, poverty and marginality in 18th century England', Somerville College, Oxford, unpublished paper.

    1987. 'Prisons for the poor: English bridewells, 1555–1800', in *Labour, law and crime*, ed. F. G. Snyder and D. Hay.

Innes, J. M. and Styles, J. 1986. 'The crime wave in recent writings on crime and criminal law', *Journal of British Studies*, 25.

Jackson, R. V. 1990. 'Government expenditure and British economic growth in the eighteenth century: some measurement problems', *Economic History Review*, 43.

Jeremy, D. 1977. 'Damming the flood: British government efforts to check the outflow of technicians and machinery, 1780–1843', *Business History Review*, 51.

John, A. H. 1955. 'War and the English economy, 1700–63', *Economic History Review*, 7.

Jones, J. R. 1980. *Britain and the World, 1649–1815.*

Kelsall, R. K. 1938. *Wage Regulation under the Statute of Artificers.*

Kennedy, P. 1983. *The Rise and Fall of British Naval Mastery.*

Knorr, K. E. 1944. *British Colonial Theories, 1570–1850.*

Kussmaul, A. 1981. *Servants in Husbandry in Early Modern England.*
Lambert, S. 1971. *Bills and Acts.*
Langford, P. 1976. *The Eighteenth Century.*
Lenman, B. 1977. *An Economic History of Modern Scotland, 1660–1976.*
Levack, B. P. 1987. *The Formation of the British State. England, Scotland and the Union, 1603–1707.*
Lieberman, D. 1989. *The Province of Legislation Determined.*
Lipson, E. 1934. *The Economic History of England. The age of mercantilism.*
McKay, D. M. and Scott, H. M. 1983. *The Rise of the Great Powers, 1648–1815.*
Mackesy, P. 1989. 'Strategic problems of the British war effort', in *Britain and the French Revolution, 1789–1815*, ed. H. T. Dickinson.
MacLeod, C. 1988. *Inventing the Industrial Revolution.*
Mathias, P. 1983. *The First Industrial Nation.*
Mathias, P. and O'Brien, P. K. 1976. 'Taxation in England and France, 1715–1810', *Journal of European Economic History*, 5.
Meyer, J. 1980. 'The second hundred years war', in *Britain and France: ten centuries*, ed. D. Johnson *et al.*
Neal, L. 1990. 'A tale of two revolutions, 1789–1819', Working Paper 90–1663 BEBR, University of Illinois, Urbana-Champaign.
O'Brien, P. K. 1988. 'Political economy of British taxation, 1660–1815', *Economic History Review*, 41.
    1989. 'The impact of the revolutionary and Napoleonic wars 1793–1815 on the long run growth of the British economy', *Review Fernand Braudel Center* 12.
O'Brien, P. K. and Engerman, S. L. 1991. 'Exports and the growth of the British economy from the Glorious Revolution to the Peace of Amiens', in *Slavery and the Rise of the Atlantic System*, ed. B. Solow and S.L. Engerman.
O'Brien, P. K. and Pigman, G. 1992. 'Free Trade, British hegemony and the international economic order in the nineteenth century', *Review of International Studies*, 2.
O'Gorman, F. 1986. 'The recent historiography of the Hanoverian regime', *Historical Journal*, 29.
Orth, J. 1987. 'The English combination laws reconsidered', in *Labour, Law and Crime*, ed. F. G. Snyder and D. Hay.
Padfield, P. 1979. *Tides of Empire. Decisive naval campaigns in the rise of the West.*
Palmer, S. H. 1978. 'Calling out the troops. The military, the law and public order in England, 1650–1950', *Journal of the Society for Army Historical Research*, 56.
Porter, R. 1982. *English Society in the Eighteenth Century.*
Pressnell, L. S. 1956. *Country Banking in the Industrial Revolution.*
Rose, R. B. 1961. 'Eighteenth century price riots and public policy in England', *International Review of Social History*, 6.
Rudé, G. 1981. *The Crowd in History. A study of popular disturbances in France and England, 1730–1848.*
Rule, J. 1986. *The Labouring Classes in Early Industrial England, 1750–1950.*
Saville, R. 1984. 'Studies in government, finance and the economy, 1760–1800', *Report B/00/23/0036/i to E.S.R.C.*
Schaeffer, R. K. 1981. 'The entelechies of mercantilism', *Scandinavian Economic History Review*, 29:2.

Schmitt, A. 1953. 'The idea and slogan of Perfidious Albion', *Journal of the History of Ideas*, 14.

Silbener, E. 1972. *The Problem of the War in 19th Century Economic Thought.*

Styles, J. 1983. 'Embezzlement and the law', in *Manufacture in Town and Country before the Factory*, ed. M. Berg *et al.*

Sugarman, D. (ed.) 1983. 'Introduction and overview', in *Legality, Ideology and the State.*

Taylor, A. J. 1972. *Laissez-faire and State Intervention in Nineteenth-Century Britain.*

Thomas, R. P. and McCloskey, D. 1981. 'Overseas trade and empire, 1700–1860', in *The economic history of Britain since 1700*, ed. R. Floud and D. McCloskey, I.

Trebilcock, C. 1969. 'Spinoff in British economic history: armaments and industry, 1760–1914', *Economic History Review*, 22.

White, L. H. 1984. *Free Banking in Britain. Theory, experience and debate, 1800–1845.*

Williams, J. B. 1972. *British Commercial Policy and Trade Expansion.*

Williamson, J. G. 1984. 'Why was British growth so slow during the Industrial Revolution?', *Journal of Economic History*, 44.

7   Crime, law and punishment in the Industrial Revolution

David Philips

Introduction

Thomas Carlyle, in many of his writings in the 1820s and 1830s, drew attention to the dramatic changes which the Industrial Revolution was bringing to the society around him. '[B]ut cannot the dullest hear Steam-engines clanking around him?', he wrote in *Sartor Resartus* in 1838, 'at home not only weaving Cloth, but rapidly enough overturning the whole system of Society ...?' Among the many areas which were 'overturned' and 'revolutionized' in the period between 1780 and 1860 was the handling by the British state of the issues of crime, the criminal law, law-enforcement and punishment.

In late-eighteenth-century England, Wales, Scotland and Ireland, the systems of criminal law, law-enforcement and punishment in force were very different from those we associate with the modern state. The criminal law – the so-called 'Bloody Code' – gave central prominence to capital punishment, with over 200 offences, most of them offences against property, punishable by death. There were few secondary punishments, other than death or transportation, for serious offences, and long-term imprisonment was not used as a punishment in itself. But, if the criminal code and punishments were harsh, the means of law-enforcement were weak and uncoordinated, and the system contained apparent contradictions. There were no full-time paid uniformed police forces; policing agencies were local, decentralized and mostly unpaid. Control of law and order and the local policing agencies was largely in the hands of unpaid landowners acting as Justices of the Peace. In England and Wales, there was no state authority charged with the responsibility of prosecuting all offences committed. Prosecution was essentially a private matter; the responsibility to prosecute rested with the victim of the offence, and if he or she chose not to prosecute, the offence went unpunished. An extensive system for the procuring of royal pardons for condemned people ensured that many of the death sentences passed were never executed.

Herein lies the central paradox of the system. The 'Bloody Code' prescribed hanging on a large scale; yet the weak police agencies meant that many offenders were never caught; private prosecution meant that many more were never prosecuted or convicted; and the system of pardons meant that many of those convicted were never actually hanged. Douglas Hay has shown that this system was less irrational than it may appear to us; the men who ran the system were concerned to catch and punish only a proportion – say, one in ten or one in twenty – of offenders; those people were to be punished severely to make an example of them and deter all other potential offenders. Exemplary punishment of a selected proportion, rather than punishment of all offenders, with lesser penalties proportioned to the seriousness of the offence, was the keynote of the system (Hay 1975a). (Hay's work has been criticized (Langbein 1983b; King 1984; Innes and Styles 1986), but it has also been well supported (Beattie 1986), and his argument still seems to me to make better sense of the late-eighteenth-century system than do the arguments of his critics.)

In the eighty years between 1780 and 1860, this system of criminal law, law-enforcement and punishment changed dramatically, largely as a result of Britain's experience of the Industrial Revolution and in response to the political and social effects of the French Revolution. Broadly speaking, we can identify five important areas in which this change took place; these areas overlapped and interacted with each other. They were: (1) policing (2) magistracy (3) prosecution (4) criminal law (5) punishment. These changes took place within an atmosphere, especially from the 1790s onwards, of growing fear about the perceived threat posed to respectable society by a supposed 'criminal class' and a fear on the part of the propertied classes of possible serious popular disorder or even revolution. These fears were clearly related to changes being brought about by industrialization and the concomitant growth of large urban concentrations of population; they also drew sustenance from the French Revolution from 1789 onwards, and the threat which this posed to all ruling classes. Some would argue that an atmosphere of 'moral panic', to heighten the urgency of the need for reforms in the area of law and order, was deliberately fostered by certain 'moral entrepreneurs' who then offered themselves and their own schemes of reform as the solutions to those fears (see Becker 1963; Philips 1980, 1983; Davis 1980). I shall deal separately with the five areas outlined above, but such separation is an artificial one, for the purposes of analysis; the five areas related to common issues, and frequently overlapped with each other. I shall also deal largely with England and Wales; Scotland had its own legal system and different developments; Ireland was also quite distinct, and in this

Table 7.1. *Indictable committals to trial, England and Wales, 1805–1842*

Year	Committals [a]	Committals [b]	(1805 = 100)
1805	4,605	49	100
1811	5,337	53	108
1816	9,091	82	167
1821	13,115	109	222
1826	16,164	125	255
1831	19,647	141	287
1836	20,984	140	286
1841	27,760	174	355
1842	31,309	194	396

[a] Indictable Committals   [b] Committals per 100,000 of population
Source: Porter 1847, 642; Censuses 1801–51.

period, raised many large but different problems of law and order, policing and rebellion – though it is useful to make some comparative reference to Irish policing experiments.

The common background to moves for reform in all five areas was a perceived increase in levels of crime and disorder; in London, one sees this from the middle of the eighteenth century; in fast-growing provincial towns, it begins in the 1780s and reaches a peak in the 1830s and 1840s. In 1810, for the first time, the government published official figures of committals to trial for indictable (more serious) offences, and these figures show a very clear and rapid increase – much greater than the increase of population – for the first half of the nineteenth century (see Table 7.1).

Many contemporaries took these rising figures of committals to trial as a clear indication that the Industrial Revolution was leading directly to an increase in the commission of crimes. G. R. Porter, the Board of Trade statistician, saw the figures as showing that 'the continued progress of our country in its economical relations' appeared to be accompanied by 'the still greater multiplication of its criminals' (Porter 1847, 641). The young Socialist Friedrich Engels stated that 'the incidence of crime has increased with the growth of the working-class population and there is more crime in Britain than in any other country in the world', this growing crime being a sign of 'the social war' between classes in England (Engels 1845, 146, 149). Many commentators claimed that the problem of crime and disorder was, predominantly, a problem of the urban and industrial areas – a claim which modern research would broadly support (Gatrell and Hadden 1972; Philips 1977; Rudé 1985; Emsley 1987).

But these criminal statistics do not necessarily show that there was an increase in crimes being *committed*, rather than an increase in crimes being *prosecuted* and hence coming to official attention. A parliamentary committee investigating this question in 1827, stated that

in the opinion of the Committee, a portion only of the accession to the Criminal Commitments, is to be deemed indicative of a proportionate increase of Crime; and that even of that portion, much may be accounted for in the more ready detection and trial of culprits, also in less disinclination to prosecute, in consequence of improved facilities afforded at the courts to prosecutors and witnesses, and of the increased allowance of costs. (*Criminal Commitments and Convictions Report* 1827, 9)

Recent historical research has supported this view that much of the increase was due to greater police and prosecution activity rather than to increased commission of offences (Gatrell and Hadden 1972; Philips 1977; Emsley 1987). But there is no doubt that there was a marked rise in *prosecuted* crime and an increase of concern, fuelled by these data, which helped to produce the changes in all five areas under discussion.

Policing

The period 1780–1860 saw Britain undergo a dramatic change from an 'unpoliced society' to a 'policed society' (Silver 1967). In 1780, England and Wales were policed only by 'old police' agencies – parish constables appointed by each local parish from its ratepayers, night watchmen for the larger towns, and various *ad hoc* private or public forces set up for particular areas. By 1857, every part of England and Wales was legally required to be policed by either a county or a borough police force, with the greater London area being covered by the Metropolitan Police Force. Scotland and Ireland had gone through a similar change, with Scotland being policed by county and burgh forces, and Ireland policed by a single Constabulary for the entire country, plus a Metropolitan Police for Dublin. The early landmarks in this change were: a 1785 Bill for a police force for London, which failed to pass (it was adopted for Dublin in 1786, but was not a success there); the 1822 establishment of constabulary forces for the counties of Ireland; and the 1829 Act which established the Metropolitan Police in London – the first major English police legislation, which became the model for subsequent forces. These were followed by: the 1835 Municipal Corporations Act, which required every municipal borough in England and Wales to establish a borough police force; the 1836 Act establishing one single Irish Constabulary (from 1867, the Royal Irish Constabulary) for all of Ireland; the 1839 Rural (or County)

Constabulary Act which *permitted* (but did not compel) those counties in England and Wales which wished to, to establish a county force (only about half of the counties opted to do so, over the next seventeen years); and finally the 1856 County and Borough Police Act which made some form of police force (county or borough) obligatory for all areas of England and Wales. Scottish Acts of 1833, 1847 and 1857 established burgh and county forces for Scotland.

In recent years, the nature of these reforms in policing, and the reasons for them, have attracted considerable historical attention. The 'Whig' view of police history, which sees these reforms as essentially a straightforward case of progress, with the reforms being a necessary and rational response to social change, is represented in the works of Reith (1938; 1943; 1956), Radzinowicz (1948; 1956a; 1956b; 1968), Critchley (1967) and Tobias (1967, 1979). To Radzinowicz, the history of the English criminal law is 'the history of progress'; in Reith's more extreme, teleological view, opposition to a police force on grounds of civil liberty was simply 'the product of long-sustained, skilful propaganda by vested interests with heavy commitments in the freedom of crime from control by law' (Radzinowicz 1948, ix; Reith 1943, 28). A 'revisionist' view, which emphasizes the importance of the fear of disorder and the needs of the new industrial capitalist society, can be found in Silver (1967) and Storch (1975), and, to some degree, in Philips (1977, ch. 3; 1980) and Jones (1982, 1983). Storch offers the strongest version of this view; the establishment of new police forces 'resulted from a new consensus among the propertied classes that it was necessary to create a professional, bureaucratically organized lever of urban discipline and permanently introduce it into the heart of working-class communities' (Storch 1975, 61). Reiner (1985, ch. 1) sets out the major issues and participants in this historiographical controversy; Emsley (1983; 1987, ch. 8) gives a balanced account of both main approaches. Miller (1977) compares the early development of the police forces of London and New York; while Palmer (1988) offers a comparative study of developments in England and Ireland over this period, leaning towards the issue of fear of public disorder as the main reason for police reform. Foster (1982) examines the permissive 1839 Rural Constabulary Act and the establishment and operation of county forces between 1839 and 1856. Carson and Idzikowska (1989) analyse the development of Scottish policing over this period.

Whatever position one adopts, it is now clear that it would be a mistake to take at face value the criticisms made of the 'old police' agencies. Contemporary criticism, in the late eighteenth and early nineteenth centuries, came predominantly from reformers – men like Jeremy Bentham, Patrick Colquhoun, Edwin Chadwick – who had an interest in denigrating the 'old police' in order to promote their own reforms (see, e.g. Colquhoun 1795; Chadwick 1829; *Constabulary Force Report* 1839 – largely written by Chadwick). Recent research shows that the much-maligned parish constables could be fairly efficient in small towns, villages and parishes (Philips 1977; Sharpe 1984; Emsley 1987). In these places, constables still retained a close, face-to-face relationship with people in the community, which could secure the necessary cooperation in order to arrest offenders and prevent normal crime (such as thefts and assaults) getting beyond a tolerable point. Where they were notably unsuccessful was in rapidly growing large towns, where such a sense of community had been lost, and also in dealing with serious disturbances and large-scale organized crime. This was aggravated by the rapid growth of segregated working-class and slum areas in London and all the large industrial towns, in the first half of the nineteenth century. However, property-owners dissatisfied with the 'old police' could still take measures to protect their property short of establishing government-run, paid police forces. From the 1770s to the 1850s, property-owners all over England came together to establish thousands of local 'Associations for the Prosecution of Felons' – private associations, to which they paid subscriptions, which assisted them to catch and prosecute offenders (Philips 1989; King 1989; Shubert 1981). Some of these associations established their own private police forces, paid for by subscription; so, too, did many towns and parishes, who set up their own small paid police forces under local Improvement Acts or the general Lighting and Watching Act of 1833 (Storch 1989; Davey 1983).

The pressure for substantial police reform came, above all, from the reformers and from urban mercantile and industrial interests concerned to protect their growing amounts of movable property against theft. And, throughout the period from the outbreak of the French Revolution in 1789 to the end of Chartism as a mass movement in 1848, there was the fear of disorder, riot or revolutionary activity among the lower orders of the growing towns. What held that pressure at bay and prevented substantial reform of the English police for the forty-four years between 1785 (when the government Bill for a police for London had to be withdrawn) and 1829 (when Home Secretary Robert Peel successfully passed his Metropolitan Police Act) was the longstanding English distrust of placing a strong, centralized police force under the control of the central government. The new industrial working class had every reason to fear that the 'new police' force would be an agency of repression, and therefore to oppose it, as they did, both before and after 1829. But they had no power to decide the outcome of the debates in parliament; nor did those middle-class radicals or the few libertarian Whig MPs who opposed a police force on grounds of civil liberty. What prevented the establishment of a police force in England before 1829 was the solid resistance of backbench Tory country squires who effectively deployed arguments about the threat to the 'Englishman's liberties', to block such moves. When Peel succeeded in finally overcoming this resistance and passing his Act in 1829, he did so by playing on the anxieties of his class about disorder, revolution and those rising criminal statistics (see Table 7.1, p. 158; Philips 1980).

Subsequent police legislation also owed something to fears of popular disturbances and of organized working-class activity. The Reform Bill riots of 1831–2 helped to produce the police provisions of the Municipal Corporations Act of 1835. The Rural Police Act of 1839 was pushed through a parliament worried by Chartist disorders in that year, which also passed acts to set up police forces for Manchester, Birmingham and Bolton – three important industrial towns without the necessary municipal government for a borough force, which faced the threat of serious Chartist disturbances (Mather 1959; Philips 1977; Palmer 1988).

It is instructive to compare, as Palmer (1988) does, the English police developments with those in Ireland over the same period. The British parliament was always readier to legislate for a police to keep down the rebellious Irish than to impose such a force on the 'freeborn Englishman'. They did so under such legislation as the Dublin Police Act of 1786, the Peace Preservation Act of 1814 (which created the Peace Preservation Police for Irish counties proclaimed to be 'disturbed'), the Irish Constabulary Act of 1822 (which set up Irish county forces), and the Irish Constabulary Act of 1836 (which established the Irish Constabulary for the entire country) (Palmer 1988). Furthermore, the Irish Constabulary was a centralized, paramilitary force, armed with carbines and pistols, and stationed in barracks, positioned strategically across Ireland. By contrast, the Metropolitan Police, and all subsequent English borough and county forces, were carefully dressed in a non-military uniform (blue tailcoat and trousers, with a glazed black top hat, strengthened with a thick leather crown) and were not given firearms; their normal weapon was the truncheon (and, occasionally, the cutlass). The long period of resistance to 'new police' forces in England was ultimately unsuccessful, but it was not without influence on the final outcome. When police forces became the norm throughout England from 1857, they were decentralized, non-military, unarmed forces, not the paramilitary, centralized single force which policed Ireland – and for which many English reformers had been campaigning since the late eighteenth century.

Magistracy

England had been governed locally, since the sixteenth century, by an unpaid magistracy – the Justices of the Peace, drawn from the country gentry who assumed the task without payment as a part of their status. Meeting four times a year in Quarter Sessions, they administered their counties, fixing county rates and providing for county services such as roads, bridges, gaols and asylums. Sitting more frequently in Petty Sessions in their own districts, they dispensed poor relief, licensed alehouses, granted bastardy orders, directed the parish constables, and generally administered local affairs. They also played an important part in the administration of justice. In Quarter Sessions, the collective bench of county magistrates heard indictable cases – cases serious enough to go before a jury, but not including capital offences which had to be heard at the Assizes by the judges on circuit. In Petty Sessions, the JPs, sitting alone or with one or two other JPs, disposed of summary offences – offences which could be tried by JPs alone without a jury – and also heard committal proceedings, in which they would decide whether or not to commit the person for trial on indictment (before a jury) at Quarter Sessions or Assizes (Webb and Webb 1906; Moir 1969; Landau 1984).

The landed class jealously guarded their privileges as unpaid magistrates. An Act of 1744 restricted the position to people who owned land worth at least £100 a year (or had the right to the immediate reversion of property worth £300 a year); since it was unpaid, the position could only be filled by men with sufficient time to devote to unpaid public service (see Cirket (ed.) 1971 for an example of the duties performed by a conscientious magistrate). A landowner took his position on the magisterial bench as of right, and, by the mid-eighteenth century, it was almost unheard-of for any JP to be dismissed by the government. These arrangements allowed landowner-JPs to administer local government and justice in most parts of the kingdom with very little interference from London. As unpaid and tenured officials, they could not be controlled by central government in the manner of a paid bureaucracy, and the landed class stoutly defended the principle of an unpaid magistracy.

But the system required a sufficient supply of conscientious landowners to make it work, which proved to be a serious problem in the case of a large and rapidly growing city such as eighteenth-century London. The increasing amount of crime and disorder sparked a demand for more JPs, but the spread of the city – especially the development of separate and distinct areas for the upper and lower orders – means that supplies of men of the proper status failed to match the demand. By the 1780s, critics were fiercely attacking the magistracy of Middlesex (the county into which most of London fell), claiming that positions were being filled by lower-class 'trading justices', concerned to use the position to make money from the fees payable to magistrates and their clerks. From the 1750s, the half-brothers Henry and John Fielding, and their successors, had been established as unpaid magistrates at an office in Bow Street, to hear cases and to administer a small force of Bow Street policemen (the 'Bow Street Runners'). But the first serious breach in the principle of the unpaid magistracy came in 1792 with the Middlesex Justices Act, which set up seven new Police Offices for the Metropolis, with three stipendiary (salaried) magistrates, and a small force of paid police under the magistrates' authority, at each Office (Philips 1980; Radzinowicz 1956b).

There was opposition to this act, as there had been to the 1785 Police Bill, on the grounds that this would give too much power to the government and would threaten civil liberties. But the opposition was defeated – by 1792 the threat of French revolutionary ideas among the lower orders, and the problem of maintaining order in London's growing metropolis were enough to overcome such objections to placing paid magistrates and a small number of paid police under government control. By the 1850s, there were twenty-three such stipendiary magistrates (who came to be called Police Magistrates, sitting in Police Courts) for London; they took over all the normal magisterial functions for the metropolis, and decided vast numbers of cases, especially when the range of summary jurisdiction was extended (see below). They came to be appointed from barristers of seven years' standing – unlike the normal JPs who had no special legal training (Davis 1984).

Following the creation of the London Police Magistrates in 1792, the principle of appointing stipendiary magistrates was extended to other urban and industrial parts of England and Wales, and for the same reasons – the difficulty of finding unpaid JPs to do the increasingly onerous and important tasks involved in controlling large working-class populations. In the first half of the nineteenth century, individual stipendiary magistrates were appointed for Manchester, Birmingham, Leeds, Liverpool, Sheffield, Cardiff, Merthyr Tydfil and the industrial areas of Staffordshire. The Municipal Corporations Act of 1835 allowed all corporate boroughs to appoint stipendiary magistrates, but relatively few chose to do so (Maitland 1885; Moir 1969; Philips 1976). In Ireland, stipendiary magistrates were created for Dublin in 1795, and in 1814 to take charge of the magistrates and the Peace Preservation Police in 'disturbed' districts (Palmer 1988). But in England and Wales outside London, stipendiaries did *not* take over most of the magisterial duties. In 1842, dissatisfaction with the efficiency of unpaid JPs in dealing with the Chartist disorders of that year, led Home Secretary Sir James Graham to propose to Peel's cabinet a scheme to employ salaried assistant barristers to assist county Quarter Sessions; but strong opposition to such a proposal from Tory gentry led to it being dropped (Mather 1959, 64–5).

So, although stipendiaries did make a difference to the magistrates' courts outside London, it was only in London that they really changed the composition and functioning of the courts. The vast majority of magistrates, outside London, continued to be the unpaid lay JPs – propertied gentlemen in the counties and middle-class councillors in the corporate boroughs (Zangerl 1971). In industrial areas short of corporate towns – such as the coal and iron area of the 'Black Country' of South Staffordshire, where there were not enough landed gentlemen to go round – industrialists were appointed as JPs. These men then found themselves sitting in judgment on their own employees in many cases involving issues such as industrial thefts, Master and Servant Act offences (see below), and cases of 'truck' payment (payment of wages in goods rather than cash) – a situation which provoked considerable working-class resentment against the employers being able to sit as judges in their own cause (Philips 1976).

So, only in London was the magistracy totally changed in this period, into a group of salaried and legally trained officials, hearing a vastly increased number of cases with the extension of summary jurisdiction (see below). Elsewhere, although a professional element had entered the system during the first half of the nineteenth century, lay unpaid JPs continued to enforce the law in the provinces.

Prosecution

There were two distinct and important ways in which government legislation, in the period 1750–1860, made it easier to prosecute offences.

Increased reimbursement for indictable prosecutions

The system of prosecution in England and Wales was one which relied almost entirely on private initiative (see Maitland 1885; Radzinowicz 1956a; Philips 1977; Hay 1983, 1984; Hay and Snyder 1989). If the victim of the crime did not pursue the prosecution, nothing happened. Only in a tiny number of cases (murder, treason, coining) did the authorities take responsibility for carrying through prosecutions. Prosecution was a costly business – in time, energy and money – which discouraged potential prosecutors. From 1752 onwards, a series of statutes progressively extended the reimbursement available to prosecutors, in order to encourage more victims of offences to prosecute. The most important statutes were: the 1778 Act which offered an allowance to all prosecutors and witnesses in felony prosecutions, even if there was no conviction; an 1818 Act which extended that allowance in felony cases to prosecutors and witnesses for all expenses incurred in the prosecution even before an appearance in court; and the 1826 Act which extended the allowance still further for prosecutions for felonies and some misdemeanours (Philips 1977, ch. 4; Radzinowicz 1948, 1956a, 1956b, 1968).

These changes did not remove all financial obstacles to prosecution, and a prosecutor still had to pay the costs initially and hope for reimbursement from the court. The allowance made by the court might still fall well short of the full costs incurred by a prosecutor, including the payment for legal representation, in a complex case. One reason for the popularity of Associations for the Prosecution of Felons (see above) was that they would pay the difference between the court's allowance and the total cost of a prosecution (Philips 1989). But these changes did make it much easier for victims to prosecute in simple offences, and they seem to have encouraged many more potential prosecutors to come forward and prosecute – thus swelling the official statistics of crimes prosecuted.

Despite pressure on this issue, the government never went so far as to appoint officials to act as public prosecutors in England and Wales – as was the case in both Scotland and Ireland. Instead, as police forces spread around the country, they increasingly took on themselves the role of prosecution in place of victims. By 1860, this was becoming the norm (Philips 1977; Hay 1983, 1984; Maitland 1885).

Extension of summary jurisdiction

From the late eighteenth century, the government began to legislate to transfer indictable offences to summary jurisdiction (tried by one or more magistrates without a jury), and to create new offences to be tried summarily by magistrates alone. The advantage of this, for the authorities, was that it was quicker, cheaper and easier to prosecute offences summarily than on indictment (see Emsley 1987, ch. 7; Hay 1975b: 313–23; Philips 1976; Magarey 1978; Munsche 1981, ch. 4; Jones 1982: ch. 7; Styles 1983).

A series of Acts in the second half of the eighteenth century permitted magistrates to try summarily such offences as: poaching game, under the Game Laws; 'embezzlement' by outworkers of their employers' raw materials; and the formation of workers' 'combinations' (trade unions), under the Combination Acts of 1799–1800. In the first half of the nineteenth century, there was a great extension of summary legislation. A series of Acts transferred the prosecution of most simple larcenies to summary trial. The Larceny Act of 1827 made it possible, for the first time, to try summarily people accused of some larcenies (of animals, trees, shrubs); the Juvenile Offenders Acts of 1847 and 1850 transferred the trial of juveniles (under the age of 16) charged with larceny, to summary jurisdiction. Most important in this period was the Criminal Justice Act of 1855, which allowed summary trial of larcenies of the value of less than 5 shillings where the accused agreed to it, and of larcenies of more than 5 shillings where the accused pleaded guilty. This led to a large increase in summary prosecutions for larceny, and in the total number of larcenies prosecuted, both summarily and on indictment.

Another series of Acts of the 1820s and 1830s created a wide range of discretionary offences to be so tried. The malicious Trespass Act of 1827 provided summary punishment for trespassing on private grounds and damaging any property, including fruit or vegetables growing in a garden – thus making children's stealing of fruit an easily punishable offence. The Vagrancy Act of 1824 'proved to be one of the most flexible, useful and criminal-making statutes of the century' (Jones 1982, 206–7). It created a wide range of offences which could result in the convicted person being defined as (in ascending order of wickedness): 'an Idle and Disorderly Person', 'a Rogue and Vagabond', and 'an Incorrigible Rogue'. The Vagrancy Act spread a very wide net, and included in its offences: able-bodied people who would not work; people begging or selling in the street without a licence; people found in public 'not having any visible means of Subsistence, and not giving a Good Account of himself or herself'; people committing acts of obscenity or using obscene language in public; common prostitutes; people gambling in public; people found in enclosed premises for unlawful purposes, or possessing housebreaking implements or an offensive weapon. The Act gave the police wide powers to arrest and hold people on suspicion, and to have them summarily convicted for being a 'suspected Person and a reputed Thief' – a power which first entered the law in section 17 of the Middlesex Justices Act of 1792, the Act which created the stipendiary magistrates for London. Most of the offences under the Vagrancy Act are offences only insofar as they are defined as such by authority; after 1829, the discretion to define such offences and arrest people for them, was increasingly wielded by members of the new police forces, who made wide use of these new discretionary powers to arrest large numbers of working-class people in streets and public places of the growing towns (see Storch 1975; Magarey 1978; Jones 1982: ch. 7; Roberts 1988).

The Metropolitan Police Acts of 1829 and 1839 added further to these discretionary police powers. The 1829 Act allowed a policeman to arrest, without a warrant, all loose, idle and disorderly Persons whom he shall find disturbing the Public Peace, or whom he shall have just Cause to suspect of any evil Designs, and all Persons whom he shall find between Sunset and the Hour of Eight in the Forenoon lying in any Highway, Yard, or other Place, or loitering therein, and not giving a satisfactory account of themselves. (10 Geo. IV, c.44: clause 7)

The 1839 Act gave the police powers to arrest people attending unlicensed theatres, cock-fights, dog-fights, bear-baitings, badger-baitings and gaming houses; or found in a thoroughfare or public place flying a kite, playing any game 'to the annoyance of the Inhabitants or Passengers' or making a slide in the ice and snow (2&3 Vic., c.47: clauses 46, 47, 49, 54; Magarey 1978).

The availability of these summary statutes, enshrining a broad discretion, enabled prosecutors to secure a conviction even when they lacked the evidence to convince a jury. The North Shields and Tynemouth Association for Prosecuting Felons, in 1835, brought several suspected thieves before a friendly magistrate

and the facts were not clearly proved so as to send them to be tried by a Jury although there was no Doubt of their Guilt and on that account they were committed for various periods as Vagrants and reputed Thieves to hard labour in the House of Correction.

Two years later, working with a co-operative superintendent of police and the magistrate, they had another five suspected thieves summarily convicted in this way (Philips 1989).

The Master and Servant Act of 1823, another summary act of the 1820s, was supposed to provide remedies for breach of the contract of employment by either the employer or the employee. But, whereas a breach by the employer was only a civil wrong for which the employee could sue for damages, a breach by the employee was a criminal offence for which he or she could be convicted, and fined or imprisoned. The act (which was not repealed until 1875, as the result of a trade union campaign against it) was not used by all employers; but it was widely used by coalowners against the miners they employed, especially as a strike-breaking weapon, and by employers in the West Midlands metal industries against their employees (Simon 1954; Philips 1976; Woods 1982).

The general effect of this substantial extension of summary jurisdiction was a vast increase, both in the total numbers of people prosecuted for all offences, and in the proportion of those tried summarily, rather than on indictment. In 1855, the London Police Magistrates dealt with 97,090 cases, of which they tried 77,712 (80 per cent) summarily; only 19,278 (20 per cent) were sent for trial on indictment (Davis 1984, 312). The great extension of summary legislation endowed the new police forces of the towns with wide discretionary powers to arrest and prosecute people for broad ranges of behaviour in public. These powers were used as a weapon of surveillance and control over the urban working class and their normal leisure pursuits – drinking, gambling, blood-sports, games played in the street, or just standing and talking in the street. The creation of the Metropolitan Police Force led to a huge increase, in the early 1830s, of people arrested and dealt with summarily, for discretionary offences; the creation of the subsequent local police forces led to similar increases in all the major towns and cities of Britain (see Storch 1976; Magarey 1978). Discretionary summary legislation, wielded by the new police forces, was an important way of disciplining the new urban workforce.

Reform of the criminal law

One of the most striking changes of this period was reform of the criminal law of Britain. Within a short period, it moved from a system which enshrined capital punishment at its centre, to one in which capital punishment was used infrequently and only, in effect, as a punishment for murder (Radzinowicz 1948, 1968; critiques of this interpretation by Palmer 1976 and McGowen 1983, 1986; for the working of the old eighteenth-century system of criminal law, see Hay 1975a, 1982; Beattie 1986; Langbein 1978, 1983a; King 1984; Innes and Styles 1986).

As late as 1808, the full 'Bloody Code' of the eighteenth century was still in force in England. Death *could* be inflicted for more than 200 offences (mostly against property), but in fact usually was not, since a well-developed system of royal pardons existed, and a pardon could be secured on recommendation of the trial judge or the exercise of patronage. The frequent award of such pardons, plus the weak system of law-enforcement and the liberal criminal procedure, made the system rather arbitrary – one might even say capricious; many offenders escaped the death penalty. But the central image of the system remained that of the gallows, with people being hanged at places like Tyburn in London, as part of great public spectacles. The system worked on the principle that it did not aim to catch and hang *all* offenders, provided that *some* people were caught and hanged to serve as a deterrent example to others. Public executions at Tyburn were abolished in 1783 because the sheriffs of London and Middlesex considered that they had lost their deterrent power: 'our processions to Tyburn are a mockery upon the aweful sentence of the law and ... the final scene itself has lost its terrors and is so far from giving a lesson, of morality to the beholders that it tends to the encouragement of vice' (quoted in Ignatieff 1978, 88). But executions continued to be held in public in England until 1868, with London executions now being held outside Newgate Prison (Cooper 1974).

There had been criticisms of the efficacy of a penal system based on capital punishment from the mid-eighteenth century: in the 1760s by the Italian legal reformer Cesare Beccaria and the English jurist William Blackstone; in the 1770s by the English legal reformer William Eden and the prison reformer John Howard; and from the 1770s onwards by the reformer of criminal law, punishment, police and many other institutions, Jeremy Bentham (Radzinowicz 1948; Beccaria 1764; Ignatieff 1978). But a serious campaign to abolish capital punishment in Britain only got under way in the British parliament in 1808, under the auspices of the Benthamite MPs Sir Samuel Romilly and Sir James Mackintosh. They met a great deal of conservative opposition to their campaign, especially from the House of Lords, and they achieved little concrete success. In 1808, they succeeded in abolishing the death penalty for picking pockets; but, by 1820, that remained their only significant achievement.

However, the campaign had important side effects. In the 1820s, the Home Secretary, Robert Peel, introduced a series of Acts to consolidate the criminal laws, which significantly reduced the number of capital offences on the statute books (Radzinowicz 1948). Following the First Reform Act, the Whig governments of the 1830s carried this much further with dramatic reductions in capital punishment, particularly in 1837 and 1841. After 1841, the death penalty was, in effect, being executed only for cases of murder (and, very rarely, treason) (Radzinowicz 1948, 1968). In the space of two decades, the Criminal Code changed from one in which death was the central punishment to one in which it became reserved only for the most serious offences and was put into force infrequently. The main reasons for this change, and the punishments which replaced the gallows, are discussed below.

Changes in secondary punishments

The development of secondary punishments in this period, and particularly the development of the penitentiary prison, has attracted some notable recent historical writing. In 1975, Foucault (English translation 1977) set out his famous and controversial thesis that this period saw a major shift from a system of essentially physical punishments in the eighteenth century, to one of largely mental and psychological punishment in the nineteenth century; he talks largely about France, but includes substantial references to both Britain and the USA. Rothman (1971) had already propounded a similar idea about the development of American penitentiaries; and this general thesis was applied very effectively to England by Ignatieff (1978). Ignatieff drew on some earlier studies of the development of the English penitentiary prison (Webb and Webb 1922; Rusche and Kirchheimer 1939; Henriques 1972). Although there has been some criticism of the details of Ignatieff's work (even by Ignatieff himself), the essence of his thesis has been confirmed by subsequent work. (See Ignatieff 1981; Henriques 1979; Tomlinson 1978, 1980, 1981, McConville 1981; DeLacy 1981, 1986; Evans 1982; Harding et al. 1985: Part 3; Priestley 1985; Forsythe 1987; Emsley 1987: ch. 9.)

An important area of secondary punishment used by Britain between 1787 and 1867 was transportation to the Australian colonies (Shaw 1966; Robson 1965; Hughes 1987; Nicholas (ed.) 1988). Transportation to the American colonies of Virginia and Maryland had been used, from 1718 until it was stopped by the outbreak of the American Revolution in 1775 (Beattie 1986; Morgan 1987; Ekirch 1987). Between 1787 and 1867, nearly 162,000 men, women and juveniles were transported, and, at its peak in the first half of the 1830s, about 5,000 convicts a year from Great Britain and Ireland (about two-thirds of them from England and Wales) were transported to Australia (Shaw 1966).

But transportation, though offering some opportunity for the judicial authorities to scale down the rate of capital punishment, could never serve as the complete penal answer for Britain. As the numbers of people convicted began to increase rapidly (see Table 7.1, above), and as the numbers hanged, or otherwise physically punished, declined – especially from the 1820s – there was an urgent need for some other large-scale means of punishment. The answer was found in Britain, as in France and the USA, in the development of long-term custodial sentences in the penitentiary prison.

Before the late eighteenth century, imprisonment was not widely used as a means of punishing serious offences. Prisons and gaols lacked individual cells, and lumped their inmates together in large dungeon-like rooms; the majority of inmates were there for debt, or awaiting trial, execution or transportation. The idea of imprisonment as a form of punishment in itself, was little developed; although the house of correction (or 'Bridewell') had been established in the sixteenth century to punish inmates by putting them to hard labour, this was used mainly for short sentences imposed on people for lesser offences of vagrancy and public order (Innes 1980, 1987; Ignatieff 1978, ch. 2; McConville 1981, chs. 1–3; Harding et al. 1985, ch. 4).

Serious change began with pressure from John Howard and other reformers in the 1770s. In 1777, Howard published *The State of the Prisons in England and Wales*. In his subsequent work, Howard stated that 'many of those unhappy wretches [now being hanged in England], by regular steady discipline in a penitentiary house, would have been rendered useful members of society' (Howard 1789, 221). Howard had assisted William Blackstone and William Eden to draft the Bill which became, in 1779, Britain's first Penitentiary Act; but, though parliament passed this act to establish two national penitentiaries (one for men and one for women), it was never implemented. Problems in finding a suitable site delayed the building of a penitentiary until, in 1787, the resumption of transportation to New South Wales removed the urgent pressure of the need to accommodate long-term convicts in something more durable than the hulks (disused warships) in which they were being 'temporarily' housed. The plan for a national penitentiary was shelved. In 1791, Jeremy Bentham revived the idea with his plan for the Panopticon ('all-seeing') penitentiary, in which his 'simple idea in Architecture' would enable the prisoners to be placed under constant surveillance by their jailers, making the prison 'a mill for grinding rogues honest, and idle men industrious' (Bentham 1791). This plan was adopted by the British government, but, once again, problems with finding a suitable site (and, Bentham darkly hinted, the prejudice against him of King George III) prevented the Panopticon being built. (In 1811, when the idea was finally abandoned, the government compensated Bentham for the failure to implement it with £23,000.)

But, in the meantime, while efforts to establish a national penitentiary were languishing in the 1780s and 1790s, a number of reforming county magistrates – Sir George Onesiphorus Paul in Gloucestershire, the Duke of Richmond in Sussex, Thomas Butterworth Bayley in Lancashire – were remodelling their local prisons along penitentiary lines: essentially, separating and classifying prisoners into a number of classes, putting the prisoners into solitary confinement in separate cells, and setting them to regular hard labour. A national penitentiary was finally built at Millbank, on the banks of the Thames in London, between 1812 and 1816, incorporating these elements – classification, solitary confinement and hard labour. It did not follow Bentham's exact Panopticon design, but enshrined his principle of ease of inspection and surveillance of the prisoners. Millbank proved to be very expensive to build, and was not a success as a prison; but, following its opening, a number of other prisons were modified to incorporate penitentiary principles (Ignatieff 1978; McConville 1981; Harding et al. 1985; Moir 1957).

The campaign for reform of punishment through the penitentiary drew its strength from two very different ideologies. Religious evangelicals, both Anglicans and Dissenters, saw the penitentiary as a way of forcing repentance on criminals, by putting them to work and leaving them alone (under surveillance) for long periods to reflect on their wrongdoing.

Utilitarian followers of Bentham, though starting from non-religious premises, agreed on the value of hard labour, surveillance and solitary confinement in reforming criminals. To those who campaigned, like Sir Samuel Romilly, to replace the arbitrary and capriciously enforced eighteenth-century 'Bloody Code' with a system of lesser penalties enforced more uniformly, the penitentiary held the answer to deal with the perceived threat of ever-rising crime.

There were two basic models to which the British government could look in building new national penitentiaries – both derived from systems already introduced into American prisons. The 'Separate System' had been in force since the 1790s in the Philadelphia Quaker penitentiaries of Walnut Street and Cherry Hill. Here the prisoners spent their entire time in solitary confinement, working on their own in their cells, leaving the cells only to take exercise or go to chapel – even these were done in solitude. The 'Silent System' was used in the penitentiaries of New York State – Auburn and Sing Sing. In this system, prisoners slept in solitary cells, but worked in association under a rule of total and complete silence; any attempt to talk to, or look at, another prisoner was punished by flogging. Though the two systems differed in their prescription of labour – solitary in the separate system, and associated in silence in the silent system – they shared the same essential aims: to prevent communication between prisoners; to prevent old, hardened offenders corrupting first offenders new to the prison culture; and, by leaving the prisoners in silence and solitude, to force them to look into their souls, reflect on their wrongdoing, and repent.

In the 1830s, there was a fierce debate in Britain about which of these two systems to adopt for a new national penitentiary. The 1835 House of Lords Select Committee into prisons recommended the separate system, and the prison inspectors William Crawford and Rev. Whitworth Russell ensured that the new national penitentiary should be built on that plan. That new penitentiary, opened in 1842, was Pentonville, the 'model prison', purpose-built to embody in stone the fullest realization of the penitentiary idea (Henriques 1972; Ignatieff 1978; Tomlinson 1980).

Pentonville was built on what was to become the standard radial plan, with four blocks of cells radiating from a central hall, from which the corridors and cell doors of all the blocks could be easily kept under observation. It housed 450 prisoners, each in his own cell, where he ate, slept and worked; he only left his cell (with his face masked) to take exercise in a solitary exercise yard, and to go to chapel, where he sat in a partitioned compartment which prevented him seeing his fellow-prisoners. The chaplain was given a role of importance in Pentonville and in all similar separate system regimes, as the long periods of solitude were seen as good for softening up the prisoner and making him receptive to the chaplain's message of religion and repentance. The day at Pentonville was divided into rigid blocks of time, signalled by bells – set times for sleeping, waking, exercise, chapel, meals, labour – with strict enforcement of punctuality and rigorous discipline.

The key to Pentonville's regime was the use of solitary confinement for a long period to break the convict's spirit and make him repent. The Reverend John Clay, chaplain of Preston Prison, a separate system penitentiary, praised the way in which

a few months in the solitary cell renders a prisoner strangely impressible. The chaplain can then make the brawny navvy cry like a child; he can work on his feelings in almost any way he pleases; he can, so to speak, photograph his thoughts, wishes and opinions on his patient's mind, and fill his mouth with his own phrases and language. (Quoted in Ignatieff 1978, 197–8)

In Pentonville, they initially kept prisoners for eighteen months in this sort of solitary confinement, but soon found that a disconcerting number of them were going insane; the eighteen months was reduced, in 1848, to twelve, and, in 1852, to nine months. In the 1850s, the more extreme features of the Pentonville system, such as the masks while exercising and the partitioned chapel stalls, were removed.

Long-term prisoners did not normally serve their full terms in Pentonville; from 1844, after their eighteen months in solitary, they were given a conditional pardon and sent to the Australian colonies as 'exiles' – the pardon being conditional on their not returning to Britain during the term of their sentence. (The free settlers of the Port Phillip District around Melbourne, which had not been a convict colony, reluctantly received nearly 2,000 of these exiles and nicknamed them 'Pentonvillains', blaming all local crime on them.) As it became clear that the Australian colonies were no longer prepared to accept either convicts or exiles, the government, in 1853, formally replaced transportation with sentences of penal servitude to be served in the newly built public works prisons, such as Portland (completed 1849), Dartmoor (1850), Portsmouth (1852) and Chatham (1856) (Tomlinson 1981; McConville 1981; Harding et al. 1985).

All the new prisons placed great emphasis on the importance of the prisoners being made to do some form of hard labour. In separate cells, they were made to turn a weighted hand crank for a set number of revolutions, weave on a handloom, make shoes or pick oakum; in associated silent systems, they were put on the treadwheel or made to do shot drill; in the public works prisons, they were set to breaking rocks and other hard outdoor manual labour on public works. Respectable mid-nineteenth-century English society saw the criminal – like the vagrant and the able-bodied pauper – as someone lacking in a proper sense of the value of work and time. The enforced labour, and the strict enforcement of punctuality by the bell, were meant to instil into the prisoner a proper sense of the work ethic and of time thrift, in the hope that this would help to turn him into a useful and productive member of society. In this sense, the mid-nineteenth-century penitentiary was designed to complement other new institutions of industrial England – the factories and Poor Law workhouses, perhaps also the schools and Sunday Schools – in their attempts to instil into their inmates a sense of time-discipline and a strong work ethic (see Thompson 1967; Longmate 1974; Laqueur 1976).

Pentonville was initially hailed as a great success as a 'model' prison. By 1850, ten new prisons had been built on the Pentonville model, and many others converted to emulate its regime. The most rigid features of the Pentonville system were dropped in the 1850s, and aspects of the penitentiary modified; but, even though the authorities soon lost faith in the reformative potential of the separate system, the typical large English prison thereafter was a radial cellular construction, modelled on Pentonville. Many of the prisons in use in England today were built in the nineteenth century, on the Pentonville model.

Conclusion

By 1860, the British systems of criminal law, law-enforcement and punishment were notably different from what they had been in the late eighteenth century. Our familiar modern institutions of police forces and custodial prisons were firmly in place; capital punishment had been removed from the Criminal Code, effectively for all crimes except murder; stipendiary, legally trained magistrates, especially in London, exerted an important influence in an area previously dominated by unpaid laymen; and the process of prosecution had become 'official', and thereby been rendered easier, cheaper, more efficient and far more wide-ranging and intrusive than ever before.

These changes took place during the classic period of the early Industrial Revolution, 1780–1850, and are clearly related to the events of that period; it is more difficult to say with certainty just how closely the changes can be related to the process of industrialization itself. Similar changes – e.g. the development of the penitentiary prison and of modern police forces – can be found during this period in other countries of Europe and the USA. Clearly, these cannot be tied simply to the Industrial Revolution, though the nature and timing of the changes – especially in the case of the police – *is* closely related to the specific experience of industrializing Britain. Similarly, the climate of anxiety and fears – of

working-class riots, and of popular political or revolutionary activity –
which helped to push through the reforms, is not simply a product of the
Industrial Revolution, but owes much to the legacy of the French Revolution.

But this 'revolution' in the machinery of law-enforcement and punishment was related to the wider process (including the First Reform Act,
the New Poor Law, and factory and public health legislation) in which
the governing class of Britain adjusted to the changes and problems of
industrialization. The fierce resistance of the landed class to the proposed
reforms in policing, criminal law and punishment, is evidence that many
of them would have liked to continue the old system of law-enforcement
and administration. But that system depended on the exercise of
informal authority by landed JPs over their own local, semi-autono-
mous, areas. By the early nineteenth century, the sheer scale of the
problem in London and the growing industrial and commercial towns
made this no longer a realistic option for dealing with the problems of
crime and social order. The squire and parson might be able to run the
local village through their personal authority and a few parish constables, but more organized, institutional means were needed to police
and control the working-class concentrations of Manchester, Birmingham and Leeds.

The new factory system, in Lancashire and the West Riding, brought
together thousands of workers in concentrations potentially dangerous
to public order. 'I shall not be surprised if it shall be necessary to
organise some kind of local force in the manufacturing districts for the
Protection of Property', wrote Peel in 1826, after a serious outbreak of
Lancashire machine-breaking. The authorities had already had to cope
with the problems of working-class industrial and political action in the
Luddite attacks of 1811–16, and in the political campaign which culminated in the 'massacre of Peterloo' in 1819. Episodes during the Chartist
period, such as the 'Plug Plot' general strike of August–September 1842 –
involving strikes in most of the industrial areas of England, which briefly
threatened the authorities' control of those areas – reinforced this point.
Friedrich Engels hailed this as a milestone in the 'social war' in England;
the Tory sheriff of Lanarkshire, Archibald Alison, reacted equally apo-
calyptically:

If the past increase and present amount of crime in the British islands be alone
considered, it must afford grounds for the most melancholy forebodings ...
Meanwhile, destitution, profligacy, sensuality and crime advance with unheard-
of rapidity in the manufacturing districts, and the dangerous classes there massed
together combine every three or four years in some general strike or alarming
insurrection, which, while it lasts, excites universal terror. (Alison 1844, 1, 3)

The image of the 'dangerous classes' of the city threatening to erupt onto the respectable propertied citizens in a torrent of crime and disorder, had already been evoked by Patrick Colquhoun, in arguing the urgent need for a police force for London in the 1790s. Colquhoun stressed that the rapidly expanding city had lost the character of a face-to-face community, in which the upper class could control the lower orders. This was exposing large amounts of valuable commercial property to the depredations of the anonymous and dangerous hordes who inhabited the growing slums, and who also, 'upon any fatal emergency (which God forbid!) would be equally ready as their brethren in iniquity, were, in Paris, to repeat the same atrocities if any opportunity offered' (Colquhoun 1795). This image was taken up, applied to the whole country, and firmly imprinted on the mind of the propertied classes, by a police reformer, Edwin Chadwick. In his influential *Constabulary Force Report* of 1839, Chadwick argued the need for a national police force, by emphasizing the dangers of allowing hordes of criminals from the urban slums to migrate freely around the country, committing crimes as they went; he also argued that a strong police force would check the growing powers of trade unions. The police reforms of the 1830s and 1850s, extending the London police reform to the borough and county authorities of the provinces, owe much to these sorts of fears.

Urbanization – in the form of the continued growth of London and its suburbs, and in the rapid growth of the industrial and commercial towns – posed problems with which the old system of law and order could not easily cope. Silver (1967) has pointed out that the rulers of pre-industrial England could tolerate a degree of disorder without too much inconvenience, but that there was less scope for this in the densely packed towns, and more sophisticated economy, of early nineteenth-century England. Manufacturers, merchants and shopkeepers demanded of the government more efficient protection for their property; this generated pressure for police forces, for replacement of the capital laws with more uniformly enforced lesser penalties, and for more efficient means of prosecution and adjudication of criminal charges. These pressures and needs did not, of course, automatically produce changes in the law and institutions; and the process of reform, in all the areas discussed, was neither simple nor straightforward. But the reformers – Bentham, Howard, Colquhoun, Peel, Chadwick – were able to use this urban middle-class pressure, along with the anxieties about disorder, to overcome the substantial opposition among the landed class to the proposed reforms. The governing class of Britain found itself, reluctantly, forced to adopt many of the reformers' solutions, extending the power of the state substantially, through the development of new official institutions. Police forces and penitentiary prisons, under some degree of Home Office control, replaced parish constables and local gaols; stipendiary magistrates invaded the province of the gentleman-JP; discretionary summary legislation put powerful weapons into the hands of police in dealing with the urban working class.

The implementation of these reforms was never a smooth, uniform process, and the timing of the eventual legislation rarely coincides neatly with the events which produced them. The substantial initial opposition within the ruling class to reform of the criminal law and the establishment of police forces, delayed the passage of the relevant laws. And, once the laws were passed, there was often considerable resistance – especially from the working class, as the people most affected – to the new police forces and penitentiaries. The opposition and resistance meant that the shape which the reforms took usually involved some element of compromise: relatively weak, decentralized, unarmed police forces for England, rather than the national, Irish Constabulary model which the reformers favoured; some stipendiary magistrates, but not the entire supersession of the lay Justices of the Peace by officials; some modifications to the strictness of the original penitentiary regime. But the overall result was a transformation, by 1860, of the machinery of criminal law, law-enforcement and punishment into their recognizable form in the elements of our modern state.

REFERENCES

Alison, A. 1844. 'Causes of the increase of crime', *Blackwood's Edinburgh Magazine*, 56, 1–14.

Beattie, J. M. 1986. *Crime and the Courts in England 1660–1800*.

Beccaria, C. 1764. *An Essay on Crimes and Punishments* (English trans., 3rd edn. 1770).

Becker, H. 1963. *Outsiders: Studies in the sociology of deviance.*.

Bentham, J. 1791. *Panopticon: Or the Inspection House*, in *The Works of Jeremy Bentham*, ed. J. Bowring, IV, 1843.

Carson, W. G. and Idzikowska, H. 1989. 'The social production of Scottish policing, 1795–1900', in *Policing and Prosecution in Britain 1750–1850*, ed. D. Hay and F. Snyder, 267–97.

Chadwick, E. 1829. 'Preventive police', *London Review*, 1, 252–308.

Cirket, A. F. (ed.) 1971. *Samuel Whitbread's Notebooks, 1810–11, 1813–14*.

Colquhoun, P. 1795. *A Treatise on the Police of the Metropolis*; 6th edn. 1800.

Constabulary Force Report 1839. 1st Report of the Commissioners appointed to inquire as to the best means of establishing an efficient Constabulary Force in the Counties of England and Wales. *Parliamentary Papers*. 1839 (169), XIX.

Cooper, D. D. 1974. *The Lesson of the Scaffold. The Public Execution Controversy in Victorian England*.

Criminal Commitments and Convictions Report 1827. 1st Report from the Select

Committee on Criminal Commitments and Convictions. *Parliamentary Papers. 1826–7* (534), VI.

Critchley, T. A. 1967. *A History of Police in England and Wales 900–1966.*

Davey, B. J. 1983. *Lawless and Immoral. Policing a country town 1838–1857.*

Davis, J. 1980. 'The London garotting panic of 1862: a moral panic and the creation of a criminal class in mid-Victorian England', in *Crime and the Law. The social history of crime in Western Europe since 1500*, ed. V. A. C. Gatrell, B. Lenman and G. Parker, 190–213.

    1984. 'A poor man's system of justice: the London Police Courts in the second half of the 19th century', *The Historical Journal*, 27, 309–35.

DeLacy, M. 1981. 'Grinding men good? Lancashire's prisons at mid-century', in *Policing and Punishment in 19th Century Britain*, ed. V. Bailey, 182–216.

    1986. *Prison Reform in Lancashire, 1700–1850. A study in local administration.*

Ekirch, A. R. 1987. *Bound for America. The transportation of British convicts to the colonies 1718–1775.*

Emsley, C. 1983. *Policing and its Context 1750–1870.*

    1987. *Crime and Society in England 1750–1900.*

Engels, F. 1845. *The Condition of the Working Class in England*, trans. W. O. Henderson and W. H. Chaloner, 1958.

Evans, R. 1982. *The Fabrication of Virtue: English prison architecture, 1750–1840.*

Forsythe, W. J. 1987. *The Reform of Prisoners 1830–1900.*

Foster, D. 1982. *The Rural Constabulary Act 1839. National legislation and the problems of enforcement.*

Foucault, M. 1977. *Discipline and Punish: the birth of the prison*, trans. A. Sheridan.

Gatrell, V. A. C. and Hadden, T. B. 1972. 'Criminal statistics and their interpretation', in *Nineteenth Century Society: essays in the use of quantitative methods for the study of social data*, ed. E. A. Wrigley, 336–96.

Harding, C., Hines, B., Ireland, R. and Rawlings, P. 1985. *Imprisonment in England and Wales. A concise history.*

Hay, D. 1975a. 'Property, authority and the criminal law', in *Albion's Fatal Tree: crime and society in eighteenth-century England*, ed. D. Hay, P. Linebaugh and E. P. Thompson, 17–63.

    1975b, 'Crime, authority and the criminal law: Staffordshire 1750–1800', unpublished Ph.D. thesis, University of Warwick.

    1982. 'War dearth and theft in the 18th century: the record of the English courts', *Past and Present*, 95, 117–60.

    1983. 'Controlling the English prosecutor', *Osgoode Hall Law Journal*, 21, 165–86.

    1984. 'The English criminal law and its prosecutors', *Modern Law Review*, 47, 1–29.

Hay, D. and Snyder, F. 1989. 'Using the criminal law 1750–1850. Policing, private prosecution, and the state', in *Policing and Prosecution in Britain 1750–1850*, ed. D. Hay and F. Snyder, 3–52.

Henriques, U. 1972. 'The rise and decline of the separate system of prison discipline', *Past and Present*, 54, 61–93.

    1979. *Before the Welfare State: Social administration in Early Industrial Britain.*

Howard, J. 1777. *The State of the Prisons in England and Wales.*

1789. *An Account of the Principal Lazarettos of Europe.*

Hughes, R. 1987. *The Fatal Shore. A history of the transportation of convicts to Australia, 1787–1868.*

Ignatieff, M. 1978. *A Just Measure of Pain. The penitentiary in the Industrial Revolution 1750–1850.*

1981. 'State, civil society and total institutions: a critique of recent social histories of punishment', *Crime and Justice: an Annual Review of Research*, 2, pp. 153–92, reprinted in *Social Control and the State*, ed. S. Cohen and A. Scull, ch. 4, 1983.

Innes, J. 1980. 'The King's Bench prison in the later eighteenth century: law, authority and order in a London debtor's prison', in *An Ungovernable People: The English and their law in the 17th and 18th centuries*, ed. J. Brewer and J. Styles, 250–98.

1987. 'Prisons for the poor: English bridewells, 1555–1800', in *Labour, Law and Crime. An historical perspective*, ed. F. Snyder and D. Hay, 42–122.

Innes, J. and Styles, J. 1986. 'The crime wave: recent writing on crime and criminal justice in eighteenth-century England', *Journal of British Studies*, 25, 380–435.

Jones, D. 1982. *Crime, Protest, Community and Police in Nineteenth-Century Britain.*

1983. 'The new police, crime and people in England and Wales 1829–1888', *Transactions of the Royal Historical Society*, 5th ser., 33, 151–68.

King, P. 1984. 'Decision-makers and decision-making in the English criminal law, 1750–1800', *The Historical Journal*, 27, 25–58.

1989. 'Prosecution associations in 18th century Essex', in *Policing and Prosecution in Britain 1750–1850*, ed. D. Hay and F. Snyder, ch. 2.

Landau, N. 1984. *The Justices of the Peace 1679–1760.*

Langbein, J. 1978. 'The criminal trial before the lawyers', *University of Chicago Law Review*, 45, 263–316.

1983a. 'Shaping the 18th century criminal trial: a view from the Ryder Sources' *University of Chicago Law Review*, 50, 1–136.

1983b. 'Albion's fatal flaws', *Past and Present*, 98, 96–120.

Laqueur, T. W. 1976. *Religion and Respectability. Sunday Schools and working class culture 1780–1850.*

Longmate, N. 1974. *The Workhouse.*

McConville, S. 1981. *A History of English Prison Administration, 1750–1877.*

McGowen, R. 1983. 'The image of justice and reform of the criminal law in early nineteenth-century England', *Buffalo Law Review*, 32, 91–125.

1986. 'A powerful sympathy: terror, the prison, and humanitarian reform in early 19th century Britain', *Journal of British Studies*, 25, 312–34.

Magarey, S. 1978. 'The invention of juvenile delinquency in early nineteenth century England', *Labour History*, 34, 11–27.

Maitland, F. W. 1885. *Justice and Police.*

Mather, F. C. 1959. *Public Order in the Age of the Chartists.*

Miller, W. R. 1977. *Cops and Bobbies: police authority in New York and London, 1830–1870.*

Moir, E. 1957. 'Sir George Onesiphorus Paul', in *Gloucestershire Studies*, ed., H. P. R. Finberg, 195–224.

1969. *The Justice of the Peace.*

Morgan, K. 1987. 'English and American attitudes towards convict transportation 1718–1775', *History*, 77, 416–31.

Munsche, P. B. 1981. *Gentlemen and Poachers. The English Game Laws 1671–1831*.

Nicholas, S. (ed.) 1988. *Convict Workers. Reinterpreting Australia's past*.

Palmer, J. J. N. 1976. 'Evils merely prohibited: conceptions of property and conceptions of criminality in the criminal law reform of the English Industrial Revolution', *British Journal of Law and Society*, 3, 1–16.

Palmer, S. H. 1988. *Police and Protest in England and Ireland 1780–1850*.

Philips, D. 1976. 'The Black Country magistracy 1835–60. A changing elite and the exercise of its power', *Midland History*, 3, 161–96.

   1977. *Crime and Authority in Victorian England: The Black Country 1835–1860*.

   1980. '"A new engine of power and authority": The institutionalization of law-enforcement in England 1780–1830', in *Crime and the Law. The social history of crime in Western Europe since 1500*, ed. V. Gatrell, B. Lenman and G. Parker, 155–89.

   1983. '"A just measure of crime, authority, hunters and blue locusts": the "revisionist" social history of crime and the law in Britain, 1780–1850', in *Social Control and the State*, ed. S. Cohen and A. Scull, 50–73.

   1989. 'Good men to associate and bad men to conspire: associations for the prosecution of felons in England 1760–1860', in *Policing and Prosecution in Britain 1750–1850*, ed. D. Hay and F. Snyder, 113–69.

Porter, G. R. 1847. *The Progress of the Nation*.

Priestley, P. 1985. *Victorian Prison Lives. English prison biography 1830–1914*.

Radzinowicz, L. 1948. *A History of English Criminal Law and its Administration from 1750*, I.

   1956a. *Ibid.*, vol. 2.

   1956b. *Ibid.*, vol. 3.

   1968. *Ibid.*, vol. 4.

Reiner, R. 1985. *The Politics of the Police*.

Reith, C. 1938. *The Police Idea*.

   1943. *British Police and the Democratic Ideal*.

   1956. *A New Study of Police History*.

Roberts, M. J. D. 1988. 'Public and private in early nineteenth-century London: the Vagrant Act of 1822 and its enforcement', *Social History*, 13, 273–94.

Robson, L. L. 1965. *The Convict Settlers of Australia*.

Rothman, D. 1971. *The Discovery of the Asylum: social order and disorder in the new republic*.

Rudé, G. 1985. *Criminal and Victim. Crime and society in early nineteenth-century England*.

Rusche, G. and Kirchheimer, O. 1939. *Punishment and Social Structure*.

Sharpe, J. A. 1984. *Crime in Early Modern England 1550–1750*.

Shaw, A. G. L. 1966. *Convicts and the Colonies*.

Shubert, A. 1981. 'Private initiative in law enforcement: associations for the prosecution of felons, 1744–1856', in *Policing and Punishment in 19th Century Britain*, ed. V. Bailey, 25–41.

Silver, A. 1967. 'The demand for order in civil society: a review of some themes in the history of urban crime, police, and riot', in *The Police: six sociological essays*, ed. D. Bordua, 1–24.

Simon, D. 1954. 'Master and servant', in *Democracy and the Labour Movement*, ed. J. Saville, 160–200.

Steedman, C. 1984. *Policing the Victorian Community. The formation of English provincial police forces, 1856–80*.

Storch, R. D. 1975. 'The plague of the blue locusts: police reform and popular resistance in Northern England, 1840–1857', *International Review of Social History*, 20, 61–90.

  1976. 'The policeman as domestic missionary: urban discipline and popular culture in Northern England 1850–1880', *Journal of Social History*, 9, 481–509.

  1989. 'Policing rural southern England before the police: opinion and practice 1830–1856', in *Policing and Prosecution in Britain 1750–1850*, ed. D. Hay and F. Snyder, ch. 4.

Styles, J. 1983. 'Embezzlement, industry and the law in England 1500–1800', in *Manufacture in Town and Country before the Factory*, ed. M. Berg, P. Hudson and M. Sonnenscher, 173–210.

Thompson, E. P. 1967. 'Time, work-discipline and industrial capitalism', *Past and Present*, 38, 56–97. Reprinted in *Essays in Social History*, ed. M. W. Flinn and T. C. Smout, 39–77. 1974.

Tobias, J. J. 1967. *Crime and Industrial Society in the Nineteenth Century*.

  1979. *Crime and Police in England 1700–1900*.

Tomlinson, M. H. 1978. 'Prison palaces: a re-appraisal of early Victorian prisons, 1835–77', *Bulletin of the Institute of Historical Research*, 51, 60–71.

  1980. 'Design and reform: the "separate system" in the 19th-century English prison', in *Buildings and Society. Essays on the social development of the built environment*, ed. A. D. King, 94–119.

  1981. 'Penal servitude 1846–1865: a system in evolution', in *Policing and Punishment in 19th Century Britain*, ed. V. Bailey, 126–49.

Webb, S. and Webb, B. 1906. *English Local Government from the Revolution to the Municipal Corporations Act: The parish and the county*.

  1922. *English Prisons Under Local Government*.

Woods, D. C. 1982. 'The operation of the Master and Servants Act in the Black Country, 1858–1875', *Midland History*, 9, 93–115.

Zangerl, C. H. E. 1971. 'The social composition of the county magistracy in England and Wales, 1831–1887', *Journal of British Studies*, 11, 113–25.

8　The Industrial Revolution and parliamentary reform

Roland Quinault

Parliamentary reform and industrialization

The era of the Industrial Revolution was also a time of important constitutional change in Britain. The Reform Acts of 1832 and 1867, along with other related reforms, fundamentally altered the representational system of the House of Commons and thus changed the character of parliamentary politics. The Reform Acts were partly reactions to immediate political pressures and partly responses to a long-lasting campaign for parliamentary reform. That campaign had started in the 1770s and had survived several periods of apathy and persecution. Since the reform campaign roughly synchronized with the traditional dates for the Industrial Revolution, historians have tended to regard the two developments as somehow interconnected. They have assumed that either reform and industrialization went hand in hand, or else that one change spawned the other. But the demand for parliamentary reform had originated long before the era of the Industrial Revolution (Cannon 1972). Indeed there had been periodic pleas for reform for as long as parliament had been in existence. A few minor reforms had occasionally been effected, but the Crown and the executive persistently impeded more fundamental reform until the mid-nineteenth century.

Most parliamentary reformers, in the period of the Industrial Revolution, were inspired, not by 'the shock of the new', but by the precedents of the past. They wished to restrict the power of the executive and they were inspired by the example of the reformers who had tried to limit the power of the Stuarts in the seventeenth century (Perry 1990, 125). In 1647, the Levellers had advocated representation according to population and manhood, or household, suffrage (Hill 1961, 130–1). There were five schemes for a more proportionate parliament between 1648 and 1653. They culminated in the 'Instrument of Government' which proposed new county and borough seats (Snow 1959, 425). The 'Instrument' was not enacted, but it provided a model for later reformers. At the Restoration reform was damned by its association with Cromwell, but during the 1679

Exclusion Crisis, Shaftesbury and the Whigs advocated the abolition of corrupt boroughs and the creation of extra county seats in order to make parliament more independent of the Crown. Yet there were virtually no changes to the representation after the 1688 Revolution.

The backward looking stance of the British reformers was not fundamentally changed by the French Revolution. The great majority of them continued to base their demands on what they alleged were the ancient rights of Englishmen (Dickinson 1989, 9). The only reformer who advocated a new constitution directly inspired by the American and French Revolutions was an expatriate, Tom Paine. But Paine had relatively little influence on British radicals until the 1820s and 1830s and none on the public reform campaign. Paine's interest in new political structures was matched by his interest in the new technology of iron bridges. But Paine thought that Britain's commercial economy was less stable and desirable than the more rural economies of the United States and France (Paine 1977, Introduction). Even after Waterloo, most advanced reformers, like Hunt and Place, still justified reform by reference to ancient rights, rather than modern realities (Dinwiddy 1986, 32–4).

It was not until the third decade of the nineteenth century that reformers began to discern a specific link between industrialization and parliamentary reform. In 1820, Sir James Mackintosh, an advanced Whig, observed that 'The great impulse given to English industry in the middle of the eighteenth century' had revealed 'The disparity between the old system of representation and the new state of society' and had left 'The new manufacturing interest' without adequate representation in parliament. His theory – that industrialization had made the existing system of parliamentary representation archaic – appeared to be confirmed by the passage of the 1832 Reform Act. This seemed, at least in retrospect, to owe much to the reform agitation in the new manufacturing centres. The new technology of the Industrial Revolution was even regarded as an agent of reform. In 1834, a Bolton weaver told a parliamentary select committee that steam power was 'Causing all the revolutions on the Continent and in England and all the reforms' (Bythell 1969, 206). But if that was the case, why were the political changes less revolutionary in England – where steam power was much more developed – than on the Continent? The apparent victory of the Manchester based Anti-Corn Law League, in 1846, reinforced the belief that industrialization was at the root of political reform. The leaders of the League, Cobden and Bright, were also prominent in the campaign which led up to the 1867 Reform Act.

Arnold Toynbee gave intellectual respectability to the theory that industrialization had led to parliamentary reform. Like other economic historians of the later Victorian period, Toynbee believed that economic and political developments were inextricably bound up together. His pioneering concept of the British Industrial Revolution was partly 'based on a theory of the political consequences of industrialization' (Kadish 1986, 242). It was Britain's political transformation – by successive reform acts – which prompted Toynbee to investigate its economic transformation. In his 1881 Oxford lectures, on 'Industry and Democracy', he argued that 'The growth of industry has stimulated the growth of democracy.' He contrasted the situation in 1770, when 'except as a member of a mob, the labourer had not a shred of political influence', with the position fifty years later, when the political power of the workers 'was rapidly growing owing to their concentration in large cities'. Toynbee largely attributed the 1832 Reform Act to the influence of the workers and thought that the 1867 Reform Act had given workmen 'The key of the position'. Thus in just a century, the workman had risen from the position of a serf to that of a full citizen in a free state (Toynbee 1916, 194–212).

Toynbee's theory, that industrialization led to democratization, was implicitly accepted by many subsequent historians. The growth of academic specialization ensured that the study of the Industrial Revolution became the preserve of economic historians, while the study of parliamentary reform was monopolized by political historians. Consequently, studies of the Industrial Revolution paid little attention to political change and studies of parliamentary reform made only passing references to economic change. Political historians generally assumed that economic change spawned political change, but they did not explain how it did so. Veitch, for example, produced no evidence to support his conclusion that 'The Industrial Revolution had made a Reform Act inevitable' (Veitch 1965, 352). His assertion that the inventor of the power-loom, Edmund Cartwright, did more to promote parliamentary reform than his brother John, the 'father of reform', has also been endorsed without supporting evidence (Cannon 1972, 263).

The only specific study of the influence of the Industrial Revolution on the demand for parliamentary reform concluded that its influence was very limited in the later eighteenth century (Whale 1922, 110). At that time, the Industrial Revolution was still largely in embryo. But even in 1850, much of the country was little affected by industrialization, whilst manufacturing relied relatively little on steam-power, factory production and automation (Cannadine 1984, 166). In any case, the diffusion of new technology did not necessarily lead to new political attitudes. Improved technology assisted the proliferation of the press, but many newspapers were apolitical, or opposed reform (Black 1988, 36–42). Furthermore the Stamp and Paper Duties kept the price of legal newspapers high until the mid-nineteenth century. Thus the continued existence of the unreformed parliamentary political system was not simply due to the embryonic state of the Industrial Revolution (cf. Perry 1990, 124). Indeed the unreformed system represented the economic and social realities of contemporary Britain more effectively than has often been assumed.

The unreformed parliamentary system

In the eighteenth century the English electorate was much less socially restricted than has commonly been supposed. In 1750, there were roughly 282,000 electors in England and Wales: about one-sixth of the whole adult male population. The total increased later in the century, but failed to grow at the same rate as the population. Nevertheless the electorate was surprisingly comprehensive in its social and occupational composition. About a third of the electorate were craftsmen and another fifth were semi-skilled or unskilled labourers. The rest of the electorate were mostly middle-class men engaged in the service sector of the economy. A fifth of them were retailers, a seventh were professional men or gentlemen and one-twentieth were merchants or manufacturers (O'Gorman 1989, 35–44). Thus the two largest occupational groups in the electorate were shop-keepers and craftsmen. This reflected the developed commercial character of England, which was already evident at the start of the Industrial Revolution.

The distribution of seats in parliament also did not accord with that of a pre-industrial, rural society. Over four-fifths of all MPs for England represented borough, rather than county, constituencies. Nearly half of these boroughs were located in the south-west of England where manufacturing and maritime trade had long been established. Most parliamentary boroughs were towns with significant economic and political activity. This vitality was most marked in the larger boroughs which were seaports, or old established commercial and manufacturing centres. In those boroughs, a high percentage of the electorate voted and a high proportion of elections were contested. The larger boroughs accounted for most of the increase in the total electorate of England and Wales between 1754 and 1830 (Cannon 1972, 30–3). In the 141 boroughs with freemen, or inhabitant householder, franchises, the electorates were often as wide as those of most constituencies after 1832 (Phillips 1982, 38, 203). In some large boroughs, manufacturing workers possessed significant electoral influence. In Nottingham, in the late 1770s, the framework knitters persuaded their MPs to sponsor a parliamentary bill to prevent unfair competition in their trade. When the Bill was lost in committee, the workers rioted and organized a ten-day strike (Chambers 1932, 31–9). At

Leicester, in 1790, an attempt to avoid a contested election led to serious rioting (Oldfield 1792, ii, 201). Such disturbances led Torrington to conclude that 'Old Sarum is a better and honester representation than any great manufacturing town could produce' (Mingay 1963, 266).

But few people were prepared to publicly defend the existence of defunct boroughs, like Old Sarum. Defoe noted, in the 1720s, that the MPs for Old Sarum represented merely an encampment with a farmhouse, while at Gatton: 'The purchasers seem to buy the election with the property' (Defoe 1971, 165, 193). John Wilkes urged the Commons, in 1776, to disfranchise Old Sarum and Gatton because 'They are now desolate and of consequence ought not to retain a privilege which they acquired only by their extent and populousness.' But Gatton had never been a real town and Old Sarum had been deserted for 500 years. Old Sarum was a pocket borough of the Pitt family and provided the elder Pitt with a seat in parliament for a while, but that did not stop him, or his son, from denouncing the 'rotten boroughs' in parliament. However there were relatively few boroughs which had no significant constituency.

Most so-called 'rotten boroughs' were real, if small, towns which were denounced, not for their lack of people, but for their subservience to a patron. In the eighteenth century, an increasing number of boroughs, especially in the south-west of England, fell under the control of single patrons (Phillips 1982, 52–8). These boroughs generally helped to provide a parliamentary majority for the government. This was classically the case in Cornwall, which had twenty-one parliamentary boroughs and thus many more MPs than much more populous counties like Lancashire or Yorkshire. The county's overrepresentation reflected its close tenurial connexion with the Crown, through the Duchy of Cornwall. The Tudor monarchs had created many new parliamentary boroughs on, or near to, duchy lands in Cornwall (Porritt 1903, i. 374). This attempt to strengthen Crown influence in parliament was not always successful, but many Cornish MPs still had close links with the Crown in the eighteenth century. They formed a bastion of opposition to reform in the Commons.

The eighteenth-century reformers pinned their hopes for a purer parliament, not on a redistribution of the borough seats, but on an increase in the number of county MPs. The 40s freehold qualification for the county franchise had been unchanged since the fifteenth century and had been much lowered by inflation. Consequently, many counties had large electorates which were expensive to bribe and which were not dominated by a single landowner. In 1754, the total county electorate of England and Wales was 50 per cent larger than the borough electorate (Cannon 1972, 30–3). Yet only one-fifth of all the MPs for England were county members. Each county elected two knights of the shire, so the larger counties were greatly underrepresented in relation to their population and electors. In the largest county constituencies, many of the 40s freehold electors lived in towns, or suburbs. Such voters tended to favour parliamentary reform in the 1770s. Londoners formed a majority of the Middlesex electors who supported Wilkes and the urban freeholders of the West Riding provided much of the support for Wyvill's Yorkshire Association.

Few counties were exclusively agricultural in character, for much manufacturing took place in rural areas: where there was water power and cheap labour. The manufacture of woollens – the country's leading export – was carried on in many of the counties of England and Wales. In the West Country, cloth spinning was carried out in the villages around the towns where the cloth merchants lived (Defoe 1971, 261). There was a similar situation in the East Midlands, where most of the framework knitters were farmers or rural labourers, whereas the master hosiers lived in the large towns. Even in Lancashire, the concentration of textile production in towns was still in its infancy in 1800 (Hudson 1965, 49). Mining was another growing industry which was located in county constituencies. Profits from coalmining helped members of families, like the Newdegates of Warwickshire and the Lowthers of Cumberland, to become county MPs. Very few miners were enfranchised, but many freeholders profited from mining.

Thus the unreformed electoral system, in numerous ways, reflected the interests of commerce and industry. But to what extent was this replicated at Westminster, in the membership of the Houses of Parliament? In general, only men with great wealth, or influential connexions, were able to become MPs or peers. A large majority of the members of both Houses of Parliament came from established aristocratic and gentry families. In 1774, 82 per cent of MPs came from families which provided at least two other members to the House of Commons after 1660. These 'parliamentary families' continued to supply over 70 per cent of MPs until the later 1820s (Wasson 1991, 643). Most of these families owned large landed estates, which had been in their possession for generations. The great landowning families remained the wealthiest and most influential social group in Britain during the era of the Industrial Revolution (Mingay 1963, 113; Thompson 1963, 276). But most landed parliamentarians accepted that business interests should be directly represented in the House of Commons. In 1766, the Duke of Newcastle, a landed magnate who was twice premier, acknowledged that trade was the life blood of the nation (Corfield 1987, 60). In 1793, Robert Jenkinson (who later became the prime minister, Lord Liverpool) accepted that 'In a commercial country like this, the manufacturing and commercial interest ought to have considerable weight', second only to the landed interest in the Commons.

Power rested on property, but that included personality as well as realty (Langford 1991). Money, rather than land, was the most essential commodity for a politician. In the century before the 1832 Reform Act, about half of all MPs – including landowners – had some commercial or professional interests (Judd 1972, 54–73). There was always a significant proportion of MPs whose wealth came from commerce or industry. Their numbers increased when British commerce burgeoned in the later eighteenth century. About one-sixth of all MPs from 1790 to 1830 were businessmen. Most of them were bankers or merchants in the major ports, particularly Londoners connected with the East India Company or the Bank of England. Manufacturers generally had insufficient wealth, or leisure, to enable them to become MPs. But a few wealthy brewers gained seats in parliament, such as Samuel Whitbread. He was allegedly excluded from the Whig Cabinet in 1806 because he was in trade, but this is difficult to verify. The first cotton-spinner to become an MP was Robert Peel – the father of the future prime minister – but he was followed by only a handful of others (Thorne 1986, 318). A significant number of MPs were professional men. They included a few Anglican clergymen until they were excluded in 1801, but most were lawyers. The bar provided many government ministers in the Commons, such as Addington, Dundas and Canning.

In parliament, the ascendancy of the Church was more marked than the ascendancy of the landed interest. For the Test and Corporation Acts excluded both Protestant Dissenters and Roman Catholics from holding public office. Dissenters could sometimes get round these restrictions at the local level, but they had to compromise their religious beliefs if they wanted to become MPs. The importance of the ties between the political and religious establishments has recently been emphasized (Clark 1985). Anglicans had more reason to support a parliamentary system which guaranteed their ascendancy than was the case with Nonconformists. Rational Dissenters were prominent in promulgating the concept of equal parliamentary representation (Langford 1988, 113). They also pioneered political lobbying and electoral analysis. But since Nonconformists were a small minority of the electorate and virtually excluded from parliament, they needed allies to mount a successful assault on the existing parliamentary order. Hence their long-standing and ultimately rewarding alliance with the Whigs. But it was the parliamentary union with predominantly Catholic Ireland, in 1801, which was mainly responsible for the dismantling of the Anglican political ascendancy in 1828–9.

Parliamentarians were members of a propertied and religious elite, but their wealth came from a variety of sources and most of them owed their seats to the support of a diverse electorate. They were consequently not unresponsive to shifts in popular feeling. Even Paley – a defender of the unreformed system – observed in 1785 that MPs 'Are so connected with the mass of the community that the will of the people, when it is determined, permanent and general, almost always, at length, prevails' (Christie 1984, 164). But those preconditions did not exist in the eighteenth century with regard to parliamentary reform. Those who advocated representational reform were in a minority and they always found it difficult to sustain their campaign.

London and reform

For much of the later eighteenth and early nineteenth centuries, parliamentary reform was a cause which was peculiarly associated with one part of the kingdom: London. The capital was much the largest city in the United Kingdom with a population of nearly 1 million in the early 1800s and of over 2 million in the 1850s. Yet it was grossly underrepresented in parliament in relation to its population and wealth. Before 1832, greater London had only 10 MPs: 4 for the City of London; 2 for Southwark; 2 for Westminster and 2 for Middlesex. Tower Hamlets had no representatives of its own, but it paid more than twice as much land tax as Cornwall, which had 44 MPs. However, many members for constituencies in the south-west of England lived in London and were not uninterested in its welfare (Langford 1988, 95). But this did not convince Londoners that their interests were adequately represented in parliament. Consequently they started an agitation for parliamentary reform which first attracted significant support in 1769–70.

The campaign was launched by Wilkes and Beckford with the support of long-established commercial interests in the City of London (Christie 1970, 217). Wilkes, the son of a Clerkenwell distiller, became Lord Mayor and, after a long constitutional struggle, MP for Middlesex. Beckford was a Jamaica merchant who became Lord Mayor and an MP for the City. At his election, Beckford complained that 'Pitiful boroughs send members to Parliament equal to great cities', whereas he believed that power should follow property (Stevenson 1977, 35). A decade later, the Wilkites and other Londoners provided most of the support for the Association Movement (Perry 1990, 106–7); but by then, the centre of the reform movement was Westminster, rather than the City of London. Westminster included the whole of the West End and had the largest electorate of any borough in Britain. The borough had a household franchise and many of its electors were small masters, or tradesmen. They readily joined Fox's Westminster Association which was modelled on those in Yorkshire and Middlesex. The Association endorsed Fox's plan for annual parliaments and 100 extra county MPs and also the more radical principles of equal representation and universal (male) suffrage.

The advanced programme of the Westminster Association was adopted, in 1792, by the London Corresponding Society, which owed little directly to the example provided by the French Revolution. The LCS, which was founded by a shoe-maker, Thomas Hardy, was less socially exclusive than previous reform associations. It charged low entry and subscription fees to attract support from 'The middling and smaller tradesmen and working people.' Artisans predominated in its membership, but most of its leaders and speakers were professional men. The total membership of the LCS never exceeded 5,000, which was a tiny proportion of the adult male population of London. Nevertheless, the government viewed the society with suspicion and tried to suppress it. However the LCS leaders were acquitted of treason and the society benefited from increased public hostility to the French war. Tens of thousands of spectators came to the LCS open air meetings, where the current distress was blamed on the corrupt representational system. But these gatherings were banned by the Seditious Meetings Act of 1795. However the LCS survived until further repressive measures were taken in the late 1790s.

The revival of the constitutional reform movement in London began in 1807, when Sir Francis Burdett was elected MP for Westminster with the assistance of former LCS members. For the next decade, Burdett largely led the reform campaign both in and out of parliament In 1808, the City of London, which had become Tory in the 1790s, turned against the government and towards the Whigs and reform. The demands of the war economy had strengthened unionism in many of the London skilled trades and when demand collapsed, at the end of the war, men like John Gast, the shipwrights' leader, became supporters of parliamentary reform. Gast wanted direct labour representation in the House of Commons and believed in the labour theory of value (Prothero 1979, 40–6, 86–7, 185). But it was a belief in free market economics, which prompted the tailors' leader, Francis Place, to agitate for the repeal of the Combination Acts, which was effected in 1825 (Rowe 1970, xi). It was not a trade unionist but a former West Country farmer, Henry Hunt, who became the popular leader of the advanced London radicals (Belchem 1985). Hunt presided over the Spa Fields meeting in December 1816, which initiated a national campaign in favour of universal suffrage and annual parliaments. Despite the growth of the reform movement in the industrial provinces, London remained the centre of the radical campaign. There is no convincing evidence that popular support for reform was impeded by the size or economic character of London. In the 1820s, support for reform declined dramatically in the capital, but it did also in the provinces.

The unrepresented manufacturing towns and reform

Since the creation of parliament in the Middle Ages, there had always been some important towns which had not been represented in the House of Commons. They were initially omitted for local rather than national reasons. Many towns were reluctant to be directly represented in parliament because boroughs were taxed at a higher rate than shires. In the fifteenth century, Sir John Paston noted that 'A dozen towns choose no burgess which ought to.' In 1653, the Instrument of Government proposed to enfranchise Manchester and Leeds, but no action was taken and unincorporated Manchester remained 'the greatest mere village in England' (Defoe 1971, 544). But the anomalies in town representation did not become serious until the later eighteenth century.

As late as 1700, the seven largest English towns, each with a population of over 10,000, were all parliamentary boroughs, but by 1750, a quarter of the twenty English towns with over 10,000 inhabitants were not represented in parliament. In 1801, twenty-one of the forty-nine English towns with a population over 10,000 were not parliamentary boroughs (Corfield 1982, Table 13). In addition, a high proportion of towns with a population between 2,000 and 10,000 were also unrepresented in parliament. Five of the twenty largest British towns in 1801 were unrepresented manufacturing towns: Manchester, Birmingham, Leeds, Sheffield and Paisley. But not all the growing manufacturing towns were unrepresented in parliament, as some historians have assumed (Flinn 1963, 139). The manufacturing towns of east Lancashire and the West Riding were generally unrepresented, but those of the East Midlands – Nottingham, Leicester and Derby – had been parliamentary boroughs since the Middle Ages.

Despite the growth of the unrepresented towns, there was little pressure for their enfranchisement until the confrontation between the British government and the American colonies drew attention to their plight. When the 1765 Stamp Act provoked the Americans to demand 'no taxation without representation', the defenders of the tax pointed out that many English towns were also unrepresented in parliament. At that time, unrepresented Birmingham and Manchester were as large as unrepresented New York and Boston. In the 1770s, Burgh, Wilkes and Cartwright, encouraged by the Americans' example, demanded the direct representation of all British large towns in parliament. This objective remained an integral part of the radical reform programme thereafter (Brewer 1981,

209–10, 19–20). The English reformers also adopted the American tactic of mass petitioning, which became a common feature of subsequent radical reform campaigns (Perry 1990, 123).

There was, however, an important difference between the situation in America and Britain. For whereas there was no American representation at Westminster, all the unenfranchised towns of Britain had virtual representation in parliament through their local county MPs. Such towns often successfully lobbied MPs to support Bills in which they had an interest (Langford 1989, 711). Their freeholders could vote in county elections and wielded considerable influence. The Birmingham freeholders, for example, ensured that one of the Warwickshire MPs acted as their parliamentary spokesman.

Many of the unrepresented towns were controlled by Tory oligarchies which associated elections with dissipation, disorder and Dissent. Their conservatism was strengthened, rather than diminished, by economic success. In 1782, it was claimed that the principal people in Manchester did not wish to alter a constitution which had given them a century of liberty and prosperity (Veitch 1965, 91). None of the large unrepresented manufacturing towns petitioned in favour of Pitt's 1785 reform scheme, although it included proposals for their enfranchisement. There was more support for reform in towns which were already parliamentary boroughs, but where majorities were excluded from power (Langford 1989, 713). In general, local opinion in the large unrepresented manufacturing towns 'Contributed singularly little to the demand for a moderate reform of Parliament' (Whale 1922, 110).

The French Revolution generated only limited support for reform in the unrepresented towns. The dissenters in Birmingham and Manchester were inspired, by the grant of religious equality in France, to campaign for the repeal of the Test and Corporation Acts. But they merely provoked a coercive Tory reaction, in favour of 'Church and King', in 1791–2. Manchester and Sheffield established reform associations roughly on the model of the London Corresponding Society, which attracted support from artisans. In Lancashire many handloom weavers supported parliamentary reform when trade was slack and their economic bargaining position was poor. But some weavers opposed reform, or quickly reverted to Loyalism (Bythell 1969, 206). The radicalization of the French Revolution and the outbreak of war between France and Britain enabled the Manchester loyalists to suppress the 'Jacobin' reformers with impunity (Bohstedt 1983, 107–16). For the next two decades, the reformers found it difficult and dangerous to raise their heads in Manchester. They remained active for longer in Sheffield, but in none of the northern industrial towns did constitutional reform societies survive into the new century.

In the early 1800s, there was a slow revival of support for reform in the northern manufacturing districts. This was partly prompted by the growth of trade unionism and hostility to the Combination Acts of 1799 and 1800. But there was no clear connection between trade unionism and support for reform until the 'Luddite' disturbances of 1811–12. The destruction of textile machines was an indignant response to a sharp fall in overseas demand which had occasioned unemployment and distress. But many 'Luddites' believed that political reform offered them a better chance of improving their lot than violence, or insurrection (Darvall 1969, xiv). In the East Midlands, many 'Luddites' were enfranchised and the Nottingham frame-workers drew up a parliamentary bill to protect their interests. They lobbied MPs in London, but received no support, even from Burdett. By contrast, the militant woollen croppers of the West Riding believed in direct action and attacked mills (Thompson 1968, 579–609). They had less experience of parliamentary lobbying, since the main West Riding woollen towns were not parliamentary boroughs.

The Luddite agitation attracted the attention of the veteran radical reformer, John Cartwright. He lived in London, but came from Nottinghamshire and had personal experience of the Industrial Revolution. He had briefly been a partner in a steam-powered woollen mill at Retford and had defended the patent rights of his brother Edmund to the carding machine. Thus Cartwright had no time for machine-breaking, or violence, but he organized the successful defence of thirty-eight Manchester 'Luddites' accused of administering illegal oaths (Thomis 1970, 23–4). In 1813, Cartwright toured the North, visiting 'The ruins of the constitution of national prosperity' at a time when other gentlemen were touring the ruins of castles and abbeys in search of the picturesque. His efforts to spread the reform gospel in the North bore fruit after the end of the Napoleonic wars.

In 1816–17, a severe economic depression revived support for reform in the manufacturing districts. Former Luddites and textile workers imitated Cartwright's London example and established Hampden Clubs to press for radical reform. In Middleton, in Lancashire, the Hampden Club met in a Methodist chapel and its secretary was inspired by the Puritan tradition of equality before God and the writings of John Bunyan. The textile districts were prominent in Cartwright's mass petitioning of parliament. The Manchester petition was signed by 30,000 people: a sizeable proportion of the town's adult population. When the petitions were rejected, on technical grounds, by the House of Commons, the radicals decided to select 'people's representatives' to personally petition for reform. In July 1819, Cartwright's friend, Sir Charles Wolseley, was chosen as Birmingham's 'Legislatorial Attorney'. But the Manchester reformers were advised not to follow suit, so they held an ordinary demonstration instead.

Thus the Manchester reform meeting, at St Peter's Fields, on 16 August 1819, was a local response to a national campaign led by the London radical leaders. One of them, Henry 'Orator' Hunt, presided over the Manchester meeting. This was his second visit to the city in a few months and was evidence of the increasing importance of the northern industrial districts in the reform campaign. The Manchester demonstrators were mostly artisans (especially handloom weavers) and factory operatives (of both sexes) from the surrounding cotton towns. In Lancashire, many parliamentary reformers also called for labour reforms: shorter hours, higher wages, a repeal of the Combination Acts and an end to capitalist exploitation. But the Manchester meeting remained loyal to the Cartwright tradition: constitutional agitation focused exclusively on radical parliamentary reform. The demonstrators displayed 'Cleanliness, sobriety, order and peace' in order to make the meeting 'As morally effective as possible.' However, the presence on the rostrum of 'caps of liberty' – symbols of the French Revolution – aroused the ire and fears of the local magistrates, who ordered the arrest of the reform leaders (Epstein 1989, 91). This was attempted by the local yeomanry, which had been raised to resist Jacobins and was largely composed of businessmen and shopkeepers. In the melee which ensued, eleven people, including women and young people, were killed and hundreds wounded.

The deaths turned the Manchester meeting into an event of national significance: the 'Peterloo massacre'. Journalists who had been present at the meeting, criticized the conduct of the local authorities (Read 1958, 143). But the Tory government prosecuted the reformers, not the magistrates. When parliament reassembled, the Home Secretary, Sidmouth, passed six acts which suppressed popular support for reform. After Peterloo, the authorities tried to avoid using the yeomanry to suppress political meetings. This new restraint facilitated the activities of later reform groups, such as the Chartists (Saville 1987, 25). The prime minister, Liverpool, attributed the disaffection in the industrial districts to the boom or bust cycle of production, which he thought was encouraged by the use of machinery and dependence on foreign markets. But he also believed that the French Revolution had made the lower classes lose respect for authority and old institutions. The growth of liberal sentiment – abroad, as well as at home – led Peel to wonder how much longer the Tories could resist reform.

'Peterloo' revived the dormant interest of the Whigs in parliamentary reform. Their leader, Grey, considered that the deaths at Manchester were 'By far the most important event that had occurred in the course of his political life.' But it was a younger Whig, Lord John Russell, who pressed parliament to transfer the seats of the rotten boroughs to the unrepresented manufacturing centres. His proposal was endorsed by a member of the Tory government, Croker, who noted that there were only eight towns in Britain with a population over 20,000 which were not represented in parliament (Cannon 1972, 179). In 1826, the seats of the rotten Cornish borough of Grampound were given to Yorkshire. This was the first time for nearly three hundred years that a parliamentary borough had been disfranchised for delinquency and the first time that representation had been transferred from one part of the country to another. In 1828, when Wellington rejected a similar transfer to Leeds, the Canningites resigned from the government. Palmerston believed that piecemeal enfranchisement was the only way to avoid a general scheme of reform (Bourne 1982, 283). In the spring of 1830, Russell proposed the enfranchisement of Manchester, Birmingham and Leeds: 'the capitals of the three great branches of our manufactures'. He stressed the outstanding claims of Manchester: its world trade; great wealth and population; the new railway to Liverpool; and scientists, like Dalton. Russell's proposal attracted sufficient support to convince some members of the Cabinet that public opinion had advanced on the question.

The rapid growth of the northern manufacturing districts strengthened the case for a large redistribution of parliamentary seats (Evans 1989, 6). In the decade 1821–31, Manchester, Birmingham, Leeds and Sheffield increased their population by over 40 per cent: a much faster rate of increase than that of London. By 1831, the combined population of Manchester and Salford was about a quarter of a million and it was the second largest conurbation in the United Kingdom. Yet the economic prosperity of the 1820s also largely killed the demand for parliamentary reform in the unrepresented industrial towns. In Lancashire the hand-loom weavers enjoyed an Indian Summer of prosperity and lost interest in reform. In Manchester, ironically, it was Tory businessmen (including the man who had led the yeomanry at Peterloo) who now pressed for the city's direct representation in parliament. But there was only limited support in Manchester for the 1830 reform petition (Read 1958, 176–9). In Birmingham, there was no significant reform movement until there was an economic depression in the winter of 1829–30. This prompted a Tory banker, Thomas Attwood, and local radicals to form the Birmingham Political Union to agitate for currency and parliamentary reform. They were inspired by the Catholic Association in Ireland, which had apparently secured the passage of Catholic emancipation. But that concession strengthened, rather than undermined, Wellington's government, which survived for another eighteen months. This casts doubt on the theory that the overthrow of the Anglican ascendancy led to the 1832 Reform Act (Clark 1985, 409). The BPU had limited local support until the Reform Bill was introduced and no influence on national developments until after it had been enacted (Flick 1978, 12, 37).

The passage and character of the 1832 Reform Act

It was not developments in Britain, but events abroad which were mainly responsible for the sudden revival of the demand for reform in the summer of 1830. The July Revolution in France – when the autocratic Charles X was replaced by Louis Philippe – was widely welcomed in Britain. The revolution may have influenced the last stage of the 1830 general election and it certainly provided both the government and the reformers with an object lesson in 'people power'. Brougham, who was elected in Yorkshire, declared that the French example would facilitate reform in Britain. The Home Secretary, Peel, noted that the success of the uprising in Paris 'Is producing its natural effect in the Manufacturing districts here, calling into action the almost forgotten Radicals of 1817 and 19.' So when the Lancashire colliers went on strike and stopped the cotton mills, Peel favoured concession, rather than confrontation. The dispute was peacefully resolved, but Peel was unable to quell the disorders which broke out in the rural south of England.

The 'Swing' riots outbreaks of machine-breaking and incendiarism – started in Kent and soon spread throughout south-east England in the autumn of 1830. The agricultural labourers were dissatisfied with their low wages and poor conditions, but their dislike of threshing machines was shared by many farmers (Hobsbawm and Rudé 1970, Appendix 4). It was alleged that farms were becoming factories for corn production and that farm workers were being treated no better than factory workers. However the authorities were less alarmed by the rural Luddism than by the rick-burning, which seemed pointlessly destructive. The government's inability to restore order in the Tory counties disillusioned its own supporters. The agitation also convinced Cobbett that parliamentary reform would come soon. The London radicals were angered by Wellington's refusal to concede parliamentary reform, which he now feared might lead to revolution. When rumours of a conspiracy forced the cancellation of the king's visit to the Guildhall, the government's credibility was fatally undermined. Dissatisfied Tory MPs voted against Wellington's government, which promptly resigned. Grey then formed a ministry committed to reform in order 'to prevent the necessity for revolution'. The combined effect of the French Revolution and Swing had convinced moderate opinion that parliamentary reform was unavoidable.

The Industrial Revolution was not directly responsible for the Reform Bill, but it did influence the parliamentary debate on that measure. Russell pointed out that England, though it led the world in mechanical inventions, denied representation to the northern industrial towns. Wellington retorted that the prosperity of those places was proof that they did *not* need direct representation. Peel thought that the enfranchisement of Manchester would 'open a door which I saw no prospect of being able to close'. Many Tories feared that a large transfer of seats from the rural south to the industrial north would undermine the supremacy of the landed interest and the Tory party. Yet many landowning Tory families, like the Egertons in Lancashire and the Wards in Staffordshire, had been enormously enriched by the Industrial Revolution. Peel was a mill-owner and Baring, who feared that 'The field of coal will beat the field of barley', was a leading banker.

In the event, the Reform Act did not result in a substantial shift of political power away from the rural to the urban and industrial areas. Forty-two new parliamentary boroughs were created, more than half of which were located in the industrial areas of the North and the Midlands. But most of these new boroughs had only one MP and none had more than two. Thus Birmingham and Manchester had the same representation in the Commons as small towns with 6,000 people, like Lewes and Marlow. Greater London obtained only five new boroughs and was still left grossly underrepresented. By contrast, some very small boroughs, like Cricklade, survived extinction by having their boundaries enlarged to include the surrounding rural areas. Thus some boroughs were more agricultural in character after 1832, than they had been before. More importantly, sixty-five new seats were allotted to the more populous English and Welsh counties, many of which were still predominantly rural. Consequently it has been contended that the Reform Act restored and perpetuated the power of the landed interest (Moore 1976). But this was not suggested by contemporaries and has not been proven (Woodbridge 1970, 88).

The disfranchisement effected by the 1832 Reform Act was not determined by considerations of economic vitality. Some eighty-six boroughs, with very small electorates, were wholly or partially disfranchised: most of which were in the south and west of England. Cornwall lost most seats, although it was hardly an economic backwater. At that time, more of Cornwall's population was engaged in mining than in any other county and it led the world in steam engine technology (von Tunzelmann 1978, 263). But the Cornish agricultural interest favoured parliamentary reform as a way of reducing taxation. Most of the disfranchised towns were not defunct 'rotten boroughs'. Many of them were market towns, such as East

Grinstead, while others were small manufacturing centres, like the lace-making towns of Amersham and Wendover. Some of the fishing ports which were partially disfranchised, such as Grimsby and Hythe, grew rapidly in the 1840s.

The franchise reforms of 1832 enlarged the electorate, but did not greatly change its social and occupational character. In the counties, the 40s freeholders remained the majority of the electors. The county electorate remained much underrepresented in the Commons, despite the increase in county seats (Evans 1983, 40). In the boroughs, the new £10 occupier franchise benefited the shop-keepers: a class which was already well represented in the pre-1832 electorate. The new qualification was too high to give the vote to the great majority of the working classes, but this threshold was effectively lowered as rents increased. In the twenty years after 1832, the borough electorate increased faster than both the county electorate and the total population (Woodbridge 1970, 73). However, the ending of the freeman franchise ensured that artisans had less electoral influence in some large urban constituencies after 1832 than they had possessed before it.

The 1832 Reform Act did not end the domination of parliament by the great landed families (Gash 1953, 193–201). But there was a decline in the proportion of MPs coming from established parliamentary families in the second quarter of the nineteenth century (Wasson 1991, 649). However, that decline was evident at the three general elections before the Reform Act and 'new wealth' had always accounted for a significant minority of MPs. Nevertheless the established parliamentary elite still supplied nearly 60 per cent of all MPs when the Second Reform Act was passed in 1867.

Thus the Reform Act did not make the House of Commons an accurate mirror of contemporary Britain (Gash 1979, 152–5). In 1850, less than a fifth of all Englishmen were entitled to vote: a proportion which was not much higher than it had been a century before. Yet there were relatively more voters in England, where half the total population lived in urban districts, than in rural Ireland, where the poor freeholders had been disfranchised in 1829. British industrialization and urbanization had at least ensured that a sizeable section of the population were able to meet the property qualifications for the franchise.

The Second Reform Act of 1867 has been interpreted as a way of incorporating the respectable labour aristocracy in the constitution (Smith 1966, 8–14). In the late 1830s, artisans established the London Working Men's Association which created the Chartist movement and in the 1860s, trade unionists were prominent in the Reform League. However the decision of the parliamentary party leaders to reopen the reform question was initially prompted, not directly by working-class agitation, but by the 1848 revolutions on the Continent. These resulted in a dramatic widening of the male suffrage in France and some extension in other countries. Thereafter, the electoral franchise in the United Kingdom lagged behind many continental countries (Quinault 1988, 831–51). Household suffrage was granted to the boroughs in 1867, but it was not extended to the counties until 1884. The creation of roughly equal electoral districts was also not effected until 1885. The largely hereditary House of Lords remained unreformed until 1911 and women were unable to vote until 1918. True universal adult suffrage was not fully established until 1928. Thus the process of parliamentary reform reached its culmination well after the period generally associated with the Industrial Revolution.

The Industrial Revolution was not responsible for the creation of a representative parliamentary democracy in Britain. The rapid economic development of Britain did not create the campaign for parliamentary reform, nor ensure it success in 1832. The initial reform agitation was largely occasioned by distaste for executive mismanagement and corruption. Thereafter, foreign developments, particularly the revolution in America and the later revolutions in France, provided much of the stimulus for parliamentary reform. As Seeley – Toynbee's contemporary – noted, the British liberal reform movement owed much to continental developments (Seeley 1911, 357). The downfall of the old Tory order, in 1830, owed more to unrest in the English and Irish countryside than to unrest in the industrial districts.

Nevertheless, Toynbee's thesis that industrialization led to democratization should not be entirely discarded. Economic growth allowed more people to come within the pale of the constitution without even a change in the franchise. The concentration of population and wealth in underrepresented cities and unrepresented towns generated dissatisfaction with the archaic and inegalitarian system of parliamentary representation. The dramatic growth of London and the manufacturing districts provided tangible evidence that Britain was changing and thus strengthened the case for reform. In 1831, Macaulay supported the Reform Bill on the grounds that new forms of property and new portions of society had developed, yet new people were still living under old conditions (Thomis 1976, 24). Industrialization prompted fears of economic dislocation and urbanization (at home and abroad) seemed to encourage political revolution. Many groups in British society, who were not strongly dissatisfied with the status quo, eventually concluded that parliamentary reform was a price well worth paying for political stability. The reform that was effected in 1832 was limited in fact, but not in potential. In that respect, it was similar to the concurrent economic and social changes in

Britain. There was a real, but labyrinthine, connexion between the Industrial Revolution and parliamentary reform.

REFERENCES

Belchem, J. 1985. *'Orator' Hunt: Henry Hunt and English Working Class Radicalism.*
Black, J. 1988. 'England's ancien régime?', *History Today*, 38, 43–51.
Bohstedt, J. 1983. *Riots and Community Politics in England and Wales 1790–1810.*
Bourne, K. 1982. *Palmerston: the early years 1784–1841.*
Brewer, J. 1981. *Party Ideology and Popular Politics at the Accession of George III.*
Brock, M. 1973. *The Great Reform Act.*
Bythell, D. 1969. *The Handloom Weavers.*
Cannadine, D. 1984. 'The present and the past in the English Industrial Revolution 1880–1980', *Past and Present*, 103, 131–72.
Cannon, J. 1972. *Parliamentary Reform 1640–1832.*
Chambers, J. D. 1932. *Nottinghamshire in the Eighteenth Century.*
Christie, I. R. 1970. *Myth and Reality.*
  1984. *Stress and Stability in Late Eighteenth Century Britain.*
Clark, J. 1985. *English Society 1688–1832: ideology, social structure and political practice during the Ancien Régime.*
Corfield, P. J. 1982. *The Impact of English Towns 1700–1800.*
  1987. 'Class by name and by number in eighteenth century Britain', *History*, 72, 38–61.
Darvall, F. O. 1969. *Popular Disturbances and Public Order in Regency England* (with new introduction by A. Macintyre).
Defoe, D. 1971. *A Tour Through the Whole Island of Great Britain* (new edn).
Dickinson, H. T. 1985. *British Radicalism and the French Revolution.*
Dickinson, H. T. (ed.) 1989. *Britain and the French Revolution 1789–1815.*
Dinwiddy, J. R. 1986. *From Luddism to the First Reform Bill.*
Epstein, J. 1989. 'The cap of liberty and Peterloo', *Past and Present*, 122, 75–118.
Evans, E. J. 1983. *The Great Reform Act of 1832.*
  1989. *Britain Before the Reform Act: politics and society 1815–32.*
Flick, C. 1978. *The Birmingham Political Union and the Movement for Reform in Britain 1830–9.*
Flinn, M. W. 1963. *An Economic and Social History of Britain since 1700.*
Gash, N. 1953. *Politics in the Age of Peel.*
  1979. *Aristocracy and People: Britain 1815–1865.*
Hill, C. 1961. *The Century of Revolution 1603–1714.*
Hobsbawm, E. J. and Rudé, G. 1970. *Captain Swing.*
Hudson, K. 1965. *Industrial Archaeology: an introduction.*
Judd, G. P. 1972. *Members of Parliament, 1734–1832.*
Kadish, A. 1986. *Apostle Arnold: the life and death of Arnold Toynbee.*
Langford, P. 1988. 'Property and virtual representation in eighteenth century England', *The Historical Journal*, 31, 83–115.
  1989. *A Polite and Commercial People: England 1727–1783.*
  1991. *Public Life and the Propertied Englishman 1689–1798.*
Mingay, G. 1963. *English Landed Society in the Eighteenth Century.*

Moore, D. C. 1976. *The Politics of Deference.*

O'Gorman, F. 1989. *Voters, Patrons and Parties: the unreformed electorate of Hanoverian England 1734–1832.*

Oldfield, T. H. B. 1792. *An Entire and Complete History, Personal and Political of the Boroughs of Great Britain.*

Paine, T. 1977. *Rights of Man* (introduction by Henry Collins).

Perry, K. 1990. *British Politics and the American Revolution.*

Phillips, J. A. 1982. *Electoral Behaviour in Unreformed England.*

Porritt, E. 1903. *The Unreformed House of Commons, Parliamentary Representation before 1832.*

Prothero, I. J. 1979. *Artisans and Politics in early Nineteenth Century London: John Gast and his times.*

Quinault, R. E. 1988. '1848 and parliamentary reform', *The Historical Journal*, 31, 831–51.

Read, D. 1958. *Peterloo: the 'Massacre' and its background.*

Rowe, D. J. (ed.) 1970. *London Radicalism 1830–1843: a selection from the papers of Francis Place.*

Saville, J. 1987. *1848: The British State and the Chartist Movement.*

Seeley, J. R. 1911. *The Expansion of England.*

Smith, F. B. 1966. *The Making of the Second Reform Bill.*

Snow, V. F. 1959. 'Parliamentary reapportionment proposals in the Puritan Revolution', *English Historical Review*, 74, 409–42.

Stevenson, J. (ed.) 1977. *London in the Age of Reform.*

Thomis, M. I. 1969. *Politics and Society in Nottingham 1785–1835.*

  1970. *The Luddites.*

  1976. *Responses to Industrialization: the British experience 1780–1850.*

Thompson, E. P. 1968. *The Making of the English Working Class.*

Thompson, F. M. L. 1963. *English Landed Society in the Nineteenth Century.*

Thorne, R. G. 1986. *The History of Parliament: The House of Commons 1790–1820.*

Toynbee, A. 1916. *Lectures on the Industrial Revolution of the Eighteenth Century in England.*

Veitch, G. S. 1965. *The Genesis of Parliamentary Reform.*

von Tunzelmann, N. 1978. *Steam Power and the British Industrial Revolution to 1860.*

Wasson, E. A. 1991. 'The House of Commons, 1660–1945: parliamentary families and the political elite', *English Historical Review*, 106, 635–51.

Whale, G. 1922. 'The influence of the Industrial Revolution (1760–90) on the demand for parliamentary reform', *Transactions of the Royal Historical Society*, 5, 101–31.

Woodbridge, G. 1970. *The Reform Bill of 1832.*

9   Margins of the Industrial Revolution

Eric Richards

Introduction

The cumulative economic advances achieved in the Industrial Revolution required growing and shifting contributions from outlying economies and regions far beyond the recognized centres of industrialization. Manchester, Birmingham, Glasgow, Belfast and Leeds dominated the picture of industrializing Britain. But the Industrial Revolution was also occurring in such places as Wicklow, Montgomeryshire, St Austell, Tiree, King's Lynn, in towns and villages across Europe, and as far away as Australia. Even on the most distant margins of a widening economic world there were visible responses to the broader process. Sometimes reluctantly these places became component parts of the increasingly articulated market system that was intrinsic to the success of British industrialization. Moreover, for the distant and marginal zones of this system, the economic consequences were sometimes even more revolutionary and disruptive than those experienced at the industrial 'core'.

Regional specialization (in company with other forms of specialization) has been seen by many historians as the engine of economic growth (Pollard 1973). In Britain geographically concentrated production in both agriculture and manufacturing had existed for centuries. But there occurred a clear intensification of regional specialization at the end of the eighteenth century. This tendency could be seen most obviously in the new manufacturing centres which generated disproportionate advances in productivity and the fastest growth in employment. They became poles of attraction to migrants from less favoured zones, from the margins of industrialization where the creation of employment opportunities often ran well behind the growth of local population. Through specialization, mechanization, geographical concentration of production and the rapid expansion of inter-regional trade flows, the industrializing economy generated great improvements in productivity. For the outlying margins

I wish to thank Dr Joanna Bourke for her thoughts on the first draft of this paper.

new opportunities for economic specialization were created. In the long run the increasingly articulated economic system offered the means of material betterment for the majority of the people in most places.

But transformation was uneven in its form and in its rewards. Seen from Cornwall or Derry or Stornaway or Adelaide, the character of industrialization was quite different from the perspectives of Lancashire, Lanarkshire or London. Often the margins were drawn into the widening economic network on terms which seemed to be dominated by the more industrial, more populated and more dynamic centres. And although the margins themselves contributed to the acceleration of productivity improvement, they were also condemned, at least in the early phases of industrialization, to a greater dependence on non-industrial output.

British industrialization, therefore, was like a growing octopus extending its tentacles into reaches ever further from its centre. While the centre itself shifted and changed no region or distant island remained undisturbed by its touch – sometimes squeezing the life out of distant sub-economies, sometimes feeding new opportunities. Compelling demands were created which directed local economic activity to serve the centre. The tentacles reached out for labour supplies, raw materials and markets. Eventually, economic change penetrated the hidden corners of economic inertia and distance, and activated sub-economies at home and abroad. The simultaneity of such change was part of the endless motion of industrialization and is difficult to analyse (Langton 1984). Here we examine some of its expressions at the margin, at different times and in different places.

But first, what was the centre? Asking where the Industrial Revolution began is as frustrating as asking when it began. Hopkins has argued that the rise of industry should be set in a broad pattern of economic development which began in London in the late seventeenth century and 'expanded during the classic phase of industrialization' (Hopkins 1988: 6). The phenomenon was neither balanced nor uniform and by 1820 certain sectors and certain regions had emerged to dominate the first phases in the revolution in industry (Crafts 1987, 1). Essentially it took the form of 'clusters' (O'Brien 1986, 297). 'The advance of productivity in a few industries did indeed enable Britain to sell around half of all world trade in manufactures' by 1850 and to account for one third of the world's industrial production. Thus from a handful of locations manufacturing radiated powerful consequences for the rest of the economy (within and beyond Britain) which were themselves uneven. Indeed it is agreed that gains in productivity were substantial but restricted to a narrow range of sectors, and consequently, to a narrow geography, by industrialization (Crafts 1985, 3–7; Crafts 1989, 424).

It is common to regard these core locations in the Industrial Revolution as the focal points for advanced technology and the accumulation of capital. One school of thought regards such growth poles as self-perpetuating, thereby causing a divergence in the status of economic regions and consigning the margins to relatively lower incomes and semi-permanent 'backwardness'. Once industrialization proper was underway forces of concentration became irresistible. Industrialization elsewhere became more rather than less difficult, and the problems of the outlying regions were exacerbated, their disadvantages multiplied (Williamson 1965; Holland 1967). Hence 'the plight of peripheral regions experiencing population growth unaccompanied by industrialization' (Hunt 1986, 68; O'Brien 1986, 135).

An alternative school of thought, usually adopting a longer time span, emphasizes the integrating and balancing characteristics of industrialization. Cumulative imbalance, in this view, was countered by the extension of the benefits of specialization to connecting regions. New opportunities for industrial development were created as time passed and new comparative advantages were revealed and explored. In this optimistic scenario the system takes on the character of an equilibrating mechanism which ultimately distributes the benefits of growth from the centre to the margins. Thus the optimistic version of British industrialization sees regional trends smoothly converging and improving, within perhaps a generation, while the opposing view perceives a substantial divergence in economic structure and welfare to the disadvantage of the marginal regions. This difference in perception is partly a consequence of the different time-frames adopted in the analyses, and partly also of the bewilderingly kaleidoscopic nature of the changes experienced by marginal zones in the classic period of industrialization.

The core may be regarded as the industrializing and manufacturing centre of the economy, the employment-generating focus of the process. By definition, therefore, the margins were those zones not participating in that process or else those which were pressed to perform functions ancillary or secondary to those of the centre. The most obvious feature of the system was the shifting nature of both centre and margins. London, for instance, eventually shifted its function increasingly towards commercial and financial services in the late nineteenth century (Lee 1986, 30, 140–3).

East Shropshire

'Pre-industrial growth' is growth occurring primarily but not exclusively in manufacturing industries, often supplying national and even international markets, but usually located in the countryside in cottages rather than factories, and employing cheap and probably primitive equipment, and little capital. In the period, roughly 1700–75 that kind of growth was widespread in the British Isles, even in areas which were subsequently rendered marginal. Particularly, but not only in textiles, the growth took place almost entirely within the old domestic frameworks for manufacturing. In Scotland, for instance, 'the growth points of the economy lay in the cottage' and this remained the logical mode of expansion at the prevailing levels of technology (Smout 1983, 63). It was, in most places, a fragile or ambiguous form of industrialization and much of it was snuffed out in the later phases of the process (Clarkson 1985). An instructive exception to these tendencies was the case of east Shropshire.

Shropshire's was an unusual economy. Its industrial career exemplified the shift from centre to periphery as the British economy grew. A large landlocked agricultural county, relatively remote from the main centres of population, Shropshire emerged spectacularly into industrial leadership in the mid-eighteenth century. Shropshire experienced the usual spread of proto-industry and the local economy rested upon a long tradition of commerce in the cloth trade and on metal working. Although there were important industrial developments as early as the 1690s there can be no mistaking the sharp acceleration in iron production in the 1750s. Deep in the county's rural heartland, at Coalbrookdale, there was a sudden multiplication of coke-blast furnaces, and during the following fifty years Shropshire maintained its role as the greatest iron-producing centre in the British Isles. Possibly triggered by high wartime prices for iron, the expansion witnessed a flowering of entrepreneurship of which the illustrious Darbys remain the best example. By the 1770s (when east Shropshire ironmasters were accounting for about 40 per cent of all British production) they had overcome several fundamental technical obstacles: using coal and coke they surmounted the bottleneck of charcoal supplies; employing Newcomen steam technology they ended the old dependence on rainfall; by using local railroads they connected their works with the River Severn, the main trading artery. In a mere thirty years, from 1760 to 1790, output quadrupled (Trinder 1981, 34).

East Shropshire became one of the original core locations of Britain's industrialization, exerting all the centripetal forces associated with the role. Like the Carron works in Scotland and the textile factories of Derbyshire and Lanarkshire, the spectacular industrial development in Shropshire sprang from a rural setting. Local landowners fed the ironmasters with raw materials and capital (and there was even some direct entrepreneurial participation). By 1800 about 200 steam engines were at work on the coalfield and labour migrated to the centre. William Ferriday, a mining agent, remarked in February 1755, 'They are mustering up all that can be met, of any sort of size, old or young, none escapes them.' Attracted by high wages to this rural enclave, labour came from distant parishes in Shropshire, from across the Welsh border, from the Black Country, even from Ireland. As late as 1810 migration into the region was a prime cause of the rapid growth of the local population (Trinder 1981, 181–4).

By this time, however, the east Shropshire cradle of the iron trade had already begun to relinquish its dominance. It lost its status as a core district and gradually slipped into an increasingly marginal relationship with the rest of industrial Britain. The transition had been long and difficult but exemplified a pattern of industrialization which had virtually completed its cycle before most of Britain had even joined the process. Nor was this simply a matter of an aborted 'proto-industrialization'. East Shropshire had experienced genuine transformation before being overtaken by the passage of comparative advantages to other regions, in the first instance to south Staffordshire.

This loss of industrial leadership was set in a context of absolute growth of iron output in Shropshire which came to a peak in 1869. But its share of national production fell decisively from 27 per cent in 1796 to 10 per cent in 1830 and to 4 per cent by 1860. Contractions during recurrent recessions became increasingly severe; the county's industrial population became too large and its industry lost its competitive edge. In essence the Salopian ironmasters were unable to keep pace with newer enterprises in South Wales and south Staffordshire. They continued to utilize old furnaces constructed in the previous century and their operations were set too deeply in the countryside. The Shropshire industry was tied to water supplies and transport facilities which were no longer appropriate to the latest iron-making technologies. Moreover the local coal and ironstone deposits were being depleted. As the local historian says, by 1815 east Shropshire was becoming 'an outlying part of an economic region centred between Birmingham and Wolverhampton' (Trinder 1981, 135–6, 146). The core had become marginalized.

The signals of relative decline were visible enough to the local community, its population swollen by the premature expansion in the earliest days of industrialization. There was a decline of enterprise and a relegation to a secondary servicing role: 'Shropshire became more and more a supplier of semi-finished iron and even of raw materials to the Black Country ironworks.' Staffordshire began importing Shropshire ore which it could utilize more profitably, mainly by virtue of better transport facilities in the new age of canals and railways. Wages in the Shropshire iron trades now fell behind: by 1845 they were 20 per cent lower than those paid in south Staffordshire and outmigration followed. A local commentator recollected that the decline of the coalfield had 'driven numbers, who cast many lingering looks behind them, from their birth-places and the scenes of their childhood, to seek employment in south Staffordshire, South Wales and other mining districts. It was painful to witness the departure of so many men of bone and muscle, but their bettered circumstances soon reconciled them to the change' (Trinder 1981, 155, 203). Like other regions which had taken an early lead in the Industrial Revolution Shropshire's main contribution had 'petered-out' (Pollard 1973, 30).

The rise and relative decline of the iron industry in Shropshire had been a kind of giantism in the local economy. In its prime it had created substantial linkages which induced expansion in, for instance, mining, river transport, rail, road and canal investment, and in local agriculture. But the rest of Shropshire's economy remained extremely narrow and, in some cases, contracted in scale during the period of expansion at Coalbrookdale. There were attempts at industrial diversification. For example, there had been some expansion in the local pottery trade and a revival of the Salopian glass industry in the 1790s; there was an ambitious plan to create an integrated chemical works (led by Lord Dundonald) and a cotton manufactory operated in the district. Clearly there had been a general testing of the economic possibilities of the region but without much success. The chemical industry made no progress and the glass industry soon faded from view, its skilled labour migrating to St Helens (Plymley 1803, 340–2).

The local salt industry typified the problems of Shropshire producers as they faced industrial competition from beyond the county. Various small salt producers had operated in Shropshire since the thirteenth century, supplying local markets in the manner common in many parts of Britain. Using antiquated evaporative methods of production some suppliers marketed their salt as far away as Bishop's Castle and Welshpool but they mainly catered to the needs of the county town, Shrewsbury, transporting their product by donkey and cart. Yet by 1800 the industry was dead and all its saltworks shut down and wasted, killed off by the dramatic recent improvements in the competitive power of Cheshire producers to the north. Superior in quality and cheaper in price, Cheshire salt, with the aid of better transport systems, was now able to penetrate and conquer the Salopian market. The Cheshire producers were also assisted by the salt tax which burdened high-cost small-scale producers elsewhere. At the centre of these market shifts were the combined effects of industrial deregulation, improved transport and economies of scale achieved in the Cheshire salt industry. Peripheral salt producers, such as those in

Shropshire, could not live with this intensity of competition at the time when Shropshire's own iron industry had exerted similarly destructive effects on its competitors (Stamper 1983–4, 77–82).

The consequences of early industrialization in Shropshire were reflected in the responses of other producers. For instance, the original impact of the expansion of ironmaking in east Shropshire was felt by local landowners and farmers as early as the 1760s. Resources of land and capital were channelled into coalmining, and agricultural output was itself stimulated by the demands of an expanded industrial population. Moreover, some of the immigrant population was absorbed directly into agriculture, itself responding to better prices in the last quarter of the century. 'First generation migrants often worked on the farms, in the coalfield, or took jobs which involved the care of animals', their sons subsequently recruited into the mines and coalworks (Trinder 1981, 184). The growth of industry fuelled the progressive commercialization of agriculture and the local responses (in terms of tenurial and technical change) are well documented. Equally formative were the shifting extensions of markets for Salopian agriculture. Remote districts of the county were being drawn into the widening matrix of inter-county trade which eventually caused the reconstruction of its agriculture. For instance, the north Shropshire plain began to supply foodstuffs to the expanding colliery district of east Denbighshire. By 1800 north Shropshire was helping to feed Lancashire: at a time when the cotton county was able to produce less than a third of its grain requirements and imported supplies from Furness in the north and from Shropshire to the south (Marshall 1808, 256). Similarly, the growth of Wolverhampton and Dudley created further market opportunities for Shropshire producers (Bythell 1969, 45 n.5; Checkland 1960).

Certain districts in north Shropshire responded to such opportunities, and commercial agriculture thrived. Yet they were unable to maintain their market advantages indefinitely, particularly when falling transport costs widened the effective hinterlands of towns and 'cracked-open' local monopolies in the countryside (Turnbull 1987, 537). Thus in 1824–6 during local controversy (concerning the anticipated extension of the canal system to link Birmingham, Liverpool and Manchester through Shropshire) it became clear that the 'natural monopoly' of food producers in north Shropshire was about to be breached. Until that time the region had been 'the furthest point the Manchester people can come for their supply'. It was thought that 'a greater facility of intercourse' would injure the local agricultural interest (Richards 1974). There could be no resisting the new transport systems and Shropshire producers were repeatedly required to respond to altering market conditions. Generally the response was positive and by the 1840s much of Shropshire's economy was recon-firmed in its agricultural role, supplying a widening radius of food deficit areas in north and midland England. Concurrently its own precocious industrial sector had been weakened, superseded by districts better endowed in resources and transport, and better equipped with modern capital stock. Shropshire in company with a number of other regions including parts of Essex, Berkshire and Norfolk, appeared to withdraw from industry by rediscovering a comparative advantage in agriculture (Berg 1985, 117). To use Clarkson's embarrassing phrase, Shropshire opted for 'agriculturization' and became an inner margin (Clarkson 1985, 38).

Regional specialization in the British Isles

The fact that east Shropshire began as a core industrial region and lapsed into a marginal zone within sixty years argues against the notion that the process was necessarily unidirectional. Nor was geography or the rough dictates of comparative advantage sufficient to determine all outcomes. Shropshire and Staffordshire were at the crossroads of early industrial-ization yet local responses, even from villages and towns within a few miles of each other, were often entirely different. A study of three small market towns each subject to similar economic stimuli, suggests that the transition from 'localism' to 'industrialism' depended, in part at least, on local leadership and social structure as much as on comparative advan-tage of an economic kind (Denholm 1988). Similarly proximity to markets was not uniformly decisive: the failure of the once-successful textile and iron-making industries of the rural Kentish Weald suggests that closeness to London was not enough (Coleman 1983, 444; Short 1989). Indeed the inability of some regions to resist competition remains one of the great unanswered questions in the history of industrialization (Mokyr 1976; 1980, 445–7). There is no definitive explanation of why some regions waxed while others waned during the great shifts of the industrial economy in the late eighteenth and nineteenth centuries. But an early start in industrialization was, on the evidence of Shropshire and elsewhere, evidently no guarantee of continuing industrial expansion and leadership.

Regions poorly or negatively integrated into the expansion of industrial output and income might be close-in or remote from the centre, and their status could change over time. They became part of the shifting patterns of regional specialization. While large territories benefited directly from regional specialization, other areas were never within the core, and whole regions which had once been part of older cores (but which now followed paths of stagnation or even retrogression) returned in time to the periphery. Cornwall, Cumbria and districts in the southern Pennines followed a trajectory similar to that of Shropshire during the course of British industrialization (Marshall 1989). Other zones, within Britain and beyond, began on the periphery and were able subsequently to draw themselves into newly beneficial connexions with the centre. The variety of this experience was integral to the process itself. The ramifications for marginal zones of the growth of productivity at the centres of industrialization were, therefore, both positive and negative. Yet it is extraordinarily difficult to draw up a balance sheet for these consequences at either the aggregate or the regional level. It seems certain, however, that the redistributive effects of changing regional concentrations of production were considerable and could be negative. As Turnbull observes, new transport systems penetrated old autarkies: 'Some of the stimuli would be at the expense of other regions as part or even the whole of their trade was redistributed to other places' (Turnbull 1987, 545).

The history of Britain's regions shows the severe effects of these accelerated redistributions of industrial productive capacity. For instance the 'peripheralizing influences' clearly affected the south-west of England. In this region the long-established woollen cloth industry, which showed substantial growth in the 1790s and 1800s, subsequently fell into stagnation and decline, unable to cope with the new competition from northern England and elsewhere (Randall 1989). In this rapid cycle of growth and decline the local population was often left without the means of livelihood and compelled by poverty to leave the region. In essence, the west country producers came into competition with Leeds and Huddersfield which were favoured by cheaper fuel and better transport facilities both for their inputs and their markets. These 'adverse natural circumstances', according to the industry's historian, were 'not countered until too late by exceptional energy among manufacturers' (Mann 1971, 193). Industrialization in Yorkshire, given the size of the prevailing market and the competition from cotton, implied and indeed required a reciprocal de-industrialization in Wiltshire, and much of the south-west retrogressed towards a far higher dependence on agriculture (for which it may have been better adapted).

A similar fate overtook that other old textile centre, East Anglia. The once thriving textile complex of the New Draperies which had employed thousands in combing, spinning, weaving, dyeing and finishing was already in decay by the mid-eighteenth century. While the old worsted trade fell into permanent decline, growth in the silk industry in Norwich provided some compensation until the 1820s. By then, however, the English silk industry had begun to concentrate in the north-west and Coventry, and this, together with the effects of free trade on marginal producers, 'shattered the industry's protective shell'. As Coleman points out, the Lancashire industry boomed and generated huge employment growth, at the very time when East Anglia was denuded of practically all industry. This region now released migrants to London and the north-west, and eventually overseas. By 1850 East Anglia had become 'an overwhelmingly agricultural region' and 'in the process many wage-earning families had known greater poverty than was experienced by their counterparts who depended on the new factories of the north-west' (Coleman 1962, 127). In industrial, though not agricultural, terms, East Anglia had been consigned to the margin. The problem with the agricultural option was that, *ceteris paribus*, it generated less growth in employment than industry, and less than required by prevailing levels of population growth. A region specializing in agriculture, even if heavily commercialized, was unlikely to be able to support the increments of population growth occurring in the nineteenth century. Where agriculture remained stagnant or peasant-based it was usually associated with rural squalor.

The decay of rural industry became ubiquitous over the nineteenth century. The fact that the growth of productivity was greatest in the mechanized textiles trades meant that the impact was swiftest in the most widespread of those industries early on and was particularly severe in its impact on female employment in rural locations (Snell 1985; Hunt 1981, 23; Collins 1982, 146). Histories of the economies of English rural communities suggest that, in some places, expansion continued for several decades after 1750. In Mokyr's words there was an 'extended coexistence of the "old" and the "new"' and in some industries the traditional sector played a positive role in the growth of the economy (Mokyr 1976, 372; Hudson 1989, 8; Samuel 1977). But by 1850 it was a losing battle: in such trades as framework knitting, handloom weaving, nailmaking, and even in brickmaking, the new transport systems (especially railways) eventually brought craftsmen into direct competition with a mass-production technology. Mills summarizes the transition: 'With a declining share of the country's industry and commerce, the rural areas became increasingly dependent on agriculture. By the end of the century many rural areas bore the hallmarks of depressed areas – falling population, low incomes, unemployment and underemployment, and a lack of investment whether in old or new industries' (Mills 1973, 15).

This euthanasia of cottage industries was the logical consequence of the overwhelming competitive power of industrialized manufacturing in the centres of the new urban nation. It is not difficult to regard the process as a great exercise in Schumpeterian 'creative destruction'. Recent research suggests that this form of de-industrialization was virtually universal (Berg 1985, ch. 5). As Houston and Snell put it:

judging from the experience of a wide range of cottage industries in East Anglia, Kent, Sussex, and other areas of southern England, and parts of Lancashire and Cheshire, Wales, Ireland, Scotland, Flanders, Hesse, east Westphalia, Silesia, Wurtemberg, Norway, parts of France (to say nothing of areas outside north-western Europe) deindustrialization might seem to have been the *usual* pattern for protoindustrial regions

or indeed rural cottage industry at large (Houston and Snell 1984, 490). Possibly the only significant exception was London where small-scale urban workshop production continued to expand well into the nineteenth century (Stedman Jones 1971, 337; Samuel, 1977).

It is also well known that the early consequences of British industrialization on Western Europe were no less alarmingly destructive of old industries. Eventually, of course, new industrial growth developed in many parts of the Continent, but in the interim the impact was often deadly. As the work of Crouzet indicates, the blizzard of British competition wiped out old European manufacturing creating, perhaps, a *tabula rasa* for a new growth later. 'By 1800 continental Europe was threatened by pastoralism and the fate of India in the 19th century. In fact countries like Spain, Portugal and Sweden which fell into the orbit of England during the wars suffered a crisis or a collapse of their traditional industries without any compensating rise of new ones' (Crouzet 1964, 577; Clarkson 1985, 36). As Pollard puts it, 'Regional specialization associated with modernization, for example in pottery, in cutlery, in toolmaking, or in woollen textiles, was tantamount to de-industrialization elsewhere' (Pollard 1973, 638). As British industrial competition penetrated markets, at home and abroad, it caused disruption and decay. 'Rural areas became more exclusively agricultural than they had been for centuries' though this was often now a prelude to out-migration and/or a renewed degree of specialization in new economic activities (Tilly 1979, 36). The irresistibility of the competition was demonstrated by the ineffectiveness of most of the efforts made by neo-mercantilist governments to protect their industries. Cullen's remarks about Ireland serve for most of Europe: 'Specialization, a large scale of production, and the external economies associated with the intense localization of the woollen industry in Yorkshire and of cotton in Lancashire created a rapidly improving competitiveness against which protection could not prove an adequate answer' (Cullen 1976, 113–23). Nor should the degree of competition from machinery be underestimated. In 1817 Robert Owen remarked of Scotland that 'There is machinery at work in one establishment in this country, aided by a population not exceeding 2,500, which produces as much as the existing population of Scotland could manufacture after the mode in common practice fifty years ago' (Owen 1817, II, 54). Even within the most dynamic industrial counties, such as Lancashire and Warwickshire, there were areas subject to the forces of rural decay (Martin 1984).

The essential point is that the process was manifestly unequal and uneven. Not only in continental Europe but also within the British Isles, the people of certain regions were required to shoulder much more of the burden of adjustment than others. In the end it expressed itself in rather severe differences in regional economic welfare some of which persisted into this century. Hunt has no doubt that certain types of industrial decay were closely connected with 'the remarkable regional variations in prosperity that became one of the outstanding characteristics of the nineteenth century labour market' (Hunt 1981, 28). These forms of regional retardation should be recognized in any discussion of trends in national living standards during industrialization (Coleman 1962, 115; Richards 1988, 193).

Unfortunately the margins are the least well documented theatres of the Industrial Revolution even though they were not always on the 'geographic periphery'. For instance, as Cullen remarks of his own country in the nineteenth century, 'The growth of population accompanied by a decline in domestic industry, signified that Ireland was becoming more rural, more agricultural, than it had been' (Cullen 1972, 119). But some parts were affected more severely than others. Much of the pre-industrial growth in eighteenth century Ireland had been highly unstable and ephemeral (Almquist 1979, 699–718) and much of the transformation of the Lagan valley region into a factory production centre was achieved at the expense of textile manufacturers in the Ulster countryside (Collins 1982, 146). The experience of the flax-growers and flax-spinners of the north-west of Ireland followed the path of expansion in the 1750s and 1760s and then suffered rapid decline as textile technology passed through several revolutions. Consequently 'the entire basis of the standard of living in the rural communities ... was eroded in the first 20 years of the nineteenth century, leading many to migrate to the great textile town of Paisley in the Scottish lowlands' (Collins 1981). Elsewhere in Ireland the same story was repeated including the collapse of woollen production in the 1820s and the inexorable decline of a whole array of trades (including hats, gloves, carpets, crockery, candles, paper) broken by the competition of cheaper and better imports (Mokyr 1985, 12–14, 288–90; Beckett 1966, 243; Clarkson 1985, 35–6). By 1830 the flannel trade of Wicklow was virtually dead; between 1818 and 1840 the woollen manufacturing of Kilkenny declined by 90 per cent. Imports of British leather and footwear killed the Irish industry despite the fact that Ireland was a large supplier of the original raw material. Often the decline of domestic industry was agonisingly gradual as handworkers continued to toil at lower and lower rates as the only alternative to starvation (Freeman 1957, 6). The destruction of domestic industry in Mayo compounded the vulnerability of the people during the great famine (Cullen 1972, 119). Handknitting, embroidery and lace-making in the cottages of Donegal was virtually erased by the mechanized competition of Leicester, and efforts to resurrect home industries in Ireland (as in the Scottish Highlands) at the end of the century all failed in the face of ever stiffer competition. Thus, outside Belfast, much of Ireland became less industrial, a trend which was reinforced by the relative success of its trade in agricultural products. Between 1800 and 1826 Irish exports of grain and provisions doubled and the growing output of butter, pork and bacon (as well as of live cattle) demonstrated a shift of output in response to higher prices (Beckett 1966: 243). This agricultural growth, though a positive response to market opportunities, did not provide a reliable base sufficient to generate a cumulative growth of income in Ireland.

The list of regional casualties in the British Isles was long. While East Anglia was being de-industrialized to the advantage of the West Riding, whole areas of West Wales, Derbyshire, Cornwall and many parts of upland Britain were being divested of their rural, low-productivity, domestic industries which had no way of resisting the competition of modern factory production (Collins 1978, 603). In many of these places the early promise of industrial progress was dashed in the years after Waterloo. The case of north Wales was eloquently represented in the words of A. H. Dodd: 'Hardly a district however backward or remote, but could, in the early days of George III, show signs of change startling enough to give some substance for the wildest dreams of material progress.' But as industrialization became concentrated (in Lancashire, for example) 'the products of these better-equipped regions ousted one local manufacturer after another from the home market' and brought North Wales into ever closer dependence on the great industrial centres (Dodd 1951, viii, x).

The Scottish Highlands

Within the British Isles, in the century after 1750, there were therefore several regions which despite experiments to revive or stimulate industry, eventually found themselves bereft of secondary production. They were left with economies which, in some cases, were saddled with a swollen population and from which migration was inadequate. They were re-affirmed in a greater degree of agricultural dependence than before. They were subject to pressures (transmitted through a better integrated national market) which induced them to specialize in the production of raw materials for the core districts of the Industrial Revolution. In some districts the consequences were expressed in terms of cumulative retro-gression in most sectors of the local economy and, for many communities, an increasingly precarious economic structure. These were the true margins of the Industrial Revolution where, in terms of economic welfare, the consequence of industrialization at the centre was retardation on the rim. A full demonstration of this proposition would, of course, require comparative statistics of *per capita* incomes, which do not exist. Moreover, some regional retardation was eventually mitigated by demo-graphic adjustments which included out-migration, later marriage and higher levels of celibacy. Some districts, marginalized in the early phases of industrialization, eventually developed patterns of growth which brought them into the industrial core. But none of this should divert attention away from the undeniable retardation that afflicted several regions over most of the nineteenth century.

The plight of the Scottish Highlands illustrates the peripheral experi-ence in especially dramatic tones. Industrialization in the south of the British Isles let loose such forces upon the Highlands that its entire economic structure was dislocated. The process operated upon an economy which, until about 1750, had been relatively insulated from broader economic currents (Smout 1983, 47–8). Its poverty was notorious and the region remained hostage to recurrent 'famine' or 'destitution' even into the nineteenth century. The old Highland economy is poorly recorded, partly because most of its output did not enter a market. 'Pure household production lasted in greater purity and vigour in the Highlands than in the more commercialized south' (Gray 1957, 44). Only partial specialization and differentiation in employment had occurred. Tailors, shoemakers, wrights and carpenters were separate occupations and were paid directly in food for their services. Almost everything else was pro-duced within the family economy – wool came from the family sheep, was spun, dyed, woven and fulled in the household. Houses were built by the occupants, without squared timber, glass, mortar, slates or a single nail. Everything else was made of wood or leather with an absolute minimum of equipment: there were virtually no carts, mills or even sickles; grain was usually handpicked not cut with an implement. All this indicates an extreme minimum in terms of the substitution of capital for labour and a low propensity to import. A few specialized tasks were performed by travelling tinkers (Teignmouth 1836, I, 318–20).

Most Highland agriculture (excluding the lowland fringes of the north east coasts) was self-subsistent in form though some districts were dependent on periodic meal imports. Low levels of agricultural produc-tivity were associated not only with low living standards but also with recurrent famine which continued into the nineteenth century (Richards

1982, part 1). The main export was live cattle which had been favoured by the greater access to English markets after 1707. Cattle production, labour intensive in most places, produced a flow of revenue to landlords in the form of rents but tended to leak out of the region by way of landlord consumption in the south and by expenditure on meal supplies and luxury imports. As late as 1836 Lord Teignmouth was able to describe the typical condition of so much of the Highlands:

Almost all the articles of ordinary use are fabricated by themselves. Every cottage in Isla, and very generally through these regions, has its spinning wheels; the yarn is spun, is sent to the loom, and woven into shirts, sheeting and other articles of dress. Wrights, smiths, tailors, shoemakers etc. are similarly maintained by clusters of farms. (Teignmouth 1836, 318)

The quickening of economic activity beyond and within the Highlands, from the 1770s was demonstrated in a range of local developments, some shortlived, some permanent. They were cast upon a context in which the rapid growth of population was greatest (often a doubling in fifty years in the poorest parts (i.e. the north-west and the Hebrides) and from which out-migration was least effective.

In the late eighteenth century there was pronounced expansion in certain sectors, largely responding to external markets and better prices. The West Highlands was perhaps the last area of Britain to receive the influences associated with the 'improvement' movement in agriculture. Under the stimulus of rising prices, cattle production expanded as part of 'the search for animals' to satisfy southern demand (Smout 1983, 55). On the low lands in the east there was an expansion of wheat farming (especially in Caithness and Easter Ross) also for export to the south. More dramatic was the rapid growth of kelp production along the western seaboard. Kelp was a seaweed which was reduced to soda-ash by severely labour-intensive methods to be used as a raw material for the soap and glass industries of the Industrial Revolution in Glasgow and Lancashire. The price of kelp multiplied ten-fold between 1750 and 1810 and many districts of the West Highlands committed themselves almost totally to its production. This was clearly a backward linkage of the Industrial Revolution. So also, in a less direct fashion, was the expansion of the herring fishery which developed partly in response to the food needs of the slave economy, especially in Jamaica. At its height the West Indian market consumed 60,000 barrels of herrings per annum (Thomson 1849). In addition, from the 1770s onwards, there were numerous state and private experiments to sponsor broadly based economic activity in the Highlands. New capital investment was channelled into coal production, mineral exploration, salt making, cotton manufacturing, wool mills and linen production. New villages at several locations were developed as new growth points. Of these ventures the most successful was linen production which brought extensive domestic employment to several rural areas. But eventually the most pervasive expansionary influence was that derived from the shortfall of wool supplies for southern manufacturers. The sharp rise in wool prices brought great urgency to the switch of land use in the Highlands to satisfy the demand for wool. All this was in train before 1800. In a sense the shift in demand schedules associated with industrialization in the south created powerful incentives for a thorough reconnaissance of the Highland economy for ways in which it could meet the opportunities generated. In many cases that was a literal exploration of the region by southern farmers, surveyors, managers and capitalists (Richards 1982, part 2).

The outcome of this reconnoitring eventually took a specific and, indeed, very constricting shape. Most of the new growth proved to be short-lived. For instance, the kelp industry slumped catastrophically when the lowering of import duties exposed the Highland producers to the competition of barilla from Spain, Sicily and Tenerife. Even worse, the soap and glass makers (assisted by the repeal of the salt tax) now turned decisively to the use of synthetic soda manufactured from the common salt of Cheshire by means of the new Leblanc process. Technology and free trade conspired to destroy the kelp trade; prices collapsed in the 1820s and something like 40,000 West Highlanders were rendered redundant (Wilson 1842, I, 229). Similarly, the fishing industry suffered severely, partly because of the abolition of slavery in the West Indies (and the associated loss of markets), partly because of the migration of the herrings out of the western lochs. Moreover, virtually all the recent enterprise designed to break into the circle of industrialization proved incapable of sustained development. They were abject failures, part of the long sad history of aborted efforts to bring industry to the Highlands. At the same time there was an almost total destruction, by competition from machine industry, of the old domestic manufacturing structure. For instance, linen spinning and weaving were eradicated by the 1840s in most places, and by then the knitted stocking industry in Aberdeenshire was also dead. In 1836 Lord Teignmouth observed the failure of enterprise almost everywhere in the Highlands, from Tobermory to Campeltown and to Inverness, and he attributed the problem to the competition of Glasgow (Teignmouth 1836, I, 322–3).

One of the most self-destructive aspects of the Highland problem in this transition was the extraordinary appetite for imported goods that developed among the ordinary people of the Highlands. Economists are aware of this phenomenon in the onset of development in peasant economies

(Myint 1967, 41–2). The Highlanders shifted much of their consumption towards imported manufactures, and local ministers of the church roundly condemned the enticements of cheap and gaudy southern products. As in parts of Ireland the people who once dressed in home-produced clothes now dressed in imported fabrics (Cullen 1972, 106). Eventually the dress of the Highlanders became virtually the same as Lowlanders (Dixon 1886, 130). The trend affected practically all the economy – imported coal was substituted for peat in many parts, timber and slates were introduced into building, tea and sugar into the houses (Gaskell 1980, 10–11, 49). As a contemporary reported in 1836:

The steam looms of Glasgow and Paisley have stopped the village weaver in his employment; the manufacturers of Sheffield and Birmingham have discharged its smith; the taste for fashionable furniture, to which the improved dwellings of our agriculturists naturally led, has shut up the workshop of its carpenter, and the love of dress, so universally diffused in the present age, has levelled the domicile of its tailor, and the stall of the maker of Highland shoes. (NSA 1835–45; xiv, 1–8)

In terms of regional income there was in this process a two-edged sword at work. Competition from the south reduced economic activity in the region by the direct loss of markets. But, equally, it increased Highland imports of manufactured goods which were cheaper and more attractive than local products. Industrialization awakened consumption appetites which were the more remarkable since they developed in a time of low per capita incomes. It was a phenomenon common in regions on the margin and was one of the most striking testimonies to the irresistibility of industrial manufacturing.

The only fully successful sectors to emerge in the Highland economy were sheep-farming and, to a lesser degree, the large arable producers to the east. Vast tracts of the Highlands were converted into great sheep-farms devoted exclusively to the production of wool for the Yorkshire textile mills. Income derived from sheep-farming was very narrowly distributed and its leakage out of the region was high. With only the weakest of linkages into the local economy, and employing virtually no local labour apart from small numbers of shepherds, the success of wool production had little fructifying effect within the Highlands. The benefits were restricted to the sheep-farmers (who were few in number), the landlords (who mainly consumed rather than invested their windfall gains), and the producers and consumers of woollen textiles in the national economy at large. By extreme specialization, in sheep-farming, there was a massive increase in productivity and income to a single sector of the Highland economy, a sector which had little feedback effects on the existing labour force and capital infrastructure of the Highlands. The social effects in the Highlands were severe and the resulting controversy has generated one of the most energetic debates in modern Scottish history (Richards 1985).

In essence, the dictates of regional specialization were imposed on the Highlands in the shape of a vast structural change. In its course much of the old economy of the region and most of its inhabitants, were rendered redundant. But the population in most of the western parishes continued to increase until the 1850s. What had started out as a peasant society on the periphery of the national economy had been drawn into close relations with the industrial core. The effect was to intensify its marginality in several senses: in particular, many of its people were extruded to the physical margins of their own region while the inland territories were taken over by the sheep-farmers. They became coastal crofters living a peasant existence on inadequate allocations of land. Some of them turned to part-time fishing but possessed too little capital for real success. Many resorted to seasonal migration to the great fishing ports outside the region, or to railway construction or domestic service in the south which often helped to sustain their homes in the Highlands. Others migrated permanently to Inverness, or Glasgow or England, or to North America and to the most distant margins of the British world. For the most part the Highlanders who remained were restricted now to congested crofting settlements with no apparent potential for economic development. The nation at large, and the process of industrialization in particular, had benefited from the structural change imposed on the Highlands. The associated burden of adjustment was carried by a society least able to cope: the imperatives generated by industrialization within a marginal region such as the Highlands brought little benefit to the people of the Highlands. The solution, painfully gradual though it was, was for most of them to leave the region.

The smoothness of the adjustment to economic adversity, in the north of Scotland and elsewhere, depended largely on the responsiveness of the people to better opportunities outside the region, even abroad. Often they were extremely reluctant to leave their declining region, partly from attachment to what little land (or trade) they had been able to hang on to; poverty itself was a cause of immobility, and the older generation generally resisted drastic change such as permanent migration. Rural districts in northern Scotland (and even in England) in the late nineteenth century were surprisingly poor hunting grounds for emigration agents (Armstrong 1988, 108–16).

Australia

The most distant margin of the British world, a margin to which many Highlanders eventually departed, was colonial Australia. Hartwell once remarked that the Australian wool industry was called into life by 'the Yorkshire industrial revolution and the consequent demand there for imported wool' (Hartwell 1971, xii). The irony was that many of the Scottish Highlanders found themselves manning sheepruns in the antipodes having been eliminated from their own economy by precisely the same forces that had caused the Highland clearances. The added irony was that, by the 1880s, it was the competition of wool producers in Australia that decisively undermined sheepfarming in Scotland. The forces released in the industrial core of Britain now determined the shape and size of economic activity across the globe, even in the furthest antipodean margins.

Several Australian colonies were created in the central decades of the British Industrial Revolution and they became classic examples of British society on the periphery. At such a distance the imperatives generated by industrialization in Britain were less immediate but can still be read in the genesis of these infant economies in the outback. In a sense, of course, colonization itself was a response to the needs of the metropolitan core. At least it may be said that colonization was often made feasible by the opportunities for trading with industrializing Britain. A 'vent for surplus' and the prompt identification of staples for export were paramount in the thinking of practically all colonial planners.

Creating colonial economies in the antipodean wilderness was highly variable. For example, the convict economy of New South Wales, founded in 1788, required several decades before it aspired towards civilian status. Instrumental in this evolution was a cadre of British merchants who, by breaking the East India monopoly, were eventually able to connect Australia with the extending tentacles of British trade through India. Sydney, by 1810, was linked through Calcutta to London and Glasgow thereby providing the prerequisite for the development of a range of exports. New South Wales and Van Diemen's Land were soon yielding skins, whale oil, and then wool to the British market. Before long, even on this remote margin, the infant colonial economies were beginning to oscillate in response to the movements of the British trade cycle.

In Britain and Europe (and indeed in Asia) old economies and industries, as we have seen, were compelled to confront and adjust to the challenge of industrialization by the beginning of the nineteenth century. In Australia (ignoring the fragile aboriginal economies which were easily dispersed from areas of white settlement) entirely new economies were established in a context of development mainly defined in Britain. A perfect example of colony making of this sort was South Australia in the 1830s. The initial steps involving the testing of the local possibilities, potential export production and links with the evolving trade network, had been undertaken. The creation of the South Australian economy, *sans* convicts, was powerfully influenced by the ideas of the theorist of colonies, Edward Gibbon Wakefield (1796–1862). He produced a blueprint for colonization in 1829 and South Australia was its first practical test. It entailed a systematically balanced programme of land sales, capital imports and immigration. Within the plan were central economic assumptions about the primary producing function of a new colony. It must be self-sufficient in foodstuffs and produce primary products (the predictions included wool, rice and wheat as well as opium for the China trade) to exchange for the manufactures of Britain. Lord Brougham's maxim that 'Every axe driven into a tree in British North America set in motion a shuttle in Manchester or Sheffield' (quoted in Rolph 1844) coloured the thinking of all colonists including those in the remote antipodes.

No colony, however distant and experimental, could escape the commercial embrace of industrial Britain. Thus the new South Australian economy eventually produced three basic staples for export – wheat, wool and copper. Among its many immigrants in the mid-nineteenth century were economic refugees from the Scottish Highlands and miners from the declining copper industry of Cornwall. But the most striking characteristic of the new economy was that it remained essentially 'pre-industrial' in form for the following hundred years. Its great export staples produced few backward or forward linkages for the generation of secondary industry: the economy remained geared almost exclusively to primary production. Secondary industry in a narrow band, protected by distance from Britain, remained entirely ancillary – that is, such activities as machinery maintenance and brewing, and a range of simple food processing for the local market. All local manufacturing was severely constrained in scale and market. For everything else the infant colony remained dependent on manufactured imports, overwhelmingly derived from Britain. Year after year, for almost a century, South Australia was supplied by ships laden with 'Manchester goods' too cheap for local producers to mount serious competition against even in their own market (Richards 1975).

South Australia, like many other old and new economies on the outer margins of the trading world, was effectively restricted, in the context of *laissez-faire*, to simple forms of economic production, the scope of which was determined by the ease of importing manufactures from Britain. South Australia was one of the economies which found great difficulty in initiating its own industrialization partly because it fared well on primary production, partly because import-substitution was simply too difficult. Of course, some colonies eventually rebelled against this 'colonial' function and erected protective systems by which to nurture their industries. But even as late as 1889 it was still possible to say that 'The manufactories of New South Wales are to a great extent located in England, as goods are simply discharged upon the Circular Quay, Sydney, and warehoused there' (Brown 1889, 34).

The colonial margins of the Industrial Revolution experienced diverse consequences. The original native economies were generally destroyed by the impact of white settlement. The settler economies were usually restricted to primary production and unable to develop manufacturing sectors until the twentieth century. But, in Australia, this hardly amounted to retardation since the productivity of the export-based primary production was highly competitive and sustained by large capital imports from Britain. Living standards were generally higher than in Britain itself which was, of course, the pre-requisite for the longest-distance migration in human history. This brought 1.6 million people from the British Isles to Australia in the nineteenth century. But the colonies were marginal in the sense that they had virtually no control over their own economic destiny and, in that century, had little chance of developing an industrial structure of their own. Like many other parts of the formal and informal empire, the Australian colonies responded to the needs of the core. Their economies were created within the framework of *laissez-faire* but, given high productivity and the associated high living standards, the adjustments were relatively smooth. The reach of the metropolitan tentacles brought benefits as well as restraints to these outer margins and they developed an inter-dependence with the industrial centre.

Conclusion

The common element in the experience of the margins of the Industrial Revolution – in regions such as Shropshire, Wiltshire, West Wales, Tipperary, the Scottish Highlands, Portugal and South Australia – was the way in which their economies were reshaped by forces activated within the industrial core in Britain. The 'price signals' transmitted from the earliest stages effectively redefined the widening range of economic relationships (O'Brien 1985, 779).

It is possible to take an optimistic (and also a deterministic) view of this process. For instance, Pollard has given the highest prominence to the essential role of regional specialization in the cumulative success of industrialization, both within the British Isles and, subsequently, for the economic integration of Europe. He contends that 'ultimately the whole of Britain became modernized and industrialized, but the path followed by each region was different and was determined at each point in time by its interrelation with the rest' (Pollard 1973, 638).

This optimistic formulation is no doubt true in terms of the imperatives of economic growth and the ultimate benefit which accrued to the national economy as a whole. Nevertheless it ignores the difficulties encountered by marginal regions whose adjustments were too slow or too inefficient to partake for generations in the benefits of economic growth. It is a view which gives insufficient allowance to temporary retardation (or even semi-permanent retrogression) in the regional experience. Some areas, of course, were able eventually to hoist themselves out of their initial marginality. But for a number of regions, the Scottish Highlands most obviously, the broader process seemed to cause a divergence from the rest of industrializing Britain.

There were several categories of 'casualties' in the Industrial Revolution. Capitalists such as the sugarmakers and the canal owners went into financial decline. Entire occupational groups such as the nailmakers, framework knitters, handloom weavers, lace-makers and many others undoubtedly suffered. To these we should add a group of marginalized regions within which were concentrated many of the negative adjustments required by industrialization. Indeed one of the most important historical questions that arises is how marginal regions coped with the combination of economic adversity and population growth. Very often it fell to the remnants of the 'traditional sector' to support the residual surplus population as best they could (cf. Heywood 1981, 278).

The path of adjustment for many retarded zones on the margin (often exacerbated by continuing population growth) was depopulation until a point of convergent living standards was achieved. Population loss sometimes became a substitute for economic growth. Smout indeed has suggested that the rising per capita incomes in both Ireland and the Scottish Highlands in the late nineteenth century were partly a consequence of 'the removal from the workforce of much surplus labour' by emigration 'from the periphery to the core' (Smout 1980, 261). Solow expressed the point more forcibly when she said that 'It took the death of two million people to bring Irish agricultural productivity, and incomes, up towards levels in Britain' (Solow 1984, 852; Mokyr 1980, 458). Of Wales, Thomas says that the rural exodus was a requirement of industrialization and 'a necessary consequence of economic growth' (Thomas 1962, 2). Implicit in this view is the notion that regions on the margin benefited little from industrialization and, indeed, that their people shouldered a disproportionate share of the problems of industrialization. It may be that the classic Industrial Revolution itself contained a historical counterpart of the present day north–south polarity in the structure of international and interregional relations. Then as now there may have been a systematic bias which favoured the industrial producers at the centre over the producers of raw materials on the periphery (Fishlow 1978).

The intensification of competition from the centre was the common factor on the margins where the level of secondary production was diminished. This, of itself, was not necessarily a mark of retardation or even declining living standards because, in principle, the process of industrialization opened other avenues of specialization to all connecting regions. In reality, the decline of local pre-industrial industry was associated with diminishing employment opportunities and a cumulative decline in output. The evolving patterns of specialization left some regions permanently bereft of the prospect of population resurgence and little chance of rehabilitating their industrial structures.

To say that there were margins in the Industrial Revolution is merely to say that the process was unequal, and to recognize the extraordinary reach of the tentacles of industrialization. It does not explain why the experience of connecting regions diverged in this manner (Coleman 1983, 444; Pollard 1981, 76). Towards this result we need a better taxonomy of the regional paths adopted during industrialization. It is evident already that there were rising regions, declining regions, and regions which both rose and fell, over the period 1750 to 1850. Such a taxonomy (which is merely the first step towards explanation) would have to cater also for regions which switched categories as the national economy matured, especially in the late nineteenth century.

It is improbable that the advances in national productivity in the course of industrialization could have been achieved without the turmoil of regional adjustment. Industrialization in the new centres of British industry undoubtedly made economic life in certain regions, such as the West Highlands, parts of East Anglia and West Wales, more difficult for most of the people for many decades. Until large-scale out-migration reduced their populations in the late nineteenth century, it is likely that their living standards diverged from those of the industrial core (Hunt 1981, 28). For some regions in Britain the results of the Industrial Revolution were at best equivocal and at worst debilitating. Drawing a rough average through the national experience does scant justice to the regional diversity that was part and parcel of the general process. These variations need to be accommodated in the classic debates about the course of living standards in the Industrial Revolution.

Different countries and different regions 'experienced different paths of transition from an agricultural to an industrial economy' (Crafts 1989, 428). The antipodean margins managed to achieve high living standards despite their constricted economic possibilities. But for some regions, even within the British Isles, the paths led nowhere except to depopulation and industrial decline. To recognize these variant paths is also to recognize that the phenomenon itself was neither a unilinear nor simply a national process.

REFERENCES

Almquist, E. L. 1979. 'Pre-famine Ireland and the theory of European proto-industrialization: evidence from the 1841 census', *Journal of Economic History*, 39, 699–718.

Armstrong, W. A. 1988. *Farmworkers*.

Beckett, J. C. 1966. *The Making of Modern Ireland*.

Berg, M. 1985. *The Age of Manufactures 1700–1820*.

Brown, J. C. 1889. *Plan and Practical Letter to Working People concerning Australia, New Zealand and California*.

Bythell, D. 1969. *The Handloom Weavers*.

Checkland, S. G. 1960. 'Corn for South Lancashire and beyond 1780–1800', *Business History*, 2, 4–20.

Clarkson, L. A. 1985. *Proto-industrialization: the first phase of industrialization?*

Coleman, D. C. 1962. 'Growth and decay during the Industrial Revolution: the case of East Anglia', *Scandinavian Economic History Review*, 10, 115–27.

1983. 'Proto-industrialization: a concept too many'. *Economic History Review*, 2nd ser., 36, 435–48.

Collins, B. 1981. 'Irish emigration to Dundee and Paisley during the first half of the 19th century', in *Irish Population, Economy, and Society*, ed. J. M. Goldstrom and L. A. Clarkson, 195–212.

1982. 'Proto-industrialization and pre-famine emigration', *Social History*, 7, 127–46.

Collins, E. J. T. 1978. 'The economy of upland Britain 1750 to 1850', in *The Future of Upland Britain*, ed. R. B. Tranter, 2 vols., 586–651.

Crafts, N. F. R. 1985. *British Economic Growth during the Industrial Revolution*.

1987. 'The Industrial Revolution: economic growth in Britain, 1700–1860', *Re-Fresh*, 4, 1–4.

1989. 'British industrialization in an international context', *Journal of Interdisciplinary History*, 19, 415–28.

Crouzet, F. 1964. 'Wars, blockade and economic change in Europe 1792–1815', *Journal of Economic History*, 24, 567–88.

Cullen, L. M. 1972. *An Economic History of Ireland since 1660*.

Cullen, L. M. (ed.) 1976. *The Formation of the Irish Economy*.

Denholm, A. F. 1988. 'The impact of the canal system on three Staffordshire market towns 1760–1850', *Midland History*, 14, 59–76.

Dixon, J. H. 1886. *Gairloch*.

Dodd, A. H. 1951. *The Industrial Revolution in North Wales*.

Fishlow, A. et al. 1978. *Rich and Poor Nations in the World Economy.*

Freeman, T. W. 1957. *Pre-Famine Ireland.*

Gaskell, P. 1980. *Morvern Transformed.*

Gray, M. 1957. *The Highland Economy.*

Hartwell, R. M. 1971. *The Industrial Revolution and Economic Growth.*

Heywood, C. 1981. 'The role of the peasantry in French industrialization 1815–80', *Economic History Review*, 2nd ser., 34, 359–76.

Holland, S. 1976. *Capital Versus the Regions.*

Hopkins, T. 1988. 'British imperialism: a review and revision', *Re-Fresh*, 7.

Houston, R. and Snell, K. 1984. 'Proto-industrialization? Cottage industry, social-change, and Industrial Revolution', *Historical Journal*, 27, 473–92.

Hudson, P. (ed.) 1989. *Regions and Industries. A perspective on the industrial revolution in Britain.*

Hunt, E. H. 1981. *British Labour History 1815–1914.*

    1986a. 'Wages', in *Atlas of Industrializing Britain 1780–1914*, ed. J. Langton and R. J. Morris, 60–8.

    1986b. 'Industrialization and regional inequality: wages in Britain 1760–1914', *Journal of Economic History*, 46, 935–66.

Langton, J. 1984. 'The Industrial Revolution and the regional geography of England', *Transactions of the Institute of British Geographers*, ns 9, 145–67.

Lee, C. 1986. 'Regional structure and change, and services', in *Atlas of Industrialising Britain, 1780–1914*, ed. J. Langton and R. J. Morris, 30–3, 140–3.

Mann, J. de L. 1971. *The Cloth Industry in the West of England from 1640 to 1880.*

Marshall, J. 1989. 'Stages of industrialisation in Cumbria', in Hudson 1989, 132–55.

Marshall, W. 1808. *The Review and Abstract of the County Reports to the Board of Agriculture*, I.

Martin, J. M. 1984. 'Village traders and the emergence of a proletariat in South Warwickshire, 1750–1851', *Agricultural History Review*, 32, 179–88.

Mills, D. R. 1973. *English Rural Communities: the impact of a specialised economy.*

Mokyr, J. 1976. 'Growing up and the Industrial Revolution in Europe', *Explorations in Economic History*, 13, 371–96.

    1980. 'Industrialization and poverty in Ireland and the Netherlands', *Journal of Interdisciplinary History*, 10, 429–59.

    1985. *Why Ireland Starved.*

Myint, H. 1967. *The Economics of the Developing Countries.*

NSA 1835–45. *New Statistical Account of Scotland*, 15 vols.

O'Brien, P. 1985. 'Agriculture and the home market for English industry 1660–1820', *English Historical Review*, 100, 773–800.

    1986. 'Do we have a typology for the study of European industrialization in the XIXth Century?', *Journal of European Economic History*, 15, 291–333.

Owen, R. 1837. *The Life of Robert Owen, written by himself.*

Plymley, J. 1803. *General View of the Agriculture of the County of Shropshire.*

Pollard, S. 1973. 'Industrialization and the European economy', *Economic History Review*, 2nd ser., 26, 636–48.

    1981. *Peaceful Conquest.*

Randall, A. 1990. *Before the Luddites: custom, community and machinery in the English woollen industry 1770–1809.*

Richards, E. 1974. 'The Leviathan of wealth in West Midland agriculture 1800–1850', *Agricultural History Review*, 22, 136–52.
    1975. 'The genesis of secondary industry in the South Australian economy to 1876', *Australian Economic History Review*, 15, 107–35.
    1982. *A History of the Highland Clearances*, I, *Agrarian Transformation and the Evictions 1746–1886*.
    1985. *A History of the Highland Clearances*, II, *Emigration, Protest, Reasons*.
    1988. 'Regional imbalance and poverty in early nineteenth century Britain', in *Economy and Society in Scotland and Ireland 1500–1939*, ed. R. Mitchison and P. Roebuck, 193–209.
Rolph, T. 1844. *Emigration and Colonization*.
Samuel, R. 1977. 'Workshop of the world: steam power and hand technology in mid-Victorian Britain', *History Workshop*, 3, 6–72.
Short, B. 1989. 'The de-industrialisation process: a case study of the Weald, 1600–1850' in Hudson (ed.), 1989, pp. 156–74.
Smout, T. C. 1980. 'Centre and periphery in history: with some thoughts on Scotland as a case study', *Journal of Common Market Studies*, 18, 256–71.
    1983. 'Where had the Scottish economy got by 1776?' in *Wealth and Virtue*, ed. I. Hont and M. Ignatieff.
Snell, K. D. M. 1985. *Annals of the Labouring Poor*.
Solow, B. 1984. 'Review', *Journal of Economic History*, 44, 839–43.
Stamper, J. M. P. 1983–4. 'The Shropshire salt industry', *Transactions of the Shropshire Archaeological Society*, 64, 77–82.
Stedman Jones, G. 1971. *Outcast London*.
Teignmouth, Lord. 1836. *Sketches of the Coasts and Islands of Scotland and the Isle of Man*, 2 vols.
Thomas, B. (ed.) 1962. *The Welsh Economy*.
Thompson, J. 1849. *The Value and Importance of the Scottish Fisheries*.
Tilly, C. 1979. *Consciousness and Class Experience in 19th Century Europe*.
Trinder, B. 1981. *The Industrial Revolution in Shropshire*.
Turnbull, G. 1987. 'Canals, coal and regional growth during the Industrial Revolution', *Economic History Review*, 2nd ser., 40, 537–60.
Williamson, J. G. 1965. 'Regional inequality and the process of national development: a description of the patterns', *Economic Development and Cultural Change*, 13, 3–84.
Wilson, J. 1842. *A Voyage round the Coasts of Scotland its isles*, 2 vols.

10   Social aspects of the Industrial Revolution

John Stevenson

I

Few paragraphs have done more than Dickens's famous depiction of 'Coketown' in *Hard Times* to envision the social repercussions of industrialization: the creation of a mass urban society, governed by the regime of the factory and the pace of the machine, an environment polluted and despoiled, and its inhabitants rendered anonymous and dehumanized. Indeed, as we know, the changes which are subsumed under the umbrella title of the Industrial Revolution were soon overlain by a complex process of comment, criticism and assessment. Dickens was only one of a number of figures in the early Victorian period whose views have often been summoned to give evidence about the social dimension of economic change (Tillotson 1954; Perkin 1969; Wiener 1981). Other writers cited in this context usually include Carlyle, Disraeli, Kingsley, Mrs Gaskell, Engels and Tocqueville. All writing in the period from the 1830s to the 1850s when the effects of industrial change figured largely in the national debate known as the 'Condition of England' question, they reflected the first public recognition that Britain was to some significant degree a different society to what it had been in the past. They also serve to remind us that discussion of the social repercussions of industrialization did not occur until well into the 'classic' first Industrial Revolution. Consider the social criticism of the period *prior* to the 1830s. The most notable examples from the very end of the eighteenth century, such as Frederick Eden and David Davies, were certainly interested in social evils such as poverty, squalor, underemployment, crime and demoralization. But these observers were primarily concerned with the agricultural labourer and the rural poor (Eden 1797; Davies 1795). Similarly, William Cobbett in *Rural Rides* followed Eden and Davies in examining the plight of the agricultural labourer in the south, rather that the workers in the towns of the North and the Midlands. When Cobbett's testimony is called on, it is to give evidence about the repercussions of economic and social change on the land. If a single sentiment can be said to inform so prolific an author it is, at least as far as his social criticism is concerned, that the conditions he saw about him in the rural counties of early-nineteenth-century England represented a disastrous deterioration from the situation he had known in the golden age of his youth, by implication the years of the third quarter of the eighteenth century prior to the long wars against Revolutionary and Napoleonic France. What pervades his writing on the state of the common people is the allegation that in the space of half a century, the countryside had become depopulated, its remaining population pauperized, demoralized, and deprived of the wholesome fruits of their own toil, and that a once organic relationship between farmers and labourers had been replaced by the cash nexus (Cobbett 1830). In spite of the fact that his focus differed from that of the early commentators on urban and industrial conditions, Cobbett remains one of the most potent critics of the effects of economic and social change as a whole: an extended lament about a rural world that had been lost.

Between them, Cobbett and Dickens provide the two sides of what might be called the conventional picture of the social impact of industrialization, the loss of an older rural world of security and prosperity, contrasted with the squalor and degradation of the new mass society of the factory towns. It is a view that remains deeply rooted, but in recent years historians have sought to qualify the stark contrasts offered by the first commentators on Britain's transition to an industrial society. In particular, they have sought to refine the view of the Industrial Revolution as a discrete phase of development occurring, approximately, in the century before 1850. Michael Fores has sharply reminded us that much of the customary terminology of 'revolution' rests upon shaky or at least questionable assumptions. Although we need not go as far as Fores in regarding the Industrial Revolution as a 'myth', it is necessary to recognize that historians tend to use the phrase in different ways. Sometimes it is applied to the rapid growth of specific sectors of manufacturing industry, particularly cotton and iron, from the later eighteenth century, and with them the growth of factories and the use of steam power. It is also taken to stand for the structural shift in the economy over a longer period which saw Britain's transition from a primarily agricultural society to one in which manufacturing and mining played the larger role. Overlapping with these views is that of the Industrial Revolution as marking a decisive change in which the economy as a whole moved from a state of gradual or intermittent growth into a more rapid and continuous advance in national income, or 'self-sustained growth' (Fores 1981; Musson 1982; More 1989, 72–3).

For historians concerned with the social consequences of industrialization, the central difficulty lies in evaluating the effects of a process which is now seen as both complex and protracted. As a result it is no longer possible to accept without major modification the view of an earlier generation of historians that the century prior to 1850 witnessed an overwhelming transformation of social life in both industry and agriculture (Hammond and Hammond, 1912, 1917). For example, the view that the Industrial Revolution was paralleled by an agricultural revolution which brought about radical changes in techniques, organization and social relations over a relatively brief period of time has been so heavily qualified that it can no longer be sustained. The gradual and long-term nature of change in agriculture and rural life is now well-recognized (Chambers and Mingay, 1966; Jones, 1981; Hueckel, 1981). Moreover, many of the social changes traditionally subsumed under the heading of the Industrial Revolution have been seen increasingly as part of longer-term processes often existing in complex relationship to economic growth. Accordingly, there has been a shift in emphasis in writing about the social aspects of industrialization from a concentration upon the impact of change in the most advanced sectors of the economy towards a broader and more balanced assessment of society as a whole. While many recent high-level texts on British society follow a conventional chronology in beginning the modern era in the latter half of the eighteenth century, most now accept that the eighteenth century witnessed only the beginning of processes which were to take much of the next century to spread to the economy and society at large (Rule 1986; Porter 1982). For example, Ashton depicted the last years of the eighteenth century as the decisive point at which economic activity began to develop:

After 1782 almost every available statistical series of industrial output reveals a sharp upward turn. More than half the growth in the shipments of coal and the mining of copper, more than three-quarters of the increase of broadcloths, four-fifths of that of printed cloth and nine-tenths of the exports of cotton goods were concentrated in the last eighteen years of the century. (Ashton 1948)

Modern work on economic growth, however, would characterize an economy growing only gradually until the 1820s, with little evidence of revolutionary change outside of an advanced industrial sector which as late as 1841 accounted for less than a fifth of the male labour force (Crafts 1985). Moreover, studies of the eighteenth century have increasingly suggested the importance of urbanization, commercial expansion, and the development of a consumer-oriented society as part of a long lead-in to nineteenth-century industrialization (Chalkin 1974; Plumb 1973).

But as well as differentiating and attenuating the pace of economic growth, recent work has also favoured a more segmented approach to social history and to the relationship between economic and social change. This has permitted historians to evaluate major themes in British social development from the eighteenth century in a way which allows the effects of economic change to be put into perspective (Royle 1987). Hence if we examine some of the broader social aspects of the 'classic' century of the Industrial Revolution we can discern the extent to which earlier preoccupations with an overwhelming and cataclysmic sequence of events have been replaced by a more sophisticated awareness of the complexity of the social response.

II

The received version of the social consequences of the Industrial Revolution is inseparable from the idea of population growth. Whatever emphasis is given to the long-term development of the economy, there was a major discontinuity in the form of population increase. Taking England and Wales alone population rose from 6.5 million in 1751 to 17.9 million in 1851 (Tranter 1973). The trebling of population – if we take the figure to 1861 (20.1 million) – in just over a century is the most startling concomitant of economic growth. But, as has long been recognized, there is a major historical debate centred on the question of whether population growth was caused by economic growth or merely coincided with it (Lee and Schofield 1981). England and Wales did not possess the only rapidly increasing populations in the eighteenth and early nineteenth centuries, other European populations were also growing including those in places such as Ireland, Scandinavia and eastern Europe where industrialization was clearly not responsible for population increase. Until quite recently, explanations centred on a lowering of death rates seen as the result of a complex interaction of factors. There may have been a more beneficial climatic regime, which in turn assisted a run of good harvests for much of the early part of the eighteenth century. Improvements in food supply and transport eliminated the prospect of famine and combined with a healthier climate to reduce mortality rates. Death rates from disease, most notably plague, but also other potential killers such as tuberculosis, typhus, smallpox and influenza, also fell. At present it is not clear to what extent the lowering of death rates from some of these diseases was the result of an autonomous decline in the virulence of the diseases or of increased resistance of human hosts to infection as a result of better food supplies and improved environmental conditions. It may well have been a combination of the two. But these were not effects confined to England and Wales or even to Europe, and showed few signs of having been primarily associated with Britain's role as the first industrial nation. One authority has suggested that 'there is no convincing evidence to support *any* of the widely voiced explanations for the decline in mortality which underlay the growth of population and labour supply in the late eight-teenth and nineteenth centuries' (Tranter 1985, 216). Indeed, in so far as a link might be posited with one of the most obvious symptoms of economic development, the growth of the towns, it might be argued that the tendencies pulled in the opposite direction. Death rates were customarily higher in the growing towns and cities of the eighteenth and early nineteenth centuries than in the countryside. Indeed, urban populations were only able to grow through a net influx of population from the countryside. On this reading, it was the parts of the country *least* affected by economic change which were providing the surplus population to swell the urban populations. Left to its own natural rate of increase, eighteenth-century London, like most other growing towns of the eighteenth and early nineteenth centuries, would have stagnated or even fallen in popu-lation. Only an influx of between 8,000 to 12,000 people a year permitted the capital, and in smaller order, the other early industrial towns and cities, to increase in size (Rudé 1971, 6–7).

But a new complexion has been given to the question of the relationship between the course of economic change and the rise of population for England and Wales. The estimates from the Cambridge Group indicate that the birth rate accounted for about 70 per cent of net population increase in the late eighteenth and nineteenth century and that the decline in death rate on its own would have achieved much lower rates of population increase than actually occurred. It was the increase in fertility which marked England and Wales out from the rest of Europe. During the eighteenth century the growth rate of population in England and Wales was not especially high by European standards as the mortality rate declined in common with much of the rest of the Continent. Only at the end of the century, when fertility also rose, did the population of England and Wales begin to grow more rapidly than other European countries. The explanation for this increase in fertility lies almost entirely with declining ages of marriage and levels of celibacy, what has been called the trend 'towards earlier and more universal marriage' (Wrigley and Schofield 1983, 132). In turn, the favoured explanations for this trend lie in the realm of economic growth and changes in employment. These may, for example, have altered the character of employment from 'living-in' to wage labour in such a way that the restraints on early marriage were eased. Other possibilities are that changes in the distribution of the labour force from agriculture to manufacture and from crafts and trades to semi-skilled and unskilled work, from low wage areas in the south to higher wage areas in the north, and the shift from country to town, enhanced the possibilities of marriage overall. E. A. Wrigley has argued that it was economic opportunity in a growing economy which provides the key to resolving the 'conundrum' of increasing marriage, higher birth rates, and the rapid acceleration of population growth from the late eighteenth century. But as Tranter has pointed out, a study of the changing character of employment, the proportion of the population at work, and the possible increases in per capita real wages reveals as many questions as answers to the reasons for rapid population increase from the late eighteenth century, and the need for further localized population studies (Tranter 1985, 100–7; Lee and Schofield 1981; Wrigley 1983). Moreover, economic growth, as defined by Wrigley, was by no means exclusively or even primarily *industrial* growth, much of it was commercial expansion based on the capital, the burgeoning ports, and as has been highlighted in the recent literature on eighteenth-century towns, in the prospering centres of consumption, leisure and civic life in the provincial capitals, spas and resort towns (Corfield 1982; Borsay 1989).

But many features of the demographic pattern in Britain remain tenuously linked, at best, with industrialization. The elimination of famine mortality lies far too early to be affected by it. Even the extent to which the onset of a steeper fall in mortality from the mid-eighteenth century can be attributed to economic growth is open to debate with variables in the virulence of disease and human resistance to infection forming a complex set of unresolved problems. As we have seen above, fertility is more likely to show some relationship with economic growth, although the nature of that growth and its specific industrial character is far from clear. Finally, it is worth noting that whatever the extent of the relationship between population growth and what we refer to as the Industrial Revolution, it is clear that some of the other major discontinuities in population history are not easy to correlate in any precise way with the course of economic growth. For example, it is at least arguable that if there was a major turning point in the course of the population history of England and Wales which seems to have occurred in the latter half of the eighteenth century, around the date at which historians might wish to date the origins of the Industrial Revolution, the next major discontinuity lies uncomfortably in the 1870s when lower levels of marital fertility began to occur and mean family size began to fall. For the demographic and social history of the late nineteenth and twentieth centuries, this is a change of major significance with wide consequences for household size, per capita family income, and the development of many of the cultural features we associate with twentieth-century attitudes towards the role of women, the nurturing of children and the development of the small, highly privatized domestic household. Although explanations can be advanced which link this crucial development to patterns of economic growth, they are unconvincing. Not for the first nor the last time, demographic history tends to take on a time-scale independent of obvious economic indicators or influenced by ones so subtle and complex that we are not yet able to represent them independently of other factors (Tranter 1985, 107–23).

If the population history of England and Wales only partly fits the conventional chronology of the Industrial Revolution, the same might be said for the history of urbanization. On the face of it, this might seem surprising, for the one feature that does appear to coincide with the conventional idea of an Industrial Revolution starting at some point in the late eighteenth century and ending its first phase at some point around the middle of the nineteenth is the increasing percentage of the population living in urban areas. Over half the population lived in towns by 1851 and by the end of the nineteenth century almost 80 per cent. In the space of just over a century Britain was transformed from a predominantly rural and small town society to an urban one. By 1851 there were sixty-three towns in England and Wales with over 20,000 inhabitants, in 1801 there had been only fifteen. Moreover, the balance had shifted decisively away from the most dynamic urban centre of the seventeenth and eighteenth centuries, London. In 1801 London was the largest city in Europe if not in the world, half as big again as Paris and only challenged by the cities of the Far East in size. With a population of about a million it dwarfed its nearest domestic rivals and was more than ten times the size of the largest provincial cities. Moreover London's share of the *total* urban population was still rising until the late eighteenth century. In 1650 it was estimated that 7 per cent of the total population lived in the capital, compared with 11 per cent by 1750. London continued to grow, but after 1801 it took a declining share of a growing urban population, as the highest rates of urban growth were registered in the new centres of commercial and manufacturing growth. The fastest growing cities of the early nineteenth century were Liverpool, Manchester, Birmingham, Leeds and Sheffield, some of which recorded growth rates in excess of 40 per cent in the single decade, 1820–30. Amongst the second rank towns, Bradford, Salford, Oldham, Preston and Wolverhampton were amongst those showing the most rapid increase. The broad impact of economic growth can also be seen from the evidence that the four most industrialized counties (the West Riding of Yorkshire, Staffordshire, Warwickshire and Lancashire) increased their share of the total population from 17 per cent in 1781 to 26 per cent in 1861.

The suggestion that London's relative decline as *the* urban environment of England and Wales dates from the first half of the nineteenth century is a reminder that until then the problems of urban growth remained identified with the capital rather than anywhere else. Eighteenth-century literature developed the image of London as the 'overgrown monster' or the 'dropsical head', drawing to itself the population of the countryside and the provinces, corrupting them with dreams of luxury and plenty, and often leaving them forced to turn to lives of vice and crime. London became the focus of national concern about crime, tumult and disorder, on account both of its vast size and its opportunities for crime. Thus London was the epitome of the evils of the urban environment. Cobbett was only trading on a well-established image in his famous description of London as the 'Great Wen' as, literally, a great cyst (Landa 1980). Even with the huge increase in the size of the provincial manufacturing and commercial cities, London remained the giant metropolis, almost too vast to comprehend, and the setting still, as in *Oliver Twist*, of novels of social condemnation. Indeed London's dominant role in the literature of anti-urbanism was not one ever to be fully displaced. Just as Mayhew's articles for the *Morning Chronicle* in 1848–9 on the labouring poor in London formed part of the chronicle of distress in the 'hungry forties', concern about criminality and the poor in London was to resurface increasingly from the 1860s (Stedman Jones, 1971). The British version of 'Potomac Fever' – the preoccupation of the London-based media with events on their own doorsteps – was to ensure that metropolitan conditions and concerns retained considerable prominence.

As easily the largest urban centre, London had a crucial role in the national economy. Some years ago the case was made for London as an 'Engine of Growth' in the early modern and eighteenth-century British economy, witnessed by its dramatic demographic growth, but also by the effects of its demands upon the country as a whole for specialized agricultural and manufactured products. By the end of the eighteenth century, much of the agriculture of the southern half of England was devoted to the supply of London. The supply of its needs for products as diverse as coal and cheese reached into the furthest corners of the land. Eighteenth-century writers had already developed a fertile line of discourse about the extensive trade which reached even beyond the nation's shores to supply the breakfast tables of London with tea, sugar, coffee and fine tableware. But London was more than a centre of consumption; as late as 1851 it was still the largest manufacturing centre in the country, its port far and away the largest in tonnage of traffic, and some of its manufacturing enterprises, such as its brewing and refining industries, amongst the largest in the country. In 1861 London employed almost a million workers engaged in manufacturing, 14.9 per cent of the total for the country as a whole (Stevenson 1977 (a) xxii). It might be argued that the mid-nineteenth century saw the playing out of London's role as a major manufacturing centre with a number of its principal industries, such as shipbuilding, about to go into terminal decline. But provincial dominance of manufacturing was never complete and industrial production in London increased again in the twentieth century.

But urbanization is not in itself the major preoccupation of those concerned with the social repercussions of industrialization. The argument has always revolved around the rise of disruptive new patterns of work, the factory and machine-driven production – which Dickens articulates so memorably in Coketown. It is, however, now well established that the development of the steam-powered factory system belongs to the nineteenth century, rather than to the eighteenth, and to the second half of the century rather than the first. Musson has cited figures which show that the total steam horse-power in British industry had probably reached no more than 35,000 hp by 1800, had risen to perhaps 300,000–400,000 by 1850 but had reached over 10 million hp by 1907 (Musson 1982). Probably fewer than 12 per cent of the British workforce was employed in factories by 1850 and as late as 1871 the average size of a manufacturing establishment was less than twenty employees. If Coketown were to be taken as a 'typical' picture of British industrialization in the mid-nineteenth century it would have to be regarded as premature, a feature likely to be found in some sectors, notably cotton, but still far from general. Indeed, craft and unmechanized trades were still the most numerous, there were more shoemakers than coalminers in 1851, and coalmining was itself hardly exemplary in its use of powered machinery, relying primarily on muscle power for the hewing and underground movement of coal. Similarly, trades such as the Sheffield cutlery industry remained virtually unmechanized, apart from powered grinding wheels, and was organized on a small workshop basis well into the twentieth century (Taylor 1988).

Although between 1801 and 1851 agriculture ceased to be the principal sector of the labour force, declining from 35.9 per cent to 21.7 per cent, it is evident that this was part of a process which had seen the rise of mining and manufacturing to almost 30.0 per cent by 1800 and was to see agriculture shrink considerably further after 1851, to approximately 8.0 per cent by 1901. In absolute terms, the number of those employed on the land was actually higher by the early nineteenth century. The rural population growth which fuelled emigration to the towns and overseas, also produced the pauperization and underemployment which commentators on the rural world described but in many cases failed to understand. Genuine depopulation, in the sense of a fall in the *absolute* numbers of the rural population was, *pace* Cobbett, only to be found in a few specialized cases. Goldsmith's famous *Deserted Village* was based on the creation of a new park at Nuneham Courtenay. This entailed the destruction of an old village and the movement of its inhabitants to a 'model' village on a new site beyond the Park (Batey 1968; Emery 1974). Enclosure, as we now know, did not necessarily lead to a reduction in the labour force required, whatever other effects it may have entailed (Chambers and Mingay 1966; Turner 1984). A relative decline of the rural population and of the agricultural labour force had certainly taken place by 1851, but it was exactly that, relative, leaving a substantial body of over 2 million agricultural workers in 1851, still by far and away the largest single occupational group.

If the spread and scale of manufacturing operations by the middle of the nineteenth century can be exaggerated, there remains a powerful line of argument from Dickens, through the Hammonds, to writers such as E. P. Thompson, that, where it occurred industrialization disrupted an older and, implicitly, better way of life (Hammond and Hammond 1925; Thompson 1968). To the Hammonds 'the rise of great industry' led to the loss of freedom and skills, an 'intellectual and moral chasm' between rich and poor, individuals dehumanized by the factory system, and an ugly and brutish life in the industrial towns (Hartwell 1966, xxi). Thompson's highly influential *The Making of the English Working Class* reiterated this view. While accepting the case made by Hartwell and others that there might have been some overall improvement in material living standards in the half century before the 1840s, it was bought at a price of 'intensified exploitation, greater insecurity, and increasing human misery'. Such 'slight improvement' as took place was suffered 'as a catastrophic experience' (Thompson 1968, 231). But catastrophe seems too strong a phrase to describe a process which we have come to see as protracted, piecemeal, and subject to highly complex variations of environment and experience. On the ground the Industrial Revolution was often experienced as a gradual quickening of economic activity during the course of the eighteenth century. As early as 1728 Defoe had noted that the 'great towns of Manchester, Warrington, Macclesfield, Hallifax [sic], Leeds, Wakefield, Sheffield, Birmingham, Froome [sic], Taunton, Tiverton and others ... they are full of Wealth, and full of People, and daily increasing in both; all of which is occasioned by the meer Strength of Trade, and the growing Manufactures establish'd in them'. Even with the acceleration which took place from the end of the eighteenth century or, in some cases, rather later, the long-term character of the growth of manufacturing did permit some adjustment to change. Moreover, economic growth was occurring frequently in places which were established settlements, giving them the ability to make some response to the new conditions.

While it would be pointless to minimize the problems posed of poor sanitation, inadequate housing and pollution, it is equally dangerous to ignore the attempts made to ameliorate them. To take one example, Sheffield rose from a population of approximately 9,000 in 1736 to over 40,000 by the 1790s. This rapid growth did not prevent some refurbishment and development of civic amenities. An Assembly Rooms and theatre were built in 1762, a new market in 1786, and a number of new, large chapels established by the early nineteenth century. Although these may have touched the life of the labouring classes only very marginally, it would be a profound error to suggest that older, even unincorporated communities were completely swamped by the growth of population. Indeed, several showed some vigour in responding to new needs, the booming silk town of Macclesfield saw the building of an impressive Sunday School institution serving over 2,000 pupils by 1812; the opening of a town dispensary in 1814; a private Act of Parliament 'for the better Lighting, Watching and Improvement' of the town in the same year; and in 1823 the reorganization of the market area and a rebuilt Town Hall. In 1825 a further Act appointed Police Commissioners to improve the town's paving and lighting. Modest and limited these improvements may have been but they serve to demonstrate that some attempt was being made to grapple with the consequences of rapid urbanization even if on an *ad hoc* basis and with antiquated instruments (Davis 1961; Malmgreen 1985). It is extremely misleading to use the language of the 'frontier town' or 'urban chaos' to describe the reality of the experience of urban growth in most parts of England and Wales in this period. The true frontier towns, communities built up almost from nothing on the basis of industrial development were rarer than is often recognized, most urban development took place within the framework of existing administrative structures, often inadequate no doubt, but often showing more resilience than they have been given credit for. Incorporation, especially after 1835, provided the mechanism by which a more rapid and systematic response became possible. Even where there was mushroom growth, as in the middle and late Victorian boom towns such as Middlesbrough and Birkenhead, what is surprising is not how little was achieved in a short space of time, but how much. Middlesbrough was represented by a solitary farmhouse in 1821, by 1862 it had almost 20,000 inhabitants and 75,000 by 1891. The efforts of the Pease family to establish a plan for the new settlement ensured some order in its development and a complement of churches. First generation Middlesbrough has been described as 'quite civilized' by the standards of the time (Bell and Bell 1972, 186). Although presented with appalling problems of housing and living conditions with the opening of the Cleveland iron ore fields after 1851 and a huge influx of population, some attempt was made to furnish the town with an infirmary, parks, schools and public buildings (Briggs 1963).

This impression of something less than wholesale catastrophe in the face of an urban population explosion is reinforced by the work of Anderson on the structure of the urban communities in early-nineteenth-century Lancashire. Anderson shows that there was a remarkably strong development of close kinship relations in the cotton towns, partly as a defence against the major vicissitudes of life, sickness, unemployment and death. Far from the migrant to the early industrial town being thrown into a maelstrom of an anarchic and 'soulless' environment, many sought out kin or neighbours for support and sought to live near people from the same area as themselves. A recent overview of urban life between 1776 and 1851 has argued that 'the family survived, intact, the continuing process of change shaped by urbanisation and industrialisation'. Indeed, the early experiences of town life may have strengthened a purely instrumental kin-relationship before the development of the neighbourly solidarities and sense of 'community' later to be associated with working-class urban life (Anderson 1971; Walvin 1984). The new industrial settlements may have been as much 'slums of hope' where survival strategies produced strong new relationships and better opportunities as they were areas of acute social deprivation. In practice they could be both. The birth of the working-class community with its associated mores, communal self-help, and often vigorous informal economy was as much the product of industrialization as the dreadful physical environment which many had to endure (Benson 1989).

But to what extent was industrialization purchased at the price of a fall in material living standards? To an extent, as Thompson's remarks, cited above, indicate, something of the steam has gone out of the debate. There is now at least partial agreement that there was scope for some rise in material living standards even in the first phase of industrial growth before 1850. 'Pessimists' have tended rather to concentrate their argument on the 'quality of life' in the face of what we know of national indices of output and consumption. But the experience of particular families and groups of workers is still difficult to assess because of the nature of the evidence. There are very few actual records of hours and days worked by individuals, or detailed evidence of expenditures on food, housing and other necessities. It is even more difficult to make an accurate assessment of household 'income' as a whole, taking into account non-mainstream earnings and non-money exchanges of goods and services. Those records that do exist provide us only with examples for specific households in particular localities. That being said, in so far as the broad movements of prices and wage rates can be taken into account, we can, perhaps, isolate some of the main features in the debate. There was an overall rise in real incomes per head in the country as a whole and a large-scale subsistence catastrophe such as that which affected Ireland in the 1840s was avoided. Britain was able to sustain a trebling of population in the century before 1861 and feed it largely from its own resources. Clear evidence of rising real incomes for the working classes is most apparent for the later nineteenth century, but evidence for the period before 1850 is more patchy. This is particularly true if we look at shorter periods and particular groups. To take only one example, the Revolutionary and Napoleonic Wars occupy a crucial twenty-three years in the middle of the era of the Industrial Revolution. Here there is substantial evidence that particular periods of harvest crisis and inflated food prices produced a fall in real wages of a substantial magnitude. Compared with the relatively 'normal' year of 1790, real wages were as much as 10 per cent down in 1795 and down by as much as 20 per cent in the even worse crisis of 1800–1. Although neither of these episodes produced 'famine', they produced extensive hardship and considerable contemporary comment about the need to relieve the unparalleled hardships of the labouring classes (O'Brien and Engerman 1981; Wells 1988). Similarly, the postwar depression with its high unemployment, and the early 1840s, stand out as episodes of short-term deterioration in whatever direction long-term trends were pointing.

To these temporal fluctuations must be added the plight of those who failed to benefit from economic growth or were adversely affected by it. One group were the pauperized agricultural labourers whose real wage rates seem barely to have improved much before the mid-nineteenth century. But in the light of what we now know about population growth, occurring on the land as well as in the towns, it has become difficult to see the agricultural labourer as a 'victim' of economic growth, still less of industrialization, rather more of the effects of overpopulation and chronic underemployment in rural areas. A more telling case can be made for the groups rendered technologically obsolescent by mechanization, those whose skills, traditions and values were placed under pressure by economic change. The struggle of individual groups of workers, particularly skilled artisans, to defend their status and earnings was often a losing one in a period of rapid technological change and economic development. Whatever long-term series and aggregate statistics may tell us, the experience of particular trades and occupations, notably those such as the handloom weavers and wool croppers, could be one of a deterioration in both status and earning power (Rule 1986). It is apparent that the sheer complexity of the mosaic of occupational groups and their differing circumstances will always provide ammunition for both 'optimists' and 'pessimists', at least in the period before 1850. The situation becomes even more complex if we add to the male-centred concept of principal occupation that of family earnings. Again, the ability of women and children to find work in changed technological and economic circumstances would have played a critical part in the standard of living of particular families.

If some aspects of the standard of living debate remain almost intractably difficult to determine in the earlier part of the nineteenth century, there are advantages to be gained in using the more sophisticated analyses of 'poverty' that became available in the latter part of the nineteenth century. The work of men such as Rowntree and Booth to measure poverty and establish standards of minimum requirements provide important pointers to how we might consider the standard of living and the likely experience of poverty earlier in the century. Rowntree's findings of a family 'poverty cycle' were based on a rigorous assessment of human needs measured in terms of the income required to purchase food and shelter. His argument, based on the York survey, was that the majority of the working class was likely to suffer poverty at three phases in their lives: as young children, when household per capita income might prove insufficient to meet minimum human needs; as adults with a numerous young family, for the same reason; and when elderly and too old to work. In many respects, this age-old pattern of fluctuating life fortunes, present in preindustrial society and still evident in the twentieth century, was the major influence on the actual experience of millions of households. If, at the end of the nineteenth century, when a rise in average real wage rates of a substantial degree is incontestable a third of all working-class families were living below a minimum standard of human needs and approximately a half of all deaths occurred in the workhouse, we might be wise not to exaggerate the rise in real living standards, measured solely in terms of averages, that had occurred. As a result, the standard of living debate remains finely poised. The sheer complexity of circumstances affecting individuals and households defies succinct generalization. Problems of evidence about wages and prices, and especially about regularity of employment and household income bedevil the argument. The influence of changes over time, periods of price fluctuation, trade boom and slump, and the fortunes of particular groups of workers, as well as the operation of the 'family cycle' of changing demands upon households permit a wide range of interpretation. Long term, however, a powerful argument remains that it was only through economic growth that Britain avoided the wholesale pauperization which population growth brought to Ireland and much of rural Europe during the nineteenth century. As Hartwell noted some years ago, to a large extent 'the problems caused or inherited by industrialization were solved by industrialization, by the productivity of the new industrial system' (Hartwell 1966, xxi). Whatever the hardships caused along the way, economic growth and industrialization held the key to a wider affluence for a greatly enlarged population, even if sections of the population had to wait until the twentieth century to reap the benefits.

But what of the voice of the common people themselves – those absorbing the effects of economic change and the abstract movements of wage and price indices? Almost from the beginning of the study of industrialization, historians have sought access to the attitudes of the artisans, labourers and their families in the protest movements which appear to dominate so much of the story of early industrialization. No account of the social impact of economic change is complete without its reference to machine-breakers, food-rioters, and agricultural unrest. The early historians of the process, notably the Hammonds, placed the rise of crime and protest on the agenda as one of the symptoms of a crisis-torn and profoundly disordered 'new civilization'. High points in their account of the experiences both of the skilled textile workers and the agricultural labourers were the great episodes of popular protest, the Luddite outbreaks in the Midlands and the North in 1810–12 and the 'Captain Swing' disturbances in the early 1830s through much of the southern England. Both were seen as doomed, defensive actions by workers faced with economic change which threatened their livelihood (Hammond and Hammond 1917, 1919). This emphasis upon the degree to which economic change was resisted and marked by violent protest has become a significant debate with the burgeoning studies of crime and disorder in recent years. To some extent the Hammonds received support from the work of E. P. Thompson through his discussion of the Luddites in *The Making of the English Working Class* and in his analysis of food riots and other protests in the eighteenth century. What Thompson added was a powerful argument that these forms of protest were a symptom of the breakdown of an older, paternalistic 'moral economy' of work and reward, of pricing and retailing, which was being ruthlessly discarded with the adoption of laissez-faire economics (Thompson 1968, 1971). Thus skilled workmen were forced into violent confrontation with their masters and, ultimately, with the authorities to resist the introduction of new machinery or the use of machinery in ways which abrogated traditional norms of independence and reward. In the same way food riots reached a crescendo as consumers were exposed to the operation of full effects of free trade and marketing in foodstuffs, culminating in the large waves of disturbances which affected the country in 1795–6 and 1800–1, the greatest and the last, of such nation-wide protests.

But a generation of research into the nature and motives of popular protest has led historians to adopt a somewhat more cautious attitude to these manifestations of protest. Luddism was undoubtedly a major and protracted episode of unrest, but we now know that it rests against a background of sporadic and varied responses to machinery and new work practices. The work of Hobsbawm and Rule have placed the most well-known episode of machine-breaking by the Luddites into a context in which attacks upon machines formed part of a wider repertoire of bargaining and protest which can be traced as early as the seventeenth century and continued well into the nineteenth. (Hobsbawm 1968; Rule 1986). Often such attacks were not resistance to machinery itself, but attempts to regulate its use or bring pressure to bear upon masters by threatening damage to an important capital asset. The Luddite outbreaks have thereby lost something of the apocalyptic significance with which they have been endowed both by incautious proponents of economic change and by those who wish to see them as defenders of a 'traditional' way of life. The Luddites were not blind opponents of machinery; in the hosiery districts where machine-breaking began on an extensive scale in March 1811 hostility was directed against masters who underpaid or produced the cheaper 'cut up' stockings using unskilled labour. None of these grievances were new in 1811, but unemployment, wage cuts and depressed trade as a result of the closure of the American market to British goods and the effects of the Continental System brought grievances to a head. As significant, other attempts to achieve favourable regulation of the trade had failed, forcing the workmen to turn to violent means of coercing the masters. Even so, the attacks were selective, aimed primarily at the masters who were seen as exploitative and 'unfair'. It is as absurd to see the Nottinghamshire Luddites as opponents of machinery as it is to see them as a 'quasi-insurrectionary movement' (Thompson 1968, 604). It is perhaps more sensible to see most of the machine-breaking in the East Midlands as part of a protracted period of what Hobsbawm graphically described as 'collective bargaining by riot'. The point is reinforced by the recurrence of machine-breaking in the area in 1814 after its suppression by the deployment of troops and the making of frame-breaking a capital offence in February 1812. When attempts by a United Committee of Framework Knitters to promote a Bill to regulate the trade failed and the workmen were prosecuted under the Combination Laws, frame-breaking was resumed and continued sporadically until 1816. In Yorkshire, similarly, the spread of machine-breaking amongst the croppers came after the frustration of attempts to regulate the trade by other means and during a season of particularly high prices and unemployment. The campaign against shearing frames had been waged from the end of the eighteenth century using a wide variety of means, in which violence was only one strand, although the one which has attracted most attention (Stevenson 1979, 155–62).

Violence attracts attention, but in the case of the Luddites it is important that it should be seen in the context of varying attempts to adjust to economic and technological change. Luddism marked a phase in that adjustment, provoked by exceptional circumstances of economic warfare and a poor season. But before, during and after the Luddite outbreaks workmen sought more prosaic means of coping with the changes taking place. The textile districts saw a series of strikes, combinations and negotiations between workmen and employers, including the first strikes by the cotton spinners of Lancashire. The spinners conducted strikes in 1799, 1800, 1802 and 1803. In 1810 they carried on a four-month stoppage supported by subscriptions totalling £17,000 drawn from several parts of the north. Only a fraction of the ink devoted to Luddism has been expended on one of the most impressive examples of early trade union organization, the strike by the Scottish and north of England cotton weavers in late 1812, in which 40,000 looms remained idle for six weeks over an area from Cumbria to Aberdeen. Concentration on Luddism should not obscure the most obvious feature of these years, the ability of workmen to organize themselves and to deploy a range of tactics, of which violence and machine-breaking could play a part, in order to make the best accommodation they could to change. If these actions were often defensive, they were not exclusively either backward-looking or unsuccessful. Records of individual disputes even under the restrictions of the Combination Laws of 1799 and 1800 reveal that it was possible for workmen to behave as something other than helpless victims (Stevenson, 1979, 151–5).

Similarly, it remains too simple to see food riots as a symptom of mass deprivation brought to new depths in the last years of the eighteenth century. In spite of much abuse of the term 'famine', famine proper was a distant memory by the time Britain embarked on the beginnings of industrialization in the latter part of the eighteenth century. The last 'killing famine' in the form of a classic 'crisis of subsistence' had occurred as far back as the 1620s in England, though more recently in Scotland. Food riots, which more properly should be termed price-riots, appear to have developed from the early modern period, only reaching epidemic proportions in the latter part of the eighteenth century. Primarily an urban phenomenon, they marked the response of consumers to an increasingly market-oriented trade in foodstuffs. That being said, it is notable that the major aspects of food rioting in England and Wales appear to have occurred some time after the food trade became largely deregulated and when the experience of marketing of produce of all kinds was well established. The largest outbreaks of food rioting at the end of the eighteenth century came not when people were being exposed to the market mechanism for the first time, but long afterwards. Indeed, in many parts of the country, such as the small textile towns of the south-west, price-riots had become a fairly routine part of what John Bohstedt has called 'community politics'; less a desperate reaction to deprivation than an ongoing process of negotiation with the local authorities. Moreover, as indicated above, these disturbances were very largely a small-town phenomenon, a feature of the small market town or the proto-industrial 'industrial village'. Although it is the case that in the later harvest crises, particularly that of 1800–1, price-riots began to affect the larger industrializing communities more markedly, this was a relatively short-lived phenomenon. Price riots on a nation-wide scale became a thing of the past after the end of the Napoleonic Wars, increasingly replaced by strikes, machine-breaking, collective bargaining, and political agitation. The era of price riots was therefore largely over when the most rapid phase of industrialization began after 1815 (Bohstedt 1983; Stevenson 1979, 91–112).

There is a difficulty then in representing the various forms of violent protest that occurred in the century or so after 1750 as part of a response to industrialization, if we mean by that phrase the coming of the factory system and the development of large factory towns. Historians have sometimes been guilty of lumping together all episodes of violence and disorder, from whatever cause or occasion as part of the reaction to industrialization. In practice this was far from the case. Price-riots and machine-breaking belonged to strategies of protest and negotiation which had a long history and were to reach a peak in the years between 1795 and 1816 as much because of the peculiar and difficult conditions of the Napoleonic Wars as any direct consequence of industrialization. Similarly, a tendency to invoke the unrest surrounding the agitation for parliamentary reform, especially in the years between 1816 and 1821, as part of a reaction to industrialization, is liable to confuse rather than clarify. The forcible dispersal of the reform meeting at St Peter's Fields in August 1819 – 'Peterloo' – is often taken to symbolize a whole era. In fact, the violence inflicted was wholly the responsibility of the authorities for a clumsy and inept attempt to control an otherwise peaceful mass meeting for reform. What remains striking about the early agitation for parliamentary reform was less that it produced large-scale, violent and insurrectionary movement but rather that it saw the fashioning of peaceful forms of organization and pressure, political societies, mass demonstrations, petitioning, and the development of an effective radical press. A similar confusion affects the protracted period of agitation on the part of the

Chartists. That the late 1830s and 1840s were a period of political tension is in no doubt; at least on occasions the Chartists appeared to threaten a major alteration in the balance of political power. What was evident, however, was the utilization of what were essentially means of peaceful protest, the mass petition, demonstrations, the articulation of grievances via the Chartist press, notably the *Northern Star*. Moreover the nature of the contribution of new factory workers to the agitation was through industrial action. The rolling strike wave which affected many parts of the north in the summer of 1842, known as the 'Plug-plot' riots, was notable as an example of industrial workers using strike action, backed up with a degree of intimidation, to combat wage-cuts, longer hours and truck payments.

Ultimately it became a General Strike for the Charter, having been initiated very much in the tradition of earlier stoppages which used machine-breaking and intimidation. The scale of this effort was greater, perhaps, than ever before, a consequence of the severity of the depression in 1842. But in spite of its capture for a time by the Chartists, it remained essentially a strike movement in which the organizers went to some pains to insist on their orderly and law abiding nature. That the organizers were unable to prevent some violence occurring and that the authorities reacted with some severity, arresting over 1,000 people and killing several in clashes with troops, should not prevent us from seeing the development of trade union-like responses from the workers involved. Apart from what appears the more genuinely quasi-insurrectionary movement in South Wales in the autumn of 1839, and what look like insurrectionary attempts in Dewsbury and Sheffield in January 1840, much of the 'unrest' of the Chartist era lay within the context of collective bargaining (Jones 1981). In so far as 'physical force' Chartism had a core of support it seems to have drawn it from the declining trades, the handloom weavers, nailmakers and the like. Cotton operatives, potters, engineers and miners were less well represented in direct agitation for the Charter with weaker support in the more prosperous 'new' industrial communities such as St Helens, Crewe and the more prosperous parts of the textile industry. The lack of willingness on the part of some better-placed workers to join in random violence was demonstrated again in the early months of 1848. When several thousand poor and unemployed paraded about Glasgow in March 1848, calling on mills and other works to join them in protests, it was reported that the workmen manned the walls of their premises and 'bade them defiance'. Two days later when similar disturbances broke out in Manchester, the millworkers again refused to join in, in one instance the 'hands' issuing from the factory to beat up the protesters (Stevenson 1979, 266-7).

The development of organized political protest and an increasingly developed form of industrial action by workmen tend to militate against the idea that industrialization brought only despair, disorganization and wretchedness to the factory operatives. On the contrary, what is evident at local level is the richness and fertility of workers' responses, including the foundation of many of the most significant institutional and cultural features of the Victorian period, the Co-operative movement, temperance groups, mechanics' institutes, Building Societies and Savings Clubs, as well as trade unions, religious associations and political groupings. Indeed, one of the most trenchantly-argued studies of the working-class in this period from an avowedly Marxist perspective suggests that in places such as Oldham, the 'working class' were already obtaining control over the levers of local power by the 1840s (Foster 1974). In Sheffield, another stronghold of popular radicalism, the principal effort of the local Chartists was devoted to getting representatives elected to the town council. Such developments serve as a reminder that the dense network of working class organizations which we normally associate with the age of mid- and late-Victorian 'stability' have their origins much earlier. Some historians have argued that the 1840s mark a decisive break in which an insurgent working-class movement was compromised and defeated. From this perspective, the employment of the power of the state to suppress the Chartists coerced a still highly vulnerable workforce into accepting the dominant economical and ideological assumptions of Victorian capitalism. Whether this defeat was primarily the result of a failure of the early working-class to develop an appropriate ideology to cope with the realities of the 'new civilization' is still a matter for debate amongst some historians (Stedman Jones 1971; Saville 1987). Others would argue, however, that radical alternatives had never captured the degree of support in the 1830s and 1840s which would make such an interpretation viable. Piecemeal, reformist action had already become part of the response of working-class leaders and their followers, even while others sought a more full-blooded reconstruction of the world about them. Accommodation and adaptation, a working with rather than against, had long roots, not least in the early trade societies which formed the most important and persistent forms of working-class organization in the early industrial towns. In this context it was hardly surprising that many trade unionists in the 1840s were somewhat ambivalent towards Chartism, a movement they saw as increasingly tainted with 'unrespectable' violence and whose larger aims diverted them from more immediate concerns about wages and conditions of work. Causes which offered more immediate prospects of attainment, the anti-Corn Law agitation, factory reform, and mitigation of the New Poor Law often tempted ambitious and committed working-class men as much, if not more than Chartism (Stevenson 1982, 29–32).

Such a perspective fits in with the general thrust of scholarship in recent years which suggests a more evolutionary perspective in both the social and political repercussions of industrialization. If there was no sharp break between a period of 'insurgency' and one of 'acquiescence', or at least if the break was very much less so than has sometimes been suggested, we can see that the roots of 'labourism' and reformism lie not in some abrupt change of direction after the 1840s but in the responses to industrialization almost from its outset and in the nature of British industrialization as a whole. It was a relatively long-drawn out process, which provided opportunities for adjustment and accommodation from an early stage. Political clubs of working men, trade societies, friendly societies and benefit clubs, religious groups dominated by the working class, and attempts to influence the existing political establishment through peaceful agitation, all had their origins in the eighteenth century and with the development of a more sophisticated working class in the course of the next century were to develop characteristic forms of organization and response which survived into the twentieth. Much of the debate about why there was no political upheaval in Britain in the nineteenth century analogous to that which occurred on the Continent and why it failed to develop a strong Marxist party in the late nineteenth and early twentieth centuries hinges on the peculiar nature of British industrialization. Its protracted and uneven character has been seen as playing a major part in allowing the emergence of strong sectional interests within the working class, the development and elaboration of vertical ties of deference and association, the cultivation of local affinities to region, town and workplace, and, ultimately, the acceptance of a reformist political stance (McKibbin 1984; Kirk 1985).

III

Any review of the social consequences of the Industrial Revolution has to come to terms with both its image and its reality. The public recognition that Britain was becoming an industrial nation dates, as we have seen, from the early Victorian period. In practice, however, even as late as 1850, much of what would be defined as industrialization had still to occur. But for something like another century, the debate upon the effects of industrialization was carried on in terms which took its character from the ruralist lament of Cobbett and the urban concerns of the 'Condition of England' novelists. Glossed increasingly with nostalgia, the rural world was counterposed to the squalor and misery of urban life. Sensitive evocations of rural life in both painting and literature became popular, generally more affirmative, affectionate and less openly condemnatory than those of Cobbett, seen for example in the writings of Flora Thompson, published on the eve of the Second World War (Thompson 1939). Side by side, intensified by the inter-war depression, lay the powerful image of landscape despoiled by industrialization, of which Llewellyn's *How Green Was My Valley*, turned into a highly emotive film in 1941, is perhaps the epitome. Similarly, the compendium compiled by the great lyric poet of the British wartime documentary cinema, Humphrey Jennings, *Pandaemonium* (Jennings 1985) speaks volumes for the received cultural impact of industrialization. From 1937 Jennings collected items which testified to the impact of the 'Machine' from the late seventeenth century to the end of the nineteenth. It was motivated by his belief that 'the coming of the Machine was destroying something in our life '; his political beliefs he described as 'those of William Cobbett' (Jennings and Madge eds. 1985, xii). Nor were such views surprising for writers and artists who lived in a world still shaped by the Industrial Revolution and recognisably similar to that witnessed by the first generation of critics of industrial society. When Priestley toured the country on his *English Journey* in the autumn of 1933, one of the 'Englands' he found was:

the nineteenth-century England, the industrial England of coal, iron, steel, cotton, wool, railways; of thousands of rows of little houses all alike, sham Gothic churches, square-faced chapels, Town Halls, Mechanics Institutes, mills, foundaries, warehouses ... a cynically devastated countryside, sooty dismal little towns, and still sootier grim fortress-like cities. This England makes up the larger part of the Midlands and the North and exists everywhere ... (Priestley 1934, 398–9)

It was the same 'England' that Orwell found in Wigan and Sheffield in the later thirties and could, of course, be found in industrial South Wales and central Scotland.

When Priestley and Orwell saw it, it was an industrial England 'on short time' in the inter-war depression, whose decay and dereliction were to inform planners and policy makers during the thirties and were to be released in a flood of optimistic plans for the future during the Second World War. There was little doubt that what was to be swept away was the legacy of 'Coketown'. In its 'Plan for Britain' special issue in January 1941 the photo-documentary magazine *Picture Post* carried a double spread which contrasted the urban squalor of the industrial landscape with the new 'planned' vision of ordered redevelopment, high-rise flats, unpolluted water and access to the countryside. Rebuilt cities and slum clearance would replace the damage wrought by more than a century of industrial growth (Stevenson 1987). To some extent these proposals were put into effect, but in many parts of Britain the legacy of the Industrial Revolution remained substantially intact into the 1950s and 1960s. It meant that in many industrial areas, certainly outside the largest cities and the show-piece 'New Towns', there was a continuum of environment and experience with the nineteenth century. Only with the mass development of towns and cities from the 1950s, the wholesale destruction of hundreds of acres of nineteenth-century housing, and the radical shrinkage of the industrial base upon which many of the older communities depended did large segments of the British population break the links with the world conjured up by Dickens. The very proximity of that world ending, in some cases, barely the day before yesterday is a reminder that in dealing with the Industrial Revolution in its classic phase up to the mid-nineteenth century, we are, in fact, analysing only the beginnings of a process whose repercussions in the social sphere are only now beginning to be put into full perspective.

REFERENCES

Anderson, M. 1971. *Family Structure in Nineteenth Century Lancashire*.
Ashton, T. S. 1948. *The Industrial Revolution, 1760–1830*.
Batey, M. 1968. 'Nuneham Courtenay: an Oxfordshire 18th century Deserted Village', *Oxoniensia*, 33, 108–24.
Bell, C. and R. Bell. 1972. *City Fathers: the early history of town planning in Britain*.
Bohstedt, J. 1983. *Riots and Community Politics in England and Wales, 1790–1810*.
Borsay, P. 1989. *The English Urban Renaissance: culture and society in the provincial town, 1660–1770*.
Briggs, A. 1963. *Victorian Cities*.
Chalkin, C. W. 1974. *The Provincial Towns of Georgian England*.
Chambers, J. D. and Mingay, G. E. 1966. *The Agricultural Revolution, 1750–1880*.
Cobbett, W. 1830. 1967. *Rural Rides*.
Corfield, P. 1982. *The Impact of English Towns, 1700–1800*.
Crafts, N. F. R. 1985. *British Economic Growth during the Industrial Revolution*.
Davies, D. 1795. *The Case of the Labourers in Husbandry*.
Eden, Sir F. M. 1797. *The State of the Poor*, 3 vols.
Emery, F. 1974. *The Oxfordshire Landscape*.
Emsley, C. 1987. *Crime and Society in England, 1750–1900*.
Fores, M. 1981. 'The myth of a British Industrial Revolution', *History*, 66.
Foster, J. 1974. *Class Struggle and the Industrial Revolution. Early industrial capitalism in three English towns*.
Hammond, J. L. and B. 1912. *The Village Labourer*.
    1917. *The Town Labourer*.
    1925. *The Rise of Modern Industry*.
Hartwell, R. M. 1966. 'Introduction', in J. L. and B. Hammond, *The Rise of Modern Industry*, 9th edn.
Hueckel, G. 1981. 'Agriculture during industrialization', in *The Economic History of Britain since 1700*, I, *1700–1860*, ed. R. Floud and D. McCloskey, 182–203.
Jennings, H. 1985. *Pandaemonium, 1660–1886*, ed. M. L. Jennings and C. Madge.
Jones, E. I. 1981. 'Agriculture, 1700–80', in *The Economic History of Britain since 1700, I, 1700–1860*, ed. R. Floud and D. McCloskey, 66–86.

Kirk, N. 1985. *The Growth of Working Class Reformism in mid-Victorian England.*

Landa, L. A. 1980. 'London observed: the progress of a similie', in *Essays in Eighteenth Century English Literature.*

Lee, R. E. and Schofield, R. S. 1981. 'British population in the eighteenth century', in *The Economic History of Britain since 1700*, I, *1700–1860*, ed. R. Floud and D. McCloskey, 17–35.

McCloskey, D. 1981. 'The industrial revolution 1780–1860: a survey', in *The Economic History of Britain since 1700*, I, *1700–1860*, ed. R. Floud and D. McCloskey, 103–27.

McKibbin, R. 1984. 'Why was there no marxism in Great Britain?' *English Historical Review*, 94, 297–331.

Malmgreen, G. 1985. *Silk Town: industry and culture in Macclesfield, 1750–1835.*

Marsh, J. 1982. *Back to the Land: the pastoral impulse in Victorian England from 1880 to 1914.*

More, C. 1989. *The Industrial Age: economy and society in Britain 1750–1985.*

Musson, A. E. 1982. 'The British Industrial Revolution', *History*, 67.

O'Brien, P. K. and Engerman, S. L. 1981. 'Changes in income and its distribution during the Industrial Revolution', in *Economic History of Britain since 1700*, ed. R. Floud and D. McCloskey, I, pp. 164–81.

Perkin, H. 1969. *The Origins of Modern English Society.*

Plumb, J. H. 1973. *The Commercialisation of Leisure in Eighteenth Century England.*

Porter, R. 1982. *English Society in the Eighteenth Century.*

Priestley, J. B. 1934. *English Journey.*

Royle, E. 1987. *Modern Britain: a social history, 1750–1985.*

Rudé, G. 1971. *Hanoverian London, 1714–1808.*

Rule, J. 1986. *The Labouring Classes in Early Industrial England, 1750–1850.*

Snell, K. D. M. 1985. *Annals of the Labouring Poor: social change and the agrarian England, 1660–1900.*

Stedman Jones, G. 1971. *Outcast London. A study of the relationship between classes in Victorian Society.*

Stella Davies, C. 1961. *A History of Macclesfield.*

Stevenson, J. 1977a. 'Introduction', in *London in the Age of Reform*, J. Stevenson (ed.), xiii–xxvi.

   1977b. 'Social control and the prevention of riots in England', in *Social Control in Nineteenth Century Britain*, ed. A. P. Donajgrodski, 27–50.

   1979. *Popular Disturbances in England 1700–1870.*

   1982. 'Early trade unionism: radicalism and respectability, 1750–1870', in *Trade Unions in British Politics*, ed. B. Pimlott and C. P. Cook.

   1987. 'Planners' Moon? The planning movement and the Second World War in Britain', in *War and Social Change*, ed. H. Smith, 58–77.

   1988. 'The New Jerusalem', in *The Making of Britain: echoes of greatness*, ed. L. Smith, 53–71.

Swenarton, M. 1981. *Homes Fit for Heroes: the politics and architecture of early state housing in Britain.*

Taylor, S. A. 1988. 'The Sheffield cutlery trades, 1870–1914', University of Sheffield Ph.D. thesis.

Thompson, E. P. 1968. *The Making of the English Working Class.*

1971. The moral economy of the English crowd in the eighteenth century', *Past and Present*, 50, 76–136.

Thompson, F. 1939. *Lark Rise to Candleford*.

Tillotson, K. 1954. *Novels of the Eighteen-Forties*.

Tranter, N. 1973. *Population since the Industrial Revolution: the case of England and Wales*.

1985. *Population and Society, 1750–1940: contrasts in population growth*.

Turner, M. 1984. *Enclosures in Britain, 1750–1830*.

Walvin, J. 1984. *English Urban Life, 1776–1851*.

Weber, A. F. 1899. *The Growth of Cities in the Nineteenth Century*.

Wells, R. 1988. *Wretched Faces: famine in wartime England, 1793–1803*.

Wiener, M. J. 1981. *English Culture and the Decline of the Industrial Spirit, 1850–1980*.

Wrigley, E. A. 1983. 'The growth of population in eighteenth-century England: a conundrum resolved', *Past and Present*, 98.

Wrigley, E. A. and Schofield, R. S. 1983. 'English population history from family reconstitution: summary results, 1600–1799', *Population Studies*, 37, 2.

11 Technological and organizational change in industry during the early Industrial Revolution

G. N. von Tunzelmann

Introduction

Four propositions about the Industrial Revolution have been advanced:
  (i) that the Industrial Revolution represented a 'great discontinuity' in economic growth, possibly the most important;
  (ii) that industrialization represented a 'great discontinuity', but capitalism did not;
  (iii) that the Industrial Revolution was a case of 'balanced growth';
  (iv) that organizational change, notably the rise of the 'factory system', was at least as important as technological change in the Industrial Revolution.

These views may seem difficult to reconcile, but they have in fact formed the major argument of four distinct papers by Max Hartwell (1967, 1970c, 1969, 1971, ch. 9; 1970b). This chapter reappraises those views for their logical and historical consistency. For this, conventional economic analysis is of little use, which may be one reason why so few generalizations about industry during the early Industrial Revolution have yet emerged. Complexity is inevitable, but I aim to reduce such complexity as far as possible by applying a similar approach to four separable aspects of industrial change. For reasons of space, the scope of this chapter is largely limited to the early Industrial Revolution (eighteenth century) and to England rather than Great Britain. For the same reason, the important issue of the role of labour in industry is not dealt with in detail (for surveys see Dobson 1980; Malcolmson 1981; Rule 1981).

What is done here is to split industry into four spheres, described as 'techniques', 'processes', 'operations' and 'marketing'. Each sphere represents a specific choice out of the range of possibilities historically available – the four functions of 'technology', 'organization', 'management/ finance' and 'products'. The basic argument is that a 'Great Discontinuity'

I am most grateful to the editors and to Joel Mokyr for extensive help with a rough early draft.

must involve a sizeable shift in all the feasible options realistically attainable, i.e. the functions just mentioned.

By doing this, I aim to go 'inside the black box' of the firm in conventional economics (the phrase comes from Rosenberg 1982). It is, however, only a component of a broader model derived from classical economics (Adam Smith, Ricardo, Malthus, etc.; see von Tunzelmann 1989).

Technology

The most likely arena for any radical change is that of technology. T. S. Ashton quoted a schoolboy essay as saying that, 'about 1760 a wave of gadgets swept over England' (Ashton 1948, 48). A fuller treatment of technology and technological change than space permits here is contained in a complementary study (von Tunzelmann 1990a), which also concentrates more on the early nineteenth century than the eighteenth century as here.

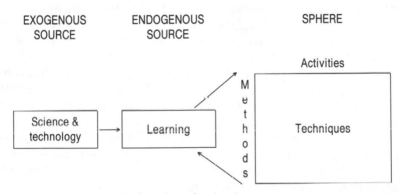

Figure 11.1   The function of technology

In Figure 11.1 the specific choices of technique are charted as particular 'methods' (on the vertical or input axis) to achieve particular outputs, here termed 'activities'. Methods are thus ways of doing things, and activities are what is done. New types of activities are often known as 'product innovations', and new methods as 'process innovations'. The central issue is the adoption of new 'gadgets' – process innovations principally in the form of machine technologies.

The summary by Landes (1969, 41) is well known:

the substitution of machines – rapid, regular, precise, tireless – for human skill and effort; the substitution of inanimate for animate sources of power, in particular, the introduction of engines for converting heat into work, thereby opening to man a new and almost unlimited supply of energy; the use of new and far more abundant raw materials, in particular, the substitution of mineral for vegetable or animal substances.

The latter two will be related here to the first principle, of mechanization.

In the language of Figure 11.1, most work by economists on the diffusion of innovation looks at the spread of a new method in one particular activity. What Landes is instead emphasizing is the diffusion of mechanization etc. across a whole range of activities.

Landes, along with much popular opinion, concentrates on the labour-saving characteristics of machinery. It will be argued here that this is a misleading depiction of the main thrust of eighteenth-century technical changes. In the first place, there was comparatively little incentive in terms of input prices to substitute capital for labour. Most studies of the standard of living have indicated that the average price of labour as reflected in real wage rates failed to rise substantially until the 1820s at least; although there were two notable exceptions. In the north of England – though not in the south – wages rose quite sharply in the late 1750s and early 1760s (von Tunzelmann 1979), closing though not yet eliminating the gap with southern wages. It was in this period, and especially in the north, that some of the most famous inventions of the Industrial Revolution were made, and the link between rising (if still low) wages and invention may have been more than coincidental, although it has never actually been proven. Not only did the most famous inventions in spinning happen to take place then, but societies like the Society of Arts additionally offered prizes for improved spinning technology (none of which went to the most famous) (Smelser 1959, 82–5). A second period of labour shortage arose at the end of the eighteenth century, associated with the French and Napoleonic Wars, when at one time or another half a million men were engaged in the armed forces. In these years, the most serious disputes involved the substitution of unskilled for skilled labour. Any labour shortages may have necessitated substituting capital for labour in the short run, but in the longer run were generally met by population growth until the beginning of the nineteenth century (Wrigley and Schofield 1981; Coleman and Schofield 1986). Generally there was a surplus of unskilled labour, aided by Irish immigration to meet short-run shortages (Pollard 1978).

The price of capital did, however, fall; particularly in the second quarter of the eighteenth century, when interest rates roughly halved – from a customary 10 per cent or so in the seventeenth and earlier centuries down to the 5 per cent that became the widespread business custom of the later eighteenth and nineteenth centuries (periods of war excluded). The price of capital to industry is a compound of the relevant interest rate –

usually (imperfectly) related to money-market conditions – and the purchase price of capital equipment such as machinery. The latter declined
because of the inventions and innovations being discussed here. This
makes it difficult to separate cause from effect, as the falling price of
capital may have been either cause or result of technical progress. The net
outcome was evidently a cheapening of capital. Adam Smith drew attention to the capital-saving nature of innovation: 'all such improvements in
mechanicks, as enable the same number of workmen to perform an equal
quantity of work, with cheaper and simpler machinery than had been
used before, are always regarded as advantageous to every society' (Smith
1776/1976, 289). The shift of emphasis by classical economists from
division of labour to capital formation occurred in the 1830s (Berg 1980),
and reflected a shift around that time from capital-saving to labour-saving
technical change.

That capital-saving was the intention and not simply the outcome is
attested by MacLeod's exhaustive study of patenting in the seventeenth
and eighteenth centuries (MacLeod 1988, ch. 9). MacLeod has painstak-
ingly analysed each patent for the explanation given by the patentee of his
goals. Of the total of 4,480 patents traced between 1660 and 1799,
MacLeod found 1,862 that gave a sufficient specification of their goals as
to allow classification. Only 93 of these claimed to be saving labour,
whilst 690 claimed to be saving capital, and a further 116 to be saving
time. There were of course political objections to emphasising the saving
of labour in a pre-modern economy characterized by underemployment
and labour surpluses. Even with generous reclassification to include
patents that may have been 'effectively labour-saving' although they did
not claim to be, MacLeod raises the labour-saving total to only 362,
barely half the number that did actually claim to be capital-saving (cf. also
Hartwell 1967, 28).

Moreover, many innovations that at first sight do not appear capital-
saving may in fact turn out to be so (Samuelson 1965). Ashton (1955,
110–11) notes that, although the steam engine was big and bulky and
expensive to purchase, it could save the firm from investing in an alternative power source whose capital cost was even higher – a team of
horses, say. Ashton thus talks of the ability of innovation to 'liberate
capital'. Many such capital-saving advances were thus found outside of
Adam Smith's case of 'cheaper and simpler machinery'; for instance in
energy supply, in transportation and distribution, and in organization.
For example, improvements in shipping allowed more journeys to be
made each year in ships that changed little in size (Ville 1986), through
wharfside loading, steam tug handling, etc. Again, the shift from domestic
'putting-out' systems of manufacture, which could tie up goods in process

for many months, to factory production, could greatly economize upon working capital, even if it were at the cost of increasing fixed capital.

The savings of time may have been even more critical than saving capital in these very changes. While time savings are often incorporated within capital-saving, or sometimes labour-saving, technical advance, I believe that there is a strong case for giving them special emphasis. In part this was because of an increasing awareness of time ('clock time', to use the phrase of E. P. Thompson 1967) in the eighteenth century, especially with the rise of the factory. Workers sensed this through having to attend punctually, for long hours, six days a week. Their employers sensed it through increasing competition for delivery dates. Private costs to individual firms of losing sales could be very large in terms of lost reputations, even when the social costs of irregular production were quite low. In part it was because working (circulating) capital was generally much larger than fixed capital in the eighteenth-century economy (see below), implying that any savings on these items – the work in progress – had a marked impact on total production costs. It was the savings of time that accounted for the introduction of chlorine for bleaching cloth – reducing to a matter of days or even hours what had previously taken months to achieve by leaving the cloth out in the sun. Production processes in preindustrial Britain were normally laborious and time-consuming (Clarkson 1971), and the industries that underwent early industrialization were those that speeded up most (von Tunzelmann 1990b). A much-quoted figure reckons that Cort's puddling and rolling processes from the 1780s eventually raised the speed of throughput twenty-five times (Harris 1988). Though many similar instances could be quoted, especially in textiles (Pollard 1978, 155–8; von Tunzelmann 1990b), they have not yet received their due share of attention from economists or historians. They can be seen either as a shortening of the time required to produce a given product or as a higher level of output from a given quantity of resources over a particular period of time. If time is saved, so usually are the more traditional resource inputs – capital as just noted (especially working capital); labour, such as the halving of labour time for the production of superfine broadcloth in the woollen industry between 1780 and 1830 shown by Gregory (1982, 90); and land, as in bleaching (Wolff 1974).

Speeding up any single activity could additionally place strains on other levels of activity to catch up. The most famous example of this sequence of speed imbalances is that between weaving and spinning in textiles – the adoption of the 'flying shuttle' in weaving increased demands for yarn supplies, which were not easy to meet in the prevailing 'domestic' system of production without getting spinning to speed up as well. So successful was the latter (through the jenny, water frame, mule, etc.) that the reverse strain eventually came to be felt on the weaving sector, leading towards the power-loom. A similar seesaw of 'challenge and response' occurred in the iron industry, between smelting and refining (blast furnace and forge).

The two remaining aspects of Landes's case, concerning raw materials and energy, deserve equal attention. Raw materials previously available in only limited quantities could be extended in two ways – in breadth by tapping new sources of supply, as for instance using the under-cultivated areas of the American South to grow cotton (Wilkinson 1973; E. L. Jones 1988), and in depth by developing new substitutes, especially the substitution of coal for timber as fuel and of iron for timber in machinery (cf. Clapham 1926, ch. 1). New energy sources, notably the stationary steam engine, continued the trend to the use of coal, and promoted increased speeds of operation in two ways: through the greater reliability of delivery dates as compared with water, wind and similar energy alternatives (von Tunzelmann 1978, ch. 6; Gregory 1982), and through the opportunity they provided to raise the running speeds of the machinery driven (von Tunzelmann 1978, chs. 7–8).

Until the 'wave of gadgets' most process innovation was organizational rather than technical, such as the adoption of the longwall system for mining coal (Ashton and Sykes 1929); and this will be covered in the next section. Aside from such process innovation, the whole area of *product* innovation has received less than due attention. Product innovation is habitually underestimated by economic historians, if only because it is usually difficult to reduce it to some straightforward measure (Mokyr 1975). There was a long initial period during which most innovation was of the 'product' type. As A. P. Wadsworth pointed out, 'Two centuries of industrial growth lay between the introduction of a cotton manufacture into England and the first Lancashire cotton factories' (Wadsworth and Mann 1931, 3). Such product innovations could be 'major' like the adoption of cotton or 'minor', such as finer or fancier kinds of cloth. Nor did product innovation cease as the Industrial Revolution proper began. MacLeod 1988 found nearly as many patents claimed to improve quality as save capital over the period 1660–1799. The interaction of such product innovation with process innovation in the form of machinery was various. In cotton spinning, for example, the mule (invented by Crompton in the late 1770s) allowed the spinning of yarns of a quality barely conceivable by hand methods. However, in cotton weaving, the power-loom diffused most rapidly in the coarser and plainer products (von Tunzelmann 1978; Temin 1988).

While economic circumstances such as rising wages might encourage substitution of a known capital-intensive technique for the current labour-intensive technique, normally the range of technical possibilities was unknown. Firms would have to search for new methods or new activities. This search process (Crafts 1977) is regarded here as a process of technological learning. Again Adam Smith can act as our mentor – in the course of his celebrated discussion of the division of labour in the opening pages of the *Wealth of Nations* he states:

All the improvements in machinery, however, have by no means been the invention of those who had occasion to use the machines. Many improvements have been made by the ingenuity of the makers of the machines, when to make them became the business of a peculiar trade; and some by that of those who are called philosophers [scientists] or men of speculation, whose trade it is not to do any thing, but to observe every thing ... (Smith 1776/1976, 21)

These three forms of 'learning' can be described as learning by using, learning by doing, and learning by learning. In present-day firms they would be classified as Research and Development (R&D) – clearly an anachronism for the eighteenth century although the goals are much the same and the procedures little different apart from the lack of organized laboratories.

Learning by using (the term employed by Rosenberg 1982, ch. 6) arises in firms introducing process innovations, particularly through acquiring skills in adapting bought-in equipment to the firm's own needs. For example, in spinning cotton on the mule, the skilled spinners had to devise ways of working the mule so that all the individual operations (at least five) could be synchronized (Catling 1970). Learning by doing arises, as Smith states, when upstream activities (like constructing the machinery) split off and those undertaking them broaden their expertise. This happened in the machine tool industry later in the nineteenth century (Rosenberg 1963), and similarly with the simpler hand tools of the eighteenth century. Both learning by using and learning by doing are likely to be dominated by incremental rather than radical technical change, and indeed there is much evidence that the cumulative effects of such incremental changes were at least as powerful as the better-known big breakthroughs in advancing technology during the Industrial Revolution. These types of learning, which will be briefly encountered again later in examining the division of labour, are therefore regarded as 'endogenous' avenues to change.

The exogenous element comes from the spontaneous advance of science, including basic technological research ('know-why' and not just 'know-how'). An obvious possible cause suggests itself, in the so-called Scientific Revolution, conventionally dated to the years from 1660. However, the view of most historians of science is that the direct links from new science to applied industrial technology before the mid-nineteenth century were weak, and in fact just as powerful in the reverse direction (e.g. Hall 1974; von Tunzelmann 1990a). Some economic historians however dispute this generalization (especially Musson and Robinson 1969). The most significant connection, in my view, was methodological – the advocacy of the 'experimental method' in the Scientific Revolution was widely imitated by engineers, agriculturalists and many others during the eighteenth century. One of the consequences was also the greater use of scientific instruments in industry and increased quality control, e.g. the use of thermometers and hydrometers in brewing (Mathias 1959, cf. Price 1984). Thus exogenous learning was also largely incremental so far as industry was concerned – it did not take many direct findings from the Scientific Revolution, but it did take some equipment and many of the new scientific procedures and standards.

Organization and organizational change

The relative impacts of technological and organizational change, investigated by Hartwell (1970b, 1971, ch. 12), remain one of the most obscure – though clearly important – issues in explaining industrial growth up to the present day. Even more obscure are their interactions.

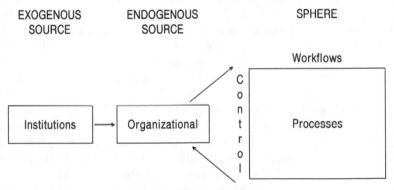

Figure 11.2   The function of organization

That this question is far more than academic may become more obvious by beginning at the level of 'exogenous' change in Figure 11.2. The external impetus comes from 'institutions', by which is meant not just particular kinds of organizations (for example, the banking system, the government, etc.), but the whole way in which society and economy are constructed (Matthews 1986 and Hartwell 1967, use the term in a similar way). An alternative term is 'ideology', but the word often carries derogatory implications akin to brain-washing. The meaning here is the 'climate of opinion' – but associated with the more concrete notion of organizational forms and behaviour.

In this respect, many historians associate the Industrial Revolution with the rise of capitalism, or more explicitly *laissez-faire* capitalism. Some of the world's most celebrated political tracts have attempted to define capitalism and account for its rise. We take the essence of capitalism to be the economic and social system in which effective ownership and control of production is in the hands of those possessing substantial capital, i.e. the financial and/or managerial elites. By *laissez-faire* we mean an economic system in which capitalists are given virtually free rein to make use of the power that they derive from such ownership and control; in particular, the government imposes few or no restraints on the exercise of such power.

Capitalism comes in many forms, of which *laissez-faire* is the starkest but not necessarily the most widespread. Analyses of long-run institutional change indeed emphasize its changing character – for example Lazonick (1988) contrasts this classical British 'proprietary capitalism' with the American 'managerial capitalism' that usurped it in the late nineteenth century, and again with the Japanese 'network capitalism' that appears to be superseding the latter in our own day.

Before going any further into establishing the consequences for industrial and economic growth, we have to ask whether such a system as *laissez-faire* capitalism emerged at the time of the Industrial Revolution. When writers like Arnold Toynbee at the end of the nineteenth century began to popularize the notion of an Industrial Revolution, they actually defined it not in terms of indications of industrial growth, but as the spread of liberal economic doctrines (Toynbee 1884; Hartwell 1965; Cannadine 1984). Indeed, in each period from the Industrial Revolution itself up to the present day, there have been those who have emphasized the technological/industrial nature of the Industrial Revolution and others who have emphasized its institutional/ideological nature (von Tunzelmann 1985). It follows in turn that, while the technological side and the institutional/organizational side of the Industrial Revolution are often conflated, we ought really to disentangle their effects.

The question of whether *laissez-faire* existed or emerged during the second half of the eighteenth and first half of the nineteenth centuries has in turn given rise to a significant historical debate (summarized usefully in Taylor 1972). It has been common to see the early Victorian period, especially, as the heyday of free enterprise, guided in part by Benthamite doctrines of utilitarianism. It is also possible to put the opposite interpretation on the selfsame period and see it as the beginnings of a new phase of governmental intervention, in which Benthamism also had a role.

'Victorian values' were as confused in Queen Victoria's time as they are today: what some see as a period of liberalization, others see as a new era of regulation.

To be a little more precise about industry, the same early Victorian period witnessed a surge in local-government provision of services, including industrially based services like lighting, gas and water (Hassan 1985; Matthews 1986a). Although the more extensive adoption of municipal services ('gas and water socialism') came in the last quarter of the nineteenth century, Eric Jones (1988) goes so far as to speculate that there was a fairly neat offset between the rise of private enterprise in manufacturing and the rise of public enterprise in services.

The way to industrial success through becoming a favourite at court had tailed off, as the power of the Crown itself had tailed off, by the early eighteenth century (MacLeod 1988). But 'mercantilist' regulations could persist in industry and trade through the exercise of power by guilds, trading monopolies and such like. North (1981) asserts that the decisive albeit slow change of the eighteenth and nineteenth centuries was the emergence of better property rights; but this was not the same as *laissez-faire*. North does not specify for whom the property rights were 'better', i.e. more secure indeed any answer to such a question leads back to the broader standard-of-living debates. North's concern is with the reduction of the so-called 'transaction costs', which can be thought of most simply as the costs of decision-making in various market or non-market environments. As yet, there is little direct evidence on whether transactions became cheaper for firms (though see Millward 1981). A more dynamic and persuasive argument might be that the balance of advantage shifted towards entrepreneurs and innovators, but this too needs to be demonstrated.

For manufacturing, the key organizational change was the advent of the factory. Yet even to describe the factory as the 'key' is not to assert that it was, or soon became, the pervasive form of organization in manufacturing, nor that there is any agreement about what a 'factory' was. Once again, it is quite feasible to define the factory from a technological perspective or from an institutional/ideological perspective, and both have been used by differing writers ever since. Andrew Ure, a fervent supporter of the factory system and of *laissez-faire*, adopted a technological definition, by stressing the physical concentration of plant around a centralized power source (Ure 1835). By his own admission this would exclude almost every large-scale activity (including ironworks, chemical works, breweries, calico printing works, etc.) other than textile mills (Crouzet 1985). Quite frequently a congregation of plant and equipment for the purpose of manufacturing a specific product could lack a connecting 'technological' link, such as a centralized power source – Adam Smith's pin factory need not have required any inanimate power. Conversely, a centralized power source could have driven plant and equipment under diversified ownership and control; for example, the so-called 'cottage factories' of the Coventry silk trade in the 1840s, where a row of independently owned cottages were all powered by a single steam engine located at the end of the street. Others, as shown in the next section, have therefore stressed the nature of factory discipline and authority – centralized and hierarchical management rather than centralized technology.

The view I am advancing here is that the *interaction* between technology and organization is their most important characteristic. Such interactions are suggested in Figure 11.2 with the control types set out in columns, representing 'inputs', and the flow of work emanating from each form of control set out in the rows, as 'outputs'. The factory system involved more centralized control and thus a vertical shift in the diagram, but also a step towards continuous batch or flow production, i.e. a horizontal movement to the right (Chapman 1967; Crouzet 1985). Again, speed was of the essence, and this came from introducing machinery and steadily speeding it up; although the capacity for raising speeds in the domestic system should not be under-estimated (Pollard 1965; Gregory 1982). Flow production developed in fits and starts depending on the location of technical change and the integration of differing activities (Sigsworth 1958).

The processes by which this move towards flow production was set in motion were predicted in the celebrated opening pages of a work so often lambasted for its preindustrial focus (e.g. by Landes 1986), namely Adam Smith's *Wealth of Nations* (1776/1976). Smith listed three types of gain from the division of labour, as in his model pin factory:

   (i) the specialization of function increases dexterity, i.e. skill;
  (ii) specialization saves the time and trouble of setting up new tasks – a time-saving advance;
 (iii) the simplification of individual tasks paves the way to new inventions – a dynamic 'learning' advance.

The second and third of these factors have received less attention than they warrant: they take us back to the sphere of technological change in ways that may now be more evident. Most interest has focused on the question of skill and its relationship to the pace of work. It will be noted that Smith's position here is an optimistic one, that the division of labour was 'enskilling', although in Book V of *The Wealth of Nations* he also stresses problems of increasing worker boredom (i.e. diminishing returns to 'enskilling'). The issue was elaborated by Marx (1867) in volume I of

Capital and more recently by Braverman (1974), who concentrated on a fourth 'gain' from the division of labour, originally put forward by Charles Babbage (1832) (more famous in our day as the acknowledged inventor of the computer). The Babbage principle was that division of labour allowed tasks to be sub-divided according to skill requirements, so that masters could divide and rule – not only was there a static gain from allocating the simpler tasks to cheap unskilled workers, but there was a dynamic benefit from 'deskilling' the expensive skilled employees (mostly adult males). Not only did machinery replace skilled and often unionized labour, in ways noted earlier, but – according to Marx and Braverman – with machinery the rate of work became machine-paced rather than employee-paced, and was being constantly intensified. For example, the economics of the steam engine permitted a rise in machine speeds, particularly with the adoption of the high-pressure steam engine, to which workers had passively to adjust (Marx 1867; Samuel 1977; von Tunzelmann 1978, ch. 7).

Out of Braverman's seminal study developed a largely sociological literature on 'labour process', reflecting both control and workflow issues (Littler 1982). The chief point of debate has been whether Braverman was correct to see a constant tendency towards 'deskilling', or whether instead Adam Smith was correct to emphasize 'enskilling' (or both). That issue itself turns on whether dynamic control rested ultimately with the masters (as in 'deskilling') or their employees (for 'enskilling'), which takes us on to questions of management. In addition, one should consider 'capital process' as well as 'labour process', i.e. the ways in which the machinery as well as the workforce is controlled and organized, as for example with the steam engine and with textile machinery. This too takes us back to the interactions with technological change and forward into managerial decision-making.

The core of Marx's approach to capitalist industrialization is to emphasize the tension between the 'forces of production', i.e. technology, and the 'social relations of production', i.e. organization. The class struggle which in Marx directs and redirects history arises from this tension. The present argument diverges from Marx, however, in seeing such tension as endemic rather than as passing through successive ideological stages – a constant ebb and flow between technology and organization. The development of new forms of control allows the development of new technologies that permit increased operating speeds, but those speeds themselves, taken far enough, necessitate further changes in control systems (Pollard 1965; Beniger 1986).

Management and finance

The question of how industrialization emerged from the medieval economy, of how capital and capitalism in their modern form originated, with immediate producers turned into wage labourers, has been at the forefront of historical and long-term economic analysis since the models of Smith and Marx. Most attention has come to focus on the preindustrial period of the seventeenth and early eighteenth centuries, the period classified by Marxists as one of 'primitive accumulation'. The following paragraphs are based on the conclusions of a survey by Berg (1985).

Some historians have asked how pools of funds sufficient to sustain industrialization were recruited (what Marx called the problem of 'primitive accumulation'). That is, the critical issue is seen as finance, and the main focus has been on landowners and merchants, especially overseas traders pursuing the 'Great Discoveries'. It needs to be asked how any such pools of funds were directed to industry rather than merely lining the pockets of rich merchants. One possible answer was, of course, for the merchants to have become manufacturers themselves, but although a number of inland merchants or their relations did so, it seems to have been rare for overseas traders. The implication, often unspoken, is of a penetration by controlling capital into small-scale handicrafts, which developed through the capitalist producers' initiatives into industrial crafts based on traditional technologies ('manufactures' in the literal sense, i.e. by hand, as opposed to later 'machinofacture'), in rural or urban workshops. However the artisans in many areas long clung to their independence.

Others have emphasized the 'domestic' or 'putting-out' systems of manufacture rather than workshops. In industries like textiles, the materials circulated around the houses of individual cottage-based producers, who successively processed them into the finished items of clothing (etc.), but they remained throughout the property of the merchants rather than the producers. This 'proto-industrialization', as some describe it, has been explained in various ways. Some focus on a contrast between arable and pastoral regions, with the underemployed peasantry of the latter acting as a basis for an expandable labour force. Some concentrate on demographic factors – induced population growth being the source of labour. Most emphasize the low labour costs and elastic labour supply (seasonal employment, semi-subsistence farming, etc.) of the emerging rural manufacturing areas, seized on by merchants and landlords. However, the occasional periods of labour shortage such as for spinning in the 1760s seem to have *encouraged* putting-out, because of difficulties in supervising the spinners (Wadsworth and Mann 1931, 276). Furthermore, many labour-surplus areas found putting-out a dead end of impoverishment (Houston and Snell 1984). The low labour costs nevertheless helped the system to accumulate capital, i.e. from internal as well as external sources, based on a web of indebtedness. Towns may have remained the locus of marketing, finance and mercantile activity, but manufacturing had been driven to the countryside by high labour costs and perhaps guild restrictions (Mokyr 1976; Rule 1981).

Division of labour was by product rather than by process: 'By the early nineteenth century there were twenty nailmaking districts in the West Midlands, each making a different kind of nail or spike' (Berg 1985, 294). Such regional specialization of products could also lead to specialization of processes, however. Rising marginal costs as the region of production had to be extended ultimately encouraged centralization; so that again workshops and 'embryo-factories' could arise from such beginnings (Pollard 1965; Tann 1970), aided by the specialization in processes which allowed machines to replace human skills, as in the 'jenny factories' in Lancashire from the 1770s (Marx 1867; Edwards and Lloyd-Jones 1973; Rosenberg 1982, ch. 2).

There was no necessary linear progression from any of these industrial structures to the factory (Berg 1985; Hudson 1986). Even in the same general region, some 'successful' activities were led by merchants (e.g. Yorkshire worsteds) and others by producers (e.g. Yorkshire woollens); conversely there were important examples of 'failure' led by merchants (e.g. West Country woollens) and others by producers (e.g. Devon serges). The enduring nature of organizational forms other than the factory has been stressed by Sabel and Zeitlin (1985), and indeed a fashionable current argument claims that we may now be witnessing a return to structures more like 'putting-out' (e.g. Piore and Sabel 1984). Moreover the putting-out system has much in common with the even more fashionable Japanese model of 'network capitalism' alluded to above, if the large manufacturing firm at the nucleus of the Japanese network is replaced by the large inland merchant. However, the Japanese seem to have solved the problem that proved to be the running sore of 'putting-out' – how to preserve quality of product and adequate speeds of production, when the domestic workers were physically far removed from any managerial control from the nucleus. As a management option for the early Industrial Revolution, present opinion favours the view that, if it suited the local distribution of income and wealth, putting-out was adopted to cope with the (slow) changes of product under way; the factory later solved its more manifest shortcomings.

Another species of division between owners and managers arose at an early stage where the former were landowners: their respective duties varied across the country and through time, and financial means for ensuring that either side carried out its responsibilities, had to be evolved. Scale was likely to be larger and more capital-intensive methods feasible. Agriculture and mining plus some transportation were the most affected (Pollard 1965, ch. 2; Flinn 1984, ch. 2; Allen 1988). Separation of ownership from management added another tier to the hierarchy, superimposed on the internal links between colliery manager or estate steward, mine 'viewer' or tenant farmer, and subcontractors or employees.

In manufacturing, Marglin (1974) argued that the preindustrial worker was a member of a hierarchy, but a hierarchy that was linear (masters, journeymen and apprentices) and in due course each lower level would move up. The worker sold the products and so controlled both product and process. This was replaced in industrial England by a pyramidal hierarchy in which few if any advanced. The worker lost control, first of product through the adoption of putting-out (the capitalist enforced specialization and separation from markets); second of process by the subsequent shift to the factory system (under putting-out the worker could still work at his or her own pace, delay production, turn in poor-quality work, or embezzle the materials, so the factory arose to regulate discipline and provide supervision). 'Part of the advantage of the putting-out system over the former handicraft methods had been the division of labour, and the specialization and the inventive talent which it encouraged, but this process, once begun, set up its own pressure for further progress which demanded further concentration, perhaps in a central manufactory' (Pollard 1965, 34).

Instead of the technological definition of the factory along the lines of Ure, Marglin is led to define it in organizational terms, in its capability for the exercise of hierarchical control by the capitalist. According to Marglin, the factory system was not at first technically or economically superior to earlier forms of organization, but it did involve a shift of power from employees to capitalist masters. An indication that the factory was adopted for its social rather than technical advantages comes from the casual historical evidence put forward by Marglin that factories appeared earlier than new technology in some areas. A less extreme version of the organizational hypothesis is that the factory did not initially necessitate technical change but did carry economic advantages from the outset (Cohen 1981).

Coleman (1973, 5) sees the labour intensity and family basis of putting-out as a fundamental obstacle to mechanical innovation. Many historians would probably agree that Marglin and North go too far in divorcing technological change in the guise of new machinery etc. from organizational change in the guise of the factory. If the factory is itself *defined* technologically, as by Ure in the manner already noted (also Landes 1986; S. R. H. Jones 1988), this argument for the need to stress technological change becomes even more apparent, although it then becomes something of a tautology. Few convincing reasons apart from the rise of new technologies have been advanced for the need to *increase* control in the later eighteenth century (changes in quality of materials and products have been suggested (Millward 1981; Hudson 1986) but these in turn may partly have resulted from new technologies). Adopting the factory may have been required to reap economies of scale from 'indivisible' new technologies like the steam engine. Alternatively the factory may have been the locus of technological learning: yet much of the early textile machinery – for example, Hargreaves's spinning jenny or Crompton's mule – were originally planned to be powered as well as operated by men and women in cottages, while others again (like Paul and Wyatt's spinning machinery, Arkwright's water frame or Cartwright's power loom) were initially animal-powered (von Tunzelmann 1978). The jenny in activities such as woollen spinning actually permitted the domestic system to survive longer. Nevertheless, most advances were eventually absorbed into factories, and subjected to continuing modification from learning by using and learning by doing. A sensible compromise is that of Pollard (1965, ch. 1) that in some industries or activities technological factors predominated and in others organizational ones; although it is their interactions which are emphasized here, and most in need of greater exploration. Heaton's earlier judgement may well be valid:

The modern factory system ... embodies the use of capital, the congregation of workpeople, the division of labour, and the exercise of supervision. Each of these factors has great value in itself, but the major part of the economic advantage of the factory springs from the use of machinery capable of performing work quickly, and the use of power which can make the machinery go at high speed. Until these elements of speed became possible, the factory system did not possess any very great advantage over the cottage industry.

Heaton also pointed out that the earliest Yorkshire factories did *not* differ in their machinery or power from cottage industry (Heaton 1920, 352–3).

With the putting-out system, finance and marketing were organized on a capitalist basis, revolving around the merchant, but the actual manufacturing remained traditional – but with a factory system the latter not only became capitalist in structure but became the hub of industry. Thus the capitalistic factory united – for a time – ownership and managerial control.

The development of formal managerial techniques such as accountancy have been analysed by Pollard (1965, ch. 6) and Hartwell (1970b and 1971, ch. 12). Pollard concluded that cost accountancy was primitive,

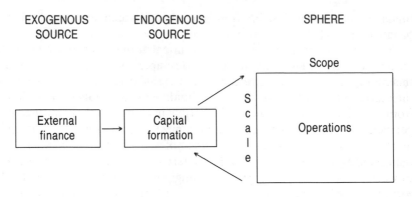

Figure 11.3   The functions of management and finance

partly because costs of labour and capital were not the main obstacle. The advent of the factory created a demand for reckoning fixed capital accounts, but the profession supplied little response, and rather passively supported a high rate of profits, 'ploughed back' into growth as in the loop of Figure 11.3.

An important issue that arises is that, if the managerial advantages were compelling, was finance the real constraint on moving to a factory system? For the capital itself, the major study again is by Pollard (1964; reprinted in Crouzet 1972). Pollard noted first that capital requirements for early factories were kept low, for example by use of cheap local materials for building the plant, and by the somewhat rudimentary nature of the machinery. Secondly, banks were becoming more important in the eighteenth-century economy, including the so-called 'country banks', but they still provided more working capital than fixed capital. Previous writers had seen this as a crucial limitation, but Pollard adopted Habakkuk's dictum 'that financial institutions adapt themselves to meet the principal economic needs of their period and that English banks concentrated on the provision of working capital because that was what industry needed . . . ' (Habakkuk 1962, 175). Bank funds helped assist the *movement* of goods, allowing speed-up, rather than setting up their production in the first place (Cameron 1982). Thirdly, the needs for capital in manufacturing could be met by the traditional flow of trade credit of the merchant-based system. To acquire the funds needed to set up a factory involved a prospective manufacturer inserting himself into this circulation of trade credit (in reverse direction to the flow of products from raw material to finished consumer good), and for a time running larger 'creditor' balances (owed to suppliers) than 'debtors' (owed to him by those further down the line). This interim stockpiling of funds in the manufacturer's firm would facilitate a leap into factory production.

To substantiate one's credibility as a worthy prospect, it was often required to match such trade credit with one's own funds, and partly for this reason much of the literature on capital formation rightly dwells on the search for matching resources: from landowners or one's own land, from wealthy contacts, from friends and relatives, and from 'sleeping partners'. In industries not emerging from a merchanting background, moreover, the workshop manufacturer might have to be the source rather than the recipient of credit (Weatherill 1982). In mining the ratio of fixed to working capital was exceptionally high, but ownership by large land-owners (some of whom allegedly believed that coal 'grew' underground in the same way as their crops on the surface!) generally met or underpinned these needs. Finally, trade credit might prove especially inadequate when fixed capital was needed to erect a mill, despite all the economies effected in costs of plant and equipment (Richardson 1989). Banks became increasingly important for funding from about the 1830s, replacing mer-chant and other traditional sources, as Hudson (1986) has shown in a detailed study of the Yorkshire woollen industry. Nevertheless, the major point is as Pollard stresses – the existence of what we would now call a network of credit, corresponding to the network of production in the preindustrial system. This of course is the similarity to the modern Japanese pattern.

The 'revolution' in finance – banking in the late seventeenth century (e.g. setting up the Bank of England) and public finance in the eighteenth century (Dickson 1967) – thus had little direct effect on industry until late in the Industrial Revolution. The more immediate influence of the 'Finan-cial Revolution' was the general cheapening in credit that helped influ-ence the direction of technological change discussed earlier.

The 'plough-back' mechanism for the growth of industrial firms shown in Figure 11.3 has long been stressed, with attention frequently drawn to high rates of abstinence from consumption by early mill-owners, low rates of wages for their workers and so on. The basic idea seems well supported by the historical evidence, although perhaps somewhat overstated (Hudson 1986). The financial opportunities discussed above (trade credit, banks, etc.) were often called in to oil the wheels when 'plough-back' broke down or when commercial crises erupted. In a perfect capital market it might not matter whether the funds came from internal or external sources, but in the historical circumstances, the ability to find internal funding from profits gave greater insulary from external con-straints such as fluctuations in interest rates (Ashton 1959) and fluc-tuations in the availability of funds occasioned by war or financial crisis

(Chapman 1972; Williamson 1985). Despite the growth of insurance, eighteenth-century business became increasingly risky, as the increasing distances implied by trade and specialization failed to be matched by improvements in the availability of commercial information (Hoppit 1987).

Once the leap into factory production had been taken, the role of both internal funds (from profit plough-back) and external funds (from banks etc.) was to permit survival and growth of the manufacturing firm. These are taken in the diagram to be reflected in changes in size (down the vertical axis) and in product type (horizontally), with the opportunity to effect economies of scale (vertically) or economies of scope (horizontally). The latter could be either through a proliferation of specific product types, such as the variety of qualities and designs of cloth produced by a weaver, or more broadly through the range of activities carried out, e.g. spinning as well as weaving in textiles. By comparison with the textile industries of other industrially advanced countries, the British cotton sector is normally regarded as being vertically *dis*integrated – throughout the nineteenth century and into the twentieth the spinning and weaving segments were less often to be found in the same firm as in the USA, for example, and indeed for sizeable periods of time this segregation of spinning and weaving seemed to be increasing (Taylor 1949; contested by Lyons 1986). Temin (1988) links the product and process dimensions in arguing that the higher average quality of yarn spun in Britain accounted for the lower degree of vertical integration between spinning and weaving than in the USA, though without really showing why or indeed accounting for the higher British yarn count. In the early days many textile mill-owners actually shared a single plant, e.g. renting a single floor of a mill.

It is conventional to see this vertical and horizontal disintegration as weakening the managerial effectiveness of the British system because of the lack of control over materials and sales, although neither eighteenth-century nor present-day evidence gives unequivocal support to integration. The iron industry, for instance, was highly integrated both vertically and horizontally, well before the Industrial Revolution (Hyde 1977), but late to develop. In textiles, industrialists did not usually integrate forwards into marketing, because merchants had carved out that role; nor were industrialists as horizontally diversified as merchants or merchant-manufacturers. But first-generation industrialists, especially though not exclusively in rural areas, had to provide 'infrastructure' on a scale unknown to later generations, including railway and canal transportation, farms, housing, schooling, medicine, finance (monetary system), retailing (the notorious truck shops), and even police (Pollard 1965, 198–206).

In regard to size, the customary nineteenth-century firm employed somewhere from six to fifteen employees (Crouzet 1985), even in relatively highly capitalized undertakings. With only isolated exceptions, the shift to larger plants and firms did not occur until the turn of the century. Although the size implications of new machinery are the most commonly emphasized factor behind the *technological* explanations for the factory (Landes 1986), this evidence suggests that they arose later in the day.

Entrepreneurs and markets

The entrepreneur from this vantage point is far more than the profit maximizer of conventional economic theory, because that involves maximization subject to *given* constraints. If the constraints are drawn sufficiently tightly, this approaches a tautology. The success of an entrepreneur in the real world is not gauged by the degree to which he or she operates within particular limited horizons, but by the degree to which the entrepreneur can overreach them. Maximization subject to constraints is at best the function of management (Lazonick 1981a) – and if these constraints are regarded as tight, not very good management at that – whereas entrepreneurship consists of altering the constraints, of broadening the horizons (Pollard 1965, ch. 1).

Several recent studies have sought to identify the entrepreneur and his or her social origins. There is a general agreement that most came from middle-class rather than working-class backgrounds – that for a variety of reasons including the need to raise finance it helped to have well-to-do connections. Within the 'middle class' (if there was such a thing) the origins may have been lower middle class striving for recognition and economic reward (Perkin 1969; Payne 1974, 1978) or it may have been middle middle class (Honeyman 1982; Crouzet 1985), perpetuating industrial leadership through what Crouzet calls 'endogenesis'. Through inheritance, 'endogenesis' remained high in later generations (Howe 1984). If one assumes that talent is more or less equally distributed across the social scale, the inference is that access to capital was most important. Though the supply of capital in aggregate was normally large enough, and the demands kept modest, the social class of an aspirant entrepreneur acted as a 'screening' device. However there were a number of notable people who overshot any such boundaries, and a considerably larger number favoured by capital availability who failed to meet the requirements. Though the 'self-made man' from the working class is largely a myth, skilled workers could succeed in industries which continued to be dominated by large numbers of small firms, producing diversified goods often on a one-off basis, and demanding intimate knowledge of production methods – examples being lace, mechanical engineering, secondary metals, and pottery (Crouzet 1985, ch. 6). Immigrants and other minority groups such as religious sects have often been noted, but the factors responsible are still the subject of much debate (technical know-how of immigrants? social motivation? ideals of self-discipline? etc.).

The above discussion emphasizes the *range* of talents required (Wilson 1957; Flinn 1966). The entrepreneur welds together and directs the various functions (von Tunzelmann 1989). The role of innovation can be exaggerated – not all the entrepreneurs were in the heroic mould (Crouzet 1985). Although capital may often have been the ultimate constraint, it was in some respects the most straightforward to 'buy in', from sleeping partners or equivalent sources. Given the capital, the entrepreneur 'ran his own show' (Gough 1969, 17). What we have yet to consider is the talent for spotting marketable opportunities – what products to produce, how and where to sell them, how and where to obtain the material and other inputs. The widening of the market associated with developments of internal transportation (particularly coastal shipping) and international transportation (opening up the New World) has sometimes been described as a Commercial Revolution. But although the pattern of commerce was largely in place before the heyday of the Industrial Revolution, the great growth of commerce may have been the result rather than the cause of industrialization (Mokyr 1985, 21–3). Entrepreneurs were thus initially able to take advantage of these greatly enlarged market opportunities, but beyond that might use these advances to 'make' markets, by manufacturing new products or new qualities of products. How much of this was a 'supply push' from the producers and how much a 'demand-pull' from their customers is briefly considered in the next section.

Market forces may thus have stimulated growth, but they also helped bring about industrial decline in many less-favoured regions (Berg 1985, ch. 5). Moreover, it was to offset the more unbridled consequences of *laissez-faire* that new forms of regulation needed to be adopted.

Products and demand

Demand is a function of the price of the product, the relative price of other products (substitutes and complements), real incomes and their distribution across individuals, and exogenous shift factors of which 'tastes' are usually thought most important. Product price has to be treated especially carefully, since observed market prices are the outcome of market interaction between 'supply prices' set by the circumstances of production as detailed above, and 'demand prices' set by the circum-

EXOGENOUS   ENDOGENOUS   SPHERE
SOURCE   SOURCE

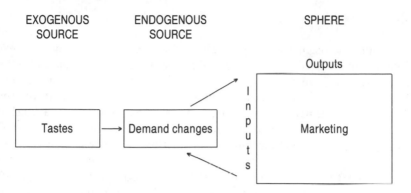

Figure 11.4   The function of products

stances of consumption such as tastes. Much of the literature which has argued for a demand-side explanation of the Industrial Revolution has in fact fallen into this simple trap (see the critique by Mokyr 1977), and consequently ascribed to demand what is probably a mixture of supply and demand.

To explain industrialization through rising incomes, permitting a shift in consumption patterns towards manufactured items (to middle-range 'decencies' rather than high-range luxuries, cf. Eversley 1967), runs two gauntlets. First, the coincidence in timing of rising per capita incomes and of changing consumption patterns has to be verified, and our current evidence is ambiguous (see Crafts 1985 for the most extensive analysis of eighteenth-century growth trends). Second, and even more difficult, one has to prove that any observed increase in average incomes is the *cause* of industrialization, whereas most interpret rising incomes as the *effect* of such industrialization. Genuinely exogenous changes in tastes are thus extremely difficult to observe, though a number of possibilities have been suggested. There is no space to elaborate through examples (but see McKendrick et al. 1982 for changes in fashion in clothing, pottery, etc.), although attention can be drawn to two aspects: changes resulting from extending the size of the market through the 'Commercial Revolution', which trickled down to both inputs and outputs; and changes in the *rate* of consumption, e.g. how frequently clothes were purchased, complementing the changes in the *rate* of production shown in the discussion of technology. Entrepreneurs could be active agents in both these aspects of changing demand. However, marketing remained generally in the hands of the merchants and middlemen (Jones 1984; Weatherill 1986).

K

Conclusion

As said at the beginning, it has not been possible to avoid some complexity, but I have tried to minimize this by using a similar method for each manufacturing function, i.e. technology, organization, management/ finance and products. In each sphere there is a simple matrix relating 'inputs' to 'outputs', an endogenous factor changing this relationship, and an exogenous factor doing the same. The data add up to the same totals in each of the four functions, but they disaggregate in different ways.

Suppose, for example, we are considering the cotton textile industry. In the sphere of marketing, as the specific set of choices made about 'products' (see Fig. 11.4), the firms will have inputs of raw cotton and other materials, and outputs of cotton yarn, cloth, etc. In the sphere of techniques, i.e. the specific choices for 'technology' (Fig. 11.1), the methods would be various types of hand and machine methods (the distaff, the spindle, the jenny, the mule, etc.) and the activities the particular areas that these relate to (spinning, weaving, etc.). In the sphere of processes, within the range of possibilities for 'organization' (Fig. 11.2), the control types would be putting-out, factory, etc., and the workflows the production processes in each (e.g. discontinuous vs. continuous spinning). Finally, the sphere of operations (Fig. 11.3) has already been covered for this example – the size of cotton firms and their degree of vertical integration. I have at times gone beyond this taxonomy to note some of the links, including feedback links, among these various functions.

How far does this get us towards answering some of the broad issues hinted at in my introduction? In the absence of quantitative data there is only so much that a qualitative investigation can tell us, and what particularly is lacking here is an assessment of how the whole range of activities in the economy (and outside) interrelate. As in much of Hartwell's work, I have aimed here to look at the general picture rather than sectoral breakdowns. Most of the recent quantitative evidence suggests (i) that economic growth was slow until well into the nineteenth century (Harley 1982; Crafts 1985), and (ii) that it took place unequally across sectors of the economy (McCloskey 1981; Crafts 1985, 1987). From this it may be concluded (i) that there was growth in breadth rather than growth in depth in the eighteenth century ('Smithian' growth through widened markets, to use the phrase of Rostow 1975), and (ii) that there was unbalanced rather than balanced growth. The classical economic model in which my taxonomy is nested requires unbalanced *levels* of output across sectors, but balanced *rates of growth* in accord with demand, though the latter does not imply *equal* rates of growth. Thus unbalanced growth (a supply-driven phenomenon, cf. Hartwell 1971, ch. 9) and balanced growth (demand-pull) are not necessarily incompatible.

To assume that there were no feedback links from the exogenous factors is obviously a great simplification (as Hartwell 1967 points out, the exogenous changes were by no means completed before industrialization, and may have actually accelerated in response to industrialization), but does suggest that we can think of the early Industrial Revolution as the outcome of a substantial change in each set of exogenous conditions – loosely referred to as the 'Scientific Revolution', the 'Rise of Capitalism', the 'Financial Revolution', and the 'Commercial Revolution', with varying degrees of impact as noted. These substantial changes in exogenous circumstances meant that the Industrial Revolution took place in an environment that was different in kind and not just in degree from what preceded it. Indeed marked changes in the rate of economic growth do not seem to have occurred until much later, when technical and other advances were sufficiently diffused. In other words, my argument supports the idea of a 'Great Discontinuity', at least for the English economy, not so much because of any sudden disruption as because change had become the norm, whereas before the Industrial Revolution change was the exception. It was a world in which time was speeding up, and the nature of innovation reflected that.

This analysis rejects the view that capitalism was less the issue than industrialism, because capitalism was precisely the factor underlying changes in organization, management and finance. By the same token, it provides qualitative support for the view that organizational changes vied with technological changes for importance in the early English Industrial Revolution. Indeed, the fact that some have chosen to define the Industrial Revolution in organizational rather than technological terms helps account for differing views over the degree of 'discontinuity'. There is, however, comparatively little to be gained from trying to determine whether technological change preceded or exceeded organizational change (or *vice versa*), since each interacted over time with the other. The lumpiness of investments in new technologies encouraged the factory system, and in turn the factory required high levels of output to break even. In a dynamic sense, changes in control helped new technologies to achieve higher output speeds; and in turn higher speeds, new materials and quality shifts eventually demanded changes in control. Tensions between technological change and organization, between organizational change and finance, and so on, had arisen in individual instances on many occasions before the Industrial Revolution; but now all were changing in response to the 'exogenous' changes and to changes in one another, as a 'moral economy' based on accepted (if sometimes violated) rights and responsibilities gave way to a competitive 'market economy'.

This chapter has concentrated on the social and economic causes of industrialization: the social consequences were to be fought out for decades to come. The subjection to factory discipline, rising speeds of operation, 'deskilling' from mechanization and 'alienation' from product and process have been regarded as defining the labour process in industrial society (Braverman 1974); although the struggles of trade unions in the nineteenth century are better seen as continuing to stake workers' claims over conditions and pace of work rather than as simple capitulation (Lazonick 1981b). In association with political factors – which may not have been wholly independent – and the accumulation of capital and control by the factory masters, these brought about the 'making of the English working class' (Thompson 1963; Morris 1979). An eighteenth century dominated by struggles between agriculture, commerce and industry, gave way to a nineteenth century in which the major class issue lay within industry, between employers and employees.

REFERENCES

Allen, R. C. 1988. 'The growth of labor productivity in early modern English agriculture', *Explorations in Economic History*, 25, 117–46.

Ashton, T. S. 1948; rev. edn 1968. *The Industrial Revolution, 1760–1830*.

1955. *An Economic History of England: the 18th century*.

1959. *Economic Fluctuations in England, 1700–1800*.

Ashton, T. S. and Sykes, J. 1929. *The Coal Industry of the Eighteenth Century*.

Babbage, C. 1832. *On the Economy of Machinery and Manufactures*.

Beniger, J. R. 1986. *The Control Revolution; technological and economic origins of the information society*.

Berg, M. 1980. *The Machinery Question and the Making of Political Economy, 1815–1848*.

1985. *The Age of Manufactures, 1700–1820*.

Braverman, H. 1974. *Labor and Monopoly Capital*.

Cameron, R. 1982. 'Banking and industrialisation in Britain in the nineteenth century', in *Business, Banking and Urban History: essays in honour of S. G. Checkland*, ed. A. Slaven and D. H. Aldcroft, 102–11.

Cannadine, D. 1984. 'The present and the past in the English Industrial Revolution', *Past and Present*, 103, 131–72.

Catling, H. J. 1970. *The Spinning Mule*.

Chapman, S. D. 1967. *The Early Factory Masters: the transition to the factory system in the Midlands textile industry*.

1972. *The Cotton Industry in the Industrial Revolution*.

Clapham, J. H. 1926. *An Economic History of Modern Britain: the early railway age, 1820–1850*.

Clarkson, L. A. 1971. *The Pre-Industrial Economy in England, 1500–1750*.

Cohen, J. S. 1981. 'Managers and machinery: an analysis of the rise of factory production', *Australian Economic Papers*, 20, 24–41.

Coleman, D. and Schofield, R. 1986. *The State of Population Theory: forward from Malthus*.

Coleman, D. C. 1973. 1973. 'Textile growth', in Harte and Ponting (1973) *Textile History and Economic History*, 1–21.

Crafts, N. F. R. 1977. 'Industrial Revolution in England and France: some thoughts on the question "why was England first?"', *Economic History Review*, 2nd ser., 30, 429–41. Reprinted with comments in Mokyr, ed. (1985), pp. 119–36.

1985. *British Economic Growth during the Industrial Revolution*.

1987. 'British economic growth 1700–1850: some difficulties of interpretation', *Explorations in Economic History*, 24, 245–68.

Crouzet, F. (ed.) 1972. *Capital Formation in the Industrial Revolution*.

1985. *The First Industrialists: the problem of origins*.

Dickson, P. G. M. 1967. *The Financial Revolution in England: a study in the development of public credit in England, 1688–1756*.

Dobson, C. R. 1980. *Masters and Journeymen: a prehistory of industrial relations, 1717–1800*.

Edwards, M. M. and Lloyd-Jones, R. 1973. 'N. J. Smelser and the cotton factory family: a reassessment', in Harte and Ponting, 1973, 304–19.

Eversley, D. E. C. 1967. 'The home market and economic growth in England, 1750–80', in *Land, Labour and Population in the Industrial Revolution*, ed. E. L. Jones and G. E. Mingay, 206–59.

Flinn, M. W. 1966. *Origins of the Industrial Revolution*.

1984. *The History of the British Coal Industry*, II, *1700–1830: The Industrial Revolution*.

Floud, R. C. and McCloskey, D. N. (eds.) 1981. *The Economic History of Britain since 1700*, I.

Gough, J. W. 1969. *The Rise of the Entrepreneur*.

Gregory, D. 1982. *Regional Transformation and Industrial Revolution: a geography of the Yorkshire woollen industry*.

Habakkuk, H. J. 1962. *American and British Technology in the Nineteenth Century: the search for labour-saving inventions*.

Hall, A. R. 1974. 'What did the Industrial Revolution in Britain owe to science?', in *Historical Perspectives: studies in English thought and society*, ed. N. McKendrick, 129–51.

Harley, C. K. 1982. 'British industrialization before 1841: evidence of slower growth during the Industrial Revolution', *Journal of Economic History*, 42, 267–89.

Harris, J. R. 1988. *The British Iron Industry, 1700–1850*.

Harte, N. B. and Ponting, K. G. 1973. *Textile History and Economic History: essays in honour of Julia de Lacy Mann*.

Hartwell, R. M. 1965. *The Industrial Revolution in England*.

Hartwell, R. M. (ed.) 1967. *The Causes of the Industrial Revolution in England*.

1969. 'Economic growth in England before the Industrial Revolution', *Journal of Economic History*, 29, 13–31, reprinted in Hartwell (1971), ch. 2.

Hartwell, R. M. (ed.) 1970a. *The Industrial Revolution*.

1970b. 'Business management in England during the period of early industrialization: inducements and obstacles', in Hartwell (ed.) (1970a), 28–41.

1970c. 'The Great Discontinuity', *University of Newcastle History Journal*, 1, reprinted in Hartwell (1971), ch. 3.

1971. *The Industrial Revolution and Economic Growth*.

Hassan, J. A. 1985. 'The growth and impact of the British water industry in the nineteenth century', *Economic History Review*, 2nd ser., 38, 531–47.

Heaton, H. 1920. *The Yorkshire Woollen and Worsted Industries: from the earliest times up to the Industrial Revolution*.

Honeyman, K. 1982. *Origins of Enterprise: business leadership in the Industrial Revolution*.

Hoppit, J. 1987. *Risk and Failure in English Business, 1700–1800*.

Houston, R. and Snell, K. D. M. 1984. 'Proto-industrialization: cottage industry, social change and the Industrial Revolution', *Historical Journal*, 27, 473–92.

Howe, A. 1984. *The Cotton Masters, 1830–1860*.

Hudson, P. 1986. *The Genesis of Industrial Capital: a study of the West Riding wool textile industry c. 1750–1850*.

Hyde, C. K. 1977. *Technological Change and the British Iron Industry, 1700–1870*.

Jones, E. L. 1988. *Growth Recurring: economic change in world history*.

Jones, S. R. H. 1984. 'The country trade and the marketing and distribution of Birmingham hardware, 1750–1810', *Business History*, 26, 26–42.

1988. 'Technology, transaction costs, and the transition to factory production in the British silk industry, 1700–1870', *Journal of Economic History*, 47, 71–96.

Landes, D. S. 1969. *The Unbound Prometheus: technological change and industrial development in Western Europe from 1750 to the present*.

1986. 'What do bosses really do?', *Journal of Economic History*, 26, 585–624.

Lazonick, W. 1981a. 'Factor costs and the diffusion of ring spinning in Britain prior to World War I', *Quarterly Journal of Economics*, 96, 89–109.

1981b. 'Production relations, labor productivity, and choice of technique: British and US cotton spinning', *Journal of Economic History*, 41, 491–516.

1988. 'Business organisation and competitive advantage: innovation and adaptation in three industrial revolutions', mimeo.

Littler, C. R. 1982. *The Development of the Labour Process in Capitalist Societies: a comparative study of work organization in Britain, Japan and the USA*.

Lyons, J. S. 1986. 'Vertical integration in the British cotton industry, 1825–1850', *Journal of Economic History*, 45, 419–26.

McCloskey, D. N. 1981. 'The Industrial Revolution 1780–1860: a survey', in Floud and McCloskey (1981), 103–27.

McKendrick, N., Brewer, J. and Plumb, J. H. 1982. *The Birth of a Consumer Society: the commercialization of eighteenth-century England*.

MacLeod, C. 1988. *Inventing the Industrial Revolution: the English patent system, 1660–1800*.

Malcolmson, R. W. 1981. *Life and Labour in England, 1700–1780*.

Marglin, S. 1974. 'What do bosses do?: the origins and functions of hierarchy in capitalist production', *Review of Radical Political Economy*, 6, reprinted in *The Division of Labour*, ed. A. Gorz.

Marx, K. 1867. 1887. *Capital*, I (1st English edn 1887).

Mathias, P. 1959. *The Brewing Industry in England 1700–1830*.

Mathias, P. and Postan, M. M. (eds.) 1978. *The Cambridge Economic History of Europe*, VII, pt I.

Matthews, D. 1986. 'Laissez-faire and the London gas industry in the nineteenth century: a new look', *Economic History Review*, 2nd ser., 39, 244–63.

Matthews, R. C. O. 1986. 'The economics of institutions and the sources of growth', *Economic Journal*, 96, 903–18.

Millward, R. 1981. 'The emergence of wage labor in early modern England', *Explorations in Economic History*, 18, 21–39.

Mokyr, J. 1976. 'Growing-up in the Industrial Revolution in Europe', *Explorations in Economic History*, 13, 371–96.

1977. 'Demand vs. supply in the Industrial Revolution', *Journal of Economic History*, 37, 981–1008, reprinted in Mokyr (1985), pp. 97–118.

Mokyr, J. (ed.) 1985. *The Economics of the Industrial Revolution*.

Morris, R. J. 1979. *Class and Class Consciousness in the Industrial Revolution, 1780–1850.*

Musson, A. E. and Robinson, E. 1969. *Science and Technology in the Industrial Revolution.*

North, D. C. 1981. *Structure and Change in Economic History.*

Payne, P. L. 1974. *British Entrepreneurship in the Nineteenth Century.*

1978. 'Industrial entrepreneurship and management in Great Britain', in Mathias and Postan (eds.), 180–230.

Perkin, H. J. 1969. *The Origins of Modern English Society, 1780–1880.*

Piore, M. J. and Sabel, C. F. 1984. *The Second Industrial Divide: possibilities for prosperity.*

Pollard, S. 1964. 'Fixed capital in the Industrial Revolution in Britain', *Journal of Economic History*, 24, 299–314, reprinted in Crouzet (1972), pp. 145–61.

1965. *The Genesis of Modern Management: a study of the Industrial Revolution in Great Britain.*

1978. 'Labour in Great Britain', in Mathias and Postan (1978), 97–179.

Price, D. de S. 1984. 'The science/technology relationship, the craft of experimental science, and policy for the improvement of high technology innovation', *Research Policy*, 13, 3–20.

Richardson, P. 1989. 'The structure of capital during the Industrial Revolution revisited: two case studies from the cotton textile industry', *Economic History Review*, 2nd ser., 42, 484–503.

Rosenberg, N. 1963. 'Technological change in the machine tool industry, 1840–1910', *Journal of Economic History*, 23, 414–46.

1982. *Inside the Black Box: technology and economics.*

Rostow, W. W. 1975. *How It All Began: origins of the modern economy.*

Rule, J. 1981. *The Experience of Labour in Eighteenth-Century Industry.*

Sabel, C. and Zeitlin, J. 1985. 'Historical alternatives to mass production: politics, markets and technology in nineteenth-century industrialization', *Past and Present*, 108, 133–76.

Samuel, R. 1977. 'The workshop of the world: steam power and hand technology in mid-Victorian Britain', *History Workshop*, 3, 6–72.

Samuelson, P. A. 1965. 'The theory of induced innovation along Kennedy-Weiszäcker lines', *Review of Economic Statistics*, 47, 343–56.

Sigsworth, E. M. 1958. *Black Dyke Mills: a history.*

Smelser, N. J. 1959. *Social Change in the Industrial Revolution: an application of theory to the Lancashire cotton industry, 1770–1840.*

Smith, A. 1776. 1976. *An Inquiry into the Nature and Causes of the Wealth of Nations*, ed. R. H. Campbell, A. S. Skinner and W. B. Todd (1976).

Tann, J. 1970. *The Development of the Factory.*

Taylor, A. J. 1949. 'Concentration and specialization in the Lancashire cotton industry, 1825–50', *Economic History Review*, 2nd ser., 1, 114–22.

   1972. *Laissez-faire and State Intervention in Nineteenth-Century Britain.*

Temin, P. 1988. 'Product quality and vertical integration in the early cotton textile industry', *Journal of Economic History*, 48, 891–907.

Thompson, E. P. 1963. *The Making of the English Working Class.*

   1967. 'Time, work discipline and industrial capitalism', *Past and Present*, 38, 56–97.

Toynbee, A. 1884. *Lectures on the Industrial Revolution of the eighteenth century in England.*

Ure, A. 1835. *The Philosophy of Manufactures.*

Ville, S. 1986. 'Total factor productivity in the English shipping industry: the North-east coal trade, 1700–1850', *Economic History Review*, 2nd ser., 39, 355–70.

von Tunzelmann, G. N. 1978. *Steam Power and British Industrialization to 1860.*

   1979. 'Trends in real wages, 1750–1850, revisited', *Economic History Review*, 2nd ser., 32, 33–49.

   1985. 'The standard of living debate and optimal economic growth', in Mokyr, ed. (1985), 207–26.

   1989. 'The supply side: technology and history', in *Industrial Dynamics*, ed. B. Carlsson, 55–84.

   1990a. 'Technical progress 1780–1860', in Floud and McCloskey, revd. edn, 1981.

   1990b. 'Time-saving technical change in the Industrial Revolution', mimeo.

Wadsworth, A. P. and Mann, J. A. 1931. *The Cotton Trade and Industrial Lancashire, 1600–1780.*

Weatherill, L. 1982. 'Capital and credit in the pottery industry before 1770', *Business History*, 24, 243–58.

   1986. 'The business of middlemen in the English pottery trade before 1780', *Business History*, 28, 51–76.

Wilkinson, R. G. 1973. *Poverty and progress: an ecological model of economic development.*

Williamson, J. G. 1985. *Did British Capitalism Breed Inequality?*

Wilson, C. 1957. 'The entrepreneur in the Industrial Revolution in Britain', *History*, 42, 101–17.

Wolff, K. H. 1974. 'Textile bleaching and the birth of the chemical industry', *Business History Review*, 48, 143–63.

Wrigley, E. A. and Schofield, R. S. 1981. *The Population History of England 1541–1871: a reconstruction.*

Postscript: an appreciation of Max Hartwell

Eric Jones

There are talking scholars and writing scholars. Max Hartwell has always been one of the former, despite his long list of books and articles. His cheery presence and staccato interjections are impossible for those around him to ignore. Energetic, direct and encouraging, he was the greatest of supervisors for anyone capable of going away and doing better next time. 'Get some bloody work done, boy', he would say, leering over the half-moon spectacles of his Pickwickian phase. Next time he would discourage chat with a donnish dismissal, sorting editorial papers the while, only to revert turn-about to his native breeziness. It was enough to make one believe, with Lindsay, that the product of a life of scholarship is not a book but a man. At any rate, few academics can have worked harder and created more positive externalities for their students. Max had a gift of turning his research students into personal friends. He almost never failed It is through his students – represented by the contributors to this book – that much of his continuing influence on economic history comes and will go on coming.

The features to notice about Max Hartwell are his bouncing energy and cheerfulness. Visited in hospital the day after a particularly gruesome operation, he was already holding forth to the nurses, who swarmed fascinated around his bed like flies in the outback where he was born. Next allied to the Life Force, then, is his Australianness. In the United States, where he has now spent an important share of his mature academic years, this provokes little by way of raised eyebrows. In England, on the other hand, there were many who were, maybe still are, ill at ease with bluntness in a don.

In the dear, dead days of the nineteen-sixties those who were tempted to dismiss him made up an odd clique. There were the social conservatives and there were the pink intellectuals, who sniffed in Oxford Common Rooms about his inconvenient trumpeting of the benefits of industrialization. Seldom can more academics have poured more cold water on a scholarly thesis. But they misplaced their man. They thought they were dealing with a 'rough-house Australian', as one of them called him.

Instead they were dealing with the great-grandson of a viticulturist, the grandson of the proprietor of the Rosemount Vineyard, the son of a teacher; with an apolitical, country Anglican altar boy, who had passed through the narrow gate of Australian academic preferment when that meant something, before and just after the Second World War; they were dealing with one of the generation influenced at the University of Sydney by the philosopher John Anderson, as well as by John Passmore, Percy Partridge and Max's special champion, the historian J. A. La Nauze; someone who had won the University Prize Medal; who had been Foundation Professor of Economic History at the University of New South Wales at the age of twenty-nine; who had resigned on a point of principle and had the guts and gall to start again, like a character from Kipling, by emigrating from downunder to the very core of English intellectual life; who was tougher than they, as able, more energetic and far more optimistic.

It was as Reader in Recent Social and Economic History at Oxford between 1956–77, as well as Professorial Fellow and Librarian of Nuffield College, that Max made his personal mark on English academic life. In him the gentrification of the Hartwells was completed, from viticulturists in New South Wales to the Wine Stewardship of an Oxford college without passing through the vintner's trade. 'Oh, Mr Hartwell, and how much do you spend on wine in a year?' asked one wine merchant. 'Seventeen hundred pounds', said Max, delighted as always to bait the Poms. The gravest error would however be to mistake the donnish manner which alternated with this irreverence for a pose. Nevertheless Max's manner has always had as much in it of the executive as of the cloistered scholar, presumably because before removing to Oxford as a don he had already presided over a department of thirty staff, giving courses to 4,000 students.

Nuffield virtually guaranteed him a flow of excellent research students; other colleges offered still more. His own record of publications may disguise the fact that Max shouldered an immense administrative burden at this period of his life. He sat, and he talked, on innumerable committees, several of them to do with libraries. For years he was a curator of the Bodleian. But he never ceased to read widely on his own account, he knew everybody, he could scent a good subject. He discussed hard with his students, who found themselves carrying out deeper primary historical research than many of those with PPE or economics degrees had thought they wanted to do. His own abiding interest in industrialisation, his curiosity as a half-outsider about its historiography, served to make his students preternaturally aware of the context of their research though he would never let them adulterate their theses with casual speculation.

The evening seminar at his house in St Margaret's Road threw graduate students in higgledy-piggledy with the dons and the outstanding foreign visitors whom Max coaxed to Nuffield (and for whom he made Oxford less unappealing than the prevalent anti-Americanism, in particular, might have done). Mixing the Fellows and students was part of college philosophy; at lunch one had to take the next place at table, sometimes placing abashed graduates of the previous summer next to the Chancellor of the Exchequer of the day. I have never found another institution willing to be thus democratic. The evening seminar set about deconstructing such new and impressive works as Deane and Cole's *British Economic Growth* and Habakkuk's *British and American Technology*. This was a democracy of the intellect, American style, boots and all. Nothing ever seemed to be left of any book except disarticulated heaps of incompatible models. What hope would there be for one's own thesis?

Looking back, Max was not so much seeking a secure place for himself to stand, seldom worth trying to find on the glossy surfaces of Oxford life, as working to establish economic history in a university abnormally given, when first he was there, to conventional political history and later to New Class social history. Economic history is an easy subject to do badly. Yet it is exceptionally hard to do well and almost impossible, so it seems, to carry off stylishly. In the Hartwellian heyday of the fifties and sixties (his classic papers on the standard of living came out in 1961 and 1963) the bandwagon of Rostowian growth did fleetingly promise that the economists might be interested. Max played up to them rather successfully but no one could have persuaded the general historians to see the subject as literature. The diet of water-powered machinery and steam boilers with which historians of those days had been force-fed never attracted people interested in another sort of power. Max put his main effort into trying to give economic history acceptable standing. Insofar as he achieved this (and when the chips were down he did not have a lot of support in Oxford) the beneficiaries were his students and anyone else who wished the subject to be taken seriously.

Outside Oxford the profession gained mightily between 1957 and 1972 from Max's editorship of *The Economic History Review*. The editorial headquarters were in college and ran like a well-oiled machine, not least because of his good fortune in having Jean Brotherhood as first and absolutely first-rate lieutenant. Max kept the *Review* in balance. Nothing would have been easier for him, given his interests and the growthmanship mood of the time, than to tilt the journal towards the modern period and the newly fashionable econometric history. But he insistently kept the coverage of the articles and the books reviewed as broad as possible. The readership among general historians, social historians and even medievalists was not permitted to melt away.

Though in everyday matters like that he is as even-handed and businesslike as can be, no-one can be more passionate than Max about his own beliefs. But then those beliefs are small-l liberal, beliefs in debate as long as it is open. He once told me that he could not live permanently in Australia because it is so conformist. Here I think is the clue: no particular set of beliefs really interests him half so much as debate itself and combating the distortions caused by the conformity of the hour. In my opinion, Max's emerging right-wing iconoclasm (we live in an age after all when the tin gods have dressed to the left) is only part conviction. Some of it is the result of being nudged that way by excesses in the other camp, with, initially, a good dose of putting it over the Poms, which they have never understood as the Antipodean tease it was.

I have seldom seen Max more delighted than when David Shapiro found him described in, I think, *Izvestia* as a 'bourgeois reactionary'. When the new economic history was meeting the Good Old English resistance to anything new, he outspokenly proclaimed himself its camp follower. Certainly he has always been the economists' economic historian and historiographer, telling them what the debates are about, explaining who had said what to whom, and of course, being Max, telling them what to believe. Having moved naturally enough into British economic history via the Yorkshire woollen industry which formed the demand side in his *Economic Development of Van Dieman's Land* (1954), he swept along enthusiastically in the 1960s with the tide of interest in economic growth. The current ran for him in two directions, into the standard-of-living debate, for which he is best known, and into promoting a vision of the Industrial Revolution as an example of growth, on which he has written most, and with respect to which he is the subject's philosopher.

As to the standard-of-living perhaps the less said the better. That debate has passed to professional philosophers like Jon Elster who, as is their way, are now being kind enough to tell us what the fuss was really all about. The Hartwell–Hobsbawm clash is widely used to show students the nature of historical debate itself: from history through polemics to historiography well within a lifetime. For myself, I always thought Max scored too easily through the poor tactics of the other side in retreating to quality-of-life arguments when they would have done better (on available evidence) to have conceded more of the historical case and moved smartly to the running sore of class in English society. Needless to say, Max would not agree. He has never thought for an instant that he could be wrong; but this misses the point that what he really did for his part was to stiffen the nature of argument in social and economic history and open the way for the quantifiers.

The grand design of the Industrial Revolution is historically, perhaps even polemically, far more important. Glancing down the list of his publications, it is easy to see that this is where his heart is. He has soaked many a blotter writing about it. He believes uncompromisingly that any growth that matters did begin in eighteenth-century England, was industrial, was revolutionary, and constituted the greatest single divide in human history. One of his recent pieces (in 1987) takes very firmly to task four of us who have dared to label these sentiments as dangerous half-truths. The measure of the man is that he would never in a thousand years let this come between us.

Index